AF779267

China's Treaty Policy and Practice in International Investment Law and Arbitration

Nijhoff International Investment Law Series

Series Editors

Prof. Eric De Brabandere (*Leiden University*)
Prof. Tarcisio Gazzini (*University of East Anglia*)
Prof. Stephan W. Schill (*University of Amsterdam*)
Prof. Attila Tanzi (*University of Bologna*)

Editorial Board

Andrea K. Bjorklund (*Montreal*) – Juan Pablo Bohoslavsky (*El Bolson, Rio Negro*) – Chester Brown (*Sydney*) – Patrick Dumberry (*Ottawa*) – Michael Ewing-Chow (*Singapore*) – Susan D. Franck (*Lexington*) – Ursula Kriebaum (*Vienna*) – Makane Mbengue (*Geneva*) – Catherine A. Rogers (*Carlisle*) – Christian Tams (*Glasgow*) – Andreas Ziegler (*Lausanne*)

VOLUME 17

The titles published in this series are listed at *brill.com/iils*

China's Treaty Policy and Practice in International Investment Law and Arbitration

A Comparative and Analytical Study

By

G. Matteo Vaccaro-Incisa

With foreword by

Vivienne Bath

BRILL
NIJHOFF

LEIDEN | BOSTON

Library of Congress Cataloging-in-Publication Data

Names: Vaccaro-Incisa, G. Matteo, 1983– author.
Title: China's treaty policy and practice in international investment law and arbitration : a comparative and analytical study / by G. Matteo Vaccaro-Incisa.
Description: Leiden ; Boston : Brill, [2021] | Series: Nijhoff international investment law series, 2351–9542 ; volume 17 | Based on author's thesis (doctoral – Université de Genève and Università commerciale Luigi Bocconi, 2014) issued under title: China's policy rationale and treaty-making on the protection of foreign investments. | Includes bibliographical references.
Identifiers: LCCN 2020055063 (print) | LCCN 2020055064 (ebook) | ISBN 9789004443907 (hardback) | ISBN 9789004443938 (ebook)
Subjects: LCSH: International commercial arbitration—China. | China—Foreign economic relations.
Classification: LCC KNQ1829 .V33 2021 (print) | LCC KNQ1829 (ebook) | DDC 341.5/220951—dc23
LC record available at https://lccn.loc.gov/2020055063
LC ebook record available at https://lccn.loc.gov/2020055064

Typeface for the Latin, Greek, and Cyrillic scripts: "Brill". See and download: brill.com/brill-typeface.

ISSN 2351-9542
ISBN 978-90-04-44390-7 (hardback)
ISBN 978-90-04-44393-8 (e-book)

Copyright 2021 by Koninklijke Brill NV, Leiden, The Netherlands.
Koninklijke Brill NV incorporates the imprints Brill, Brill Nijhoff, Brill Hotei, Brill Sense, Brill Schöningh, Brill Fink, Brill mentis, Vandenhoeck & Ruprecht, Böhlau Verlag and V&R Unipress.
All rights reserved. No part of this publication may be reproduced, translated, stored in a retrieval system, or transmitted in any form or by any means, electronic, mechanical, photocopying, recording or otherwise, without prior written permission from the publisher. Requests for re-use and/or translations must be addressed to Koninklijke Brill NV via brill.com or copyright.com.

This book is printed on acid-free paper and produced in a sustainable manner.

To my father, and his joie de vivre

Contents

Foreword XI
Acknowledgments XIV
List of Abbreviations XV
List of Illustrations XVII
Table Colors and Styles Key XVIII
Table of Cases XIX

Introduction 1

1 The Rise of a Trade and Investment Behemoth: The People's Republic of China 6
A Investment Agreements' History, Policy and the Current Shift towards Southeast Asia: an Outline 6
1. *The European Roots of BITs* 6
2 *The Changing Shift* 11
3 *BRICS and IIAs* 15
B China's Policy Evolution towards FDIs and BITs (1949–2015): Outline and Remarks 18
1. *China and FDI: Main Periods* 18
2 *From Exclusion to Resumption* 19
3 *The Shift: From Rejection to Shaping Global Standards of Investment Law* 27
4 *Chinese FTAs and Contemporary IIAs* 32
5 *Novel Topics in Chinese IIAs* 38
6 *Ongoing Negotiations: China-U.S. BIT, China-EU BIT, RCEP* 42
7 *Proposal for a New Periodization* 45
C The Quasi-Absence of Known Investor-State Disputes with China 48
D The People's Republic: What Kind of Economy? 52
E The Role of State-Owned Enterprises in Chinese Outward FDI 54
F Conclusion 57

2 Chinese IIAs: Treaty Templates and Selected Aspects of Treaty Practice 60
A Adopting the Model BIT: Policy Rationale 60
B Structure of the Chinese Model BIT 62
C Preamble, Application, and Definition of Investment 65

1 *Preamble* 65
2 *Scope and Application* 66
2.1 The Chinese Model 67
2.2 Contemporary Practice 69
3 *Definition of Investment* 70
3.1 The Chinese Template Definition of Investment 73
3.2 The Chapeau 79
3.2.1 *'In Accordance with the Laws': the* ratione legis *Requirement* 80
3.2.2 *Ratione legis in Chinese Model BITs* 82
3.2.3 *Ratione legis in Chinese IIAs* 84
3.2.4 *The Objective Criteria* 90
3.2.5 *Objective Criteria in Chinese IIAs* 92
3.2.6 *Indirect Investment* 97
3.2.7 *The Chapeau: Contemporary Practice* 102
3.2.8 *The Asset-Based List: Model and Standard Practice* 105
3.2.9 *Contemporary Practice* 108
4 *Returns* 128
D Conclusion 130

3 Analytical Review of China's Treaty Practice and Key Protection Standards 132
A Defining the Research Perimeter and the Relevant Comparators 132
B ISDS Clauses in Chinese IIAs 133
1 *Access to ISDS: The Significant Impact of Limited Consent to Arbitration* 133
2 *Express Exclusion of the MFN Clause from Covering ISDS* 134
3 *Length of Mandatory Consultations* 134
4 *Mandatory Prior Recourse to Domestic Court Proceedings* 135
5 *Mandatory Prior Recourse to Domestic Administrative Review* 135
6 *Mandatory Treaty-Based Procedural Rules: Presence and Extent* 137
7 *Dispute Settlement Mechanisms* 138
8 *Fork in the Road and Parallel Proceedings* 139
C The Expropriation Clause in Chinese IIAs 164
1 *Introduction* 164
2 *Mention and Definition of 'Indirect Expropriation'* 165
3 *Protection of 'Portfolio Investment'* 165

4 *Criteria for Lawful Expropriation* 166
4.1 Rationale of the Expropriation 166
4.2 Expropriation's Rule of Law 166
4.3 Prohibition of Discrimination 167
5 *Compensation Characteristics* 167
5.1 Overarching Characterization of Compensation 167
5.2 Timing of Payment of Compensation 168
5.3 Realizable Compensation 168
5.4 Convertible Compensation 169
5.5 Transferable Compensation 169
6 *Evaluation of the Compensation Due to Expropriation* 170
6.1 Evaluation Method 170
6.2 *Dies a quo* for the Assessment of the *Quantum* 171
6.3 Interests 173
7 *Right to Review* 173
D The Most-Favored-Nation Clause in Chinese IIAs 226
1 *Introduction and Relevant Pool of Investment Agreements* 226
2 *Structure of the MFN Clause* 227
3 *Object of Coverage* 228
4 *Ambit of Coverage* 230
5 *MFN Treatment Formulation (Positive, Negative, with Comparator)* 231
6 *Exceptions to the MFN* 231
6.1 'Subject to Domestic Law' 231
6.2 Position 232
6.3 Wording of the MFN Exceptions (Relatively to PRC Models) 233
6.4 Investment Agreements Featuring Ad Hoc Exceptions to MFN 234
7 *Non-Conforming Measures* 235
E The National Treatment Clause in Chinese IIAs 280
1 *Introduction and Relevant Pool of Treaties* 280
2 *Type of NT Clause* 280
3 *Structure of the NT Clause* 281
4 *Object of Coverage of the Clause* 282
5 *Ambit of Coverage of the Clause* 283
6 *NT Treatment Formulation (Positive, Negative, with Comparator)* 284
7 *Exceptions to the NT* 285

7.1 Position 285
7.2 Wording of NT Exceptions (Relatively to Chinese Models) 286
7.3 Relation between NT and MFN Exceptions (within the Same IIA) 286
7.4 Investment Agreements Featuring Ad Hoc Exceptions to NT 287
8 *Non-Conforming Measures* 289
F Fair and Equitable Treatment, Full Protection and Security, and Prohibition of Arbitrary or Discriminatory Treatment in Chinese IIAs 324
1 *Introduction and Relevant Pool of Investment Agreements* 324
2 *Location of FET and FPS in Chinese IIAs* 324
3 *Structure and Key Wording of FET and FPS Relatively to Chinese Models* 326
4 *FET Formulation in Chinese IIAs* 326
5 *Object of Coverage of the FET Clause* 328
6 *Additional Elements Directly Affecting FET Scope and Coverage* 328
7 *FPS Formulation in Chinese IIAs* 330
8 *Object and Coverage of the FPS Clause* 331
9 Ad hoc *Limitations to the FPS Clause* 332
10 *Prohibition of Arbitrary or Discriminatory Treatment (PAD) in Chinese IIAs* 334
11 *PAD Object and Coverage* 335
12 *PAD Ambit of Coverage* 336
13 *Relationship between PAD and Domestic Laws* 337
14 *MST in Chinese Treaty Practice* 338
15 Ad hoc *Express General Exclusions from Operation of FET, FPS, and PAD in China's Investment Treaty Practice* 339
G Conclusion 390

Conclusion 391
China's Model BITs 391
China's Investment Treaty Practice 392
China and the Proposal for an International Investment Court 395
The Contribution of This Work 397

Bibliography 399
Index 412

Foreword

The rapid development of the Chinese economy and the rise of China, first as the recipient of large amounts of foreign direct investment and then, more recently, as the source of immense amounts of investment in both the developed and developing world has focused attention on China's approach to the area of international law, particularly international investment law. China has been an active participant in the area of international investment law since the 1980s, through the negotiation of multiple bilateral investment treaties and free trade agreements with accompanying investment agreements. Notwithstanding the amount of investment into China, China has not – so far – been the target of a large number of investor-State cases, a fact for which there are a wide range of suggested reasons (some of which are examined in Chapter 1). Chinese investors, on the other hand, are becoming increasingly active in looking at investor-State dispute settlement as a way of dealing with issues arising from their investments.

The comprehensive network of international investment agreements which China has built up is of course the basis for enforcement of claims by and against China and Chinese companies. As can be expected, particularly in view of the publicity generated by the growth of China's investment, the Belt and Road initiative and the current US-China trade war, China's agreements continue to be the subject of considerable academic and political interest. A major problem, however, is that the sheer number of agreements, and the substantial changes in the form of the agreements since the first agreements with Sweden was signed in 1982, has made it difficult to compare and review the agreements as a whole.

This book is based on Dr Vaccaro-Incisa's time-consuming and painstaking comparative analysis of the contents of all of China's agreements (bar three) from 1982 to 2015. It constitutes an ambitious attempt to provide an analysis of China's international investment agreements, both in the context of the history and development of instruments of this type generally and in the context of the development of China's own policies relating to investment protection and promotion. It draws on a wide range of sources and the work of previous authors, particularly the comprehensive 2008 work by Gallagher and Shan. The book is, however, particularly interesting for the detailed work which forms the basis for the analysis and discussion of the Chinese treaties. In particular, the author takes an original approach in the systematic way in which he examines China's approach to its treaties in the context of different approaches taken by various streams of investment agreements. The comparative tables which explain the different approaches and their development are particularly helpful in allowing the reader to review the differences in approach and their changes.

The book begins, in Chapter 1, by providing context for international investment agreements generally, an overview of the development of China's treaties, and a summary of several of the major issues relating to China and international economic law, particularly the unresolved question of China as a market economy and the contested role played by China's powerful state owned enterprises. Chapters 2 and 3 provide the meat of the analysis and discussion. Dr Vaccaro-Incisa has organized and analysed the information derived from his thorough examination of the treaties by content, context and date in order to provide a comprehensive comparison of China's practice with developments and State practice in international investment law and with China's own treaty practice. An example of the interesting material that comes out of this presentation of the material can be found in Chapter 2, where the gradual evolution of China's approach to the definition of "investment" is laid out in considerable detail. The discussion is considerably enriched by commentary in the case of each treaty with the treaty practice of the state contracting with China, which provides insight into the preferences of each side to the negotiations and a better idea of what the Chinese negotiators were prepared to agree to.

Chapter 3 deals with key protection standards, including investor-State dispute settlement, national treatment, most-favoured nation treatment and fair and equitable treatment. All of these are broken down into different categories, and the analysis often provides considerable food for thought. The comprehensive review of the contested question of expropriation and how different aspects of the expropriation provision have developed in Chinese treaties over time, for example, reveals a systematic development of treaty practice in relation to the timing of the payment of compensation, but considerable variation in such elements as methods of valuation in provisions, with differences in treaty commitments across the entire time period of the treaties examined. The discussion of investor-State treaty settlement provisions in Chinese treaties is also of considerable interest, as changes in Chinese practice potentially make it easier for investors (Chinese and otherwise) to bring cases for treaty breaches other than expropriation. In particular, China's approach over time to the role of domestic dispute settlement, requirements for administrative review and provisions on "fork in the road" is clearly described and discussed. The accompanying tables are especially useful here. This chapter also deals with China's evolving approaches to the protection standards of most-favoured nation treatment, national treatment and fair and equitable treatment. The disparate approaches to national treatment, in particular, are summarized clearly and at length – thus neatly setting out some of the issues which surround this potentially contentious area.

The detailed and clearly presented information in this book describes trends in major areas of Chinese international investment treaty-making (insofar as they can be ascertained), identifies firmly-held principles and areas of flexibility, and draws conclusions in relation to policy, both long-term and current. The book does not, however, predict or to recommend particular approaches in relation to Chinese treaty-making policy. It sets out the information and the conclusions that the author draws from his analysis and provides the reader with an excellent resource for further research and discussion.

The research and analysis on which the book is based represents a significant accomplishment, which is supported both by the clear organization and presentation of the content and by the systemic way in which the material in summarized for reference in clearly laid out and easily accessible tables and charts. I confidently anticipate that the book will become a valuable resource for the many researchers, academics and writers with an interest in China's practice in this area.

Vivienne Bath[1]

1 Vivienne Bath, Professor of Chinese and International Business Law, Sydney Law School, University of Sydney.

Acknowledgments

Carrying out the research and analysis presented in this book would not have been possible without the encouragement and support of a number of distinguished colleagues, on whom I have imposed repeatedly to discuss and help refine methodology and findings.

I am immensely grateful to Professor Jurgen Kurtz, Professor Julien Chaisse, Professor Luke Nottage, and Professor Junji Nakagawa.

My former students, Alessandra Moroni and Timothée Bruneteau – both currently engaged in pursuing brilliant careers (without much surprise on my part) also provided a great deal of help.

Thanks also to Catherine Newcombe and Wojciech Giemza, for their invaluable support in reviewing and systematizing the whole work.

Finally, I would like to acknowledge and thank Mr Yun Zhang at the Department of Treaty and Law at the Chinese Ministry of Commerce, the Centre for Financial Regulation and Economic Development at the Law Faculty of the Chinese University of Hong Kong, Melbourne Law School, and the Centre for Asian and Pacific Law at the Law School of the University of Sydney.

Abbreviations

Ad.	*Addendum*
Art(s).	Article(s)
ASEAN	Association of South East Asian Nations
BBC	British Broadcasting Corporation
BIT	Bilateral Investment Treaty
BRI	Belt and Road initiative
BRICS	Brazil, Russia, India, China and South Africa
CCSAI	China-Chile Supplementary Agreement on Investment
Cf.	Compare
Ch.	Chapter
CP(s).	Contracting Party/State (or Parties/States)
DE	Germany
Ed(s).	Edited by
EEA	European Economic Area
EFTA	European Free Trade Association
e.g.	*exempli gratia*
EU	European Union
FCN	Treaty of Friendship, Commerce and Navigation
FDI	Foreign Direct Investment
FET	Fair and Equitable Treatment
fn.	footnote
FPS	Full Protection and Security
FR	France
FTA	Free Trade Agreement
G7	The Group of Seven (Canada, Germany, France, Italy, Japan, UK, US)
GDP	Gross Domestic Product
ibid.	*ibidem*
ICC	Court of Arbitration of the International Chamber of Commerce
ICSID Center	Center International Center for Settlement of Investment Disputes
ICSID	Convention International Convention for Settlement of Investment Disputes
id.	*idem*
i.e.	*id est*
IIA	International Investment Agreement
inv. rep.	investment report

IT	Italy
LCIA	London Court of International Arbitration
let.	letter
MFN	Most Favored Nation
MIGA Convention	Multilateral Investment Guarantee Agreement
MOFA	Ministry of Foreign Affairs
MOFCOM	Ministry of Commerce
NAFTA	North American Free Trade Agreement
NT	National Treatment
NY Convention	United Nations Convention on the Recognition and Enforcement of Foreign Arbitral Awards
NZ	New Zealand
OECD	Organization for Economic Co-operation and Development
p./pp.	page/page(s)
PAD	Prohibition of Arbitrary or Discriminatory treatment
para(s).	paragraph(s)
PNG	Papua New Guinea
PRC	People's Republic of China
SADC	Southern African Development Community
SAI	Supplementary Agreement on Investment
SC	Seychelles
SCC	Arbitration Institute of the Stockholm Chamber of Commerce
Sect(s).	Section(s)
TIA	Trilateral Investment Agreement
UNCITRAL	United Nations Commission on International Trade Law
UNCTAD	United Nations Conference on Trade and Development
UK	United Kingdom
US	United States
USD	United States Dollar
USSR	Union of Soviet Socialist Republics
v.	*versus*
vol.	volume
WTO	World Trade Organization
WWII	World War II

Illustrations

Figures

1 Cases registered under the ICSID Convention and Additional Facility Rules 13
2 Top 20 investor economies (2015–2016) 14
3 FDI inflows and outflows (2012–2018) 14
4 Most promising investor economies for FDI (2017–2019) 15
5 Annual growth of Chinese BITs (1982–2015) 24
6a Changes in national investment policies – trend (1992–2016) 30
6b Changes in national investment policies – number of measures (2002–2016) 31
7 Chinese outward FDI – annual flow (1992–2015) 37

Tables

1 BITs concluded by G7 States (plus Switzerland and Sweden) 10
2 First Chinese BITs 25
3 Novel topics – IIA coverage in recent Chinese IIAs (from 2008 on, selected) 39
4 Chinese and European model BITs – sequence of provisions 63
5 European and Chinese model BITs – application 68
6 Chinese model BITs – definition of investment 74
7 European and Chinese model BITs – definition of investment 76
8 PRC IIAs – *Ratione legis* in the definition of investment 84
9 PRC BITs– objective criteria in the definition of investment 95
10 Express mention of 'indirect investment' (selected IIAs) 98
11 Investment indirect ownership and/or control in recent Chinese IIAs: presence and definition 101
12 Investment definition in 2008–2009 Asia-Pacific IIA 114
13 China-Canada BIT – definition of investment 120
14 China-Chile SAI – definition of investment 126
15 Chinese model BITs – returns 128
16 Returns – Definition in PRC, UK, DE model BITs, plus PRC-DE BIT 129
17 ISDS in Chinese IIAs 150
18 Expropriation characteristics in Chinese IIAs 186
19 Compensation due to expropriation: characteristics and criteria 202
20 MFN in Chinese IIAs 244
21 NT in Chinese IIAs 296
22 FET, FPS, MST, and PAD in Chinese IIAs 354

Table Colors and Styles Key

Tables 5, 7, 12, 13, 14, 16

- *Original text featured in the 1984/1989 PRC model BIT*
- Text found in earlier PRC model BIT
- ***Text original of the 1997 PRC model BIT***
- Text from the German pre-2000 model BIT / practice
- **Text from the German post-2000 model BIT / practice**
- Text from the UK model BIT
- **Text from the US model BIT**
- *Text from the Canadian 2004 model BIT*
- ***Text from the Canadian 2006 model BIT***
- **Common / identical / equivalent wording among compared agreements**
- Wording not falling in any other category

* Further specifications in the key places under each relevant table, and/or in the related footnotes.

Table of Cases

ICJ

Border and Transborder Armed Actions (Nicaragua v. Honduras), Judgment, [1988] ICJ Reports 69.

Case concerning the Barcelona Traction Light and Power Company Ltd (Belgium v. Spain), Judgment, [1970] ICJ Reports 3.

Nuclear Tests Case (Australia v. France), Judgement, [1974] ICJ Reports 253.

ICSID

Abaclat and Others v. Argentine Republic, Decision on Jurisdiction, Aug. 4th, 2011, ICSID Case No. ARB/07/5.

Adriano Gardella S.p.A. v. Côte d'Ivoire, Award, Aug. 29th, 1977, ICSID Case No. ARB/74/1.

Ansung Housing v. China, Award, Mar. 9th, 2017, ICSID Case No. ARB/14/25.

Beijing Urban Construction v. Yemen, Decision on Jurisdiction, May 31st, 2017, ICSID Case No. ARB/14/30.

Biwater Gauff (Tanzania) Ltd. v. United Republic of Tanzania, Award, Jul. 24th, 2008, ICSID Case No. ARB/05/22.

CMS Gas Transmission Co. v. Argentina, Decision on Jurisdiction, June 17th, 2003, ICSID Case No. ARB/01/8.

Deutsche Bank AG v. Democratic Socialist Republic of Sri Lanka, Award, Oct. 31st, 2012, ICSID Case No. ARB/09/2.

Ekran Berhad v. People's Republic of China, ICSID Case No. ARB/11/15 (case discontinued in May 2011, before the establishment of the Arbitral Tribunal).

Fedax N.V. v. The Republic of Venezuela, Decision on Objections to Jurisdiction, Jul. 11th, 1997, ICSID Case No. ARB/96/3.

Fedax N.V. v. The Republic of Venezuela, Award, Mar. 9th, 1998, ICSID Case No. ARB/96/3.

Fraport AG Frankfurt Airport Services Worldwide v. Republic of the Philippines, Award on Jurisdiction, Aug. 16th, 2007, ICSID Case No. ARB/03/25.

Fraport AG Frankfurt Airport Services Worldwide v. Republic of the Philippines, Dissenting Opinion by Mr. Bernardo M. Cremades, Jul. 19th, 2007, ICSID Case No. ARB/03/25.

Garanti Koza LLP v. Turkmenistan, Decision on Jurisdiction, Jul. 3rd, 2013, ICSID Case No. ARB/11/20.

Garanti Koza LLP v. Turkmenistan, Dissenting Opinion of the Decision on the Objection to Jurisdiction for Lack of Consent by Prof. L. Boisson de Chazournes, Jul. 3rd, 2013, ICSID Case No. ARB/11/20.

Gardella S.p.A. v. Côte d'Ivoire, Award, Aug. 29th, 1977, ICSID Case No. ARB/74/1.

Inceysa Vallisoletana S.L. v. Republic of El Salvador, Award, Aug. 2nd, 2006, ICSID Case No. ARB/03/26.

Ioannis Kardassopoulos v. The Republic of Georgia, Decision on Jurisdiction, Jul. 6th, 2007, ICSID Case No. ARB/05/18.

Joy Mining Machinery Limited v. Arab Republic of Egypt, Award on Jurisdiction, Aug. 6th, 2004, ICSID Case No. ARB/03/11.

Maffezini v. Spain, Decision of the Tribunal on Objections to Jurisdiction, Jan. 25th, 2000, ICSID Case No. ARB/97/7.

Malaysian Historical Salvors, SDN, BHD v. The Government of Malaysia, Award on Jurisdiction, May 17th, 2007, ICSID Case No. ARB/05/10.

Malaysian Historical Salvors, SDN, BHD v. The Government of Malaysia, Decision on the Application for Annulment, Apr. 16th, 2009, ICSID Case No. ARB/05/10.

M.C.I. Power Group L.C. and New Turbine, Inc. v. Republic of Ecuador, Award, Jul. 31st, 2007, ICSID Case No. ARB/03/6.

Mr. Patrick Mitchell v. Democratic Republic of the Congo, Award, Feb. 9th, 2004, ICSID Case No. ARB/99/7.

Mr. Patrick Mitchell v. Democratic Republic of the Congo, Decision on the Application for Annulment of the Award, Nov. 1st, 2006, ICSID Case No. ARB/99/7.

Phoenix Action v. The Czech Republic, Award, Apr. 15th, 2009, ICSID Case No. ARB/06/5.

Ping-An Life Insurance Company of China Ltd. v. Kingdom of Belgium, Award on jurisdiction, Apr. 30th, 2015, ICSID Case No. ARB/12/29.

Saba Fakes v. Turkey, Award, Jul. 14th, 2010, ICSID Case No. ARB/07/20.

Saipem S.p.A. v. The People's Republic of Bangladesh, Decision on Jurisdiction and Recommendation on Provisional Measures, Mar. 21st, 2007, ICSID Case No. ARB/05/07.

Salini Costruttori S.p.A. and Italstrade S.p.A. v. Kingdom of Morocco, Decision on Jurisdiction, Jul. 31st, 2001, ICSID Case No. ARB/00/4.

Señor Tza Yap Shum v. The Republic of Peru, Decision on Jurisdiction and Competence, Jun. 19th, 2009, ICSID Case No. ARB/07/6.

Señor Tza Yap Shum v. The Republic of Peru, Award, Jul. 7th, 2011, ICSID Case No. ARB/07/6.

SGS Société Générale de Surveillance S.A. v. Republic of the Philippines, Decision on Jurisdiction, Jan. 29th, 2004, ICSID Case No. ARB/02/6.

Siemens A.G. v. The Argentine Republic, Decision on Jurisdiction, Aug. 3rd, 2004, ICSID Case No. ARB/02/8.

Société Générale de Surveillance S.A. v. Republic of the Philippines, Decision on Jurisdiction, Jan. 29th, 2004, ICSID Case No. ARB/02/6.

Tokios Tokelés v. Ukraine, Decision on Jurisdiction, Apr. 29th, 2004, ICSID Case No. ARB/02/18.

UNCITRAL

China Heilongjiang v. Mongolia, UNCITRAL PCA (case initiated in 2010 and now pending).

Romak S.A. (Switzerland) v. The Republic of Uzbekistan, Award, Nov. 11th, 2009, UNCITRAL PCA Case No. 2007-07.

Sanum Investments v. Laos, Decision on Jurisdiction, Dec. 13th, 2013, UNCITRAL PCA Case No. 2013-13.

S.D. Myers, Inc. v. Canada, 40 I.L.M. 1408, 1440 para. 281 (NAFTA Arb. 2000).

WTO

United States – Import Prohibition of Certain Shrimp and Shrimp Products, Appellate Body Report, Oct. 12th, 1998, WT/DS58/AB/R.

Introduction

Over the course of its long imperial history, China's inclination was always to regard international relations and power as regulated primarily through the lens of trade and influence (on a regional scale), rather than the material possession of territories across the globe.[1] The Opium Wars (1839–1842 and 1856–1860) and the 'unequal treaties' that ensued with the United States, France and the United Kingdom, the collapse of the Empire (1911) and the advent of the People's Republic (1949), all hardened China's already negative attitude towards foreign (and, in particular, Western) trade and investment,[2] then effectively discouraged. Such hostility ended in 1978, when the Chinese Communist ruling party, implicitly acknowledging that Zedong's 'Great Leap Forward' campaign contributed instead to China's 'Great Famine' (1958–1961), made way for Xiaoping's 'Open Doors' policy. By gradually rebuilding trade and investment channels with the rest of the world, that policy ultimately resulted in China's unparalleled growth over the past 40 years, fueled by foreign investment. Today, China, next to its trade weight, expresses an investment capacity superior to that of almost all OECD States – one that, in contrast to any of these, it can directly control, or anyway substantially influence. The expanding outflow of Chinese investment has thus induced China to begin revisiting its stance on the matter of foreign investment protection – a stance, as a former capital-importing State, which has been traditionally conservative (or restrictive).

1 Cf., W Bernstein, *A Splendid Exchange: How Trade Shaped the World* (Grove Press, 2008), 152–198; also, a remarkable account of the different perspective between China and Europe on this point may be found in A Carty and J Nijman, *Morality and Responsibility of Rulers: European and Chinese Origins of a Rule of Law as Justice for World Order* (Oxford, 2018).

2 In a letter to British king George III, China's long-reigning ruler, Qian Long (emperor 1735–1796), dismissed enhanced trade with British merchants in the following terms: 'Swaying the wide world, I have but one aim in view, namely, to maintain a perfect governance and to fulfill the duties of the State: strange and costly objects do not interest me. If I have commanded that the tribute offerings sent by you, O King, are to be accepted, this was solely in consideration for the spirit which prompted you to dispatch them from afar. Our dynasty's majestic virtue has penetrated unto every country under Heaven, and Kings of all nations have offered their costly tribute by land and sea. As your Ambassador can see for himself, we possess all things. I set no value on objects strange or ingenious, and have no use for your country's manufactures'; translation by E Backhouse and JOP Bland, in *Annals and Memoirs of the Court of Peking* (*from the 16th to the 20th Century*) (Heinemann, 1914), 324–325. At the time, China accepted only silver as payment for sales (which is why a few merchants began using opium as a method of payment).

© KONINKLIJKE BRILL NV, LEIDEN, 2021 | DOI:10.1163/9789004443938_002

Until recently, however, China's development into one of the most active and influential players in international investment law has often been overlooked. Notwithstanding a relatively late start (1982), China has managed to weave a web of international investment agreements (IIAs – including bilateral, trilateral, and multilateral investment treaties, as well as investment chapters in FTAs, and investment agreements flowing from framework arrangements to establish multi-stage comprehensive FTAs) whose size and reach is comparable – when not superior – to that of Germany, the UK, France, or Switzerland. The model bilateral investment treaties (BITs) of two of these States – Germany and the UK – were the principal reference points for China's own treaty models and practice. Indeed, the People's Republic has availed itself of a model BIT since 1984,[3] well before most major capital exporting economies.

Since the turn of the millennium – and, most notably, the renegotiation of the BIT with Germany, in 2003 –, China's foreign investment protection program has seen significant developments. This book aims at reviewing *inter alia* those changes introduced in the investment instruments to which China acceded between 2003 and 2015, particularly in terms of structure and wording, and their underlying policy rationale. Indeed, the investment protection regimes stipulated with Pakistan (2006), New Zealand (2008), ASEAN (2009), Peru (2009), Canada (2012), Chile (2012), Japan and South Korea (2012), and South Korea (2015) have, to date, only been analyzed separately or, in any event, never in connection with the rest of China's investment treaty practice or templates. In addition, China's approach to investment treaty making has not yet been analyzed in terms of the still ongoing gradual policy shift, from being rigidly adherent to its own model, to more open to innovations coming from trusted or more experienced States, to being possibly more flexible and relatively unbridled from rigid political directives.

This book thus endeavors to complement earlier comprehensive works that do not cover the past decade, as well as more recent but partial analyses, by comparatively reviewing Chinese models and IIAs, among themselves, as well as with those of other major players in the international investment legal field. The in-depth examination of the structure and wording of investment

---

3 See N Gallagher and W Shan, *Chinese Investment Treaties: Policies and Practice* (Oxford University Press, 2009), 35–43 and 421–437; *contra*, Q Kong, according to whom China never used a model for its BIT negotiations; see Q Kong, 'Bilateral Investment Treaties: The Chinese Approach and Practice' (1998/99) 8 *Asian Yearbook of International Law* 105, 114. However, in light of the more recent, conspicuous and uncontested work of Gallagher and Shan, it is here assumed that, at the time of Kong's writing, this piece of information was not publicly available.; on the point, see Chapter 2.

treaties seeks to offer at least a partial response to two key scholarly observations made over the last decade. Firstly, and generally, the differences among BITs have often been overlooked, as well as their impact on the evolution of international investment law.[4] Secondly, and with specific regard to China, the existing research on Chinese BITs has until recently been '... either outdated or incomprehensive, confined to a limited number of BITs with States from a particular, albeit important, part of the world'.[5] Indeed, over the past few years, scholarly attention on China – in general, across various academic fields and, specifically, in international investment law – has increased. However, this study is believed to be the first that seeks to objectively retrace a State policy by systematically analyzing the entire lot of its actual treaty practice – as opposed to interpreting the latter through official and unofficial political statements. In the case of China, this 'reversed methodology' is somewhat necessary as, on the one hand, documents relating to investment treaty negotiations are for the most part not available and, on the other, statements or comments from Chinese public officials responsible for, or otherwise involved in, these negotiations are rare and difficult to obtain.

The focus of the in-depth comparative analysis will be key traditional clauses of investment treaties. More recent clauses dealing with novel topics (*e.g.*, environment and labor) could become object of further research later in time, when these will be included in a significant body of treaties.

As mentioned, as term of reference and comparison for China's investment treaty models and practice, this study relies on templates adopted by key States in the field. This is for two reasons. First, treaty models are evidence of the 'minimum expression of consent' a particular State is prepared to offer vis-à-vis any counterpart. Second, key Western economies have long maintained the primacy in the formulation of investment protection standards. Hence, changes China introduced over time in the model texts or actual stipulations are illustrated through the analysis of detailed comparative tables elaborated *ad hoc*. Further, the analytical aspects of this research are not based on

4 In this sense, see MS Manger, 'A Quantitative Perspective on Trends in IIA Rules', in A De Mestral and C Lévesque (eds.), *Improving International Investment Agreements* (Routledge, 2013), 76–92, 91; in this sense, also, J Paulsson, 'Arbitration Without Privity', *ICSID Review – Foreign Investment Law Journal*, Vol. 10, Issue 2, Fall 1995, 232–257, at 235: "... the contents of BITs vary greatly: as much as any individual country might like to impose its own idea of a standard BIT, the varying negotiating strength of the other side has the effect of rendering most countries' portfolios of BITs quite heterogeneous ... in particular, the scope of and nature of third party access to international arbitration through BIT mechanisms are so different from one BIT to the next that one cannot speak of a dominant practice: each BIT must be examined on its own".

5 Gallagher and Shan, *Chinese Investment Treaties* (fn. 3).

external sources, such as doctrine or case law, and are thus entirely original. Indeed, it would not be easy to rely upon case law, as China has only seldom been respondent in investor-State arbitration (and, to date, it has never lost a case).[6] Chinese investors, on the contrary, have begun taking advantage of China's investment treaty network for the protection of their own investments abroad (with mixed results).[7]

By focusing on the People's Republic of China's treaty practice in international investment law, this work does not cover the treaty practice of China's Special Administrative Regions (SARs). Therefore, investment treaties concluded by Hong Kong and Macau with third countries are excluded, as well as those of each SAR with the People's Republic (the special character of these latter arrangements being self-evident for a variety of reasons – from an international law perspective, chiefly, that they do not properly qualify as treaties). By the same token, the research will not delve into China's *One Belt, One Road* initiative (already subject of intense academic scrutiny) but will of course include the relevant BITs in the comparative analysis. Also excluded, lastly, are agreements under negotiations, such as the China-US and China-EU BITs, or ASEAN-led negotiation for a Regional Comprehensive Economic Partnership (RCEP). In the perspective of a treaty-practice analysis, further study in the last two directions here excluded may be indeed appropriate in due course, *i.e.*, when the relevant agreements will be concluded.

A brief summary of the research content is provided below.

Chapter 1 opens by offering a review of the recent history of BITs (from their European origin to what is labeled as the current 'Pacific lead'), by comparatively analyzing the treaty-making activity in the field of traditional capital exporters and emerging economies. The focus then shifts to the history of FDIs and BITs in China: from exclusion to the beginning of the BIT programme, to its significant expansion, to the recent launch of the FTA programme.

Chapter 2 focuses on the three Chinese model BITs (1984, 1989 and 1997), including their structure, key concepts, and the changes China introduced over the time. This is followed by a comparative analysis of selected provisions (with particular regard to treaty scope and the definition of investment), also with the model texts of key Western States, to investigate inter-template (hence, policy) relationships, if any.

Chapter 3, the heart of this research, is entirely original. The first task is to define the perimeter of the pool of Chinese IIAs under scrutiny, to include all those that are in force, not superseded by renegotiations or more recent

6 See, *inter alia*, Chapter 1, Section C.

7 *Ibid.*

stipulations, and allow for investor-State arbitration. Hence, moving from a selection of key foreign investment protection clauses (such as investor-State dispute settlement, expropriation, most-favored-nation treatment, national treatment, fair and equitable treatment, full protection and security, and prohibition of arbitrary or discriminatory treatment), each treaty of the survey lot is contrasted against the Chinese models and contemporary practice, as well as those of key Western States, plus selected agreements of particular significance (*e.g.*, NAFTA, ASEAN investment agreement).

Given its comprehensive analysis of China's investment protection programme, and of selected clauses, this work may constitute the basis for further academic research on, or related to, this topic. Its use is also intended in the context of investment arbitration, to produce objective assessments of those aspects of China's treaty practice included herein. Indeed, investment tribunals have long sought to strengthen (if not, base) the interpretation they offer *in casu* of investment protection clauses by making reference to the treaty practice of the respondent State. However, the tribunals' analyses have not infrequently proved perfunctory and, too often, the review of a small selection of treaties out of an entire network has been deemed sufficient for drawing conclusions regarding a State's treaty practice. Such methodology hampers the strength of the reasoning that is attached to it, and, ultimately, detracts from the credibility of the ISDS system as a whole.

Lastly, taking into account the current negotiations at UNCITRAL for the reform of ISDS, this book may hopefully contribute some clarity on the investment treaty policy and practice of China, a key global player whose economic size, geopolitical magnitude, and vastness of investment treaty network, can simply no longer be ignored, or underestimated.

CHAPTER 1

The Rise of a Trade and Investment Behemoth: The People's Republic of China

A Investment Agreements' History, Policy and the Current Shift towards Southeast Asia: an Outline

1. *The European Roots of BITs*

At their origin, Bilateral Investment Treaties (BITs) were conceived as instruments for major European capital-exporting States to 'promote and protect' their businesses in poor capital-importing States.[1] Their main purpose '... was historically that of protecting investments from the industrialized party into the developing one, thereby (hopefully) attracting capital into the latter's economy'.[2] Over the last three decades, international agreements featuring foreign investment protection regimes have expanded, including chapters of Free Trade Agreements (FTAs) and self-standing agreements flowing from framework arrangements for multi-stage FTAs. All these instruments, here collectively referred to as International Investment Agreements (IIAs), are nowadays regularly concluded also between States (or even groups of States) where capital is reciprocally exported and imported. Accordingly, the definition of these arrangements has evolved in a more sophisticated and neutral fashion, as a specific type of international treaty that provides for substantive as well as procedural protection for foreign investors against so-called political risk.[3]

The first BIT was signed between the Federal Republic of Germany and Pakistan, on 25 Nov. 1959. Between 1959 and 1963, Germany virtually had a

1 Cf., R Dolzer and M Stevens, *Bilateral Investment Treaties* (Martinus Nijhoff Publishers, 1995), 1: 'BITs are European in origin'. This theoretical axiom has started to change very recently only: by the end of 2008, only 26% of all BITs were South-South, and only 9% North-North; see UNCTAD, 'World Investment Report: Transnational Corporations, Agricultural Production and Development' (2009), 33 <http://unctad.org/en/pages/PublicationArchive.aspx?publicationid=743> accessed Nov. 20th, 2019.

2 G Sacerdoti, 'Bilateral Treaties and Multilateral Instruments on Investment Protection' (1997) 269 *Recueil des cours de l'Académie de Droit International de la Haye* 251, 327–328.

3 See S Schill, 'Tearing down the Great Wall: The New Generation Investment Treaties of the People's Republic of China' (2007) 15 *Cardozo Journal of International and Comparative Law* 73, 83, even though referring to BITs only.

© KONINKLIJKE BRILL NV, LEIDEN, 2021 DOI:10.1163/9789004443938_003

monopoly on BITs.[4] The influence of Germany in shaping the key features of investment law may be inferred by looking at the stipulations concluded around certain 'peak' moments of international investment law history (with regard to the international community at large, or China in particular).[5] In 1963, the Netherlands first (in March, with Tunisia) and France soon afterward (in August, also with Tunisia) signed their first BIT. Italy followed in 1964 (with Guinea). While the Netherlands[6] and Italy[7] continued over the subsequent years their BIT programs, France halted its own for almost a decade.[8] Sweden as well figures among the early starters, as its first BIT was already concluded in 1965 (with Cote d'Ivoire).[9] The United Kingdom – more focused on treaties of 'Friendship, Commerce and Navigation' (FCN)[10] and on intra-Commonwealth trade and investment privileges – signed its first BITs in 1975 only (with Egypt and Singapore).[11]

It has been correctly noted, however, that these early agreements may be considered only as forerunners of current BITs, as they lack an investor-State dispute settlement mechanism (ISDS; and, in particular, investor-State arbitration, or ISA) alternative to the domestic courts of the host State to protect the investor from possible breaches of rights and guarantees granted in these

4 Switzerland came in second, by signing its first BIT in 1961, with Tunisia. By the time the Netherlands signed its first, in 1963, Switzerland was party to 7 BITs already.

5 See Table 1, below. For a review of the evolution of Germany's BIT models and practice, see R Dolzer and Y Kim, 'Germany', in C Brown (ed.), *Commentaries on Selected Model Investment Treaties* (Oxford University Press, 2013), 289–320.

6 With Cote d'Ivoire and Cameroon (1965), Indonesia (1968), Tanzania, Uganda, Sudan, and Kenya (1970).

7 With Malta (1967), Gabon (1968), Chad and Cote d'Ivoire (1969).

8 There will not be another French BIT until 1972 – which will be a renegotiation of that with Tunisia.

9 Cote d'Ivoire appears to have represented at the time for BITs what Chile is today for FTAs: by 1966 already, it enjoyed agreements with Switzerland, The Netherlands, Italy, Sweden and Germany.

10 Despite primarily concerned with trade, FCNs are considered the forerunners of BITs, as they usually feature, *inter alia*, guarantees on property rights and business interests of foreigners; according to Dolzer and Stevens (fn. 1), 11, however, '… the broad spectrum of close political, economic and cultural cooperation which was envisaged by FCNs (such as unrestricted right to entry and the unqualified right of national treatment) were thought to be incompatible with the new political realities [of the late 1950s]', and this brought to the end of the stipulation of FNCs in 1966 (with the conclusion of the last two: U.S.-Togo and U.S.-Thailand).

11 The first BIT the UK signed with a Commonwealth State is with Sri Lanka in 1980. Nevertheless, despite the late start, the UK has caught up quick (*e.g.*, Romania and Indonesia in 1976, Thailand in 1978).

specific treaties.[12] The first BITs combining substantive investment protection with binding ICSID arbitration were the 1968 Netherlands-Indonesia BIT (terminated)[13] and the 1969 Italy-Chad BIT (still in force).[14] In the 1990s, this type of BIT will represent the standard. By 1979, however, States had concluded only approximately 100 BITs, most of which were between major Western European States and developing States. BITs were, thus, expanding at a slow pace (as ICSID was a dormant system).[15] It was perhaps too early, for often newly independent States, to consent to the sovereign restraints a BIT implies (especially vis-à-vis ex-colonizers).[16]

As for non-European G7 economies, Japan's traditional emphasis on trade, rather than foreign investments,[17] may explain why it entered into its first BIT

---

12 For instance, approximately the first 50 BITs of Germany do not feature any ISDS, which entered the treaty practice only from 1985 (1985 BIT with St. Lucia, 1986 with Bulgaria – limited to amount of compensation due to expropriation –, 1986 with Nepal, 1987 with Hungary). For some general references, see A Newcombe, 'Developments in IIA Treaty-Making', in A De Mestral and C Lévesque (eds.), *Improving International Investment Agreements* (Routledge, 2013), 17; see also, M Langford and D Behn, 'Managing Backlash: The Evolving Investment Treaty Arbitrator?', *European Journal of International Law* (forthcoming 2017) <https://papers.ssrn.com/sol3/papers.cfm?abstract_id=2835488> accessed Nov. 20th, 2019.

13 Indonesia acceded to the ICSID convention on the same year. Art. 11 reads: 'The Contracting Party in the territory of which a national of the other Contracting Party makes or intends to make an investment, shall assent to any demand on the part of such national and any such national shall comply with any request of the former Contracting Party, to submit, for conciliation or arbitration, to the Centre established by the Convention of Washington of March 18, 1965, 1 any dispute that may arise in connection with the investment.'

14 Art. 7 reads: 'Tout différend concernant les investissements, objet du présent Accord, qui s'élèverait entre un Etat contractant (ou n'importe quelle Institution ou Organisation dépendante ou contrôlée par le même Etat) et une personne physique ou morale, ayant la nationalité de l'autre Etat, sera soumis à la juridiction du Centre International pour le règlement des différends relatifs aux investissements, conformément à la Convention Internationale de Washington du 18 mars 1965. Toute contestation ou tout différend entre les deux Etats, portant sur 1'interprétation ou l'application du présent Accord, seront réglés par la voie diplomatique'.

15 The first ICSID award was rendered in 1977, in the case involving the Italian investor *Adriano Gardella S.p.A. v. Côte d'Ivoire*, Award, Aug. 29th, 1977, ICSID Case No. ARB/74/1.

16 Such resistance on the part of developing States is exemplified by two Resolutions adopted by the General Assembly of the United Nations in 1974: 'Declaration for the Establishment of a New International Economic Order', 1974 (A/RES/S-6/3201), and 'Charter of Economic Rights and Duties of States', 1974 (A/RES/29/3281).

17 Already noted back in 1995 by Dolzer (cf., Dolzer and Stevens (fn. 1), 3) and maintained until recently (cf., Table 1).

at a later stage (*i.e.*, in 1977, with Egypt),[18] and still today it is party to 33 of them in total (only 30 of which are in force).[19] The U.S. maintained its long-standing policy based on bilateral FCN treaties even longer than the UK.[20] It consequently signed its first BITs in 1982 (with Egypt and Panama) – which is, notably, the same year as China. While the U.S. developed its first model text a few years later (in 1987), its strategy first shifted towards the conclusion of over sixty 'Trade and Investment Framework Agreements'.[21] Despite being officially labeled in a number of ways, these instruments are limited in scope as they primarily provide the context for an annual bilateral forum '... to meet and discuss issues of mutual interest with the objective of improving cooperation and enhancing opportunities for trade and investment'.[22] More systematic BIT negotiations would be pursued only in the course of the 1990s,[23] even though the overall size of the U.S. BIT network remains quantitatively modest.[24] As for Canada, the first BIT was signed with a dusking USSR, in 1988.[25]

18 Since its first BIT with Switzerland (1973), Egypt has rapidly concluded BITs will all major capital-exporters: Germany and France in 1974, Italy in 1975, The Netherlands in 1976, Japan in 1977 and the U.S. in 1982; notably, Egypt appears also to be the first developing State to have signed a BIT with another developing State (*i.e.*, the 1976 Egypt-Morocco BIT).

19 UNCTAD / Investment Policy Hub.

20 The U.S. entered into over 100 of such treaties (starting with the Treaty of Amity and Commerce with France, in 1782, and ending in 1966, with the agreements with Togo and Thailand).

21 The U.S. seems not to have ceased to conclude these agreements. For instance, in 2006 it signed a Trade and Investment Framework Arrangement with ASEAN (the text is available at: <http://www.ustr.gov/sites/default/files/uploads/agreements/tifa/asset_upload_file932_9760.pdf> accessed Nov. 20th, 2019.

22 According to the U.S. Trade Representative < https://ustr.gov/trade-agreements/trade-investment-framework-agreements> accessed Nov. 20th, 2019.

23 For a review of the early U.S. BIT program, see KJ Vandevelde, 'The Bilateral Investment Treaties Program of the United States' (1988) 21(1) *Cornell Journal of International Law* 202, 208–211. Despite the late start, the U.S. is found to have been '... at the forefront of varying the pattern started by Germany by the way of dramatically extending its length, and also by deviating from the basic pattern by way of combining matters of trade and investment in Free Trade Agreements instead of concluding solely investment-focused agreements', see Dolzer and Kim (fn. 5), 291.

24 BIT 45 signed / 39 in force / 2 terminated; source: UNCTAD / Investment Policy Hub.

25 In that year, the USSR concluded BITs also with Germany, France, Italy, the UK, the Netherlands, Belgium and Finland.

TABLE 1 BITs concluded by G7 States (plus Switzerland and Sweden) -selected years / *total number of BITs*-

	1967[26] / *63*	1983[27] / *220*	1994[28] / *>700*	2014[29] / *>2860*		
Germany	29 (>50%)	54 (>25%)	92 (>10%)	155	131	17
Switzerland	16	34	68	130	115	10
France	1	25	62	109	95	4
UK	0	22	71	107	95	1
The Netherlands	3	14	48	107	92	10
Italy	1	7	30	106	79	14
Belgium-Lux	2	14	35	104	68	8
Sweden	3	13	31	73	66	4
U.S.	0	3	33	47	40	1
Canada	0	2	10	45	31	5
Japan	0	2	4	25	19	0

A notable conceptual difference between Europe and North America (especially, since 2004) is that with the latter BITs tend to go beyond the aspect of 'promotion and protection' of investment, and to cover liberalization and free movement of capital. Nevertheless, until recently, investment liberalization was openly perceived as a '*per se* newly contentious global issue'[30] and, besides wider and deeper forms of integration among States (*e.g.*, EU, NAFTA, or ASEAN), many – especially developing States – still oppose it.[31] To date, for

26 Release of the Draft Convention on the Protection of Foreign Property.

27 Year of the signature of the China-Germany BIT.

28 Figures for 1994 are extracted from Dolzer and Stevens (fn. 1), 267–285.

29 In 2014, and after 123 years, China returned to be the largest economy in the world, overtaking the U.S. The column indicates the number of BIT signed / in force / terminated; source: UNCTAD online database; the total number of BITs in force in 2014 is provided in UNCTAD 2013.

30 C Huiping, 'China-ASEAN Investment Agreement Negotiations: the Substantive Issues' (2006) 7(1) *The Journal of World Investment & Trade: Law, Economics, Politics* 143, 144.

31 *E.g.*, ASEAN Member States accepted investment liberalization in the Framework Agreement on ASEAN Investment Area, but strictly between ASEAN members only; singular ASEAN Members (*e.g.*, Malaysia, Indonesia, Thailand and the Philippines), and other States (*e.g.*, India and China), still oppose indiscriminate liberalization.

instance, the 2004 and 2012 U.S. model BITs have, indeed, found limited practical adoption.[32]

2 *The Changing Shift*

Today, BITs are in excess of 2896 (of which, 2337 are in force), plus at least 389 trade, partnership or framework international agreements with an investment dimension (of which, 314 in force).[33] Over half of these are with (or between) European States. Currently, it appears that virtually next-to-all significant BITs have been signed: year 2017 has witnessed the conclusion of only 7 new agreements – marking the yearly lowest in a quarter century.[34] In this respect, two factors are altering the key actors in the field as well as shaping the evolution of investment agreements.

The first is political. BITs – especially those less recent yet still in force – are under intense scrutiny by law and policy makers, scholars, and public opinion all over the world. Following the surge of investment arbitral cases (ICSID and non-ICSID),[35] some decisions have revealed the potential costs for host States of breaches of treaty guarantees *vis-à-vis* foreign investors' claims. Some States have terminated their BITs, or withdrawn from the ICSID Convention.[36] Others have become concerned about (alleged) expansionary interpretations of

32 See the BITs with Uruguay (2005) and Rwanda (2005).

33 UNCTAD, 'International Investment Agreements Navigator' <https://investmentpolicy.unctad.org/international-investment-agreements> accessed Nov. 20th, 2019.

34 UNCTAD, 'World Investment Report: investment and the digital economy' (2017), 111 <http://worldinvestmentreport.unctad.org/world-investment-report-2017> accessed Nov. 20th, 2019.

35 See Figure 1, below.

36 *E.g.*, in Apr. 2007, Bolivia submitted a letter to ICSID, under Art. 71, announcing its decision to withdraw from the ICSID Convention; in Dec. 2007, Peru notified ICSID it withdrew consent for investment arbitrations in the mining and energy sectors; in Nov. 2008, Venezuela communicated to the Netherlands its intention to terminate the Dutch-Venezuela BIT; Ecuador has denounced 21 of its 25 BITs; Indonesia has also terminated 21 of its BITs; between 2012 and 2017, South Africa terminated the agreements with Argentina, Austria, Belgium, Denmark, France, Germany, Luxembourg, Netherlands, Spain and United Kingdom; 22 EU member States announced their intention to terminate all BITs concluded between them by 6 December 2019. See UNCTAD, 'Recent Developments in International Investment Agreements (2007–June 2008)' (UNCTAD Series on Issues in International Investment Agreements, 2008) <http://unctad.org/en/docs/webdiaeia20081_en.pdf> accessed Nov. 20th, 2019; UNCTAD, 'Taking Stock of IIA Reform: Recent Developments' (UNCTAD IIA Issues Note, Issue 3, June 2019) <https://unctad.org/en/PublicationsLibrary/diaepcbinf2019d5_en.pdf> accessed Nov. 23rd, 2019. For the policies of BRICS states, see further below in this Section.

perceived investor-oriented arbitral panels;[37] governments started criticizing the BITs' language, as 'intended to capture or threaten to capture a wide range of State activities',[38] resulting in States being 'legally constrained from pursuing a range of legislative strategies that significantly impair investment interests';[39] national interest groups vocally manifested against the BITs' lack of consideration for the environment and human rights.[40] Consequently, innovations in recent model and actual treaties reflect the efforts of an increasing number of States to find a new balance between two potentially competing objectives: the promotion and protection of investments, and the right to properly regulate for public welfare purposes.[41] In this context, it shall be mentioned that, in July 2017, under the push of the EU and Canada, UNCITRAL inaugurated talks under Working Group III with the goal to *i*) identify and consider concerns regarding ISDS (with particular reference to ISA), *ii*) consider whether reform is desirable and, if so, *iii*) recommend any relevant solutions (see Section 6, below, and the book's conclusion).

The second factor is economic. The equilibrium of global investment flows – which set the basis of the current BIT framework – is rapidly changing: as a sign of this, in 2012, for the first time, developing States as a whole have overtaken developed States as main recipient of FDIs.[42] Also due to the medium-term effects of the 2008–2012 global economic crisis, in 2012 Europe accounted

37 See J Paulsson, *The Denial of Justice in International Law* (Cambridge University Press, 2005), 228–62; M Sornarajah, 'The Retreat of Neo-Liberalism in Investment Treaty Arbitration', in CA Rogers and RP Alford (eds.), *The Future of Investment Arbitration* (Oxford University Press, 2009), 291; TH Yen, 'East Asian Investment Treaties in the Integration Process: *Quo Vadis*?', in RP Buckley, R Weixing Hu and DW Arner (eds.), *East Asian Economic Integration: Law, Trade and Finance* (Edward Elgar Publishing, 2011), 183–204.

38 D Schneiderman, *Constitutionalizing Economic Globalization* (Cambridge University Press, 2008), 34 and 37–8.

39 *Ibid.*

40 M Sornarajah, *The International Law on Foreign Investment* (Cambridge University Press, 2004), 259.

41 MA Clodfelter, 'The Adaptation of States to the Changing World of Investment Protection through Model BITs' (2009) 24(1) *ICSID Review* 165, 174.

42 UNCTAD, 'World Investment Report: Global Value Chains: Investment and Trade for Development' (2013), 62–72, <http://unctad.org/en/PublicationsLibrary/wir2013_en.pdf> accessed Nov. 20th, 2019; the situation lasted until 2015; since then, there is no clear trend, with developed and developing States, as a whole, repeatedly switching position; see UNCTAD, 'World Investment Report: investor nationality: policy challenges' (2016), 64–68, <https://unctad.org/en/PublicationsLibrary/wir2016_en.pdf> accessed Nov. 20th, 2019; see, also, UNCTAD, 'World Investment Report: investment and new industrial policies' (2018), 61–64, <https://unctad.org/en/PublicationsLibrary/wir2018_en.pdf> accessed Nov. 20th, 2019.

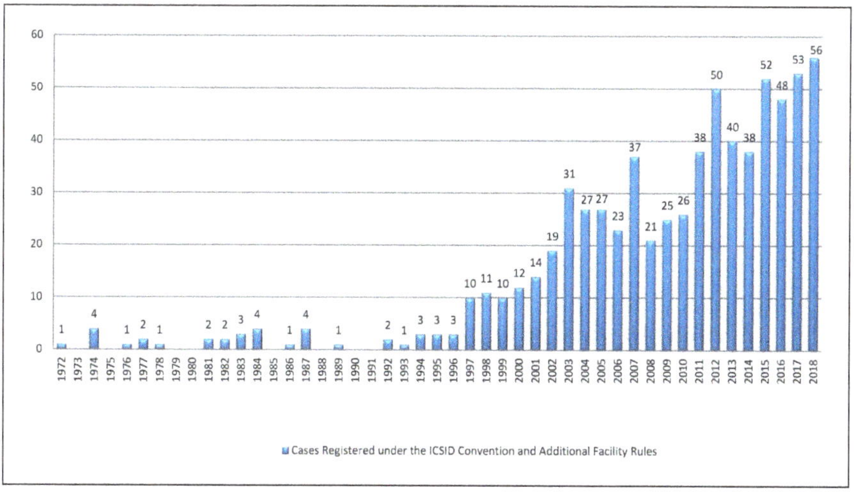

FIGURE 1 Cases registered under the ICSID Convention and Additional Facility Rules (*up to December 31st, 2018*)[43]

for almost two thirds of the global FDI decline, with FDI outflows falling over 37% (to levels similar to financially-troubled 2009, one third from the peak record of 2007), and inflows of 42% (to levels comparable to 2002).[44] While all major European States still figure among the top 20 investor economies worldwide (and are still perceived among the most promising investors abroad), the rise of new actors – most notably, China – is a fact.[45] It is significant that today the outward flow of FDI from Asia accounts for a larger share than that from the EU (roughly, 39% of the global flow), with BRICS economies, for instance, figuring as top investors in Africa[46] and in many South American States.

Hence, the roots of the international investment regime may lie in Europe; its future developments, however, may well rest on East and Southeast Asia's hands, with China playing an ever more significant role within and outside that region.

43 World Bank, 'The ICSID Caseload – Statistics' (Issue n. 1, 2019) <https://icsid.worldbank.org/en/Documents/resources/ICSID%20Web%20Stats%202019-1(English).pdf> accessed Oct. 10th, 2019.

44 *Ibid.*; see, also, Figure 3, below.

45 See Figures 2, 3 and 4.

46 UNCTAD, 'World Investment Report: Special Economic Zones' (2019), 33, <https://unctad.org/en/PublicationsLibrary/wir2019_en.pdf> accessed Nov. 20th, 2019.

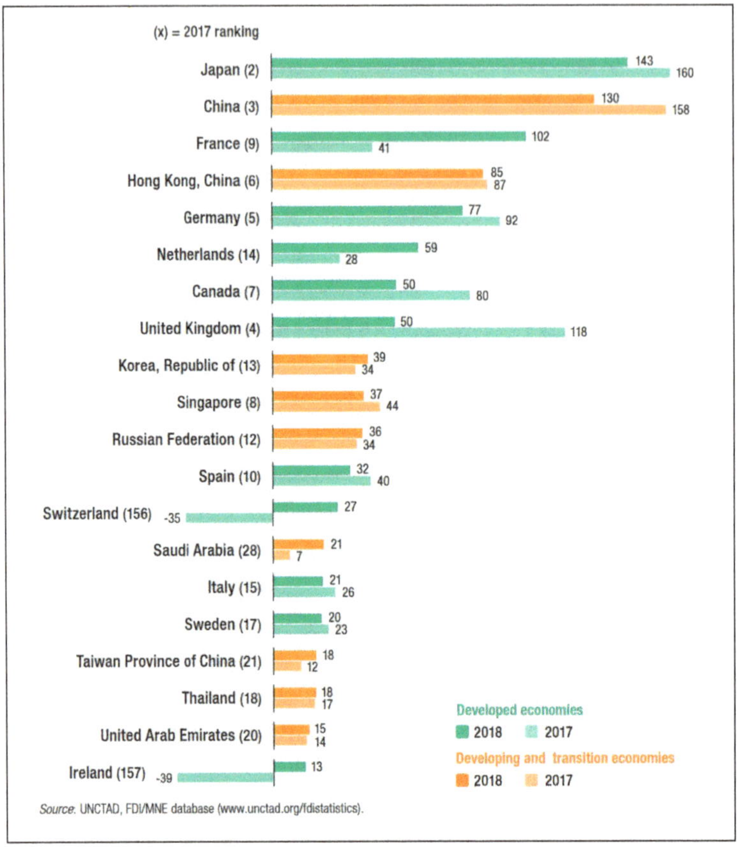

FIGURE 2 Top 20 investor economies (2017–2018) (*billion USD*)[47]

FDI inflows (2012–2018) (*billion USD*) **FDI outflows (2012–2018) (*billion USD*)**

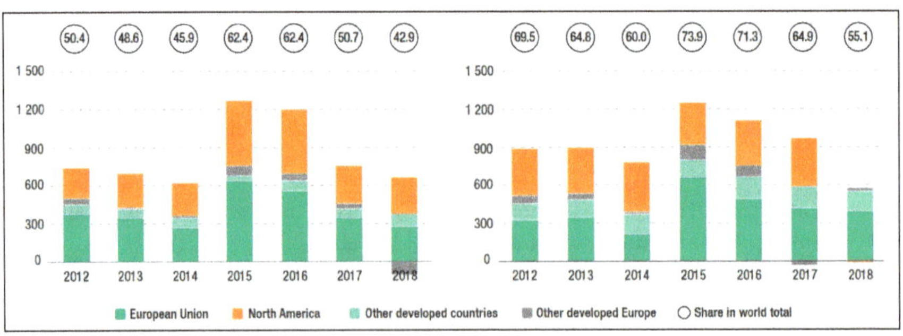

FIGURE 3 FDI inflows and outflows (2012–2018)[48]

47 *Id.*, 7.
48 *Ibid.*

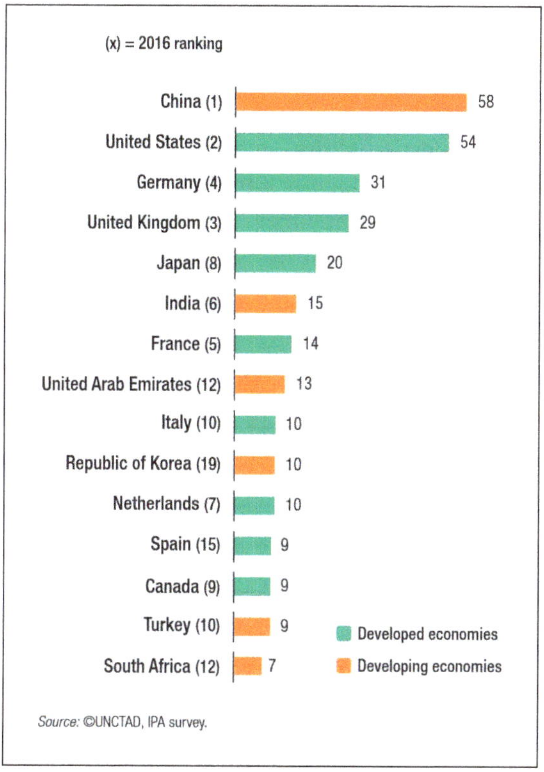

FIGURE 4 Most promising investor economies for FDI (2017–2019)[49] (*percentage of responses for States seen as top source of FDI*)

3 *BRICS and IIAs*

In 2001, Goldman Sachs gathered, under the acronym BRICS, a group of developing, large, fast-growing and most-promising economies in the long term: Brazil, Russia, India, China, and South Africa.[50] It is on the 'C' of the acronym that this work focuses, as the group's current heavyweight – under a combined demographic, economic, and geopolitical perspective. Also, China's world-wide network of investment agreements results from its relatively early engagement with international investment law (it signed the first BIT in 1982, with Sweden). China today enjoys a network of 129 BITs (110 of which in force), without considering another 16 that have been terminated in the meantime.[51] In addition,

49 UNCTAD, 'World Investment Report: investment and the digital economy' (2017), (fn. 34), 9.

50 J O'Neil, 'Building Better Global Economic BRICs' (Goldman Sachs Global Economics Paper n. 66 Nov. 30th, 2001), 3 <http://www.goldmansachs.com/our-thinking/archive/archive-pdfs/build-better-brics.pdf> accessed Nov. 20th, 2019.

51 UNCTAD / Investment Policy Hub.

there are 6 FTAs featuring a complete investment protection regime (without considering the special arrangements in place with Hong Kong, Macau, and Taiwan).[52] The comparison with the other BRICS States is revealing:

- Brazil signed its first BIT in 1994 (with Portugal) and, by 1999, it had signed another 14;[53] however, due to domestic political opposition and the local reheating of the Calvo doctrine, it subsequently announced it would not ratify any of the signed texts. Under a recently inaugurated alternative IIA policy (which excludes ISA altogether), Brazil has signed 12 agreements, mostly with South American or Lusophone States; to date, only one (with Angola) is in force.[54]
- Russia signed its first BIT in 1989 (as USSR, with Finland); over time, it has signed 84 BITs (64 of which are in force, 15 not in force, and 5 terminated);[55] notably, Russia is also the pivot of the recently established Eurasian Economic Union (EAEU; featuring an investment protection chapter with ISDS), which has in turn concluded a comprehensive FTA with Vietnam (already in force) and is pursuing negotiations with Egypt, Iran, Singapore, and Serbia.[56]
- India signed its first BIT in 1994 (with the UK) and over the following 15 years concluded 89 BITs. Of these, however, only 24 are in force,[57] 4 not yet,[58] and 61 have been terminated.[59] In 2011 (subsequent to losing a treaty-based case for the first time), India almost halted the expansion of its network, while working on updating its 2003 model (which was by and large similar to that of 1993); it ultimately released its new model BIT in late 2015. Since

52 China-Pakistan (2006), China-New Zealand (2008), China-ASEAN (2009), China-Peru (2009), Costa Rica (2010), China-Korea (2015). The investment regime of the 2015 China-Australia FTA is incomplete and currently under additional negotiations.

53 UNCTAD / Investment Policy Hub.

54 *Ibid.*; see J Kalicki and S Medeiros, 'Investment Arbitration in Brazil: Revisiting Brazil's Traditional Reluctance towards ICSID, BITs and Investor-State Arbitration' (2008) 24 *Arbitration International* 423, 431–438; see, also, M Papa, 'BRICS and Politics of Reforming Global Governance: the Case of Investment Arbitration', in G De Búrca, J Scott and C Kilpatrick (eds.), *Critical Legal Perspectives on Global Governance: Liber Amicorum David M Trubek* (Hart Publishing, 2013), 415.

55 UNCTAD / Investment Policy Hub.

56 YZ Haftel, 'BRICS and the Global Investment Regime', in SY Kim (ed.), *BRICs and Global Economy* (World Scientific Publishing, forthcoming 2019), 10–15 <https://papers.ssrn.com/sol3/papers.cfm?abstract_id=2957721> accessed Oct. 31st, 2019.

57 Including FTA arrangements featuring an investment protection chapter with Malaysia, Japan, Korea, and Singapore.

58 Including the ASEAN-India Investment Agreement, signed in 2014 and flowing from a multi-stage comprehensive FTA framework agreement of 2004.

59 UNCTAD / Investment Policy Hub.

2013, India has concluded only two BITs (only one of which entered into force, in 2017).[60]
- South Africa signed its first BIT in 1994 (with the UK as well); the BIT network formally features 50 concluded agreements. However, due to dwindling support in principle to granting special protection to foreign investment, over the last few years South Africa has denounced most of its BITs with key capital exporters, while focusing on alternative ways to promote inward foreign investment (of interest are the developments within the South African Development Community).[61] To date, only 12 BITs are in force (27 are not, while 11 have been terminated).[62]

Of these States, only India is experienced with investment treaty models (having adopted at least three, in 1993, 2003, and 2015). However, over the last decade Brazil, India, and South Africa have developed a quite controversial relationship with investment arbitration and have adopted a conservative or restrictive approach towards IIAs.

Conversely, China, which appears to have adopted a model since 1984, by 1993 was considering the adoption of its third official update.[63] Indeed, while imposing certain limitations, China has been by far the most active in pursuing a coherent international investment policy. Together with a number of domestic reforms, this has resulted in the creation of an environment sufficiently friendly to let foreign investors focus on the opportunity China represents, and

60 Haftel (fn. 56), 15–19; see, also, DJ Khambata and AN Mehta, 'Foreign Investment in India: The Unfolding Legal Story', in C Esplugues (ed.), *Foreign Investment and Investment Arbitration in Asia* (Intersentia, 2019), 55–99.

61 However, notwithstanding the release of the SADC model BIT, in July 2012, the SADC dispute settlement mechanism has been substantially altered in 2016; see EC Schlemmer, 'Dispute Settlement in Investment-Related Matters: South Africa and the BRICS' (2018) 112 *AJIL Unbound* 212; see, also, T Chidede, 'Investment Dispute Resolution under the Amended Annex 1 of the SADC FIP', *Tralac Blog* (Oct. 1st, 2018), <https://www.tralac.org/blog/article/13526-investment-dispute-resolution-under-the-amended-annex-1-of-the-sadc-fip.html> accessed Oct. 31st, 2019. In the meantime, South Africa terminated most of its BITs with EU members (*e.g.*, Denmark, France, Switzerland, UK, Germany, Austria, Spain, the Netherlands, Italy).

62 UNCTAD / Investment Policy Hub.

63 See N Gallagher and W Shan, *Chinese Investment Treaties: Policies and Practice* (Oxford University Press, 2009), 35–43 and 421–437; *contra*, Q Kong, according to whom China never used a model for its BIT negotiations; see Q Kong, 'Bilateral Investment Treaties: The Chinese Approach and Practice' (1998/99) 8 *Asian Yearbook of International Law* 105, 114. However, in light of the more recent, conspicuous and uncontested work of Gallagher and Shan, it is here assumed that, at the time of Kong's writing, this piece of information was not publicly available (on the point, see Chapter 2).

get past the hostile attitude the communist ruling party maintained for quite some time towards them.

B China's Policy Evolution towards FDIs and BITs (1949–2015): Outline and Remarks

1. *China and FDI: Main Periods*

In their comprehensive work of 2009 on China's policy in international investment law, Professors Norah Gallagher and Wenhua Shan divide the history of foreign investment in China into four periods:[64]

1. Nationalization and exclusion (1949–1978),
2. Gradual resumption (1979–1991),
3. First surge (1992–2000), and
4. Second surge (2001–2008).

With regard to the Chinese BIT program, since its inception in 1982, they propose three periods (approximately corresponding to the adoption of a new model text):

1. The 1980s, with first-generation BITs (tied, since 1984, to the first model BIT);
2. Most of the 1990s, comprising first and second-generation BITs (the latter, based on the second model BIT, of 1989); and,
3. Third-generation BITs of the late 1990s and early 2000 (mostly based on the 1997 model BIT).

It is believed that a fourth period should be added to the previous three, starting from 2006: then, China begun concluding FTAs featuring an investment chapter[65] and multi-stage FTAs comprising investment agreements,[66] as well as gradually shifting for the North American models' language and structure.[67] As illustrated in detail in Chapter 3, at the beginning, new stipulations, while

64 *Id.*, 4. Li, instead, divides the Chinese BIT program in two phases: 1982–1996 and from 1997 on, with each phase comprising a number of 'sub-phases'; cf., L Li, 'Chinese BIT Practice and Challenges' (2010) 17(4) *Chinese Journal of International and Economic Law* 114.

65 China-Pakistan FTA (2006), China-New Zealand FTA (2008), China-Peru FTA (2009).

66 China-ASEAN Investment Agreement (2009), China-Chile Supplementary Agreement on Investments (2012).

67 China-Canada BIT (2012) and China-Japan-Korea TIA (2012). Such fourth period could begin in 2003 as well, with the renegotiation of the 1983 China-Germany BIT; however, as illustrated in Chapter 2 and Three, for how innovative such an agreement has been, China will not grant similar standards again until the 2008 FTA with New Zealand; also, while grouping Chinese BITs differently, Cai concurs in that, since 2006, China's policy begun the shift for a more balanced generation of investment treaties, see C Cai, 'China-U.S. BIT

weighed carefully, appear to be the result of *ad hoc* negotiation bargains, rather than part of a systemic approach.

Nevertheless, as illustrated further below, although each generation of BITs characterizes a given period, BITs of different generations may still be found in other periods.[68]

2 *From Exclusion to Resumption*

In principle, the People's Republic's foreign policy is still today characterized by the 'Five Principles of Peaceful Co-existence', consisting of *i*) 'mutual respect for States' sovereignty and territorial integrity, *ii*) mutual non-aggression, *iii*) non-interference in each other's internal affairs, *iv*) equality and mutual benefit, and *v*) peaceful coexistence'.[69] In 1974, the Chinese Communist leadership, recently admitted to the UN, joined the initiative of developing States at the General Assembly for the adoption of the "Declaration on the Establishment of a New International Economic Order", which emphasized State sovereignty over domestic natural resources and rejected the idea that foreign investment should receive special status under international law.[70] Accordingly, the early decades of Communist rule resulted in the reaffirmation of the sovereign right to *i*) control the entry of FDI and regulate the activities of foreign investors; *ii*) nationalize foreign property without being subject to conditions such as 'public purpose, due process and compensation'; and *iii*) mandate renegotiations, revisions, or unilateral modifications of State contracts on the basis of changed circumstances or public interest.[71]

Negotiations and the Future of Investment Treaty Regime: A Grand Bilateral Bargain with Multilateral Implications' (2009) 12(2) *Journal of International Economic Law* 457, 462.

68 In this sense Gallagher and Shan, *Chinese Investment Treaties* (fn. 63), 35; view confirmed and further developed in N Gallagher and W Shan, 'China', in C Brown (ed.), *Commentaries on Selected Model Investment Treaties* (Oxford University Press, 2013).

69 Ministry of Foreign Affairs of the People's Republic of China, 'China's Initiation of the Five Principles of Peaceful Co-Existence' <http://www.fmprc.gov.cn/mfa_eng/ziliao_665539/3602_665543/3604_665547/t18053.shtml> accessed Nov. 20th, 2019. That respect for State sovereignty comes first should not surprise; even today, sovereignty in China is understood in its political dimension well before its legal articulation, with international law perceived as a 'purely pragmatic instrument, not a goal in and of itself'; in this sense, see the brief but effective review of E Pekar, 'The Chinese Investment Regime and the U.S.-China Negotiations', in W Shan (ed.), *China and International Investment Law* (Brill Nijhoff, 2014), 263–296, at 265–271.

70 General Assembly, 'Declaration for the Establishment of a New International Economic Order', 1974 (A/RES/S-6/3201).

71 Kong, 'Bilateral Investment Treaties' (fn. 63), 109; in this sense, also A Berger, 'China's New Bilateral Investment Treaty Programme: Substance, Rational and Implications for International Investment Law Making' (Paper for presentation at the American

In light of the above, and in the framework of the People's Republic's 'resentment and skepticism' towards foreign investment and its protection by international law,[72] it is not surprising that, since its establishment in 1949 and until 1978, the Chinese ruling class effectively opposed existing foreign investment on its territory, and discouraged any new. Before 1949, foreign investors in China controlled (or had significant stakes in) key sectors such as railway, mining, textiles, and navigation.[73] While early Communist governments never explicitly considered a nationalization program, by 1956 foreign investments were effectively eliminated from the Mainland – and excluded for the subsequent twenty years.[74]

The hostility toward foreign investors, their investments, and international stipulations on the matter was justified with two sets of arguments. First, China's 'century of humiliation' following the 'unequal treaties' with Western Powers[75] – which brought large segments of Chinese society to regard trade and investment treaties as 'imperialistic impositions' on China as well as other States.[76] Second, Chinese leaders viewed (and practiced) changes in the treatment of foreign investment as an effective tool to express political answers – whether as a matter of provocation or retaliation (*e.g.*, against the protracted

Society of International Law International Economic Law Interest Group Conference, Nov. 14th–15th, 2008), 7 <https://www.die-gdi.de/uploads/media/Berger_ChineseBITs.pdf> accessed Nov. 20th, 2019.

72 As put by Schill, 'Tearing down the Great Wall' (fn. 3), 77. Chinese politicians (and scholars) tended to view international law as a tool '… used by the imperialists and hegemonists … to carry out aggression, oppression and exploitation'; see Kong, 'Bilateral Investment Treaties' (fn. 63), 108. Indeed, in his presidential inauguration speech, on 20 January 1949, U.S. President Truman presented a kind of development deliberately set in opposition to the socialist model, to be achieved not through foreign property, but foreign investment. Investment is the liberal answer to the demands for a more social world that allowed to secure Western influence vis-à-vis the Soviet Union. For a study on the point, see A Escobar, *Encountering Development: The Making and Unmaking of the Third World* (Princeton University Press, 1995).

73 TN Thompson, 'China's Nationalization of Foreign Firms: The Politics of Hostage Capitalism, 1949–57', (1979) 27(6) *Maryland Series in Contemporary Asian Studies* 1, 3.

74 *Id.*, 10; exceptions being some joint ventures with USSR entities and States.

75 *E.g.*, 1842 Nanking Treaty with the UK, 1844 Wanghia Treaty with the U.S., 1844 Huagpu Treaty with France (the latter two forcibly granting MFN treatment to U.S. and French interests).

76 For a brief review of the point, see V Bath, 'Foreign Investment, The National Interest and National Security: Foreign Direct Investment in Australia and China' (2012) 34(1) *Sydney Law Review* 5, 5; more in depth, D Wang, *China's Unequal Treaties: Narrating National History* (Lexington Books, 2005).

tensions for its recognition, or in the context of the War of Korea).[77] 'Hostage capitalism' and the ensuing occasional 'retaliatory requisitions' were ultimately perceived as contributing to the goal of 'socialist transformation of capitalist industry and commerce'.[78]

Domestically, under the leadership of Mao Zedong, Communist China's early economics was deeply affected by the 'Great Leap Forward' policy, adopted between 1958 and 1962 and aimed at rapidly transforming China from a primarily agricultural to an industrial economy – resorting, *inter alia*, to collectivization of land.[79] Internationally, by virtue of the common ideological matrix, China negotiated treaties with its then-closest ally, the Soviet Union. In 1950, a (quite generic) 'Treaty of Friendship, Alliance and Mutual Assistance'[80] was signed. Subsequently, in 1958, China and the USSR concluded the 'Treaty of Trade and Navigation' (***inter alia*** granting to each other MFN treatment 'in all trade, navigation' and 'other economic relations').[81]

However, the domestic and international economic policies adopted in this period did not bring the hoped results in terms of prosperity and financial stability. The 'Great Leap Forward' has been authoritatively considered 'a very expensive disaster',[82] directly contributing to the 'Great Famine' of 1958–1961. By the late 1970s, the Chinese economy was on the brink of collapse. Thus, with

77 *E.g.*, in 1951 China took over all installations of Shell Oil Company in China, after the British government of Hong Kong took over an oil tanker the ownership of which was disputed by China; see Thompson (fn. 73), 68.

78 *Ibid.*

79 According to Zedong's views, the best way to finance industrialization was for the government to take control of agriculture, thereby establishing a monopoly over grain distribution and supply; this would allow the State to buy at a low price and sell much higher, thus raising the capital necessary for State industrialization.; see AG Walder, *China Under Mao: A Revolution Derailed* (Harvard University Press, 2015), 50–60, 152–159; also see YY Kueh, *China's New Industrialization Strategy: Was Chairman Mao Necessary?* (Edward Elgar Publishing, 2008), 116–136. This logic, which implies a net grain exporting position for China, strikingly misses the country's demography and demographics.

80 Art. 5 expresses the Treaty's purpose as to 'develop and strengthen the economic and cultural ties' between the two States; the Treaty, nevertheless, mostly reproduced the text of a 1945 agreement already concluded between the USSR and the previous Chinese government; the Treaty expired in 1979.

81 With regard to dispute settlement, Art. 16 of that Treaty provided that the parties would guarantee enforcement of arbitral awards 'with regard to disputes arising out of the commercial or other contracts of their corporate bodies or institutions, where the Parties have duly agreed to refer the dispute to an ad hoc or permanent arbitral tribunal for settlement'.

82 DH Perkins, 'China's Economic Policy and Performance', in R MacFarquhar, JK Fairbank and D Twitchett (eds.), *The Cambridge History of China*, vol. 15 (Cambridge University Press, 1991), 483–486.

the alleged adoption of the motto 'it does not matter whether the cat is black or white, as long as it catches mices',[83] Deng Xiaoping, new Party leader, in 1978 steered the 'universal truth of Marxism' to the 'concrete reality of China'.[84] With the plan to develop a 'socialist system with Chinese characteristics',[85] Xiaoping inaugurated the 'Open Doors' policy, and pushed for a number of changes in the legal framework (at both domestic and international level). In order to fuel economic growth, China then adopted an extensive plan of modernization, in which the resumption of FDI was key – also, to acquire advanced technology and management skills. In this perspective, China basic principles of foreign policy earlier mentioned were updated to expressly include three 'guiding principles of international economic cooperation and exchange': *i*) sovereignty, *ii*) equality and mutual benefit, and *iii*) reference to international practice.[86] In 1979, the National People's Congress passed the law of 'China-foreign equity joint ventures' and, in 1982, Article 18 of the Constitution was amended as follows, to include a reference to foreign investments (thus confirming their protection under Chinese law):

> All foreign enterprises and other foreign investment located in China, as well as joint ventures with Chinese and foreign investment located in China, shall abide by the law of the People's Republic of China. Their lawful rights and interests are protected by the law of the People's Republic of China.[87]

The Communist establishment was nonetheless aware that, to reduce the skepticism maintained by foreign investors and to 'win their trust and confidence', it was necessary to 'commit to international obligations through bilateral agreements'.[88] Hence, in 1982 the Chinese BIT program saw the light, with the signature of the first investment treaty, with Sweden. Another 25 BITs

---

83 See BBC, 'Deng Xiaoping', *BBC News* <http://news.bbc.co.uk/2/shared/spl/hi/asia_pac/02/china_party_congress/china_ruling_party/key_people_events/html/deng_xiaoping.stm> accessed Nov. 20th, 2019.

84 ME Marti, *China and the Legacy of Deng Xiaoping: From Communist Revolution to Capitalist Evolution* (Brassey's Washington DC, 2002), 10.

85 *Ibid.*

86 Kong, 'Bilateral Investment Treaties' (fn. 63), 110.

87 Art. 18 of the Constitution of the People's Republic of China (adopted on Dec. 4th, 1982, amended in 2004); the text is available in English at: http://english.people.com.cn/constitution/constitution.html, accessed 20 Nov. 2019.

88 As per the words of S Li, 'Bilateral Investment Promotion and Protection Agreements: Practice of the People's Republic of China', in P De Waart, P Peters and E Denters (eds.), *International Law and Development* (Martinus Nijhoff, 1988), 177–180.

were to follow by 1989, and further 68 in the course of the 1990s. Together with an assortment of additional investor-friendlier domestic regulations, China shifted its policy as well at the multilateral level, becoming a party to the Multilateral Investment Guarantee Agency Convention from its inception, in 1988, and signing the ICSID Convention in 1990.[89] All these reforms, nevertheless, did not imply the adoption of liberal economic theories; rather, they were driven by 'utilitarianism or even mercantilism', as 'China's attitude towards FDI in this period was [still] rooted in mixed feelings of attraction and aversion'.[90]

Unsurprisingly, earlier Chinese BITs mainly targeted industrialized or capital-exporting States. According to its 'discrete cultural, legal and political traditions',[91] China's first BIT with one such State was concluded with Sweden – perceived as more neutral than West Germany, France or the UK (all of which were already experienced in investment negotiations and treaty-making – having concluded, respectively, 33, 19 and 17 BITs).[92] Nonetheless, as the real target was actually the investment potential of these and other similarly-sized economies, almost all BITs China entered into for the three subsequent years were with major capital exporters, such as Germany (1983), France (1984), and Italy (1985) (see Table 2, below). The conclusion of BITs with less significant investment partners shows, on the other hand, an interesting pattern (in particular over the years 1992–1993), as it mirrors switches in diplomatic recognition, as the only China, from the Republic of China (Taiwan) to the People's Republic of China.

As noted, China, despite being a developing State, seemingly adopted a model BIT text in 1984 already, after the signature of the China-France BIT.[93] The vast majority of all subsequent BITs have adhered to such text, *in toto* or for the most part. However, more than some nationalistic 'resistance' vis-à-vis capital-exporter States, or the increasing economic leverage that the Chinese government could rely upon, the reason for such a rather strict policy, hence the ensuing relative uniformity of the BIT program, is to be ascribed to the limited power Chinese negotiators disposed of. Such limitation, in turn, rests on the complex (and strictly hierarchical) distribution of power within the Chinese government,[94] and the lengthy procedures necessary to consider

89 China ratified its signature in 1993.

90 In the words of Kong, 'Bilateral Investment Treaties' (fn. 63), 110.

91 B Shelley, *Democratic Development in East Asia* (Routledge, 2004), p. 40.

92 By contrast, in 1982 Sweden had concluded 8 BITs; see Table 1.

93 See fn. 63.

94 Revealing, in this respect, is a passage in Gallagher and Shan, *Chinese Investment Treaties* (fn. 63), 40, with regard to the negotiations for the 1997 BIT with Barbados: 'The [Request for Authorization of negotiation] suggested the State Council giving a general or standing

modifications to either the negotiators' mandate or the model text, especially at the time.[95]

Next to political considerations of all sorts, this has long been one of the reasons why, despite negotiations for a BIT with the U.S. (begun in 1983, following by the restoration of diplomatic relations in 1979, and the stipulation of the 'Agreement on Trade Relations')[96] have so far failed, notwithstanding repeated re-launches (the last two, in December 2007[97] and July 2013).[98] What the U.S. insisted on (in terms of dispute settlement, national treatment, and liberalization commitments) was not only far ahead for China's politics of the time,[99] but also technically not possible because out of the hands of the negotiators.

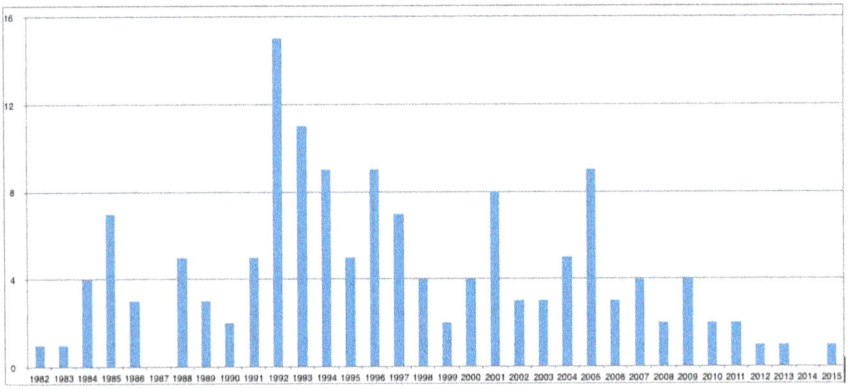

FIGURE 5 Annual growth of Chinese BITs (1982–2015)[100]

authorization on such negotiations with other States based on this text, so that the [Ministry of Foreign Trade and Economic Cooperation] and the [Ministry of Foreign Affairs] did not need to seek specific authorization on such negotiations, unless there were 'major changes' in the treaty text'.

95 For a brief description of the Chinese treaty-making process, see Gallagher and Shan, *Chinese Investment Treaties* (fn. 63), 33–34.

96 Agreement on Trade Relations between the United States of America and the People's Republic of China, signed on Jul. 7th, 1979, TIAS 9630, 31 UST 4651; the Agreement featured the MFN clause.

97 Flowing from the U.S.-China Strategic Economic Dialogue.

98 For an analysis of failures and re-launches of these negotiations, see Q Kong, 'U.S. China Bilateral Investment Treaty Negotiations: Context, Focus and Implications' (2012) 7(1) *Asian Journal of WTO and International Health Law & Policy* 181.

99 In this sense see, also, A Berger, 'Investment Rules in Chinese Preferential Trade and Investment Agreements: Is China Following the Global Trend towards Comprehensive Agreements?' (German Development Institute Discussion Paper n. 7, 2013), 6 <http://www.die-gdi.de/uploads/media/DP_7.2013.pdf> accessed Nov. 20th, 2019.

100 Original table, data extracted from UNCTAD Investment Policy Hub.

TABLE 2 First Chinese BITs[101]

BIT no.	Party	Signature	Renegotiation/new stipulation
1	Sweden	March 29th, 1982	Sep. 27th, 2004 (signed, not in force)
2	Romania	Feb. 10th, 1983	Apr. 16th, 2007
3	Germany	Oct. 7th, 1983	Dec. 1st, 2003
4	France	May 30th, 1984	Nov. 26th, 2007
		***PRC 1984 model* BIT**	
5	Belgium-Lux	June 4th, 1984	Jun. 6th, 2005
6	Finland	Sept. 4th, 1984	Nov. 15th, 2004
7	Italy	Jan. 28th, 1985	–
8	Thailand	Mar. 12th, 1985	Aug. 15th, 2009 (CAIA)
9	Denmark	Apr. 29th, 1985	–
10	Netherlands	Jun. 17th, 1985	Nov. 26th, 2001
11	Austria	Sept. 12th, 1985	–
12	Singapore	Nov. 21st, 1985	Oct. 23rd, 2008 (FTA) Aug. 15th, 2009 (CAIA)
13	Kuwait	Nov. 23rd, 1985	–
14	Sri Lanka	Mar. 13th, 1986	–
15	UK	May 15th, 1986	–
16	Switzerland	Nov. 12th, 1986	Jan. 27th, 2009
17	Poland	Jun. 7th, 1988	–
18	Australia	Jul. 11th, 1988	Jun. 17th, 2015 (FTA)
19	Japan	Aug. 27th, 1988	May 13th, 2012 (TIA)
20	New Zealand	Nov. 22nd, 1988	Apr. 7th, 2008 (FTA)
...			
128	Canada	Sept. 9th, 2012	–
–	U.S.	–[102]	–

Subsequently, while continuing to pursue investment agreements with major capital exporters (*e.g.*, the UK, in 1986), China started to enter also into BITs with developing States such as Thailand, Singapore, Kuwait, Sri Lanka,

101 Source: author, crossing references from the Ministry of Commerce of the People's Republic of China (MOFCOM) and those available on the UNCTAD Investment Policy Hub.

102 See fn. 98.

Malaysia, Pakistan, and Ghana.[103] In those with developed States, however, China quite occasionally accepted a few amendments: *e.g.*, the 1986 BIT with the UK, and the 1987 BIT with the Netherlands were the first to allow for *ad hoc* international arbitration[104] – an exception all the more noticeable as both the UK and Dutch models at the time featured arbitration only as an option.[105] China thus appears to have opted, since then, for a two-tier policy: BITs with developed States primarily served the purpose (especially, at first) of attracting foreign investment; conversely, BITs with developing States – whose text usually coincides with that of the Chinese contemporary model – were (especially, at first) primarily aimed at forging or strengthening diplomatic alliances,[106] or anyway undertaken in light of political considerations.[107] In any case, until the late 1990s, China's international investment policy has been marked by a reluctance in principle to commit to strong legal protections to foreign investment.[108] However, as China's need for primary and raw resources grew, demanding consistent Chinese outbound investment to secure it, BITs with developing States progressively shifted their focus on the protection of that flow. The same happened soon afterwards with developed States as well.

Although all early Chinese BITs were relatively conservative (or restrictive;[109] and this is reflected in the text of its first two models as well as in China's

---

103 With regard to the 1983 BIT with Romania, it should be noted that Romania has been the most active Socialist State in concluding BITs (the first, in 1976, with the United Kingdom) and has continued to be so also in the post-Socialist era (before 2012, Romania enjoyed a network of 84 BITs, almost the size of Italy's network at the time, comprising 93 agreements); thanks to the 'comradely relationship' of Socialism, and the lack of a model BIT on the part of China, the 1983 BIT between the two States relies on the experience of Romania (by 1983, already strong of 13 agreements, including all major European capital-exporters) which, since the 1980 BIT with Senegal, was not new to cover 'direct and indirect capital investments'; thus, so does the first China-Romania BIT. Neither the 1994 renegotiation, nor that of 2007, will keep such exceptional wording.

104 This is just one year after Germany stipulated its first BIT featuring unrestricted ISA (with St. Lucia, in 1985).

105 According to G Smith, 'Chinese Bilateral Investment Treaties: Restrictions on International Arbitration' (2010) 76 *Arbitration* 58. Also, LE Trakman, 'China and Foreign Direct Investment: Does Distance Lend Enchantment to the View?' (2014) 2(1) *The Chinese Journal of Comparative Law* 1, 12.

106 In this sense, see Li, 'Chinese BIT Practice and Challenges' (fn. 64), 1.

107 Also see the economic impact analysis of Chinese BITs with developing States elaborated by K Hadley, 'Do China's BIT Matter? Assessing the Effect of China's Investment Agreements on Foreign Direct Investment Flows, Investors' Rights, and the Rule of Law' (2013) 45 *Georgetown Journal of International Law* 255, 269–274.

108 In this sense, Berger, 'China's New Bilateral Investment Treaty Programme' (fn. 71), 8.

109 For a brief illustration of the difference between the 'liberal' and 'restrictive' approaches to international investment protection, and with regard to China, *id.*, 3.

material practice at the time), those with developing or socialist States featured certain typical characteristics. The focus there was more on investment promotion and encouragement, and more emphasis was placed on State sovereignty and national jurisdiction;[110] only certain provisions were quite specific (*e.g.*, definitions of investment and admission, a thorough consultation process, the exclusive and complete jurisdiction of national courts).[111] Lastly, with both developing and developed counterparts, most Chinese BITs signed until the mid-1990s provided for FET and MFN treatments, but not NT.

3 *The Shift: From Rejection to Shaping Global Standards of Investment Law*

It has been reported that the Chinese Ministry of Commerce (MOFCOM) and that of Foreign Affairs (MOFA) started considering a new model text (and to streamline the domestic process for BIT negotiations) since early 1993, in light of *i*) the evolution of the economic context, *ii*) the increasing number of investment agreements concluded, and *iii*) China's ratification of the ICSID Convention.[112] With regard to the first aspect, the principal reasons were chiefly two: *i*) the surge of outward direct investments from China and the corresponding interest to protect Chinese investors in foreign countries also by means of BITs (*e.g.*, through proper ISDS and NT clauses); and *ii*) the rise of the competition for foreign investment, attracted (back then especially) by friendly investment policies of Eastern European and South American States. For instance, with regard to ISA, China still showed a conservative attitude: when acceding to the ICSID Convention, in 1990), it consented to submit to the Centre's jurisdiction only disputes over the amount of compensation due to expropriation, in line with its traditional equivalent *ad hoc* consent to arbitration featured since the 1984 model BIT. However, following the 1993 ratification of the accession to the Convention, occasional unconditional access to ICSID arbitration was granted – the first, in the BIT with Lithuania, in November 1993.[113]

---

110 Li, 'Bilateral Investment Promotion and Protection Agreements' (fn. 98), 177–180.

111 *E.g.*, BITs with Thailand (1985), Singapore (1985), Sri Lanka (1986).

112 Gallagher and Shan, *Chinese Investment Treaties* (fn. 63), 40.

113 Nevertheless, the three subsequent BITs, with Uruguay, Azerbaijan and Ecuador – despite all these States being part of the ICSID Convention already – do not make any reference to ICSID. China's reluctance to grant unrestricted access to arbitration, ICSID in particular, seemed *inter alia* related to the importance China attaches '… to the issue of sovereignty and its suspicion about whether the Chinese Government could obtain a fair treatment if disputes were referred to an international forum, including ICSID'; see Z Yuqing, 'The Case of China', in MJ Moser (ed.), *Investor-State Arbitration: Lessons for Asia* (Juris, 2008), 155, 157.

Hence, in 1997, in the course of China's BIT talk with Canada (at the time, ultimately unfruitful), China's State Council approved some key changes to its template. The third model BIT was thus adopted amid of '... much speculation as to why at this stage China, which was attracting unprecedented sums of FDI, needed to revise its model BIT at all'.[114]

Together with a number of liberal changes in some substantive provisions, the 1997 Chinese model BIT granted unrestricted consent to international arbitration, including ICSID.[115] The 1980s' reluctance to include, *e.g.*, the NT clause (which contributed to stalling the BIT negotiations with the U.S.) had vanished: China would no longer hold objections to post-entry NT and MFN guarantees in its BITs. Such changes, implemented systematically since the year 2000, represent consequently a watershed moment in the Chinese BIT practice.[116]

Some limitations and the two-tier policy, nonetheless, persisted: for instance, NT clauses in Chinese BITs with capital-exporting States – *e.g.*, Germany (2003), Belgium (2009) – allow China to maintain existing non-conforming measures (subject to a 'best efforts' rollback promise).[117] Chinese BITs with capital-importing States – *e.g.*, Guyana (2003) – still limit the NT 'without prejudice to its laws and regulations' (thus, leaving the door open for the Parties to adopt *new* non-confirming measures).

The first agreement based on the new model text was the 1998 China-Barbados BIT.[118] Since then, the new model has been employed as template in approximately 40 new agreements – mostly, with African and South American States. It has also served as a starting point for the dozen renegotiations China concluded – mostly, with European States –, occasionally even going beyond the template (*e.g.*, the 2003 renegotiation with Germany).[119]

114 Gallagher and Shan, *Chinese Investment Treaties* (fn. 63), 39–41.

115 See Chapters 2 and 3.

116 This shift is so important that the subsequent agreements have been regarded as a *per se* new generation of Chinese BITs; cf., J Xiao, 'The ASEAN-China Investment Agreement: A Regionalization of Chinese New BITs' (Society of International Economic Law, Second Biennial Global Conference, University of Barcelona, Jul. 8th–10th, 2010), 14–15 <http://papers.ssrn.com/sol3/papers.cfm?abstract_id=1629202> accessed Nov. 20th, 2019.

117 Remarkably, even though Chinese BITs with developed countries provide on average for slightly higher levels of substantive protection than those with developing countries, China is able to make developed partner countries bear more obligations than it is itself willing to assume; see Berger, 'China's New Bilateral Investment Treaty Programme' (fn. 71), 13.

118 The 1997 China-South Africa BIT was the first where China accepted investor-State dispute arbitration for all disputes; nevertheless, not being South Africa party to the ICSID Convention, Art. 9 of the BIT features only *ad hoc* arbitration.

119 There have been exceptions: the 1999 China-Qatar BIT still features the dispute settlement provision of the 1984 Chinese model.

With the adoption of the 'Go Global' strategy, in 1999, and the new 'Outline of the 10th Five-Year Plan for National Economy and Social Development', in 2001, China increasingly focused on outbound trade and investment.[120] With regard to the BIT program, the 'centerpiece' may be considered the 2003 renegotiation of the 1983 BIT with Germany. In that innovative agreement,[121] China agreed on particularly high standards of investment protection which, whilst not replicated in subsequent agreements,[122] would pave the way to more complex negotiations for the investment discipline featured in Chinese FTAs since 2008, as well as, *e.g.*, the BIT with Canada and the Trilateral Investment Agreement (TIA) with Japan and Korea (both of 2012).

Therefore, on the one hand, China (like India, Brazil and South Africa) tends to resist rules restraining its ability to regulate foreign investments,[123] as well as those on liberalization.[124] Such a stance contributes to shaping a trend which, to some extent, is having effect globally: in 2012, UNCTAD noted how '… in general governments became more selective about the degree of FDI involvement in different industries of their economies'.[125] Even the most liberal State in this respect appears at least in part to have changed its policy: for instance, it has been noted how the U.S. too has '… dramatically shrunk virtually every right originally accorded to foreign investors …', compared to the 1989 model.[126]

120 Also, in 2003 China acceded to the WTO.

121 As considered by the OECD, 'Novel Features in Recent OECD Bilateral Investment Treaties' (OECD International Investment Perspectives, 2006) <http://www.oecd.org/investment/internationalinvestmentagreements/40072428.pdf> accessed Nov. 20th, 2019.

122 *E.g.*, with regard to the FPS standard: among the agreements concluded in 2005, the protection and security standard (termed as 'full' for the first time with France, in 1984) is 'full' only in the BIT with the Czech Republic, while 'most constant' with Spain and Portugal; in the 2006 BIT with India, FPS is not mentioned, while in the 2007 renegotiations with Cuba it is still phrased in the terms of the 1984 Chinese BIT. For the full review of this point, see Chapter 3.

123 Cf., JW Salacuse, 'Towards a Global Treaty on Foreign Investment: The Search for a Grand Bargain', in N Horn (ed.), *Arbitrating Foreign Investment Disputes: Procedural and Substantive Legal Aspects* (Kluwer Law International, 2004), 75.

124 Cf., the cautious stance adopted by Chinese scholars during the negotiations of the China-ASEAN investment agreement; *e.g.*, Huiping, 'China-ASEAN Investment Agreement Negotiations' (fn. 30), 143–163. Also, Trakman, 'China and Foreign Direct Investment' (fn. 105), 11.

125 The list of instances provided for 'specific FDI regulations and restrictions' features, along Bolivia and Benin, a number of OECD States (Canada, Italy, Hungary); sectors concerned with restrictive measures are mainly extraction, manufacture, finance and telecommunication; see UNCTAD, 'World Investment Report 2013' (fn. 43), 95–98; see, also, Figures 6 and 7, below.

126 J Alvarez, 'The Return of the State' (2011) 20(2) *Minnesota Journal of International Law* 223, 235.

A growing shift away from neo-liberalist approaches has been noted,[127] and elements of the Calvo doctrine (as per the terms framed in Chinese BITS)[128] seem again in vogue.[129]

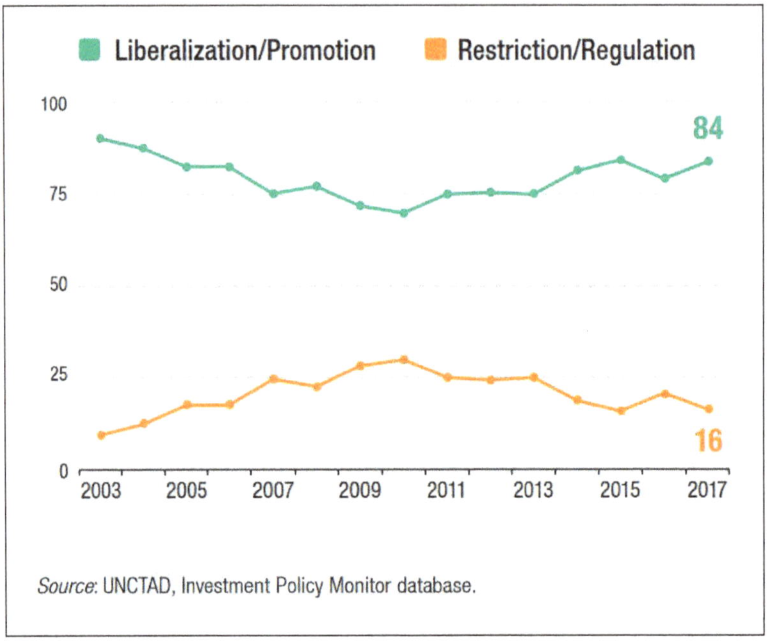

FIGURE 6A Changes in national investment policies – Trend (2003–2017)[130]

127 Gallagher and Shan, *Chinese Investment Treaties* (fn. 63), 43. According to Dolzer and Schreuer, however, '... the global policy trends in national policy developments do not point in one direction ...', referring to the opposing trends between Asia and Africa, on the one hand, and South America, on the other; cf., R Dolzer and C Schreuer, *Principles of International Investment Law* (Oxford University Press, 2012), 85, and UNCTAD, 'World Investment Report: Non-Equity Modes of International Production and Development' (2011), 94 <http://unctad.org/en/PublicationsLibrary/wir2011_en.pdf> accessed Nov. 20th, 2019.

128 *E.g.*, mandatory cooling-off periods for negotiations or, especially, preliminary evaluation by domestic courts. This aspect is typical, for instance, of Argentina's treaty practice. In its own, China chose to mandate for prior review by administrative courts; for an analysis of this point, see Chapter 3.

129 On the revival of the Calvo doctrine and the decline of the neo-liberalist approach, see W Shan, 'From North-South Divide to Private-Public Debate: Revival of the Calvo Doctrine and the Changing Landscape in International Investment Law' (2007) 27(3) *Northwestern Journal of International Law and Business* 631.

130 UNCTAD, 'World Investment Report: investment and new industrial policies' (2018) (fn. 43), 80.

Item	2003	2004	2005	2006	2007	2008	2009	2010	2011	2012	2013	2014	2015	2016	2017
Number of countries that introduced changes	59	79	77	70	49	40	46	54	51	57	60	41	49	59	65
Number of regulatory changes	**125**	**164**	**144**	**126**	**79**	**68**	**89**	**116**	**86**	**92**	**87**	**74**	**100**	**125**	**126**
Liberalization/ promotion	113	142	118	104	58	51	61	77	62	65	63	52	75	84	93
Restriction/ regulation	12	20	25	22	19	15	24	33	21	21	21	12	14	22	18
Neutral/ indeterminate[a]	–	2	1	–	2	2	4	6	3	6	3	10	11	19	15

Source: UNCTAD, Investment Policy Monitor database.
[a] In some cases, the expected impact of the policy measures on the investment is undetermined.
FIGURE 6B Changes in national investment policies – Number of measures (2003–2017)[131]

On the other hand, China has kept a more open (yet consistent) stance than any other BRICS State towards FDIs. As a result, today China has overtaken Germany for number of BITs concluded – a quite striking result for a State outright neglecting foreign investment until 1978, and that signed its first BIT in 1982. Moreover, China realized sooner than other States that competition for FDIs is no longer confined between nation-States but increasingly extends to regions,[132] and that more and more States are '… likely to submit to a regional approach in attracting FDIs'.[133] According to UNCTAD, FTAs that include investment chapters have a stronger impact in terms of increased FDI flows than standalone BITs.[134] China's move to incorporate the investment

131 *Id.*

132 According to UNCTAD, eight of the ten agreements other than BITs featuring a discipline for investment concluded in 2012 are of a regional nature, with at least 110 States currently involved into regional negotiations of some kind; *id.*, 88–100. See, also, 'World Investment Report: investment and the digital economy' (2017) (fn. 34), 110–114. See also Table 3, below.

133 See KH Wee and H Mirza, 'ASEAN Investment Cooperation: Retrospect, Developments and Prospects', in F Bartels and N Freeman (eds.), *The Future of Foreign Investment in Southeast Asia* (Routledge Curzon, 2005), 202.

134 UNCTAD, 'The Role of International Investment Agreements in Attracting Foreign Direct Investment to Developing Countries' (UNCTAD Series on International Investment Policies for Development, 2009), 110 <http://unctad.org/en/docs/diaeia20095_en.pdf> accessed Nov. 20th, 2019; on the new 'category' of 'trade and investment' agreements,

discipline into FTAs is also partly explained with the need to update the vast web of agreements weaved before the adoption of the 1997 model, nowadays unfit to its far reaching investment policy goals.[135]

4 *Chinese FTAs and Contemporary IIAs*

With the conclusion of the 2006 FTA with Pakistan, China ventured for the first time into the territory of FTAs featuring a chapter on investment protection. With regard to content, however, the chapter is far from a breakthrough, as it simply reproduces the text of the 1997 model (which nonetheless represents an upgrade with respect to the previous investment discipline between China and Pakistan, anchored to the 1984 model BIT).[136] The ice was nevertheless broken, and China was now ready to turn to more complex and diversified arrangements, such as the 2008 FTA with New Zealand; the 2009 and 2012 agreements on investments (part of multi-stage FTAs)[137] concluded, respectively, with ASEAN and Chile; the investment treaties of 2012 – bilateral, with Canada, and trilateral, with Korea and Japan; and the FTAs with Australia and South Korea, both of 2015.

To date, China has signed twelve more or less comprehensive FTAs. Only some cover investment protection as well, as briefly illustrated in the outline that follows (which does not take into account Hong Kong, Macau, and Taiwan):

- As mentioned, the 2006 China-**Pakistan** FTA features a chapter on investments; nevertheless, the text replicates the 1997 Chinese model BIT.

---

see A De Mestral and A Falsafi, 'Investment Provisions in Regional Trade Agreements: A more Efficient Solution?', in A De Mestral and C Lévesque (eds.), *Improving International Investment Agreements* (Routledge, 2013), 107–134.

135 Possibly exploiting, even if imperfectly, certain 'shortcuts', such as negotiating a modern investment regime with ASEAN as a whole (signed in 2009), without however terminating the BITs already in place (some of which, clearly outdated) with each single Member State of the organization. With regard to the negotiation of this regional agreement, see H Chen, 'China-Asean Investment Agreement Negotiations' (2006) 1(3) *Frontiers of Law in China* 423, 424.

136 However, the Amending Protocol of 2008 uniquely featured, for the time, the possibility to establish, in Pakistani territory, so-called 'China-Pakistan Investment Zones', where the Pakistani government grants specific advantages (especially, on tax and bureaucracy matters) to Chinese investors. For greater detail, see GM Vaccaro-Incisa, 'China's Policy Rationale and Treaty Making on the Protection of Foreign Investment: A Comparative Perspective, from the Model Bits to the Latest Stipulations' (Université de Genève, thèse doctorale, 2015), Chapter III, <https://archive-ouverte.unige.ch/unige:48427> accessed Nov. 23rd, 2019.

137 In Eastern Asia, the practice of signing a preliminary Framework Agreement focusing on structure and objectives of a series of subsequent agreements on specific matters (*e.g.*, investment) appears to be common practice.

- In the FTA concluded in 2008 between China and **Singapore**, rather than updating their bilateral investment protection regime (based on a 1985 BIT), the Parties formally agreed to incorporate the outcome of the still ongoing negotiations for an investment agreement between China and ASEAN (flowing, in turn, from a framework agreement for a multi-stage comprehensive FTA; see below).[138]
- China agreed instead to new clauses – and to change the formulation of some it was already accustomed to – in the investment chapter of the 2008 FTA with **New Zealand.** This regime features post-entry NT (subject to a grandfather clause for existing non-confirming measures), MFN for both pre- and post-entry stage, full FET, conditions for lawful expropriation (through the otherwise usually neglected 'Hull rule'), and *a priori* unrestricted consent to ISA; nevertheless, it does not set out the objective of progressive liberalization – otherwise quite common in Chinese IIAs since 2000, especially with developed States.[139]
- The investment chapter in the 2009 China-**Peru** FTA may resemble, at a first glance, the China-NZ FTA (especially with regard to the overall architecture of dispositions); a more careful analysis, however, shows that some provisions draw, instead, from the parties' respective template or experience (*i.e.*, respectively, the 1997 Chinese model and the 2006 U.S.-Peru FTA); the chapter features, also, a number of original formulations.[140]
- The 2009 Agreement on Investment between China and **ASEAN** (CAIA), part of a multi-stage comprehensive FTA, displays remarkable similarities with the ASEAN Agreement on Investment (ACIA), of the same year;[141] the CAIA features also commonalities with both the China-NZ FTA as well as

138 Art. 84 China-Singapore FTA.

139 For a more in-depth review, see Vaccaro-Incisa, 'China's Policy Rationale and Treaty Making on the Protection of Foreign Investment' (fn. 136), Chapter IV.

140 For a more in-depth review, see Vaccaro-Incisa, 'China's Policy Rationale and Treaty Making on the Protection of Foreign Investment' (fn. 136), Chapter V.

141 In turn, and notably, ACIA has the express goal (inserted in the recital) to create a comprehensive investment agreement that is comparable to international best practices; for a socio-political genesis of the agreement, see S Cho and J Kurtz, 'The Limits of Isomorphism: Global Investment Law and the ASEAN Investment Regime', in J Chaisse and L Nottage (eds.), *International Investment Treaties and Arbitration Across Asia*, (Brill Nijhoff, 2018) 410–441, at 422–434. For an in-depth review of the ACIA regime, see J Chaisse and S Jusoh, *The ASEAN Comprehensive Investment Agreement* (Edward Elgar Publishing, 2016); for a general introduction of the approach of Southeast Asian Nations to International Investment Law and arbitration, singularly and through ASEAN, see L Nottage, J Chaisse, and S Thanitcul, 'International Investment Treaty Arbitration Across Asia: A Bird's Eye View', in J Chaisse and L Nottage (eds.), *International Investment Treaties and Arbitration Across Asia*, (Brill Nijhoff, 2018) 3–56, at 21–52.

the China-Peru FTA (indeed, negotiations for all these agreements took place approximately within the same time frame).[142]

- The 2010 China-**Costa Rica** FTA operates a *renvoi* to the 2007 BIT between the two States (whose text is entirely drawn from the 1997 Chinese model).[143]
- The 2012 Supplementary Agreement on Investment (SAI) between China and **Chile**, part of the multi-stage comprehensive FTA signed back in 2005, replaced the 1994 China-Chile BIT (based on the 1984 Chinese model); together with the 2012 BIT with Canada (signed on the same day), it represents China's first 'North American style' agreement under both structure and wording.[144]
- The 2013 FTA with **Iceland**, driven by geopolitical considerations,[145] offers no novelty of sort and, with respect to investment protection, simply operates a *renvoi* to the outdated 1994 BIT between the parties (which is based on the 1989 Chinese model).
- The 2013 FTA with **Switzerland** does not cover investment protection at all; the single-page Chapter 9, limited to 'investment promotion', features only two (generic) provisions. The investment protection discipline is thus left to the 2009 BIT, which replaced the 1986 agreement (notably, changing the template of reference, from Chinese to Swiss).
- In 2015, **Australia** and China concluded a 9-year long FTA negotiation, stalled also because of Australia's growing concerns over international investment law and, in particular, ISA. Consequently, the treaty only contains a so-called 'early harvest' investment chapter, as elements such as MST, performance requirements, expropriation, compensation, or transfers, are still under negotiations. Moreover, ISA, while formally in place, is so far

142 For a more in-depth review, see Vaccaro-Incisa, 'China's Policy Rationale and Treaty Making on the Protection of Foreign Investment' (fn. 136), Chapter IV.

143 Art. 89 of the China-Costa Rica FTA simply reaffirms the commitments under the China-Costa Rica BIT.

144 For a more in-depth review, see Vaccaro-Incisa, 'China's Policy Rationale and Treaty Making on the Protection of Foreign Investment' (fn. 136), Chapter VI.

145 While Iceland could hardly offer much in terms of trade volumes or investment flows, it was strategic to China's quest for more influence in the Arctic: China has for long sought to join the Arctic Council (an eight-nations intergovernmental body promoting cooperation in the region) as a permanent observer – a goal frustrated in 2009 and 2011, with its request for admission rejected. It is not a case that, upon signature of the FTA with Iceland (Apr. 15th, 2013), the two Parties issued a joint statement calling for new bilateral cooperation on '… human rights, gender equality, labor issues, *Arctic affairs*, as well as cooperation on geothermal development, culture, education and tourism' (emphasis added). One month later (on May 15th, 2013), the Arctic Council eventually granted permanent-observer status to China, along with India, Italy, Japan, Singapore and South Korea. Permanent observers have no voting rights in the Council but, unlike *ad hoc* observers, are automatically invited to the Group meetings.

limited to NT disputes (while the 1988 China-Australia BIT, still in force, offers arbitration only for disputes relating to the amount of compensation due to expropriation).

- Quite peculiar is the case of **South Korea**. The FTA concluded with China in 2015 contains an investment discipline in line with other agreements in the region, to the point that some commentators considered it as an instance of Chinese 'malleability' when dealing with investment rules in FTAs.[146] What is striking, however, is that this is the *third* concurrent discipline for the protection of foreign investment, on top of the two already in place established with the 2012 TIA between China, Japan, and South Korea, and the 2007 China-South Korea BIT. The co-existence of the agreements seems to be a choice of the Parties, as the 2012 TIA expressly specify the right to '... relying on the bilateral investment agreement ... which is considered by the investor to be more favorable than this Agreement'.[147]
- In the 2017 FTA with **Georgia**, investment is only briefly mentioned in the 1-page Chapter 12 dedicated to 'areas of cooperation'. Consequently, investment protection is still clasped to the 1993 BIT, which is based on China's 1984 model (hence *inter alia* lacking NT, and limiting ISA to disputes over compensation due to expropriation).

This brief overview highlights China's strategy with regard to FTAs as one primarily concerned with trade, either with a view to offset geopolitical concerns or to secure the supply of resources.[148] Nevertheless, where an investment agreement is included (in the form of a chapter, or a separate agreement within the framework of a multi-stage FTA), it is often used as an opportunity to update old BIT regimes – when an investment rationale for doing so is felt (and the lack thereof results in a different outcome, as the cases of Iceland and Georgia show). If the BIT already in place belongs to the new generation of Chinese BITs (or, if it belongs to an old generation BIT, and yet there is neither investment nor political opportunity for further negotiations in this respect), then the FTA will either incorporate that agreement (Singapore) or operate a *renvoi* to it (Costa Rica, Iceland); but the FTA may also be kept separate and indifferent to the BIT (Switzerland). However, where investment protection regimes are negotiated, then it is no longer the case of 'BITs in FTAs with tiny

146 See H Wang, 'The RCEP and its Investment Rules: Learning from past Chinese FTAs' (2017) 3(2) *The Chinese Journal of Global Governance* 160.

147 Note to Art. 25, TIA. For an *ad hoc* piece on the TIA, see WM Choi, 'Substantive Provisions of the East Asian Trilateral Investment Agreement and their Implication', in J Chaisse (ed.), *China's International Investment Law Strategy* (Oxford, 2019), 222–242.

148 See J Nakagawa and W Liang, 'A Comparison of the FTA Strategies of Japan and China and their Implications for Multilateralism' (RCCPB Working Paper n. 11, Oct. 2011), 19 <https://papers.ssrn.com/sol3/papers.cfm?abstract_id=2169361> accessed Nov. 20th, 2019.

adaptations'.[149] Such an approach, true in the case of the first arrangement (Pakistan), has changed since 2008 (New Zealand, Peru), and even more so since 2012 (Chile, in parallel with the BIT with Canada).

The current policy shift (*i.e.*, the 'NAFTA-ization of Chinese BITS')[150] is driven by a gradualist approach on the evolution of treaty wording (as well as the addition of innovative provisions), and seems undertaken preferably against a background of asymmetric economic relationships. For the first practice with BITS, it chose a liberal Western State (Sweden) and a Socialist State (Romania), both with robust experience in the field yet neither major economies in absolute terms, nor significant economic partners for China anyway. The same approach was adopted for FTAS: the firsts, in fact, have been with Pakistan – nowadays a 'Chinese protectorate',[151] and New Zealand – a developed market economy whose dimension is, nevertheless, negligible (compared to other OECD economies, or China itself).[152]

Currently, a considerable share of foreign investment pivots on China, which has become the second largest investor world-wide,[153] as well as the second largest recipient of outward FDI (on top of overtaking recently the U.S. as the world's largest trading nation).[154] China is investing significantly in Africa, Asia, and South America, primarily to meet its energy supply needs. The 'Belt and Road' initiative (BRI), presented in 2013, is arguably China's most significant, because it entails a commitment (added, in 2017, even in the constitution) of massive outbound investments across over sixty counties located along (or adjacent to) the ancient Silk Road.[155] However, the already vast Chinese IIA network notwithstanding, there is still space for growth and improvement, as

---

149 Xiao, 'The ASEAN-China Investment Agreement' (fn. 116), 20.

150 Berger, which coined the expression to define the trend in Asian and Pacific countries of progressively adopting innovations first included in NAFTA, defines the process as 'incomplete'; see Berger, 'Investment Rules in Chinese Preferential Trade and Investment Agreements' (fn. 99), 8–11. On the 'Americanization' of Chinese BITs, see Cai, 'China-U.S. BIT Negotiations' (fn. 139), 459–501.

151 According to media sources, in 2010, when a U.S. delegate confronted a Chinese diplomat about Beijing's uncompromising support for Pakistan, the Chinese reportedly responded with a sarcastic remark: T Deen, 'China: Pakistan is our Israel', *Aljazeera* (Oct. 28th, 2010) <http://www.aljazeera.com/indepth/features/2010/10/20101028135728235512.html> accessed Nov. 20th, 2019.

152 In this sense, also, Nakagawa and Liang (fn. 148), 17–18.

153 UNCTAD, 'World Investment Report: Special Economic Zones' (2019) (fn. 46), 4. Indeed, between 2008 and 2010 China out-lended the World Bank.

154 Trakman, 'China and Foreign Direct Investment' (fn. 105), 2.

155 In October 2017, at the 19th National Congress, among the amendments to the constitution approved, the Party resolved to add the text 'pursue One Belt One Road'; see Xinhua News Agency, <http://www.xinhuanet.com//english/2017-10/24/c_136702726.htm> accessed Nov. 29th, 2019). For an overview of the BRI initiative, see H Wang, 'China's

evident, *e.g.*, from the protracted negotiations for a BIT with, respectively, the U.S. and the EU, or those at UNCITRAL for the reform of ISDS, or those for the Regional Comprehensive Economic Partnership (RCEP), in addition to a number of renegotiations sought or needed (in particular, of investment protection regimes with States part of the BRI initiative).

Further expansion and necessary modernization may, nevertheless, not come easily. Besides the specificity of each counterpart and negotiating table, China's rising outward investment flow in general faces certain skepticism and resistance abroad. This is partly the result of *i*) the still very significant role of State-owned enterprises (SOEs) in the Chinese investment outflow, *ii*) the brisk pace with which this latter has soared, *iii*) the non-positive image of China in some quarters, and *iv*) the challenges China poses to established competitors.[156] For this reason, China has been *inter alia* called to implement, next to its 'going-out' policy, a purposeful 'going-in' strategy, *inter alia* to ensure China's own economic, environmental and social development.[157]

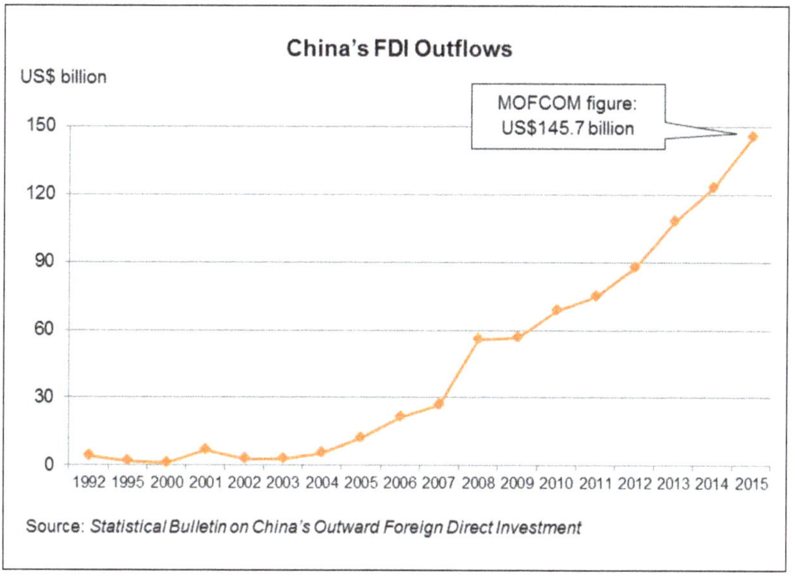

FIGURE 7 Chinese outward FDI – annual flow (1992–2015) (*billion USD*)[158]

Approach to the Belt and Road Initiative: Scope, Character and Sustainability', (2019) 22(1) *Journal of International Economic Law* 29.

156 As put in KP Sauvant and VZ Chen, 'China Needs to Complement its "Going-Out" Policy with a "Going-In" Strategy' (Columbia FDI Perspectives, May 12th, 2014) <https://academiccommons.columbia.edu/catalog/ac:185433> accessed Nov. 20th, 2019.

157 *Ibid.*

158 W Chu, 'China Takes Global Number Two Outward FDI Slot: Hong Kong Remains the Preferred Service Platform', *HKTDC Research* (Nov. 11th, 2016) <http://economists

5 *Novel Topics in Chinese* IIAs

Since the turn of the millennium, IIAs have progressively undergone a redefinition of their structure, an increase in the level of detail of several key provisions and, to a more limited extent, an expansion of the topics covered therein. The process, nonetheless, has begun with NAFTA in 1994, and it is therefore tied to the general expansion of trade agreements to reference such topics as labor, sustainable development, and protection of the environment (usually not in a cogent manner and often in the form of a *renvoi* to other *ad hoc* agreements, between the parties or multilateral).[159] The practice of adding these 'novel' elements in IIAs, however, begun spreading only a decade later, arguably following the release, in 2004, of the new U.S. and Canada model BITs, and the role the EU started to play in the field since the entry into force, in 2009, of the Lisbon Treaty.[160]

As shown in the review that follows, even recent investment regimes, whether standalone or part of an FTA, tend nonetheless not to delve into these topics.[161] In particular, when part of an FTA, the investment protection regime is often subject to general treaty exceptions – exceptions that, since the inception of GATT (1947), are aimed at preserving the regulatory autonomy of the State when exceptional events occur.[162] In principle, the increased attention States place on the regulation of trade, including exceptions, seems to point to a general belief that trade (as opposed to investment) has a more significant (or, anyway, direct) impact (or connection) with issues such as sustainable development, natural environment, and labor rights. Indeed, with the exception of certain safeguards for the protection of natural environment,

-pick-research.hktdc.com/business-news/article/Research-Articles/China-Takes-Global-Number-Two-Outward-FDI-Slot-Hong-Kong-Remains-the-Preferred-Service-Platform/rp/en/1/1X000000/1X0A804W.htm> accessed Nov. 20th, 2019.

159 *E.g.*, Article 177 of the 2008 China-New Zealand FTA (Labour and Environmental Cooperation): "The Parties shall enhance their communication and cooperation on labour and environmental matters through both the Memorandum of Understanding on Labour Cooperation and the Environment Cooperation Agreement between the Parties."

160 See, in particular, Reg. (EU) No. 1219/2012, where Parliament and Council have 'establish[ed] transitional arrangements for bilateral investment agreements between Member States and third countries', by which Member States have, in sum, accepted to halt further negotiations and expansions of their own BIT programmes. For an overview of the competence and negotiations carried out by the EU, see GM Vaccaro-Incisa, 'Protection of Foreign Investment and the EU: Framework, Legal Risks, and First Fruits', in E Mišcenic and A Raccah, *Legal Risks in EU Law* (Springer, 2016), 111–133.

161 For instance, see the study on sustainable development provisions of M Chi, 'Sustainable Development Provisions in Investment Treaties' (UN ESCAP Report, UN Publications, 2018); from the same author, also *Integrating Sustainable Development in International Investment Law* (Taylor & Francis, 2017).

162 See, *e.g.*, Article 159 (General exceptions) in Chapter 15 (Exceptions) of the China-Costa Rica FTA.

provisions of this sort are in most cases left toothless or unactionable in the context of ISA – when not expressly excluded from it.

The foregoing holds quite true in the case of the People's Republic, which first included these 'novel' topics (in a quite generic fashion) in the 2008 FTA with New Zealand.[163] The table below offers an overview of a selection of these in 15 of the most recent IIAs concluded by China, and reviews how often commitments in the fields of labor and environment have been undertaken, and where such concepts as sustainability and development are at least mentioned (and in which IIA part or provision).

TABLE 3 Novel topics – IIA coverage in recent Chinese IIAs (from 2008 on, selected)

Year	Partner	Topics			
		Labor	Environment	Sustainability	Development
2008	New Zealand		(mention)[164]	Preamble	Preamble
2008	Colombia	–	Exp.	–	–
2009	ASEAN	–	–	Preamble	Preamble
2009	Peru	–	–	–	–
2010	Libya	–	–	–	–
2011	Costa Rica	–	–	(part of FTA)	(part of FTA)
2011	DRC	–	Exp.	Preamble	Preamble
2011	Uzbekistan	–	Exp.	Preamble	Preamble
2012	Canada	–	Env. Meas. Gen. ex. Exp.	Preamble	Preamble
2012	Chile	–	Exp.	–	Economic
2012	JP-SK	–	Preamble Env. Meas.	Preamble	Preamble
2013	Tanzania	–	Exp Env. Meas.	Preamble	Preamble
2015	Australia	–	Gen ex. ISA carve-out Expert appt.	–	–
2015	SK	–	Env. Meas.	–	Economic (preamble)
2015	Turkey	–	Gen. ex. Exp.	–	Economic (preamble)

163 Similarly, M Chi, supra, fn. 161, UN ESCAP Report, p. 39–40.

164 See Article 177 of the 2008 China-New Zealand FTA (fn. 159).

Preliminarily, the table shows that, while by this time open to including terms and concepts related to the topics surveyed, China has not yet adopted a treaty policy regarding their presence or wording. Firstly, no obligation is undertaken regarding *development*, whether "sustainable" or "economic", as these, while often mentioned in one form or another (ten times out of fifteen cases), are confined to the preamble.[165] Secondly, commitments related to *labor* standards or rights are nearly absent (the only exception being a generic reference to ILO in the 2008 China-New Zealand FTA).[166]

Lastly, the one topic that appears most frequently (11 out of 15 IIAs) – and, occasionally, with some teeth – is *environmental* protection. As a matter of general framework, and drawing from the wording of the North American models (particularly, Canada), in four IIAs the Parties "… *recognize that it is inappropriate to encourage investment by waiving, relaxing, or otherwise derogating from domestic health, safety or environmental measures*".[167] The absence of a treaty policy in this respect, however, is reflected in the varied positioning of said wording amongst the treaties: from ISA consultations (Canada), to an *ad hoc* "environmental measures" provision (South Korea FTA and Japan-South Korea TIA), to a catch-all "health, safety, and environmental measures" (Tanzania), to a preambular remark (again, Japan-South Korea TIA, where the concept is in fact repeated twice, with slightly different terms). More significantly, in seven cases measures adopted for the protection of the environment are expressly characterized as exception to claims of expropriation. Of these, in four the exception is mentioned (at least) right in the expropriation clause, in the following terms: "*expropriation expressly excludes measures adopted for the protection of 'environment' as being able to constitute indirect expropriation*".[168] In the remaining three, a wording identical or equivalent to the 2004 North American models is employed, hence with the environment expressly included alongside

165 The most 'stringent' of these preambular expressions being the quite specific outcome expected from the investment agreement (within the overarching FTA arrangement) featured in the CAIA: 'Reaffirming the Parties' commitment to establish the China-ASEAN Free Trade Area … in the realisation of the sustainable economic growth and development goals on the basis of equality and mutual benefits so as to achieve a win-win outcome'.

166 See Article 177 of the 2008 China-New Zealand FTA (fn. 159).

167 This is the case with 2012 Canada (Art. 18.3 – Consultations), 2012 TIA (preamble and Art. 23 – environmental measures), 2013 Tanzania (Art. 10 – Health, safety, and environmental measures), and 2015 South Korea (Art. 12.16 – Environmental measures).

168 This is the case with 2008 Colombia (Art. 4), 2011 DRC (Art. 6), 2012 Canada (Annex B.10), 2012 Chile (Annex A).

"public health" and "safety" under the notion of "public welfare".[169] To these last three agreements, the 2015 China-South Korea FTA should be added as, while not expressly mentioning "environment", the provision, still clearly drawing from the U.S. model wording, is simplified to a catch-all "legitimate public welfare".[170] Another element to note with respect to the environment is the sequence of adaptations in IIAs of the phrasing originally featured in Article XX (General Exceptions) of GATT 1947. There, the relevant parts of the clause read: "*… nothing in this Agreement shall be construed to prevent the adoption or enforcement by any contracting party of measures: … (b) necessary to protect human, animal or plant life or health*". In the U.S. model, this wording, which is placed under Article 8.3.(c)(ii) (Performance Requirements), is developed into: "*… [treaty commitments] shall not be construed to prevent a Party from adopting or maintaining measures, including environmental measures: … (ii) necessary to protect human, animal, or plant life or health*". With minor adjustments, equivalent provisions are also found in the 2013 China-Tanzania BIT (Article 10.2 – Health, safety, and environmental measures) and in the 2015 China-Turkey BIT (Article 4 – General Exceptions). The 2015 China-Australia FTA, albeit with a different structure, articulates an equivalent concept (Article 9.8 – General Exceptions). A provision with a possibly broader scope is found in the 2012 China-Canada BIT (Article 33 – General Exceptions), where the first part of the North American models' wording is included but deprived of the limiting condition "*necessary to protect human, animal, or plant life or health*". Lastly, the China-Australia FTA originally establishes that measures "*… for the legitimate public welfare objectives of public health, safety, the environment, public morals or public order shall not be the subject of [ISA claims] …*".[171] In addition, replicating the North American models, the Parties reserved to themselves the right to request the arbitral tribunal to "*… appoint one or more experts … on any factual issue concerning environmental, health, safety, or other scientific matters …*".[172]

In sum, three conclusions can be drawn with respect to the foregoing: firstly, in recent IIAs, States seek to ensure that they maintain regulatory power to intervene in the public interest without fear of investment claims; in this perspective, and secondly, China currently seems open to including 'novel topics',

169 See 2004 U.S. model BIT, Annex B.4.(b) and 2004 CA model BIT, Annex B.13.(1)(c). This wording has been employed in 2011 Uzbekistan (Art. 6), 2013 Tanzania (Art. 6), and 2015 Turkey (Art. 5).

170 See Annex 12-B.3(b).

171 China-Australia FTA (2015), Art. 9.11 (Consultation).

172 *Idem*, Art. 9.20 (Expert Reports), equivalent to Art. 32 U.S. model BIT and Art. 42 Canada model BIT.

and to adding teeth to provisions related to environmental protection (arguably along with health, safety, and public order); and, thirdly, China remains 'reactive' (as opposed to 'proactive') to these developments, given that it has not yet adopted a treaty policy (at least, a coherent one) over any of them. Indeed, while the agreements with, *e.g.*, Canada, Australia, and Tanzania feature all of the innovations regarding environmental protection above illustrated, those with Chile, South Korea, and Turkey do not.

Thus, China's overall position on this matter seems still *in fieri*.

6 *Ongoing Negotiations: China-U.S. BIT, China-EU BIT, RCEP*

In addition to, or as part of, its chief foreign economic policy initiative, the Belt and Road Initiative (BRI), China is currently engaged in 13 FTA negotiations (and 8 FTA feasibility studies); it has ongoing BIT negotiations with key partners such as the U.S. and the EU; and it is a party to the ASEAN-led negotiations for the Regional Comprehensive Economic Partnership (RCEP).[173] Additionally, as highlighted earlier, since the turn of the millennium it has also renegotiated several older BITs.

Preliminarily, it should be noted that BITs with States parties to the BRI initiative are generally outdated (with only a handful concluded after the year 2000) and have so far been left untouched by China's general renegotiation effort. The fact that China 'does not appear to have a strong intention to bring in BRI-wide hard law obligations' arguably highlights the chiefly geopolitical and trade (as opposed to investment) characters of the project.[174] Moreover, proper investment protections can be granted via *ad hoc* contract clauses – arguably effectively so, when *i*) the investment is sought after by the host State, *ii*) the foreign investor is State-controlled, *iii*) trade and investment flows are tilted in favor of the investor's State, as so are *iv*) other economic, political, and technological factors.

With regard to RCEP – which encompasses ASEAN Member States and ASEAN's FTA partners (*i.e.*, Australia, New Zealand, Japan, South Korea, China, and India) –, the text of the investment chapter agreed upon in November 2019 by all parties except India, and currently under 'legal scrubbing', is all but groundbreaking. On the matter of foreign investment, the agreement was, as a preliminary matter, expected to at least partly address the Asian so-called 'noodle bowl' of investment treaties: as of 2019, RCEP members are parties to almost 1.000 IIAs, accounting approximately for one third of the world's total.

---

173 Source: MOFCOM, <http://fta.mofcom.gov.cn/english/index.shtml> accessed Nov. 28th, 2019.

174 Wang, 'China's Approach to the Belt and Road Initiative' (fn. 155), 43.

Instead, RCEP investment discipline is not intended to replace those already in place between and among the Parties (via BITs and ACIA).[175] Then, in terms of substantive protections, RCEP appears to be a slightly enhanced ACIA, as it further clarifies clauses such as FET, denial of benefits, and performance requirements (chiefly, by limiting their operation). Lastly, and most notably, largely due to India's opposition (and, to a lesser extent, Indonesia and Australia), the Parties agreed to exclude ISDS altogether. In this context, China confirmed a flexible approach: it accepted RCEP without ISDS, while the 2015 China-Australia FTA foresees a bilateral court system (not yet implemented), and the 2012 China-Canada BIT contemplates standard ISA.

The negotiations for a BIT with each of China's most significant trade and investment partners – the U.S. and the EU – are proving even more difficult, despite the recent conclusion of IIAs with Western States such as Chile, Canada, and Australia (which were thought to facilitate a positive outcome in the short-to-medium term here as well). In favor of the conclusion of these long-negotiated agreements, jointly with China's progressive adjustment to international investment protection standards, plays the gradual repositioning of liberal market economies towards the protection of foreign investment law.[176] On the one hand, in fact, the U.S. has "… virtually shrunk […] every right originally accorded to the foreign investor".[177] On the other, over the last

175 As noted by Chaisse, "RCEP ultimately adds just another layer to the many existing investment treaties in the region which, given RCEP's investment chapter limitations, remain more important than ever for most RECP investors. No investment claims will be made under RCEP; instead, RCEP investors will rely on old BITs to challenge host country policies.", see J Chaisse, 'The Regional Comprehensive Economic Partnership's investment chapter: One step forward, two steps back?' (Columbia FDI Perspectives, No. 271, Feb. 10th, 2020), http://ccsi.columbia.edu/publications/columbia-fdi-%20perspectives/ accessed Apr. 4th, 2020.

176 Cf., *e.g.*, L Peterson, 'Out of Order', in M Waibel, A Kaushal, KL Chung, C Balchin (eds.), *The Backlash Against Investment Arbitration* (Wolters Kluwer, 2010) 483–488; see also, Figures 6–7.

177 Cf., J Alvarez, 'The Return of the State' (Chapter 1, fn. 126), at 235; moreover, domestically, the U.S. have also been long subject to repeated calls to better regulate international investment arbitration: *e.g.*, Art. 3.G.iv U.S. Trade Act (2002), calling, *inter alia*, for mechanisms for an appellate body to provide coherence to the interpretations of investment provisions in trade agreements (available at: <http://www.gpo.gov/fdsys/pkg/PLAW-107publ210/html/PLAW-107publ210.htm> accessed Apr. 4th, 2020); *e.g.*, the 2004 Uruguay-U.S. BIT (Annex E), the 2004 Singapore-U.S. FTA (Art. 15.19) or the 2004 Chile-U.S. FTA (Art. 10.19) foresees such possibility, which has been subsequently institutionalized in the 2012 U.S. Model BIT (Art. 28.10). Also, in the context of the negotiations for the U.S.-Korea FTA, cf., *Letter on the Korea Free Trade Agreement to President Obama from 110 members of Congress*, July 22nd, 2010 (available at: <http://www.citizen.org/documents/KORUSLetterJuly2010.pdf> accessed Apr. 4th, 2020), and *Letter on the Korea Free*

few years the EU has approached investment law (and, in particular, ISA) with increasing suspicion.[178] The widespread feeling among scholars is that the treaty outcome from any pair of this 'negotiating triangle' was likely not only to influence the remaining two, but also to set standards reaching far beyond the pure bilateral (or trilateral) dimension.[179]

Both the U.S. and the EU, however, currently find themselves in situations where they are unlikely to conclude an IIA with China in the near term. With regard to the U.S., despite repeated announcements of 'major breakthroughs' over negotiations that have been on the table for over thirty years[180] and the preference of the current administration for conducting international relations on a bilateral level (as opposed to multilateral),[181] the political climate at present over trade and investment with China is lukewarm (to say the least) and anyway quite unpredictable. Negotiations with the EU face, on the other hand, three substantial roadblocks. The first is of a political and economic nature, as the ultimate goals of the Parties are significantly different: the EU wants a comprehensive IIA regime featuring advanced HR, labor, and environmental obligations – and, crucially, full market access; in contrast, China

---

Trade Agreement to President Obama from 550 organizations, Sept. 22nd, 2010 (available at: <http://www.citizenstrade.org/pdf/Korea_Opposition_Final.pdf> accessed Apr. 4th, 2020), both requesting to discard ISA from the treaty.

178 See, *e.g.*, European Parliament, Resolution on the EU-China negotiations for a bilateral investment agreement 2013/2674(RSP) of Oct. 9th, 2013, at points 41–47 (available at: <http://www.europarl.europa.eu/sides/getDoc.do?type=TA&language=EN&reference=P7-TA-2013-411> accessed Apr. 4th, 2020); specifically, at point 41 the Parliament 'Expresses its deep concern regarding the level of discretion of international arbitrators to make a broad interpretation of investor protection clauses, thereby leading to the ruling-out of legitimate public regulations; demands that the arbitrators appointed by the parties in the context of a dispute be independent and impartial, and that the arbitration provided follow a code of conduct based on the rules adopted by the UN Commission on International Trade Law (UNCITRAL), on those of the International Centre for Settlement of Investment Disputes (ICSID) or on any other international agreements and standards recognized and agreed to by the parties'.

179 With regard to the EU-China BIT negotiations see, *e.g.*, W Shan and L Wang, 'The China-EU BIT: The emerging "Global BIT 2.0"?' (Columbia FDI Perspectives, Columbia Center on Sustainable Investment, No. 128, Aug. 18th, 2014).

180 *E.g.*, in 2013, the parties jointly and publicly announced that their BIT will be negotiated under a negative list approach, and extend NT to pre-establishment.

181 Presidential Memorandum Regarding Withdrawal of the United States from the Trans-Pacific Partnership Negotiations and Agreement, Presidential Memorandum, White House, 23 Jan. 2017, <https://www.whitehouse.gov/presidential-actions/presidential-memorandum-regarding-withdrawal-united-states-trans-pacific-partnership-negotiations-agreement/> accessed Apr. 4th, 2020.

aims to secure an FTA.[182] Secondly, on the matter of investment protection, it is now established that the EU shares its competence with member States in dealings with third States whenever key components such as portfolio investment and ISDS are included.[183] Lastly, the EU's stubborn insistence, since 2015, on replacing investment arbitration with an *ad hoc* international investment court hardly meets China's interest, as it *inter alia* diminishes *i*) the State individual pre-litigation negotiating position vis-à-vis foreign investors (currently uniquely strong, in light of the unparalleled size and potential of its domestic market, and its political organization), and *ii*) the influence China can exert on the adjudicatory body (while in the context of an international court China would enjoy, at most, only one of its nationals sitting as a member).

In light of the foregoing, these three agreements, which are anyway still under negotiation, cannot be explored further in this work, which focuses on the analysis of the evolution of selected treaty provisions in China's *actual* investment treaty practice.

7 *Proposal for a New Periodization*

All the foregoing taken into account, and factoring in also *i*) elements from fields such as international relations and economics, and *ii*) the evolution of China's policy on the protection of foreign investment over the past two decades, it is believed that the periodization formulated by Gallagher & Shan in 2008 may today be partly reassessed.

The first 'nationalization and exclusion' period remains unchanged, running from 1949 until 1978. However, with regard to the subsequent three periods – *i.e.*, 'resumption' (1978–1991), 'first surge' (until 2000), 'second surge' (from 2001 on) –, Gallagher & Shan determination is arguably based on an overly *quantitative* aspect (*i.e.*, number of BITs concluded in a given period). From the economics standpoint, however, the existence of a direct correlation between *i*) number of BITs signed, *ii*) flow of foreign FDI, and *iii*) Chinese GDP growth

182 Council of the European Union, Conclusions of a comprehensive European international investment policy, Oct. 25th, 2010, at point 16 <http://www.consilium.europa.eu/uedocs/cms_data/docs/pressdata/EN/foraff/117328.pdf> accessed Apr. 4th, 2020; see also the analysis of M Bungenberg and C Titi, 'The Evolution of EU Investment Law and the Future of EU-China Investment Relations', in W Shan (ed.), *China and International Investment Law* (Brill Nijhoff, 2014) 297–370, at 361–369.

183 European Court of Justice, Opinion 2/15, EU:C:2016:992, <http://curia.europa.eu/juris/document/document.jsf?text=&docid=190727&doclang=EN> accessed Apr. 4th, 2020.

(or any other country, for that matter) is controversial (beside the fact that they all grow).[184]

Therefore, in light of:

1. China's overall policy changes over time;
2. The comparative analysis of the text of Chinese investment treaties and models (see Chapters Two and Three);
3. The relationship between China and other international investment major players, and the trends in the treaty policy and practice of these latter; and
4. The IIAs China concluded over the last two decades;

the following periodization is found to better reflect China's overall policy on the protection of foreign investment.

As mentioned, in line with Gallagher & Shan, the **1st period** (**exclusion**) ends in 1978, with the beginning of the 'Open Doors' policy. this, however, was a *political* choice, not the first investment treaty (which will follow only in 1982, with Sweden). Therefore, it seems appropriate to frame China's policy on the basis of a *qualitative* criterion, focusing on:

1. The framework political and policy choices, and
2. The actual changes introduced over time in the texts of investment treaties and models, showing China's progressive will to do 'business like all the others' (retaining nevertheless some specificities).

Consequently, the **2nd period**, or FDI '**resumption**', comes to a close *towards* the end of the '80s (as the material effects of policy choices rarely materialize overnight, this proposed periodization does not offer clear-cut dates to marking the transition from one period to the next). Indeed, in the second part of the 1980s, a number of political choices cumulatively contributed to display China's 'will of normalization' with regard to foreign investment, resulting in the beginning of the **3rd period**, here labelled '**transition**'. In addition to the points highlighted by Gallagher & Shan (for the portion of their periodization coinciding with this one), other qualifying elements are:

1. The 1986 China-UK BIT (the first featuring *ad hoc* arbitration, albeit limited to disputes concerning the amount of compensation due to expropriation,[185] as well as the first NT clause, albeit in the limited form of a 'best effort' obligation);

184 With regard to the specific Chinese perspective on the point, see Hadley (fn. 107), 262–274. For a brief review of the issue in broader terms, based on a number of prior studies, see Berger 'China's New Bilateral Investment Treaty Programme' (fn. 71), 1–2.

185 Art. 7.1 China-UK BIT (1986): 'A dispute between a national or company of one Contracting Party and the other Contracting Party concerning an amount of compensation which has

2. The 1987 China-Netherlands BIT (featuring *ad hoc* arbitration, albeit limited to disputes concerning the amount of compensation due to expropriation);
3. The 1989 model BIT (where the 'best effort' NT clause became a standard policy feature);
4. China's accession, in 1993, to the ICSID Convention (which it had signed in 1990, subject to a 'notification' appended for which it '… would only consider submitting … disputes over compensation resulting from expropriation and nationalization');[186]
5. The 1993 China-Lithuania BIT (the first allowing for ICSID arbitration);
6. The 1997 China-South Africa BIT (the first allowing for unrestricted access to ISA, albeit governed by an *ad hoc* procedure built in the treaty);
7. The 1997 model BIT (making unrestricted consent to ISA, including ICSID, a standard policy feature);
8. The 1998 China-Barbados BIT (the first featuring unrestricted consent to ICSID arbitration).

This transition period culminates with the 1998 China-Barbados BIT. This is not because the agreement is particularly significant *per se*; rather, because since then Chinese BITs (with only limited exceptions) feature unrestricted access to ISA, including ICSID arbitration, as a matter of standard. All other elements being equal, it could therefore be considered that, since then, China 'did business like everyone else'.

Consequently, the **4th period**, here named '**modern investment protection policy**', begins in 1999, with China's adoption of the 'Go Global' strategy (*i.e.*, another policy choice, not a treaty) and the focus on outbound investment. This phase is characterized by:

1. The systematic use of the 1997 model, from year 2000 on;
2. The conclusion of approximately 40 new BITs (chiefly, with African and South American States);
3. The renegotiations of over a dozen BITs (mostly, with European States);

---

not been amicably settled after a period of six months from written notification of that dispute shall be submitted to international arbitration'.

186 The legal effect of a 'notification', where understood as 'reservation' within the meaning of Articles 2 and 19 of the 1969 Vienna Convention on the Law of Treaties, is debated; see the case-law review on the point in GM Vaccaro-Incisa, 'Arbitration clauses limited to compensation due to expropriation: Relevant case-law, interpretive trends, and the case of China's treaty policy and practice', in J Chaisse, L Choukroune, S Jusoh (eds), *The Handbook of International Investment Law and Policy* (Springer, forthcoming), p. 27–36.

4. The conclusion of the 2003 China-Germany BIT;[187]
5. China's accession to the WTO, in 2003.

Lastly, the **5th period**, here labeled '**contemporary investment protection policy**', is marked by China's progressive shift toward the North American model of investment protection. While seeds of such a shift are already discernible with the 2003 BIT renegotiation with Germany and the 2006 FTA with Pakistan, the leap is taken with States in Southeast Asia and the Pacific in 2008–2009, and the conclusion of the negotiations for agreements such as the FTAs with New Zealand and Peru, and the Investment Agreement with ASEAN. These have, in turn, paved the way to the inclusion of selected new elements in China's treaty practice, for instance in the agreements concluded between 2012 and 2015 with Chile, Canada, Japan, South Korea, Australia, and Turkey.

C The Quasi-Absence of Known Investor-State Disputes with China

As noted, over the last three decades China has succeeded in attracting an impressive flow of inbound investment, although its FDI regime remains overall restrictive (relatively to liberal economies).[188] Notwithstanding this, or the comprehensive network of agreements devoted to the protection of foreign investment, as of today there is no publicly known investment award against China.[189] This is chiefly deemed to be due to three factors.

First, China appears concerned to project an image of fair host State, 'friendly' towards foreign investors – which (usually) receive handsome returns

187 For an analysis of the far-reaching implications of this renegotiation, see RH Kreindler, 'Investment Treaties and the Evolution in their Negotiation and Application: The New Germany-China BIT and its Relevance to International Financial Law Trends' (2009) 6(1) *Transnational Dispute Management* 1, 9–10.

188 China continues to rank poorly in the OECD FDI Restrictiveness Index, scoring particularly low, *e.g.*, in transportation equipment, radio and TV broadcasting, media, telecommunications, and fisheries. See the OECD FDI Regulatory Restrictiveness Index, <https://stats.oecd.org/Index.aspx?datasetcode=FDIINDEX> accessed Apr. 4th, 2020. Even the latest Foreign Investment Law, released in March 2019 and in force starting from Jan. 2020, despite certain 'noteworthy features', is considered not sufficient to alter the status quo; see Y Zheng, 'China's New Foreign Investment Law: Deeper Reform and More Trust are Needed' (Columbia FDI Perspectives, No. 264, Nov. 4th, 2019).

189 To date, only the following cases are known: *Ekran Berhad v. China*, ICSID Case No. ARB/11/15 (registered in 2012), settled before the constitution of the tribunal; *Ansung Housing v. China*, ICSID Case No. ARB/14/25, initiated in 2014, award of Mar. 9th, 2017, finding the claim manifestly without legal merit according to ICSID Arbitration Rule 41.5; *Hela Schwarz v. China*, ICSID Case No. ARB/17/19 (registered in 2017), pending. See also, M Heymann, 'International Law and the Settlement of Investment Disputes Relating to China' (2008) 11 *Journal of International Economic Law* 518.

on their investments.[190] Second, out of China's 134 IIAs in force, only about half grant unrestricted *a priori* access to ISA.[191] Among the States excluded are, *e.g.*, significant capital exporters whose investors are acquainted with ISA, like the U.S., the UK and Italy. Third, in any case, the following considerations may ultimately deter foreign investors from pursuing ISA against China.

The first is the lack of clarity over the status of certain international legal norms within the Chinese domestic legal system. For instance, it is not clear which law would govern the recognition and enforcement of (non-ICSID) investment awards. In 1987, when acceding to the 1958 New York Convention on the Recognition and Enforcement of Foreign Arbitral Awards, China attached two reservations: a 'reciprocity reservation', by which 'arbitral awards not considered as domestic awards in the state where their recognition and enforcement are sought' shall not be recognized; and a 'commercial matters reservation', under which the Convention applies only to differences arising out of legal relationships that are 'commercial' in accordance with Chinese law. Moreover, China categorizes arbitral awards differently from the New York Convention (location of the arbitration institution for China, seat of arbitration for the New York Convention).[192] And although, as recalled earlier, in 1983 China amended its constitution to include the protection of foreign investments under Chinese law,[193] the status of international treaties within the Chinese legal system remains debated, and whether investment treaties override Chinese domestic law is a matter open to question as well.[194] A 2002 regulation by the Supreme People's Court has clarified that Chinese

190 Trakman, 'China and Foreign Direct Investment' (fn. 105), 5. China is reportedly proud of its 'MianZi', *i.e.*, in the investment arbitration context, the fact of never having a case filed against it at ICSID; see Gallagher and Shan, 'China' (fn. 68), 131–181, 181. Also, international relations scholar Cui Yankun claims that the probability of expropriation in China today is 'next to nothing'; see Cui Yangkun, 'New Developments in China's Bilateral Investment Treaties', (2007) *Law and Society* 706.

191 For a detailed analysis on the point, see Chapter 3. Most IIAs in force yet not publicly available on the UNCTAD or Kluwer arbitration websites have been kindly provided, upon request, by the Treaty and Law Department of MOFCOM. I wish to thank Mr. Yun Zhang for his precious cooperation. On jurisdictional restrictions in China's BITs, see also J Willems, 'Investment Disputes under China's BITs', in J Chaisse (ed.), *China's International Investment Law Strategy* (Oxford, 2019) 444–461; and GM Vaccaro-Incisa, 'Arbitration clauses limited to compensation due to expropriation: Relevant case-law, interpretive trends, and the case of China's treaty policy and practice', *supra*, fn. 186.

192 For a review of status and enforceability of foreign arbitral award in China, see M Zhang, 'Enforceability: Foreign Arbitral Award in Chinese Courts', (2018) 20 *San Diego International Law Journal* 1.

193 Art. 18 of the Chinese constitution; cf., above (fn. 87).

194 See, *e.g.*, E Pekar, 'The Chinese Investment Regime and the U.S.-China Negotiations' (fn. 69), at 273.

administrative courts, in adjudicating international cases involving trade and investment, should apply only Chinese law.[195] This means that international trade and investment agreements must be transformed into Chinese law before they can be applied and implemented.[196] Arguably in an attempt to partly address the issue of implementation, the Supreme Court, abiding by the fundamental principles of international relations (*i.e.*, *bona fide* and *pacta sunt servanda*) held that regulations implementing international agreements should be interpreted in a manner consistent with international treaties, when more than one interpretation is possible.[197]

Secondly – and, perhaps, in order to counter these uncertainties, as well as the perceived 'Chinese lack of affinity for international arbitration'[198] and preference for other ISDS, including informal methods of dispute settlement –, China's policy seems that of concretely offsetting foreign investors' concerns (*e.g.*, that they might receive less than FET, or be subject to indirect expropriation) by according better than NT standard.[199] It is because of such an informal yet seemingly established policy that, still in 2012, the EU Directorate General for Trade considered initiating arbitration against China likely to be a 'last resort',[200] as investors conceivably benefit more from reaching a negotiated

195 Arts. 7 and 8 of the Provisions on Some Issues on the Adjudication of Administrative Cases Concerning International Trade, Aug. 29th, 2009; the regulation applies also to investments; cf., Gallagher and Shan, *Chinese Investment Treaties* (fn. 3), 51. Chinese administrative courts are a preliminary step for foreign investors wishing to pursue investor-State arbitration against China; Chinese BITs, however, usually include a time-limit for such courts to render a decision (which varies from 3 to 6 months, depending on the treaty), after which the investor may, in any case, initiate arbitration; see *ad hoc* section in Chapter 3.

196 As it nevertheless happens as well, *e.g.*, in the German and Italian legal systems.

197 Art. 9, Provisions on Some Issues on the Adjudication of Administrative Cases Concerning International Trade, Aug. 29th, 2009.

198 Kong, 'Bilateral Investment Treaties' (fn. 63), 130. Yuquing points out that '... the main reason for China's aversion to arbitration was the importance attached by the Chinese government 'to the issue of sovereignty and its suspicion about whether the Chinese Government could obtain a fair treatment if disputes were referred to an international forum, including ICSID'; see Z Yuqing, 'The Case of China', in MJ Moser (ed.), *Investor-State Arbitration: Lessons for Asia* (Juris, 2008) 155, 157.

199 Cf., the quick settlement (two months after registration of the case) in *Ekran Berhad* (fn. 162); see also LE Trakman, 'Enter the Dragon IV: China's Proliferating Investment Treaty Program' (UNSW Centre for Law, Markets and Regulation, 2011) <https://www.clmr.unsw.edu.au/article//enter-the-dragon-iv%3A--china%27s-proliferating-investment-treaty-program> accessed Nov. 20th, 2019.

200 L Rubinacci, 'EU-China Investment Relationship, Update on State of Play' (DG Trade Civil Society Dialogue, Mar. 7th, 2012) <http://trade.ec.europa.eu/doclib/docs/2012/march/tradoc_149185.pdf> accessed Nov. 20th, 2019.

settlement than they would with arbitration.[201] Moreover, concerns have been expressed '... about the unreliability of China's judicial system, which fails to enforce contractual obligations, and about the lack of transparency and uniformity in the application of the regulatory regime governing investments'.[202]

Lastly, elementary considerations of convenience, in balancing the pros and cons of potentially losing access to the world's largest single market, no doubt play a considerable chilling effect on any foreign investor that profits, or wishes to profit, from it, particularly in light of the specific nature of China's constitutional architecture and government.[203]

Nevertheless, when looked at through the lenses of treaty policy and practice, notwithstanding the cautiousness in building a foreign investment protection program, the general consideration stands for China as well, as any State '... labors under two connected handicaps whenever [it] seek[s] to regulate, unambiguously and in advance, some sphere of conduct by means of general standards to be used without further official direction on particular occasions'.[204]

---

201 Trakman, 'China and Foreign Direct Investment' (fn. 105), 3.

202 EU Parliament, text P7_TA(2013)0411, adopted on Oct. 9th, 2013, at point 10; the text is available at: <http://www.europarl.europa.eu/sides/getDoc.do?type=TA&language=EN&reference=P7-TA-2013-411> accessed 20 Nov. 2019. Beside issues of enforcement, the Parliament is nuancing also the issue of corruption; on this, see TP Bernstein and L Xiaobo, *Taxation Without Representation in Rural China* (Cambridge University Press, 2003), 109 *et seq*. Also, for a view of the general European perspective on the topic, relevant are the guidelines by EU Small and Medium Enterprises Centre 'Dispute Settlement with Chinese Companies' (2012) <http://www.eusmecentre.org.cn/guideline/dispute-settlement-chinese-companies> accessed Nov. 20th, 2019, that at 4 read: 'If a foreign company does not succeed in solving the dispute in a friendly way, as a last resort this foreign company can seek litigation. However, foreign enterprises often fear that they are likely to lose the case in court since local jurisdictions might favour local companies. Foreign companies also fear that cases in China take too long, which prevents many of them from taking the final step to file a lawsuit. Furthermore, many foreign companies believe that the corruption of Chinese courts plays a major role in terms of fair trials. And last but not least, foreign companies doubt the effectiveness of the court's ruling when it comes to the enforcement of the award.'

203 Significant is also the fact that, given China's manufacturing integration in global value chains, for a foreign investor to get offside with China may result in undermining a regional manufacturing strategy. It is quite interesting, hence, that some of the known claims initiated against China are about real estate (which are less likely to depend on international production chains).

204 '... The first handicap is our relative ignorance of fact: the second is our relative indeterminacy of aim ... human legislators can have no such knowledge of all the possible combinations of circumstances which the future may bring. This inability to anticipate brings with it a relative indeterminacy of aim'; Prof. HLA Hart, *The Concept of Law* (Oxford University Press, 1961), 232–257.

Conversely, Chinese investors' claims against host States are growing, although with mixed success (often because of the limitations of older Chinese BITs still in force).[205] Some scholars hold that resort to arbitration on the part of Chinese investors is unlikely to grow substantially in the medium term, as '... it would be too rash to apply the behaviour of multinational enterprises from OECD countries that caused a substantial increase of transnational arbitration to Chinese companies of which a considerable number are still state-owned. Unless the actual coverage of Chinese BITs will be substantially extended in the medium term, Chinese outward FDI face high political risks and diplomatic relations between China and host countries are aggravated transnational arbitration cases involving Chinese investors will remain rare'.[206] It has also been noted that Chinese companies do not usually pay attention to the presence of BITs when making investment decisions.[207] While both considerations used to hold true, they may not remain so in the future, as today China's strategy seems focused to increasing the protection of its foreign investment and investors abroad, including ISA (all the while supporting mediation at the domestic level). And such an increased attention flows *inter alia* from the transformation of China's economy.

D The People's Republic: What Kind of Economy?

The government of the People's Republic defines the country's economic system as a 'socialist market economy'.[208] Such a locution is intended to draw a distinction from other forms, such as 'State capitalism', 'market socialism' or 'mixed market economy'.[209] In the case of State capitalism, the presence of financial markets excludes the dissemination of the 'social dividend' (*i.e.*, the

---

205 *Señor Tza Yap Shum v. The Republic of Peru*, Decision on Jurisdiction and Competence, Jul. 7th, 2011, ICSID Case No. ARB/07/6; *Sanum Investments v. Laos*, Award, Aug. 6th, 2019, UNCITRAL, PCA Case No. 2013–13; *China Heilongjiang v. Mongolia*, UNCITRAL, PCA (initiated in 2010, pending); *Ping-An Life Insurance Company of China Ltd. v. Kingdom of Belgium*, Award on Jurisdiction, Apr. 30th, 2015, ICSID Case No. ARB/12/29; *Beijing Urban Construction v. Yemen*, Decision on Jurisdiction, May 31st, 2017, ICSID Case No. ARB/14/30. See also Vaccaro-Incisa (fn. 191).

206 Berger 'China's New Bilateral Investment Treaty Programme' (fn. 71), 13–14.

207 A Chen (ed.), 'Should the Four "Great Safeguards" in Sino-Foreign BITs be Hastily Dismantled? Comments on Critical Provisions Concerning Dispute Settlement in model U.S. and Canadian BITs', in *The Voice from China* (Springer, 2013).

208 EF Vogel, *Deng Xiaoping and the Transformation of China* (Belknap Press, 2011), 682.

209 PCC Huang, 'Profit-Making State Firms and China's Development Experience: "State Capitalism" or "Socialist Market Economy"?' (2012) 38(6) *Modern China* 591, 621–623.

redistribution to the society at large of the profits generated by State-owned enterprises, whether in the form of money or goods). In mixed market economies, while the market is subject to a strong regulatory oversight, the extent of State ownership and the authoritarianism of the political context are relatively limited: private ownership does not pose ideological hurdles, and it is conceptually framed among the 'means of production'; also, the market determines the economic performance, and enterprises are profit-oriented. In market socialism, a full-fledged socialist ideology is ultimately discarded, following the realization that full economic planning is unattainable, or even undesirable.

When strategizing the concept of 'socialist market economy', Deng Xiaoping envisaged the continuation of planned economy supplemented by the market in all those sectors where planning was infeasible (or a substantial failure, or competition considered beneficial). Such a mixed ownership regime harkens back to the Stalinist 'two-stage theory of revolution', and is accepted as a temporary compromise in the progressive transition to a full planned economy (which remains the ultimate systemic goal).[210] According to this approach, the market is temporarily allowed to provide commodities while 'exhausting its historical stage and gradually retransforming itself into planned economy'.[211] Private property enjoys thus full – albeit temporary – dignity, next to traditional collective village enterprises and State ownership (the management of whose companies, however, receives competitive rewards and benefits based on international standards).

The nature the Chinese economy, as socialist or capitalist, was debated already in 2006.[212] Of the former, it lacked *i*) the adherence to the 'production for use' ideology (as opposed to 'for profit'); *ii*) the dominance of the working class (in terms of control over the surplus of the economic value); and *iii*) the self-management (or 'workplace democracy'). It was not possible, however, to identify as capitalist a State where 50% of the workforce is employed in the agricultural sector, and where the State-owned economy generates about half of the GDP and plays a key role in several strategic areas. Moreover, in 2006,

210 S. Amin, '"Market Socialism", a Stage in the Long Socialist Transition or Shortcut to Capitalism?' (2004) 32(11/12) *Social Scientist* 3, 4–8.

211 KE Brødsgaard and K Rutten, *From Accelerated Accumulation to Socialist Market Economy in China* (Brill, 2017), 94–106.

212 D Schweickart, 'China: Socialist or Capitalist?' (2015) *Perspectives on Global Development and Technology* 14, 13–25; see, also, C Lin, *The Transformation of Chinese Socialism* (Duke University Press, 2006), 251–287; see, also, Y Zhao, 'Neoliberal Strategies, Socialist Legacies: Communication and State Transformation in China', in P Chakravartty and Y Zhao (eds.), *Global Communications: Toward a Transcultural Political Economy* (Rowman & Littlefield Publishers, 2008), 23–50.

China's ruling class decided to halt the privatization program and retain full public control over a number of key industries and sectors.[213] Somehow echoing the USSR's 'commanding heights' policy,[214] China decided to consolidate its 'national champions'. Differently from the Soviet version, though, China appears to be operating the necessary restructuring of State enterprises on a commercial basis and rationale, retaining ownership but substantially relinquishing operative control. The tension between the 'socialist' and 'market' components of the current Chinese economic policy is evident in the 13th 5-year-plan (2016–2020), where the earlier pledge to allow the 'market to play a decisive role in allocating resources' has been partly retrenched with the reassertion of the Party's central role in China's economic and social development.[215]

Nevertheless, the debate over the status of China's economy is arguably rather more relevant under a trade perspective, than investment.[216] Relevant here is, instead, the policy on SOEs, as it is through those that the majority of Chinese foreign investment abroad had been carried out, and still is in a very significant proportion.

E The Role of State-Owned Enterprises in Chinese Outward FDI

FDI may still be perceived in some Chinese governmental circles as a 'decidedly capitalist thing';[217] this notwithstanding, China's policy choices over the last three decades indicate that the ruling class has long understood its necessity. The tenth 5-year-plan of the People's Republic, adopted in 1999, was labeled 'Going Abroad'; the eleventh, adopted in 2006, 'Going Out'; the twelfth, of 2011, 'Go Global', and specifically indicated as priority targets for Chinese

213 Z Huanxin, 'China Names Key Industries for Absolute State Control', *China Daily* (Dec. 19th, 2006) <http://www.chinadaily.com.cn/china/2006-12/19/content_762056.htm> accessed Oct. 31st, 2019.

214 SE Bonner, *Socialism Unbound: Principles, Practices, and Prospects* (Columbia University Press, 2013), 86.

215 K Koleski, 'The 13th Five-Year Plan' (U.S.-China Economic and Security Review Commission Staff Research Report, Feb. 14th, 2017) <https://www.uscc.gov/Research/13th-five-year-plan> accessed Nov. 20th, 2019.

216 Market economy status, as opposed to 'economy in transition' or 'non market economy', determines significant differences, *e.g.*, in terms of burden of proof on antidumping investigations in the EU, the U.S., or Japan (none of which currently recognizes China as a market economy).

217 As referred to by E Cary, 'SOEs Declining Role in China's Foreign Investment', *The Diplomat* (Jul. 3rd, 2013) <http://thediplomat.com/2013/07/soes-declining-role-in-chinas-foreign-investment/> accessed Nov. 20th, 2019.

outward FDI energy, high-end manufacturing, and raw materials.[218] The thirteenth plan, adopted in 2016 and labeled 'OBOR' (acronym for One Belt, One Road), focuses on outbound investment finalized to increase terrestrial and maritime trade within the Euro-Asiatic mega-region.

For liberal (and liberalized) economies, to address first-hand strategic investment policy goals is a challenging affair: there, in principle, private investors pursue their choices autonomously on the basis of a profit-oriented criterion.[219] In the case of the People's Republic, however, governmental policy may be (more) effectively pursued through the 100+ known State-owned Enterprises (SOEs) controlled, to varying degree, by the central government (and, together with provincial SOEs, which are in excess of 100.000, generate about half of China's GDP).[220] SOEs' are of many types, ranging from fully-State-owned to collective enterprises, joint enterprises, or shareholding limited corporations. These conceptually 'necessary vestiges from the past'[221] have been (and still are) an effective means for the Chinese government to -partially- redress China's trade and investment surplus.[222] Indeed, the majority of top Chinese investors abroad are SOEs, and their combined share of Chinese FDI, while progressively decreasing, remains critical and anyway quantitatively unimaginable in any other economy. In 2005, SOEs were the source of almost the totality of Chinese FDI; by 2012, they still generated approximately the 90% of it; projections show that in 2020 SOEs will still determine around half of an overall FDI outflow exceeding 100 billion USD.[223]

As governmentally owned entities of the People's Republic, SOEs enjoy certain privileges; notably:

---

218 Raw materials currently comprises approximately 70% of all Chinese FDI, which focuses on Australia, U.S., and Canada (with operations not always successful in terms of management or profitability).

219 There are, of course, exceptions, as many States retain controlling or anyway significant stakes in domestic energy multinationals: *e.g.*, Saudi Arabia with Saudi Aramco, France with Areva and EDF, Italy with ENI, Spain with Enagás.

220 Through SOEs, China assists its strategic industries (the 'national champions'), even though the logic to prioritize profits over strategic interests is making its way. It is worth noting that, as of 2014, the 60% of Chinese FDI into the U.S. came from SOEs.

221 Cary (fn. 191).

222 The first Chinese SOE investment abroad is reported to be the 1987 joint venture between Chinese 'Sinosteel' and the Australian 'Hamersley Iron'.

223 Way up from the 84 billion USD of 2012; for a recent analysis on the point, see HY Wang and L Miao, 'China's Outward Investment – Trends and Challenges in the Globalization of Chinese Enterprises', in J Chaisse (ed.), *China's International Investment Strategy* (Oxford, 2019) 41–55, at 44; see, also, D Ritchie, 'Chinese Outward Foreign Direct Investment', *China Go Abroad* (Dec. 4th, 2013) <http://www.chinagoabroad.com/en/commentary/chinese-outward-foreign-direct-investment> accessed Nov. 20th, 2019.

a. Reduced governmental oversight over investment plans abroad (compared to that over private Chinese investors, which must seek approval of the National Development Research Council for an assortment of initiatives they intend to pursue abroad);
b. Permanent supply of low-cost financing (through the central government), and
c. Subsidies; and
d. Losses potentially covered by the State.

These 'advantages' produce a distortion in terms of international trade and investment, which is also one the reasons SOEs' FDI is looked with suspicion in many quarters abroad. Also, the regulatory framework governing Chinese SOEs is rather fragmented and outdated,[224] and the lack of clarity of certain laws is cause of frustration for foreign firms dealing with them.[225] Perceived critical issues are *i*) the lack of transparency in SOEs governance (*e.g.*, appointment of key positions); *ii*) the generally poor reports and financials; *iii*) the evaluation of SOEs domestic assets (not carried out by independent bodies); and *iv*) the apparently limited concern with health, safety and environmental regulations.[226]

In part, the above issues are influenced by a 'cultural prejudice' against Chinese firms abroad, reinforced in turn by the fact that these often aim at direct acquisitions of foreign firms, or anyway controlling shares, including in strategic sectors.[227] Consequently, investment by Chinese SOEs is perceived and received differently than that from Japan in the '70s and '80s: this latter, even when directed from the State, came in from publicly listed and

224 The principal law is Law no. 91 of 1991, currently under revision by the Asset Supervision Administration Commission of the State Council; cf., Y Wang, 'New SASAC Rules to Enhance Risk Control of Chinese SOEs' Outbound Investments' (Norton Rose Fulbright Publications, Feb. 2012) <https://www.martindale.com/investments-law/article_Norton-Rose-Canada-LLP_1451278.htm> accessed Nov. 20th, 2019.

225 Wang (fn. 155); problematic are also the repeated cases of 'fraudulent practice' emerging out of projects carried out under the supervision of multilateral development banks and institutions, and participated by Chinese SOEs; in this respect, see S Finder, 'The International Fraud and Corruption Sanctioning System – The case of Chinese SOEs', in J Chaisse (ed.), *China's International Investment Strategy* (Oxford, 2019) 397–411.

226 For a general overview of the issues surrounding SOEs, see J Chaisse, 'Untangling the Triangle: Issues for State-controlled Entities in Trade, Investment, and Competition Law', in J Chaisse and T Lin (eds.), *International Economic Law and Governance* (Oxford, 2016) 233–258.

227 See, *e.g.*, Sauvant and Chen (fn. 155); Wang and Miao (fn. 197); with specific regard to security concerns, see L Wang, 'Chinese SOEs Investment and the National Security under IIAs', in J Chaisse (ed.), *China's International Investment Strategy* (Oxford, 2019) 67–86.

transparent companies, and in the form of joint ventures or non-controlling shares (revealing awareness of, and cautiousness with, the foreign context). In addition, some investment from Chinese SOEs have reportedly been blatant failures, amid overly ambitious plans, underestimation of financial and cultural factors, and poor performances. It is estimated that with the sole operations in the U.S. and Australia, Chinese SOEs have piled over 35 billion USD of failed or troubled operations.[228]

The situation is, nevertheless, gradually changing. In 2004, the State Council replaced the old outward investment 'examination regime' with a 'registration requirement', resulting into a surge of (SOEs-driven) outward Chinese investment. In 2009, the adoption of new 'Measures for the Administration of Outbound Investment', further constrained (in principle) the Authorities' scrutiny, limiting it to safeguarding fundamental Chinese interests and China's international obligations.[229] Therefore, with respect to central SOEs' overseas investments, the 'Asset Supervision Administration Commission of the State Council' (the centrally controlled authority exercising supervision – and, where necessary, control – over all SOEs) gradually left most of the decision-making power within the SOEs. Central SOEs are currently free to decide on, and implement any, overseas investment plan within their primary business sector. The Commission only intervenes in a limited range of circumstances (*e.g.*, overseas investment falling outside the primary business scope). Political influence seems thus limited, allowing SOEs management to balance politically-driven strategic goals and company profitability.

F Conclusion

The macroeconomic and geopolitical redistribution of global power, from the Atlantic to the Pacific, visible since the turn of the millennium, is impacting international rule making for the protection of foreign investment as well. Coupled with ASEAN's prolific treaty making activity in this field (as well as in the region), China's significant ties to, and share of, the global economy, in terms of both trade and investment, have been the driving factors of this global shift.

While its IIA programme, inaugurated in 1982, has arguably become the largest of any State at the present time, China has, to date, not played a proactive

228 Cf., Ritchie (fn. 197).

229 Art. 9, 2009 Measures for the Administration of Outbound Investments.

role in terms of contributing to or shaping the evolution of rulemaking in the field.[230] As illustrated, a variety of factors – often intertwined or overlapping – have contributed to this, including:

i. The time China needed to re-adjust its stance and approach, after decades of relative isolation, towards the international legal system, as well as Western capital;
ii. China's inexperience with the international rules for the protection of foreign investments, and the consequent cautiousness in opening to standards alien to its legal tradition;
iii. The limited mandate granted, until the end of the 1990s, to Chinese IIA negotiators by central authorities, which *de facto* bound negotiators (and, arguably, negotiating counterparts) to the Chinese model;
iv. The distribution of power within the State, in terms of layers of government, including the relationship between the central and the territorial sub-units, which made (and, to some extent, still makes) domestic implementation of measures related to certain modern standards for the protection of foreign investment problematic and slow;
v. China's relatively recent shift, from a capital importing economy to a leading exporter of capital as well;
vi. Certain peculiar characteristics of Chinese investment, both domestic and international, in particular the role there played by SOEs – whose management and conduct have been determined, until relatively recently, more by political directives than economic objectives.

At the dusk of the last millennium, the progressive and very significant increase of Chinese outward investment prompted China's ruling class to bring the Mainland's treaty policy on the protection of foreign investment in line with international standards.

However, while China has since then further evolved and modernized several aspects of its treaty practice (as illustrated in detail, with reference to key standards, in Chapters 2 and 3), it has not yet assumed the role of 'rule-maker' in the field. The relatively comprehensive position that China recently outlined

230 In the field of investment law, the words of Professor Wang are still valid today: 'As [China] wishes to be viewed as a responsible member of the international community, however, it must do more to meet the rest of the world's expectations'; see G Wang, 'China's Practice in International Investment Law: From Participation to Leadership in the World Economy' (2009) 34 *Yale Journal of International Law* 586.

at the UNCITRAL table for ISDS reform seems to reflect relative comfort with the *status quo* – which dates back to a time when China was a 'rule-taker' (the point is further developed in the book Conclusion).[231]

231 See the statement (in Chinese) on the UNCITRAL website at <https://uncitral.un.org/sites/uncitral.un.org/files/wp117c.pdf> accessed Nov. 20th, 2019; and the comment of A Roberts, 'UNCITRAL and ISDS Reform: China's Proposal', *EJIL: Talk!* (Aug. 5th, 2019), <https://www.ejiltalk.org/uncitral-and-isds-reform-chinas-proposal/> accessed Nov. 20th, 2019.

CHAPTER 2

Chinese IIAs: Treaty Templates and Selected Aspects of Treaty Practice

A Adopting the Model BIT: Policy Rationale

As mentioned, it appears that China developed a model BIT since 1984 – before most OECD States, as well as all major developing States (such as, *e.g.*, India or Mexico) –, and that it subsequently adopted other two (in 1989 and 1997).[1] China, thus, understood early the possible benefits deriving from adopting a treaty template on the protection of foreign investment, such as:

- Enabling a State to clarify its foreign investment protection policy and position in BIT negotiations;
- Promoting uniformity in the State treaty practice, reducing inconsistencies within the BIT programme;[2]
- Providing a strategic negotiating advantage, as the model becomes the basis for negotiations (with the counterpart in the reacting position to an established framework);
- Promoting predictability with respect to the treatment foreign investors may expect.[3]

1 See Chapter 1, fn. 63.

2 Newcombe (fn. 12), 21; recent treaty practice suggest that States are increasingly concerned with consistency among their BITs (and, especially, clarifying limits to the application of the MFN treatment); see also Schill, 'Tearing down the Great Wall' (Chapter 1, fn. 3), 84; See also, Dolzer and Stevens (Chapter 1, fn. 1), 13: 'most BIT negotiations take as their starting point model agreements of capital-exporting countries … a central part of BIT negotiations would therefore concern modifications to such a model treaty that may be deemed desirable by the capital-importing countries'; the last element in the list is perhaps the less immediate *in concreto*: foreign investors have often little awareness of the international legal framework governing their investment; nor usually decide to make an investment on the basis of the presence (or lack) of a BIT.

3 Which is consistent with the broad objective of promoting the rule of law, also at the international level – a theme frequently touched upon by China in official statements; in this sense see J Chaisse, 'China's International Investment Policy: Formation, Evolution, and Transformation(s)', in J Chaisse and L Nottage (eds.), *International Investment Treaties and Arbitration across Asia* (Brill Nijhoff, 2018) 544–578, at 573.

© KONINKLIJKE BRILL NV, LEIDEN, 2021 | DOI:10.1163/9789004443938_004

China has always been very attentive to all the above policy aspects – the second criterion arguably carrying more weight than the others. Indeed, as shown in Chapter 3, China managed to achieve an overall remarkable degree of uniformity amongst its BITs, if one considers that:

- The early adoption of a model text (which draws from the practice and, later, models, of major European States) allowed China until recently to 'impose' its model as template in the vast majority of negotiations;
- Serious departures from the template wording in actual stipulations have been, until recently, relatively rare;
- More than half of China's BITs were concluded in the early 1990s.[4]

All Chinese models reveal strong ties with the German and British templates. Thus, while the overall BIT structure and provisions appear similar (or equivalent), some variations brought or accepted in actual stipulations, or between one model and the other, reflect the specific Chinese attitude toward the public / private international law intertwine that international investment law, as settled via international arbitration, constitutes.

The State Council seems to have adopted the first model BIT in 1984.[5] According to the information provided by MOFCOM, the Council adopted the second model in 1989.[6] Lastly, the third version was adopted in 1997, and it has remained unchanged since then (officially at least).[7] The analysis that follows focuses on the 1997 model, the innovations brought with its adoption with respect to the previous texts, and those accepted by China in subsequent stipulations.

As mentioned in Chapter One, key changes introduced in 1997 derive from the BIT talks with Canada.[8] The new model brought in several liberal changes in substantive provisions: *e.g.*, China's 1980s resistance to commit to full-fledged-NT (which contributed to the early stall of the BIT negotiations with the US) was no more. Also, China was now willing to grant unrestricted consent to ISDS, including ICSID. Nevertheless, typical 'Chinese characteristics' appear in several parts of the text, such as preamble, definition of investment, standards of treatment, standard for compensation, transfer regime and ISDS.

4 Cf., Figure 5, above.

5 Gallagher and Shan, *Chinese Investment Treaties* (Chapter 1, fn. 63), 421; English version provided by the MOFCOM.

6 *Id.*, 427; English translation provided by Prof. Shan.

7 *Id.*, 433; English version provided by MOFCOM.

8 *Id.*, 41.

The following analysis highlights each of these, focusing on the evolution of the model text.

B Structure of the Chinese Model BIT

The 1997 model BIT comprises a Preamble and 13 Articles. This is in line with the standard practice and models of European States: *e.g.*, the UK,[9] Dutch[10] and Italian[11] models have 14 articles, the German 13,[12] the French 11,[13] (see Table 4, below). To date, and with regard to negotiating templates only, China has thus not followed the US or Canada, which since 2004 have adopted more articulated models (respectively, 37 Articles and a few Annexes,[14] and 52 Articles and several Annexes).[15]

The 1997 model contains all provisions commonly found in BITs, namely:

1. Preamble
2. Definitions (Art. 1)
3. Substantive guarantees (*i.e.*, admission, Art. 2; standards of treatment, Art. 3; expropriation and compensation, Art. 4; compensation for damages and losses, Art. 5; transfers, Art. 6; subrogation, Art. 7, umbrella clause, Art. 10)
4. State-State dispute settlement (Art. 8)
5. Investor-State dispute settlement (Art. 9)
6. Treaty application clause (Art. 10)
7. Final provisions (*i.e.*, consultations; entry into force, duration and termination).

The Table below outlines the structural similarities between the Chinese model – whose number and sequence never changed throughout the models – and those the European members of the G7. The following section focuses on key aspects of the wording chosen in the Chinese model.

9 Both the 1991 as well as the 2006 models.
10 Dutch 2004 model BIT.
11 Italy 2003 model BIT.
12 Both the 1991 as well as the 2008 models.
13 France 2006 model BIT.
14 Both the 2004 and 2012 models.
15 Canada 2004 model BIT; the draft model of 2006 comprises, instead, 42 provisions.

TABLE 4 Chinese and European model BITS – sequence of provisions

Art.	PRC	UK	DE	FR	IT
1	*Definitions*	*Definitions*	*Definitions*	*Definitions*	*Definitions*
2	Promotion and protection of investment	Promotion and protection of investment	Admission and protection of investments	Promotion and admission of investments	Promotion and protection of investments
3	Treatment of investment	National treatment and most-favored-nation provisions	National and most-favored-nation treatment	Fair and equitable treatment	National treatment and the most favored nation clause
4	*Expropriation*	Compensation for losses	*Compensation in case of expropriation*	National treatment and most favored nation treatment	Compensation for damages or losses
5	Compensation for damages and losses	*Expropriation*	Free transfer	*Dispossession and indemnification*	*Nationalisation or expropriation*
6	Transfer	Repatriation of investment and returns	Subrogation	Free transfer	Repatriation of capital, profits and income
7	Subrogation	(Exceptions)	Other provisions	*Settlement of disputes between an investor and a contracting party*	Subrogation
8	***Settlement of disputes between contracting parties***	*Reference to International Centre for Settlement of Investment Disputes*[16]	Scope of application	Guarantee and subrogation	Transfer procedures

16 In the alternative UK BIT model the provision is labeled 'Settlement of disputes between an investor and a host State'.

TABLE 4 Chinese and European model BITS – sequence of provisions (*cont.*)

Art.	PRC	UK	DE	FR	IT
9	*Settlement of disputes between investors and one Contracting Party*	***Disputes between the contracting parties***	***Settlement of disputes between the contracting states***	**Special commitment**	***Settlement of disputes between the contracting parties***
10	**Other obligations**	[Subrogation]	*Settlement of disputes between a contracting state And an investor of the other contracting state*	***Settlement of disputes between contracting parties***	*Settlement of disputes between investors and contracting parties*
11	Application	**Application of other Rules**	*Relations between the contracting states*	Entry into force and termination	*Relation between governments*
12	*Consultations*	Scope of Application[17]	(Registration clause)	–	**Application of other provisions**
13	Entry into force, duration and termination	Entry into Force	Entry into force, duration and notice of termination	–	Entry into force
14	–	Duration and Termination	–	–	Duration and expiry

17 In the alternative UK BIT model the provision is labeled 'Territorial extension'.

C Preamble, Application, and Definition of Investment

1 *Preamble*

The principal purpose of a treaty is reflected in the preamble, which provides for the 'color, texture and shading'[18] of the entire stipulation. Before the adoption of the 1984 model, China had signed four BITs.[19] In those earlier agreements, preambles are quite simple:

- China's first BIT, in 1982, with Sweden, follows the traditional Swedish pattern in outlining only the desire to 'maintain fair and equitable treatment for investments';[20]
- The 1983 China-Germany BIT features, according to the German custom, the parties' effort 'to create favorable conditions for investments';
- The 1988 BIT with Australia features the *ratione legis* requirement at the preamble stage, which has become over the time quite frequent (in addition to the model language).[21]

In general, the progressive enrichment of the standard preamble appears aimed at checking expansive interpretations against any measure, regardless of its nature and public welfare effect.[22]

Officially, the text of the preamble has not changed throughout the three models. The standard language recites:

> *Intending to create favorable conditions for investment by investors of one Contracting Party in the territory of the other Contracting Party;*
>
> *Recognizing that the reciprocal encouragement, promotion and protection of such investment will be conducive to stimulating business initiative of the investors and will increase prosperity in both States;*
>
> *Desiring to intensify the cooperation of both States on the basis of equality and mutual benefits;*
>
> *Have agreed as follows: ...*

18 As magisterially synthesized in the WTO Appellate Body Report, *United States – Import Prohibition of Certain Shrimp and Shrimp Products*, Appellate Body Report, Oct. 12th, 1998, WT/DS58/AB/R, paras. 153 and 155.

19 Sweden (1982), Romania (1983), Germany (1983), France (1984).

20 This simple formulation is standard in Swedish BITs (cf., 1981 BIT with Pakistan; also, the 1978 BIT with Egypt where, however, it is associated to the typically French BIT preambular objective to 'promote the development of economic, industrial and technical cooperation').

21 *E.g.*, BITs with Nigeria (1997), Trinidad and Tobago (2002), Guyana (2003), Benin (2004).

22 In this sense, Gallagher and Shan, *Chinese Investment Treaties* (Chapter 1, fn. 63), 51.

The above text, which does not mention any specific principle or extensive commitment, outlines the three general purposes of a Chinese BIT:

1. To facilitate and attract investments;
2. To contribute to the prosperity of the contracting parties;
3. To cooperate on the basis of equality and mutual benefits.

Coherently with China's early lack of trust in international investment law and related commitments, the preamble appears to be structured to avoid 'pro-investor' presumptions or interpretations;[23] although it is there recognized that the primary purpose of the BIT is to attract investments (first principle), it is also essential that such investment shall be beneficial to the host State (second and third principles).

In actual Chinese BITs, the preamble has long reflected the model language – which was used for the first time in the 1984 BIT with Belgium-Luxembourg.[24] In nowadays practice, part of the preambular language may be found either transferred or restated in greater detail in the provision of scope (also labeled 'objectives'), giving to the text a normative character, more than simple interpretive indication.[25]

2 *Scope and Application*

With respect to their ambit of application, BITs may be divided into two 'families': on the one side, that stemming from the European practice and models, whose 'application' provision (placed towards the end of the treaty) provides that the agreement 'shall apply to ***investments***;'[26] on the other, that of the North American models, whose 'scope' provision (found at the very beginning of the treaty) determines that the BIT applies to '***measures*** adopted or maintained by a Party ….'[27] This distinction is yet to be doctrinally explored in investment law (while the definition of 'measure' has been subject to thorough scrutiny

23 *E.g.*, such as in *Société Générale de Surveillance S.A. v. Republic of the Philippines*, Decision on Jurisdiction, Jan. 29th, 2004, ICSID Case No. ARB/02/6., para. 116: 'The object and purpose of the BIT supports an effective interpretation of Art. X(2). The BIT is a treaty for the promotion and reciprocal protection of investments. According to the preamble, it is intended "to create and maintain favorable conditions for investments by investors of one Contracting Party in the territory of the other". It is legitimate to resolve uncertainties in its interpretation so as to favor the protection of covered investments'; see, also, Gallagher and Shan, *Chinese Investment Treaties* (Chapter 1, fn. 63), 50.

24 Terminated in light of the 2005 renegotiation.

25 *E.g.*, Art. 2 ('objectives') of CAIA (2009).

26 Emphasis added; this is since the very first BIT, the 1959 agreement between Germany and Pakistan (Art. 9); with regard to model BITs, the German and British expressly state so (respectively, at Art. 8 and Art. 12); the French and Italian models, despite not featuring an 'application' provision as such, follow the same conceptual pattern.

27 Emphasis added; Art. 2 of US (2004 and 2012) and Canada (2004 and 2006) models.

in trade law). In general, it may be considered that application 'to measures' implies that investments are not protected just as such (in what could today appear an 'overly ontological' approach) but in connection to an action (or omission) of the host State negatively affecting a specific investment. In this context, it is easy to discern the 'protective intent' of the investment regime, designed in principle against *lex ad hominem* (*i.e.*, in the case of foreign investment, the archetypal issue of direct expropriation, a measure with a specific target which would be illegitimate if not excused by the promotion of the broader public interest).[28] Conversely, the conceptually wider BIT application 'to investments' seems to be relying on the positive nature of the investment as such, thus focusing on the 'promotion' side of the investment regime. In this case, however, the treaty involuntarily creates a potentially problematic linguistic link between the general concept of 'promotion of public interest', core of the Sovereign legislator activity, and that, much more limited, of the treaty's 'promotion of investment'. It seems that this narrow distinction has yet escaped the attention of doctrine.

2.1 The Chinese Model

As illustrated, according to their structural features the Chinese models stem from the major European models. An analysis of the application provision (Art. 11 of any Chinese model), confirms this. As per most of the text – and thanks also to the early BITs concluded with Germany and Britain[29] – China took more than just inspiration from the British and German models. The text resembles to a considerable extent a patchwork of the British and German wording of the same provision – to which the firmest and longest-standing *topos*[30] of Chinese BITs is, *i.e.*, the explicit call for respect of domestic laws and regulations (Table 5, below, provides a comparative illustration of this).

The wording of the provision may be sectioned and highlighted as follows:

- '*This agreement shall apply to investments which are made prior or after its entry into force*' is extracted from both British and German models, which feature an identical wording, with the exception of the characterizing 'agreement' from the British model, and the 'prior' *in lieu* of 'before' from the German model; China thus operated, here, a merger;[31]

28 Expropriation is conceptually tied only to 'promotion' of the public interest, not 'protection': when the latter case occurs, we are in the field of criminal law and the activity is illegal – thus not an investment.

29 Respectively, in 1983 and 1986.

30 Ancient Greek, lit. 'place', meaning 'commonplace', doctrinally meaning 'constant practice'.

31 Interestingly, China discarded the word 'also' (in the locution 'this treaty shall also apply') opening the German provision. The word – which is nevertheless featured in the 1983 China-Germany BIT, and kept in the 2008 German model – was perhaps deemed unclear.

TABLE 5 European and Chinese model BITs – application

Art. 11 PRC model '84/'89	Art. 11 PRC model '97	Art. 12 UK '06	Art. 8 DE '08	Art. 12 PRC-DE '03
This agreement shall apply to investments which are made prior or after its entry into force by investors of either CP *in accordance with the laws and regulations of the other CP* in the territory of the Latter.	This agreement shall apply to investments made prior or after its entry into force by investors of one CP in the territory of the other CP in accordance with the laws and regulations of the CP concerned, but not apply to the disputes arose before its entry into force.	This agreement shall apply to all investments, whether made before or after its entry into force, but shall not apply to any dispute concerning an investment which arose, or any claim concerning an investment which was settled, before its entry into force.	This Treaty shall also apply to investments made prior to its entry into force by investors of either CP in the territory of the other CP consistent with the latter's legislation.	[idem as PRC '84/'89]

Original UK	*Original PRC*	Other shared wording
Original DE	Found in earlier PRC model	

- '... *in accordance with the laws and regulations of the other Contracting Party* ...' is the typical Chinese *ratione legis* condition[32] (similar to the German 'consistent with the latter's legislation');
- '... *by investors of either Contracting Party ... in the territory of the other Contracting Party*' derives from the German model;

32 According to Schill, such systematic requirement of Chinese BITs is due more to a general distrust towards international investment arbitration, than an effective desire to provide a chance of domestic redress via the domestic administrative courts; see Schill, 'Tearing down the Great Wall' (Chapter 1, fn. 3), 92–93.

- The 1997 model, in particular, by extracting additional words from the British model, adds at the end of the provision '... *but [the agreement does] not apply to the disputes arose before its entry into force*' (*i.e.*, the *ratione temporis* scope); the addition, however, reproduces only a few essential words of the original sentence (much longer), thus creating an equivalent yet more concise phrasing.

China's treaty-*bricolage* technique in building its first model BIT, since 1984, thus emerges, as well as its rationale: relying on the experience acquired by foreign powers and 'perfecting' their texts (in the sense of added simplicity and clarity) to fit China's needs.

Over the years – and models –, the 'application' provision has not gone through substantial changes. Beside the earliest stipulations, featuring the *ratione temporis* criterion only,[33] the *ratione legis* and *loci* soon appeared to complete the provision[34] – with the notable exception of the 1986 China-UK BIT.[35] It may be noted that, in the context of the re-negotiations of the 1983 China-Germany BIT, Germany did not insist on updating the definition in accordance with its own latest model (being the content substantially equivalent), but accepted to rely on the old 1984 Chinese text (which, nonetheless, constituted an update from the 1983 regime).

2.2 Contemporary Practice

Between April 2008 and August 2009, two FTAs featuring investment chapters (*i.e.*, PRC-NZ FTA and AANZFTA) and two investment agreements flowing from multi-stage comprehensive FTAs (ACIA and CAIA) were signed in the western Pacific – over an area spanning from China to New Zealand and encompassing the entire Southwest Asia and Australia –, redesigning the legal trade and investment framework of the region. These agreements, whose negotiations mostly overlapped, present remarkable similarities.

The agreements to which China is a Party reflect, however, an approach more adherent to its own model BIT – displaying China's reluctance to go through overwhelming and sudden changes in the structure of investment treaties,

33 In the 1982 BIT with Sweden, the provision simply states: 'This agreement shall apply to all investment made after July 1, 1979'.

34 *E.g.*, Art. 9 China-Germany BIT (1983): 'This agreement shall also apply to investment made from July 1st, 1979, by investor of a Contracting Party in the territory of the other Contracting Party in accordance with its laws and regulations'.

35 The 1986 China-UK BIT lacks the provision altogether (however, *ratione legis* and *loci* are featured in the definition of investment); indeed, the British model BIT, even in its latest version (2006), focuses solely on the moment when the dispute arises, not considering any *rationes*.

and the desire to maintain an overall coherent set of similar stipulations (thus the refusal to embrace *sic et simpliciter* the US model). Hence, in line with the German model, in the PRC-NZ FTA and the CAIA the *ratione loci* is expressed a first time already in the definition of investment. The *ratione temporis*, on the other hand, is left into the 'Scope' provision[36] (successor of the old model BIT-based 'Application' provision – extinct, in fact, in all four stipulations).[37] It is with the *ratione legis*, however, that it is possible to draw an element in favor of the theory for which China applies two different standards in investment agreements[38] – yet exercised in a not entirely clear fashion, along the lines 'developed' *v.* 'developing', 'capital exporter' *v.* 'capital importer', 'western' *v.* 'eastern' State. In fact, the exigency to include such criterion is much less felt in the British model, where it appears only as an exceptional condition against admission (*i.e.*, each Party 'shall admit' the investment '... subject to its right to exercise powers conferred by its laws ...'[39]). In the German model, however, it is featured twice, framed in general terms, both in the 'Promotion and protection' provision (*i.e.*, each Party shall 'admit such investments in accordance with its legislation'[40]) and in the 'Application' provision (*i.e.*, the treaty applies to investments made '... consistent with the [host State] legislation'[41]). It may not surprise that, in its models and stipulations, China systematically adhered to the more 'controlling' German approach.

3 *Definition of Investment*

The definition of investment is a key provision of all IIAs, as it essentially delimits their scope of application, provided that only qualified investments enjoy the guarantees therein offered.[42] The definition of investment, in particular, interacts with other substantive provisions (such as, *e.g.*, NT or ISDS

36 Art. 137.6 PRC-NZ FTA and Art. 2.2 CAIA; see Section C, below.

37 The 'Application' provision of the German model (Art. 8) restate the *ratione temporis* and *loci* of the BIT; in the UK model, instead, only the *ratione temporis* is mentioned (being an explicit mention of the *ratione loci* not featured at all); in all Chinese models the 'Application' provision is a merger of the British wording for the *ratione temporis* and the German wording for the *ratione loci* (see Table 5, in Chapter II, Section B).

38 On the Chinese dual standard in investment treaties, see Li, 'Chinese BIT Practice and Challenges' (fn. 72).

39 Art. 2.1 British model BIT.

40 Art. 2.1 German model BIT.

41 Art. 8 German model BIT.

42 UNCTAD, 'Scope and Definition' (UNCTAD Series on Issues in International Investment Agreements, 2011) <http://unctad.org/en/pages/PublicationArchive.aspx?publicationid

provisions), thus playing an important role in shaping the overall investment protection regime. The definition is also tightly connected to the State attitude towards investment liberalization: the broader the definition, the more protection is likely to be offered to investments.[43] From the embryonic open-list pivoting on 'capital' enshrined in the 1959 Germany-Pakistan BIT,[44] and passing through the broad notion of 'property' featured in the 1967 Draft Convention on the Protection of Foreign Property,[45] the definition of investment over the time has gone through a process of standardization. However, while all major model BITs build on a common open-ended structure and notion comprised of a chapeau and a list of instances,[46] no universally binding definition or concept of investment has been yet agreed upon.

=354> accessed 20 Nov. 2019; also, WTO, 'Report of the Working Group on the Relationship between Trade and Investment to the General Council', Dec. 9th, 2002 (WT/WGTI/6), 6.

43 *Id.*, pp. 3–5. As opposed to narrow definitions, normally preferred in investment-liberalization contexts. A narrow approach is an enterprise or transaction-based definition, focused on FDI; a broad approach is an asset-based definition, with options for the inclusion or exclusion of various categories of investments. Most BITs adopt the broad approach, as it provides for comprehensive, rule-based protection, and grants high standards of treatment for all categories of foreign investments. Since a broad definition of investment entails the liberalization of all forms of capital movement, and increases the risk of destabilizing short-term flows, a narrow definition is usually adopted in liberalization-oriented agreements. A narrow definition may fit the entire agreement and make it unnecessary to further delineate the BIT's scope and coverage; a broad definition, on the other hand, requires more flexibility, which can be achieved by structuring specific commitments within the substantive provisions dealing with pre-establishment commitments. As modern investment agreements cover both liberalization and protection aspects, the current approach seems to consist in the use of different definitions for the pre- and post-establishment phases of investments: narrow, for the former (*i.e.*, market access and investment liberalization), and broad, for the latter.

44 Art. 8.1: '(a) The term 'investment' shall comprise capital brought into the territory of the other Party for investments in various forms in the shape of assets such as foreign exchange, goods, property rights, patents and technical knowledge. The term 'investment' shall also include the returns derived from and ploughed back into such 'investment'. (b) Any partnership, companies or assets of similar kind, created by the utilization of the above mentioned assets shall be regarded as 'investment'.'

45 Art. 9.c: '"Property" means all property, rights and interests, whether held directly or indirectly, including the interest which a member of a company is deemed to have in the property of the company'; the comment attached to the text of the Draft Convention stresses, at p. 43, that the use of the term 'property' was '... meant to be used in its widest sense which includes, but it not limited to, investments.'

46 *E.g.*, German, British, Dutch, French, Italian, US models; in the Canadian model, the list of instances is closed.

According to the Oxford Dictionary, 'investment' means 'the action or process of investing money for profit', 'a thing that is worth buying because it may be profitable or useful in the future', or 'an act of devoting time, effort, or energy to a particular undertaking with the expectation of a worthwhile result'.[47] According to the Merriam Webster Collegiate Encyclopedia, 'investment' means:

> Process of exchanging income for an asset that is expected to produce earnings at a later time. An investor refrains from consumption in the present in hopes of a greater return in the future ... Investment cannot occur without saving, which provides funding. Because investment increases an economy's capacity to produce, it is a factor contributing to economic growth.[48]

The definition of investment vests critical importance in the context of ICSID arbitration, as it is evident from the numerous disputes that pivot on the relationship between the definitions of investment respectively featured in the ICSID Convention and the relevant IIA. Indeed, the former does not contain an express definition of investment.[49] The latter, in contrast, always contains a detailed definition. In German, British, Dutch, French and Italian practice, as well as in Chinese, the definition is:

- Introduced by a chapeau that provides for some overarching characteristics (such as the *ratione personae*,[50] the *ratione loci*,[51] the *ratione legis*,[52] and, on occasion, the *ratione temporis*[53] as well;
- Followed by an open-ended, asset-based series of instances enshrining the bulk of the *ratione materiae*[54] of the definition, exemplified in a list of five or

47 See Oxford Dictionaries online (www.oxforddictionaries.com).

48 See Merriam-Webster's Collegiate Encyclopedia (Springfield, 2000), 815.

49 See Art. 25 ICSID Convention, as well as the position of Dr. Aron Broches, General Counsel of the World Bank and chair of the Legal Committee tasked with the drafting of the ICSID Convention, as reported in the ICSID, *History of the ICSID Convention: Documents Concerning the Origin and the Formulation of the Convention on the Settlement of Investment Disputes Between States and Nationals of Other States* (ICSID Publishing, 1968) Volume II-1, 54, 566.

50 *I.e.*, that the investment must be made by a properly qualifying investor.

51 *I.e.*, that the investment must be made in the territory of the host State.

52 *I.e.*, that the investment must be made in accordance with the law of the host State.

53 *I.e.*, that the investment must be made after the entry into force of the agreement (most often, there are variations and exceptions).

54 That the activity carried out by the investor must indeed qualify as an investment according to the treaty definition (BIT and/or ICSID).

six categories (*e.g.*, property rights, contractual rights, intellectual property rights, concession rights), and
- Closed with the extension of protection to any alteration to the form in which assets are invested, and/or returns as well (the rest of the *ratione materiae*).

Since 2004, in the North American models the definition of investment is preceded by that of 'covered investment', which subsumes the *ratione personae, loci* and *temporis*. While Canada does not maintain a chapeau to the definition of investment, the US does, thereby adding further specifications to the *ratione personae*[55] and, most importantly, the three objective criteria of *i*) commitment of capital or other resources, *ii*) expectation or gain of profit and *iii*) assumption of risk. Albeit differently, both US and Canadian models and practice do incorporate a more comprehensive list of investment instances than European agreements, expanding the *ratione materiae* to expressly include company participation and concessions categories.[56] North American models and most practice, though, do not feature the *ratione legis* requirement in the definition of investment.[57]

Taking into account that, so far, European-styled BITs have been the legal ground of all known investment disputes, it is noteworthy that both the first texts finalized or still being negotiated and made public by the EU, as well as those of ASEAN, and most of China since 2008, are all shifting towards the North American model. This is of particular significance with regard to the definition of investment, in light of the greater detail it is therein dealt with. This may be considered also a common response coming from four key regions (US and Canada, EU, ASEAN, China – that, combined, currently command the vast majority of inward and outbound FDI worldwide), to certain interpretive trends in investment arbitration relating to the definition of investment.

3.1 The Chinese Template Definition of Investment

Like the others, Chinese model BITs link the scope of the definition of investment to the way in which the investment is made. Only assets '*invested by investors of one Contracting Party in the territory of the other contracting Party*' are covered investments under the treaty. This is significant, as China's policy with regard to admission of foreign investment has long followed a systematic

55 *I.e.*, that the investor must own or control, directly or indirectly, the investment.

56 As the list of investment instances is therein closed, the Canadian model is particularly detailed.

57 The US does, but only in relation to the concession category; see Sect. C.3.2.1, below.

'one-by-one' approval system (hence, investments not duly approved could not rely on the BIT protection).[58]

The definition of investment contained in the 1997 Chinese model BIT reproduces mainly the wording employed since 1984. The fist model, in turn, for the most part merged elements either common or distinctive of the British and German templates.

Comparative Table 6, below, outlines commonalities and differences amongst the relevant agreements (including the innovative China-Germany BIT of 2003) The subsequent sections analyze in detail specific elements of the definition of investment, such as chapeau, *ratione legis* condition, objective criteria, indirect investment, and ownership and control.

TABLE 6 Chinese model BITs – definition of investment

Art. 1.1 China model '84 and '89	Art. 1.1 China model '97
1. The term 'investment' means every kind of asset invested by investors of one CP in accordance with the laws and regulations of the other CP in the territory of the Latter, and in particular, though not exclusively, includes:	[*idem*]

58 However, this will soon no longer be the case. China's requirement that all new foreign investments obtain government approval was first partly lifted in 2013, by way of experiment, in the pilot free trade zone (FTZ) in Shanghai, pursuant to which foreign investments (unless in a sector specified in a newly issued negative list) could be registered without a preliminary government approval. This was followed by the circulation of a draft foreign investment law for comments in early 2015, which is now finalized and set to enter in force in January 2020. The law is designed to move China towards a pre-establishment negative list-market-access approach to foreign investment; see V Bath, 'The South and Alternative Models of Trade and Investment Regulation – Chinese Outbound Investment and Approaches to International Investment Agreements', in F Morosini and M Ratton Sanchez Badin (eds.), *Recalibrating International Investment Law: Global South Initiative* (Cambridge University Press, 2018); see J Huang, *International Business Law: Chinese and Comparative Perspectives* (Foreign Language Teaching and Research Press, 2017) 292–306; for a review of the previous systemic screening process, see W Shan, *The Legal Framework of EU-China Investment Relations – A Critical Appraisal* (Hart Publishing, 2005).

TABLE 6 Chinese model BITs – definition of investment (*cont.*)

Art. 1.1 China model '84 and '89	Art. 1.1 China model '97
(a) movable, immovable property and other property rights such as mortgages and pledges;	(a) movable and immovable property and other property rights such as mortgages, pledges **and similar rights**;
(b) shares, stocks and any other kind of participation in companies;	(b) shares, **debentures**, stock and any other kind of participation in companies;
(c) claims to money or to any other performance having an economic value;	(c) claims to money or to any other performance having an economic value **associated with an investment**;
(d) copyrights, industrial property, know-how and technological processes;	(d) **intellectual property rights, in particular** copyrights, **patents, trade-marks, trade-names,** technical process, know-how **and good-will**;
(e) concessions conferred by law, including concessions to search for or exploit natural resources.	(e) **business** concessions conferred by law **or under contract permitted by law**, including concessions to search for, **cultivate, extract** or exploit natural resources.
–	Any change in the form in which wassets are invested does not affect their character as investments provided that such change is in accordance with the laws and regulations of the CP in whose territory the investment has been made.

TABLE 7 European and Chinese model BITs definition of investment

Art. 1.1 PRC '84 / '89	Art. 1.1 PRC '97	Art. 1(a) UK '06[59]	Art. 1.1 DE '08[60]	Art. 1.1 PRC-DE '03
1.1 The term **'investment'** means **every kind** **of asset invested** by investors of one CP in accordance with the laws and regulations of the other CP **in the territory of the Latter,** and in particular, though not exclusively, includes:	[idem]	1(a) **'investment'** means **every kind of asset,** **owned or controlled**[61] **directly or indirectly**, and in particular, though not exclusively, includes:	1.1 the term **'investments'** comprises **every kind of asset** which is **directly or indirectly** invested by investors of one CP in the territory of the other CP. The investments **include in particular:**	1.1 the term 'investment' means every kind of asset invested **directly or indirectly** by investors of one CP in the territory of the other CP, and in particular, though not exclusively, includes:
(a) **movable, immovable property** and other property rights **such as mortgages** and **pledges;**	(a) movable and immovable property and other property rights such as mortgages, pledges ***and similar rights;***	(i) **movable and immovable property** and any other property rights **such as mortgages,** liens or **pledges;**	(a) **movable and immovable property** as well as any other rights in rem, **such as mortgages,** liens and **pledges;**	(a) [idem PRC '84]

59 Art. 1.a of the 1993 UK model BIT is identical to that featured in the 2006 model (with the sole exception of a more concise chapeau); for the sake of space and clarity, thus, the latter only is featured in the Table.

60 Art. 1.1 of the 1991 German model 1991 is contained in that, more articulated, of the 2008 model (only differences being a more concise chapeau, a simpler listing for the IP-related items, and the addition of the last sentence); for the sake of space and clarity, thus, the latter only is featured in the Table.

61 Art. 1 US 1992 model: '... investment in the territory of one Party that an investor owned or controlled, directly or indirectly ...'.

TABLE 7 European and Chinese model BITs definition of investment (*cont.*)

Art. 1.1 PRC '84 / '89	Art. 1.1 PRC '97	Art. 1(a) UK '06	Art. 1.1 DE '08	Art. 1.1 PRC-DE '03
(b) **shares,** stocks and any other kind of participation in companies;	(b) shares, debentures, stock and any other kind of participation in companies;	(ii) **shares** in and stock and debentures of a company and any other form of participation in a company;	(b) **shares** of companies and other kinds of interest in companies;	(b) shares, **debentures,** stock and any other kind of **interest** in companies;
(c) **claims to money or to any** other performance having an economic value;	(c) claims to money or to any other performance having an economic value *associated with an investment;*[62]	(iii) **claims to money or to any** performance under contract having a financial value;	(c) **claims to money** which has been used to create an economic value or claims **to any** performance having an economic value;	(c) [*idem to PRC '97*]
(d) copyrights, industrial property, **know-how** and technological processes;	(d) **intellectual property rights,** in particular copyrights, patents, trademarks, trade-names, **technical process,** know-how and **good-will;**	(iv) **intellectual property rights, goodwill, technical processes** and **know-how;**	(d) **intellectual property rights,** in particular copyrights and related rights, patents, **utility** model patents, **industrial** designs, trade-marks, plant variety rights;	(d) *intellectual property rights, in particular* copyrights, *patents* and **industrial designs,** *trademarks, trade-names, technical processes,* **trade and business secrets,** know-how *and good-will;*[63]

62 As in Art. 1.a.iii of the 1992 US model BIT.

63 Such wording has been reused, *e.g.*, in the 2005 China-Portugal BIT (while the 2001 China-Netherlands BIT makes use of the wording of the 1997 model).

TABLE 7 European and Chinese model BITs definition of investment (*cont.*)

Art. 1.1 PRC '84 / '89	Art. 1.1 PRC '97	Art. 1(a) UK '06	Art. 1.1 DE '08	Art. 1.1 PRC-DE '03
			(e) trade-names, **trade and business** secrets, **technical processes, know-how, and goodwill;**	
(e) **concessions** conferred by law, **including concessions to search for or exploit natural resources.**	(e) **business** concessions conferred by law or under contract *permitted by law*,[64] including concessions to search for, cultivate, ***extract*** or exploit natural resources.	(v) **business concessions** conferred by law or under contract, **including concessions to search for,** cultivate, **extract or exploit natural resources.**	(f) **business concessions** under public **law, including concessions to search for, extract or exploit natural resources;**	(e) *[idem to PRC '97]*[65]
	Any change **in the form in which assets are invested does not affect their character as investments**	**A change in the form in which assets are invested does not affect their character as investments**	Any **alteration of the form in which assets are invested shall not affect their classification as investment.**	*Any change in the form in which assets are invested does not affect their character as investments.*

64 Art. 1.a.v 1991 US model BIT: 'any right conferred by law or contract, and any licenses and permits pursuant to law'.

65 Employed also, *e.g.*, in the China-Netherlands (2001) and China-Finland (2004) BITs.

TABLE 7 European and Chinese model BITs definition of investment (*cont.*)

Art. 1.1 PRC '84 / '89	Art. 1.1 PRC '97	Art. 1(a) UK '06	Art. 1.1 DE '08	Art. 1.1 PRC-DE '03
–	provided that such change is in accordance with the laws and regulations of the CP in whose territory the investment has been made.	and the term 'investment' includes all investments, whether made before or after the date of entry into force of this agreement.	In the case of indirect investments, in principle only those indirect investments shall be covered which the investor realizes via a company situated in the other CP.	

Key

Original PRC Found in earlier PRC model *As in 1997 PRC model*	Original UK **Original US**	Original DE (pre-2000) **Original DE (post-2000)**	**Other shared wording**

3.2 The Chapeau

The chapeau of the definition of investment of all Chinese model BITs reads as follows:

> *The term investment means every kind of asset invested by investors of one Contracting Party in accordance with the laws and regulations of the other Contracting Party in the territory of the Latter, and in particular though not exclusively, includes …*

The wording can be dissected as follows:
- Words common to both German and British models, employed since the 1984 Chinese model, *e.g.*, the traditional '*every kind of assets*' locution in the chapeau;

- Words specific to the British model, most notably, the locution introducing the open-list (‘*and in particular, though not exclusively, includes*’);
- Words specific to the Chinese model, *i.e.*, the *ratione legis* condition and, in general, the overall articulation of the chapeau (original and unchanged since 1984).

The articulated phrasing of the chapeau has been featured since China's first BIT, in 1982, with Sweden. As such, however, it is not featured in any preceding agreements of Germany, the UK, The Netherlands, France, Italy, Sweden, Switzerland or Japan. Also, it shall be noted that, until the 2003 BIT renegotiation with Germany (the 111th investment agreement China signed, according to UNCTAD), the wording has known no alteration in Chinese agreements (and in most subsequent practice, it has been restored). It is therefore to be concluded that China attaches importance to those elements, which are apparently intended to introduce clear limits *ratione personae*, *legis* and *loci* to the BIT coverage.

3.2.1 *‘In Accordance with the Laws’: the* ratione legis *Requirement*

The ‘in accordance with law’ clause (less frequently formulated as ‘pursuant to the law’, here *ratione legis*) is a fairly typical IIA feature and can be found in the majority of models (with the exception of Canada). There are various forms by which this requirement can be established,[66] and State practice differs in the positioning and in the frequency of repetition of this clause within the overall text. The Dutch and British models deprive it of its potential pre-merit character (whether of jurisdiction or admissibility, as discussed below): in the latter, the clause appears, phrased differently, only as an exceptional condition *against* admission (each Party ‘shall admit’ the investment ‘… subject to its right to exercise powers conferred by its laws …’).[67] Together with the US, the three models resort to the wording of the clause only with reference to the concession category (as a specific instance in the definition of investment).[68] In the German model, instead, it is featured in both the ‘promotion and protection’ (*i.e.*, each Party shall ‘admit such investments in accordance with its

66 In this sense, also *Saba Fakes v. Turkey*, Award, Jul. 14th, 2010, ICSID Case No. ARB/07/20, para. 186: ‘among the mechanisms used to include this limitation is to add it into the definition of investment itself, making it clear that for the purposes of that reciprocal protection agreement only those made in accordance with the laws of the host State will be deemed investments.’

67 Art. 2.1 British model BIT.

68 *I.e.*, in the US model ‘licenses, authorizations, permits, and similar rights conferred pursuant to domestic law’; in the UK model: ‘business concessions conferred by law’.

legislation')[69] and the 'application' provisions (*i.e.*, the treaty applies to investments made '… consistent with the [host State] legislation').[70] In the French, Italian, and Chinese models, the clause is also reserved a highlighted status within the definition of investment.[71]

Preliminarily, it is to be observed that the wording is often referred to in doctrine as the 'legality requirement'.[72] Such a label, however, is misleading: framing the clause in terms of 'legality', and the investor's alleged contrary conduct as 'illegal',[73] brings the legal reasoning nearer to the criminal domain – which may not properly reflect the intention of the contracting parties. According to the Oxford Dictionary, 'illegal' means 'contrary to or forbidden by law, especially criminal law';[74] 'unlawful', on the other hand, 'not conforming to, permitted by, or recognized by law or rules'.[75] Something that is illegal is against the law, whereas an unlawful act merely contravenes the rules that apply in a particular context. Consequently, framing the issue in terms of lawfulness/unlawfulness is arguably more appropriate, as this meaning is closer to the text of investment agreements resorting to such clause, let alone the intention of State parties. It follows the indication of the issue as *ratione legis* requirement (or condition), as clearly identifying the scope of the clause in the context in which it is used (along, *e.g.*, *ratione loci* and *ratione personae*). By including in the text of the BIT the *ratione legis* clause, the intention of States is to insist on respect for domestic civil and administrative laws and regulations on investments, with particular attention to those on admission.[76]

69 Art. 2.1 German model BIT.

70 Art. 8 German model BIT.

71 In the Chinese and Italian models, in the chapeau; in the French model, in a dedicated paragraph after the list of investment instances.

72 *E.g.*, *Saba Fakes* (fn. 66), 37 *et seq.*

73 The first time this happened seems to be in *Salini Costruttori S.p.A. and Italstrade S.p.A. v. Kingdom of Morocco*, Decision on Jurisdiction, Jul. 31st, 2001, ICSID Case No. ARB/00/4, para. 46. However, the word chosen by the tribunal in the original French text is 'illicite', and that reference was not to criminal laws or conducts is evident by the reading of the whole section of the decision, which refers to '… the tender process in conformity with the legal rules applicable to invitations to tender …'. Criticism in this respect can be instead expressed towards the *Inceysa* tribunal (see below).

74 See Oxford Dictionaries online (www.oxforddictionaries.com).

75 *Ibid.*

76 On the different regimes of admissions amongst investment treaties, cf., T Pollan, *Legal Framework for the Admission of FDI* (Eleven International Publishing, 2006); in Dolzer and Schreuer (Chapter 1, fn. 127), at 88, the authors briefly illustrate the difference between admission and establishment, in that '… the right of 'admission' concerns the right of entry of the investment in principle, whereas the right of 'establishment' pertains to the conditions under which the investor is allowed to carry out its business during the

Conversely, perhaps because of the not uniform State practice, the extent and implications of this clause have been interpreted differently by arbitral tribunals, spanning from the breach of 'fundamental principles' in *Inceysa*,[77] to that of 'local laws' in *Kardassopoulos*,[78] to 'good faith mistakes' in *Tokio Tokeles*.[79] Also, it is debated whether the clause relates to jurisdiction or admissibility. On the one side, all decisions have so far been rendered in the form of decisions on jurisdiction (*Salini*), jurisdictional awards (*Inceysa, Fraport, LESI, Saba Fakes*), or awards on both jurisdiction and merit where the *ratione legis* criterion would nevertheless be dealt with in the jurisdictional section (*Desert Line*). However, doctrinal contributions have highlighted that at least in some instances the *ratione legis* clause operates at the admissibility level,[80] or may even be limited to the assessment of facts.[81] The answer to this issue may rest on the location of the *ratione legis* clause: if inserted in the scope or application provision of the treaty (alongside, *e.g.*, the *ratione temporis* and *materiae*, as per the German model), the location accordingly assumes a jurisdictional character; conversely, in the context of the definition of investment, the *ratione legis* requirement appears fit to pertain to admissibility.[82]

3.2.2 *Ratione legis in Chinese Model BITs*

As shown, by comparison with the German and British models, the opening statement of Art. 1 of the 1997 Chinese model displays only one original – yet

---

period of investment'; cf., also, D Carreau and P Juillard, *Droit international économique* (Dalloz, 2010), 361.

77 *Inceysa Vallisoletana S.L. v. Republic of El Salvador*, Award, Aug. 2nd, 2006, ICSID Case No. ARB/03/26.

78 *Ioannis Kardassopoulos v. The Republic of Georgia*, Decision on Jurisdiction, Jul. 6th, 2007, ICSID Case No. ARB/05/18.

79 *Tokios Tokelés v. Ukraine*, Decision on Jurisdiction, Apr. 29th, 2004, ICSID Case No. ARB/02/18.

80 On the 'legality' issue and its jurisdictional or admissibility character, see also (partly *contra*): S Schill, 'Illegal Investments in Investment Treaty Arbitration' (2012) 11(2) *The Law and Practice of International Courts and Tribunals*, 281–323; and R Moloo and A Khachaturian, 'The Compliance with the Law Requirement in International Investment Law' (2010–11) 34 *Fordham International Law Journal* 1473.

81 Cf., Cremades dissenting opinion attached to Fraport AG Frankfurt Airport Services Worldwide v. Republic of the Philippines, ICSID Case No. ARB/03/25, Award, Aug. 16th, 2007 (decision annulled, on grounds unrelated to the present analysis, on Dec. 23rd, 2010), at paras. 37–38.

82 For a more in-depth analysis on the point, see GM Vaccaro-Incisa, 'Objective Criteria and *Ratione Legis* Condition in the Definition of Investment: Global Trends and the Chinese Practice', in J Nakagawa (ed.), *Asian Perspectives on International Law* (Routledge, 2019).

substantial – addition. It requires the investment, in order to properly qualify as such, to be an asset invested '… *in accordance with the laws and regulations of the other Contracting Party*'. Such a requisite, not uncommon in IIAs, has been a constant for China since the conclusion of its first BIT, with Sweden, in 1982.

The scope and ambit of the clause has been arguably clarified in the 2007 amendment to the 1995 China-Cuba BIT, where the Parties agreed that 'in accordance with the laws and regulations'

> … *shall mean that for any kind of invested assets to be considered as investment protected in this agreement, it shall be* ***in accordance with any of the investment modalities defined by the legislation*** *of the Contracting Party receiving the investment* ***and registered as such in the corresponding registry.***[83]

The concern thus appears, first, procedural (rather than substantial); also, more of a civil and administrative (rather than criminal) nature. The notion of 'investment' is linked to the investor's compliance with the requirements dictated by the domestic law to operate a business, and the administrative *iter* for admission.[84] This is also consistent with China's support for the principle that 'foreign investment does promote national development very much *on the condition* that it can be effectively regulated'.[85] Designed (and understood) as such, the provision stresses the relevance of a Party's administrative regulations – as only assets invested accordingly will be considered investments covered by the BIT guarantees. In this perspective, the *ratione legis* clause seems to be operating as an admissibility requirement in cases of (alleged) violations of civil and administrative norms. The conservative reading of the *ratione legis* clause is significant taking into account China's long-followed systematic 'one-by-one' approval system.[86]

That the real concern is a uniform application of the domestic civil and administrative laws may be also confirmed by the fact that, in the 2003 renegotiation of the BIT with Germany, China, on the one hand, agreed to remove the locution '*in accordance with the laws and regulations*' from the definition of investment in Art. 1; on the other hand, it kept, at Art. 2 (investment promotion

83 Emphasis added; the portion of BIT text is reported in Gallagher and Shan, Chinese Investment Treaties (Chapter 1, fn. 63), 55.

84 In this sense, see, *e.g.*, Dolzer and Stevens (Chapter 1, fn. 1), 3.

85 C Cai, 'China', in W Shan (ed.), *The Legal Protection of Foreign Investment – A Comparative Study* (Hart Publishing, 2012), 281.

86 See fn. 58.

and protection), the condition that '*each Contracting Party shall ... admit such investment in accordance with its laws and regulations*'.[87] Moreover, while on the one hand China for the first time accepted, at Art. 9 of the model, arbitration as the *sole* mechanism for the settlement of disputes, on the other it confirmed that investors shall first refer '*... the issue to an administrative review procedure according to Chinese law ...*' before submission of the dispute to arbitration (*Ad.* 6 to Art. 9).[88]

3.2.3 *Ratione legis in Chinese IIAs*

The Chinese practice on the *ratione legis* condition is, overall, uniform. With regard to its presence in the chapeau of the definition of investment, the practice knows no exception for the first 78 agreements still in force (or signed) – *i.e.*, up to the 2001 BIT renegotiation with the Netherlands. Out of 132 IIAs in force or signed, only 8 do not feature it in the definition of investment (or covered investment), and only 2 of these also do not feature it in the application provision.[89]

Exceptions to an otherwise uniform practice pertain to recent and/or complex stipulations. Table 8, below, provides an exhaustive illustration of this.

TABLE 8 PRC IIAs – *Ratione legis* in the definition of investment

Counterpart	Signed	In force	
PRC MODEL	1984		V
1. Norway	1984	1985	V
2. Denmark	1985	1985	V
3. Austria	1985	1986	V
4. Singapore	1985	1986	V
5. Kuwait	1985	1986	V
6. Italy	1985	1987	V
7. UK	1986	1986	V

87 The same happens in the 2004 China-Uganda BIT.

88 Gallagher and Shan, in *Chinese Investment Treaties* (Chapter 1, fn. 63), at 55–56, understand this wording more narrowly, as well as the clarification provided in the China-Cuba BIT, to '... mean that to qualify as an investment protected by the BIT, it must take one of the accepted forms of foreign investment in China and register such investment with China's registration authorities').

89 The 2012 TIA with Japan and Korea, and the 2015 FTA with Korea.

TABLE 8 PRC IIAS – *Ratione legis* in the definition of investment (*cont.*)

Counterpart	Signed	In force	
8. Sri Lanka	1986	1987	V
9. Australia	1988	1988	*V*[90]
10. New Zealand	1988	1989	*V*
11. Japan	1988	1989	*V*[91]
12. Poland	1988	1989	V
13. Malaysia	1988	1990	*V*
PRC MODEL	1989		V
14. Pakistan	1989	1990	*V*
15. Ghana	1989	1990	V
16. Bulgaria	1989	1994	V
17. Turkey	1990	1994	V
18. Hungary	1991	1993	V
19. Papua NG	1991	1993	V[92]
20. Mongolia	1991	1993	V
21. Greece	1992	1993	V[93]
22. Ukraine	1992	1993	V
23. Vietnam	1992	1993	*V*
24. Argentina	1992	1994	V
25. Kazakhstan	1992	1994	V
26. Kyrgyzstan	1992	1995	V[94]
27. Armenia	1992	1995	V
28. Philippines	1992	1995[95]	*V*

90 Unusual formulation of the chapeau: "'Investment' means every kind of asset, owned, controlled or contributed by nationals of one Contracting Party and admitted by the other Contracting Party subject to its law and investment policies applicable from time to time and include …".

91 Specific formulation: 'in accordance with, or not in violation of, the laws and regulations …' of the host State.

92 But focused only on admission: '… admitted by either Contracting Party subject to its laws and regulations …'.

93 Unclear punctuation, *ratione legis* requirement seemingly referred only to admission.

94 The specific wording refers to 'assets accepted in accordance with the investment laws and regulations'.

95 Standards superseded by the 2009 CAIA.

TABLE 8 PRC IIAS – *Ratione legis* in the definition of investment (*cont.*)

Counterpart	Signed	In force	
29. Bolivia	1992	1996	V
30. Laos	1993	1993	*V*
31. UAE	1993	1994	V
32. Tajikistan	1993	1994	V
33. Croatia	1993	1994	V
34. Estonia	1993	1994	V
35. Lithuania	1993	1994	V
36. Belarus	1993	1995	V
37. Albania	1993	1995	V
38. Georgia	1993	1995	V
39. Slovenia	1993	1995	V
40. Uruguay	1993	1997	V
41. Chile	1994	1995[96]	*V*
42. Peru	1994	1995[97]	*V*
43. Azerbaijan	1994	1995	V
44. Egypt	1994	1996	V
45. Jamaica	1994	1996	V
46. Iceland	1994	1997	V
47. Ecuador	1994	1997	V
48. Oman	1995	1995	V
49. Serbia	1995	1996	V
50. Morocco	1995	1999	V
51. Israel	1995	2009	V
52. Bangladesh	1996	1997	V
53. Lebanon	1996	1997	V
54. Mauritius	1996	1997	V
55. Saudi Arabia	1996	1997	V
56. Macedonia	1996	1997	V
57. Zimbabwe	1996	1998	V
58. Cambodia	1996	2000	*V*
59. Syria	1996	2001	V
60. Algeria	1996	2003	V
61. Zambia	1996	–	V

96 Standards superseded by the 2012 China-Chile SAI.

97 Standards superseded by the 2009 China-Peru FTA.

TABLE 8 PRC IIAS – *Ratione legis* in the definition of investment (*cont.*)

Counterpart	Signed	In force	
PRC MODEL	1997		V
62. Sudan	1997	1998	V
63. South Africa	1997	1998	V
64. Gabon	1997	2009	V
65. Barbados	1998	1999	V
66. Ethiopia	1998	2000	V
67. Cape Verde	1998	2001	V
68. Yemen	1998	2002	V
69. Qatar	1999	2000	V
70. Bahrain	1999	2000	V
71. Iran	2000	2005	V
72. Rep. of Congo	2000	2015	V
73. Botswana	2000	–	V
74. Brunei	2000	–	V
75. Jordan	2000	–	V
76. Cyprus	2001	2002	V
77. Myanmar	2001	2002	V
78. Mozambique	2001	2002	V
79. Netherlands	2001	2004	–[98]
80. Nigeria	2001	2010	V
81. Sierra Leone	2001	–	V
82. Kenya	2001	–	V
83. Trinidad & Tobago	2002	2004	V
84. Bosnia	2002	2005	V
85. Cote d'Ivoire	2002	–	V

98 While no *ratione legis* condition is featured in the chapeau of the definition of investment, the addendum to Art. 1 applies the criterion to "investment of legal persons of a third state which are owned of controlled by investors of one contracting part and which have been made in the territory of the other contracting party *in accordance with the laws and regulations of the latter*", and "to reinvestments made by investors of one contracting party in the territory of the other contracting party and *in accordance with the laws and regulations* of that party". The *ratione legis* clause is also featured in the admission (Art. 2) and application (Art. 12) provisions. Consequently, applying the criterion to two particular instances, it is arguably *implied* in the general definition (*a minore ad maius*), its exclusion from the chapeau seemingly a typo.

TABLE 8 PRC IIAS – *Ratione legis* in the definition of investment (*cont.*)

Counterpart	Signed	In force	
86. Guyana	2003	2004	V
87. Germany	2003	2005	–[99]
88. Djibouti	2003	–	V
89. Latvia	2004	2006	V
90. Tunisia	2004	2006	V
91. Finland	2004	2006	V
92. Uganda	2004	–	–[100]
93. Benin	2004	–	V
94. North Korea	2005	2005	V
95. Equatorial Guinea	2005	2006	V
96. Czech Rep.	2005	2006	V
97. Madagascar	2005	2007	V
98. Spain	2005	2008	V
99. Portugal	2005	2008	–[101]
100. Belgium-Lux	2005	2009	V
101. Namibia	2005	–	V
102. Guinea	2005	–	V
103. India	2006	2007	V
104. Pakistan [FTA]	2006	2007	V
105. Russia	2006	2009	V
106. Vanuatu	2006	–	V
107. Cuba	2007[102]	2007	V
108. South Korea	2007	2007	V
109. France	2007	2010	V
110. Costa Rica	2007	2016	V

99 The *ratione legis* requirement is mentioned, however, in the promotion (Art. 2) and application (Art. 11) provisions.

100 The *ratione legis* requirement is mentioned, however, not only in the admission (Art. 2) and application (Art. 12) provisions, but also with express reference, at the end of the definition of investment, to the "change of form in which propertied are invested". It is thus arguable an argument similar to that made for the PRC-NL BIT (see fn. 98).

101 Same as the China-Uganda BIT.

102 In reality that of 2007 is labelled by the parties as an amendment of the 1995 BIT: the updates brought in almost all clauses render the amendment, however, more similar to a renegotiation.

TABLE 8 PRC IIAs – *Ratione legis* in the definition of investment (*cont.*)

Counterpart	Signed	In force	
111. Seychelles	2007	–	–[103]
112. New Zealand [FTA]	2008	2008	–
113. Mexico[104]	2008	2009	V
114. Colombia	2008	2013	V[105]
115. Mali	2009	2009	V
116. Malta	2009	2009	V[106]
117. ASEAN[107] [CAIA/FTA]	2009	2010	V[108]
118. Peru [FTA]	2009	2010	V
119. Switzerland	2009	2010	–[109]
120. Bahamas	2009	–	V
121. Chad	2010	–	V
122. Libya	2010	–	V
123. Uzbekistan	2011	2011	V
124. DR Congo	2011	–	V
125. South Korea & Japan	2012	2014	–
126. Canada	2012	2014	–
127. Chile [SAI/FTA]	2012	2014	V
128. Tanzania	2013	2014	V
129. South Korea [FTA]	2015	2015	–
130. Australia [FTA]	2015	2015	–
131. Turkey	2015	–	V

103 While the *ratione legis* clause does not figure in the chapeau of the definition of investment, it does in the definition of "invested indirectly" (point 2).

104 First BIT with a North American structure.

105 With the specification, in footnote, that in the locution "in accordance with the law", the term "law" "refers to the respective legal system of the contracting parties".

106 Particularly stringent, and explicit, is the requirement that "Investments … shall be made, and shall, for their whole duration, continuously be in line with the respective domestic laws" (Art. 2.2).

107 The 1985 BIT with Thailand features no ISDS; the BIT with Indonesia has been terminated in 2015; the FTA with Singapore expressly refers to CAIA.

108 The locution here expressly includes also "policies", which are clarified in footnote that "… shall refer to those affecting investment that are endorsed and announced by the Government of a Party, and made publicly available in a written form."

109 The *ratione legis* requirement is mentioned, however, in the promotion and admission (Art. 3) and scope of application (Art. 2) provisions.

3.2.4 *The Objective Criteria*

The 'objective criteria' are elements spelt out in the IIA, in connection with the definition of investment, aimed at directing the interpreter in ascertaining whether the investor's activity qualifies as an investment as intended by the contracting parties. The 'objectivity' of these criteria is understood not in absolute terms; rather, it relates to the express mention in the treaty text, thus the need for the interpreter to take them into account.

Among the BITS models, only the US, since its 2004 model, makes use of objective criteria, by listing three:

1. Commitment of capital or other resources,
2. Expectation or gain of profit,
3. Assumption of risk.

Rather than with the case of traditional investments (*e.g.*, concession contracts for the setting up of infrastructure, energy, or mining projects),[110] the usefulness of objective criteria emerges in relation to less immediate cases (*e.g.*, promissory notes, participation contracts, sovereign bonds), and with reference to the context that brought to the establishment of the ICSID Convention in 1965. Indeed, in the absence of a definition of investment there,[111] interpretation becomes necessary.

As mentioned, all publicly known ICSID investment disputes that have dealt with the issue of what constitutes an investment arise out of concise European BITS – which, differently from the US models since 2004, do not feature the objective criteria. The arbitral jurisprudence has yet to settle on whether the lack of an express definition of investment in the ICSID Convention delegates the defining issue entirely to the relevant IIA, or if the term, as present in the Convention, should be given a meaning of its own (whether drawn from a dictionary, or construed out of a reasonable interpretation of what an investment should constitute, *in abstracto* or *in casu*). This issue has in turn ignited another, *i.e.*, which could be and how to weigh in the objective criteria each time individuated. Two lines of thought have developed. In brief, the first school, originating with the *Fedax* and *Salini* cases,[112] tests to varying

---

110 And despite being properly elaborated for the first time in *Salini* (fn. 73), an infrastructure project.

111 See fn. 49.

112 *E.g.*, *Fedax N.V. v. The Republic of Venezuela*, Decision on Objections to Jurisdiction, Jul. 11th, 1997, ICSID Case No. ARB/96/3; *Salini* (fn. 73) (originally published in French in (2002) 1 *Journal du Droit International* 196); *Joy Mining Machinery Limited v. Arab Republic of Egypt*, Award on Jurisdiction, Aug. 6th, 2004, ICSID Case No. ARB/03/11; *Mr. Patrick Mitchell v. Democratic Republic of the Congo*, Decision on the Application for Annulment

degrees the alleged investment against a number of criteria, four (investor's commitment and investment duration, risk, and contribution to the host state development) or more (with the addition of returns and/or legality and/or good faith);[113] at the extreme, it treats each criterion as a jurisdictional requirement, the lack thereof resulting in exclusion from ICSID arbitration.[114] The second school rejects,[115] to varying extent, one or more criteria (because not expressly mentioned in the ICSID Convention, which lacks a definition of investment altogether) and, in particular, the assumption that any such criterion may be assumed as a jurisdictional bar; at the extreme, this position has come close to disregard the very dictionary meaning of the term investment.[116]

Although *in casu* most readings may be justified, the interpretive rebounds have contributed to an appearance of uncertainty that is ultimately detrimental to the foreign investment protection treaty system as a whole. Indeed, the presence of objective criteria in the IIA does not directly solve potential jurisdictional issues arising out of the lack of a definition of investment in the ICSID Convention. However, in case of doubt (and at least formally bowing

---

of the Award, Nov. 1st, 2006, ICSID Case No. ARB/99/7; *Saipem S.p.A. v. The People's Republic of Bangladesh*, Decision on Jurisdiction and Recommendation on Provisional Measures, Mar. 21st, 2007, ICSID Case No. ARB/05/07; *Malaysian Historical Salvors, SDN, BHD v. The Government of Malaysia*, Award on Jurisdiction, May 17th, 2007, ICSID Case No. ARB/05/10.

113 *E.g.*, *Phoenix Action v. The Czech Republic*, Award, Apr. 15th, 2009, ICSID Case No. ARB/06/5, paras. 100–113.

114 *E.g.*, MHS, then annulled.

115 *E.g.*, *M.C.I. Power Group L.C. and New Turbine, Inc. v. Republic of Ecuador*, Award, Jul. 31st, 2007, ICSID Case No. ARB/03/6; *Biwater Gauff (Tanzania) Ltd. v. United Republic of Tanzania*, Award, Jul. 24th, 2008, ICSID Case No. ARB/05/22; *Malaysian Historical Salvors, SDN, BHD v. The Government of Malaysia*, Decision on the Application for Annulment, Apr. 16th, 2009, ICSID Case No. ARB/05/10 (note however, the dissenting opinion of Judge M. Shahabuddeen); *Saba Fakes* (fn. 66); *Abaclat and Others v. Argentine Republic*, Decision on Jurisdiction, Aug. 4th, 2011, ICSID Case No. ARB/07/5; *Deutsche Bank AG v. Democratic Socialist Republic of Sri Lanka*, Award, Oct. 31st, 2012, ICSID Case No. ARB/09/2. It is significant that in *Saba Fakes* the criteria were reduced to three: (i) a contribution, (ii) a certain duration, and (iii) an element of risk (para. 110). The taking is significant, as in 2001 the *Salini* Tribunal made an express reference to the three criteria individuated by Prof. Gaillard (president of the 2010 *Saba Fakes* Tribunal) in 1999, to which it added the 'contribution to the host State development' in light of the ICSID preamble (cf., para. 100 *Salini* (fn. 73)). The fact that in *Saba Fakes* (fn. 294)such fourth criterion was nevertheless discarded is believed to mark a strong doctrinal response in the context of the debate over the characteristics of foreign investments.

116 *E.g.*, *Biwater* and the possibility to consider investment a 'loss leader' project (fn. 115, at para. 321).

to the interpretive criteria enshrined in the Vienna Convention on the Law of Treaties),[117] arbitrators often look at the treaty practice of States to corroborate their interpretation of the various clauses. Given the virtual impossibility of amending the ICSID Convention, the ability of a State (or group of States) to consistently steer or maintain its treaty practice with respect to certain clauses, especially after certain arbitral decisions, could be significant.

3.2.5 *Objective Criteria in Chinese IIAs*

Differently from the US with the 2004 model, China, along with the European States (until the EU took the lead on IIA negotiations), offered scarce reaction to the jurisprudential debate on the definition of investment, at least until recently. Thus, Chinese models – and the vast majority of actual treaties – do not list objective criteria to qualify the notion of investment. Since 2001, however, some criteria have progressively made their way into the Chinese practice.[118]

The first express reference to objective criteria has been agreed on the occasion of the 2003 BIT renegotiation with Germany. The criteria are not mentioned in the definition of investment *per se*, thus maintaining unaltered the typical structure and content of the provision. However, *Ad.* 1.a to Art. 1 provides the following clarification:

> For the avoidance of doubt, the Contracting Parties agree that investments as defined in Article 1 are those made for the purpose of establishing **lasting economic relations in connection with an enterprise**, especially those which allow to **exercise effective influence** in its management. (emphases added)

It has to be preliminarily noted that the wording the Parties agreed upon is exceptional, for both of them. Never has it been employed before, nor will any of them resort to it in a subsequent stipulation.[119] This is, thus, a significant

117 Arts. 31 and 32, Vienna Convention on the Law of Treaties, UN Doc. A/Conf.39/27/1155, UNTS 331/8.

118 For a more detailed illustration of this point, see Vaccaro-Incisa, 'Objective Criteria and *Ratione Legis* Condition in the Definition of Investment' (fn. 82).

119 Germany will not make use of that wording in any subsequent agreements – Iran (2002), Libya (2004), Afghanistan (2005), Timor Leste (2005), Guinea (2006), Madagascar (2006). Those with Afghanistan, Madagascar and Timor Leste feature an *Addendum* to Art. 1, which however provides as follows: '(a) Returns from the investment and, in the event of their reinvestment, the returns therefrom shall enjoy the same protection as

innovation that the China-Germany BIT of 2003 uniquely features. Arguably, both States considered such an addition necessary, in light of the sizeable two-way flow of investment.

Compared with the 2004 US model, and the doctrinal criteria debated in the case law referred to earlier, the text of the *addendum* appears to offer a compromise solution: out of the four (contribution, duration, risk and development), five (with the addition of profits/returns), or more (*e.g.*, good faith)[120] criteria individuated by the *Salini* 'school', the treaty assumes as *preconditions* the elements of 'contribution' and 'risk' (as the investment 'purpose' is 'in connection with an enterprise') but that of 'duration' (*i.e.*, 'lasting economic relations') appears *controlling* (thus potentially excluding at least some forms of venture capitalism). As of the 'effective influence' the investor may exercise, through the investment, on the management of the enterprise, it appears (contrary to Gallagher & Shan),[121] that the use of the preceding word 'especially' implies for such an 'influence' to be understood as an *inclusive* criterion (*i.e.*, to support the qualification of investment as such, when from the analysis of the other elements a clear-cut answer may not be ascertained), rather than a self-standing one. This reading is also consistent with the 25% minimum shareholding stake required by Chinese law for joint-ventures to properly qualify as 'foreign invested enterprise' (thus enjoying the related benefits).[122]

---

the investment. (b) Without prejudice to any other method of determining nationality, in particular any person in possession of a national passport issued by the competent authorities of the Contracting State concerned shall be deemed to be a national of that Contracting State.'

120 *Phoenix Action v The Czech Republic*, Award, Apr. 5th, 2009, ICSID Case No. ARB/06/5, paras. 100–113; this criterion is debatable, as the notion of good faith has very different contours in international law (as meta-legal axiom at the basis of the larger concept of international relations), civil law (where it is a typical interpretive instrument of performance of contract) and common law (where until the '70s its existence was flatly rejected, and even today employed restrictively). The ICJ itself has used the concept of good faith in a less than coherent fashion: compare *Nuclear Tests Case* (*Australia v. France*), Judgement, [1974] ICJ Reports 253, 268 ("one of the basic principles governing the creation and performance of legal obligations, whatever their source, is the principle of good faith.") and *Border and Transborder Armed Actions* (*Nicaragua v. Honduras*), Judgment, [1988] ICJ Reports 69, 105 (good faith, as a concept, "is not in itself a source of obligation."). Its consideration in connection with the definition of investment, especially in ICSID arbitration, may be questionable.

121 Gallagher and Shan, *Chinese Investment Treaties* (Chapter 1, fn. 63), 59.

122 From 1979 (adoption of the Law of Sino-Foreign Equity Joint Ventures was passed) until 1986 (adoption of the Law of Wholly Foreign Owned Enterprises), equity joint ventures were the only form of foreign investment possible in China. In 1988, with the adoption of the Law of Sino-Foreign Contractual Joint Ventures, this form of investment was

As noted, the wording featured in this respect in the 2003 China-Germany BIT is, nevertheless, exceptional. It will remain so until 2012, with China's shift for the North American template, and the stipulations with Canada and Chile.

To date, there are 9 IIAs expressly mentioning objective criteria, plus another 6 that make some reference to additional criteria without, however, expressly listing them. Out of the overall Chinese network, IIAs featuring objective criteria are a very modest percentage. If, however, the focus shifts to the period identified in Chapter 1 as 'contemporary investment protection policy' (*i.e.*, the last decade), then it is possible to see that out of the 24 IIAs concluded over the period, 12 either expressly refer to objective criteria, or feature some indication enriching the definition. Particularly consistent is the practice from 2011. Thus, it may be argued for a policy change in this respect. Table 9, below, illustrates the point.

Such apparent recent convergence of China appears to be dictated ultimately by prudence: even outside of the ICSID regime (*i.e.*, the case for the majority of Chinese BITs, which do not feature unrestricted *a priori* consent to ICSID arbitration), tribunals have provided inconsistent answers as to what constitute an investment.[123] The insertion of the objective criteria serves to guide the analysis of the interpreter over those elements expressly listed and consented to, and reduce resorting to others.

---

ultimately opened to foreigners. According to the OECD, joint ventures are still the most popular form of foreign investment in China; *cf.*, Davies, K., *China Investment Policy: An Update*, in OECD Working Papers on International Investment (OECD Publishing, 2013/01), available at http://dx.doi.org/10.1787/5k469l1hmvbt-en, accessed 20 Nov. 2019.

123 *E.g.*, Magisterial is the synthesis of the 2009 UNCITRAL case (*Romak S.A. (Switzerland) v. The Republic of Uzbekistan*, Award, Nov. 11th, 2009, UNCITRAL PCA Case No. 2007-07, paras. 180–207) provided by Dolzer and Schreurer: 'The Tribunal ... considered that the word "investment" in a BIT must have a meaning of its own. In support, the Tribunal (surprisingly) referred to the illustrative, non exhaustive definition in the applicable BIT and also to the conclusion of a trade agreement on the same day the BIT was signed. To identify the autonomous meaning of "investment", the Award turned to the Black's Law Dictionary, but subsequently decided to require three criteria: contribution, duration and risk. In this context, the Tribunal assumed that the term "investment" should be presumed to have the same meaning in the context of ICSID and outside ICSID. At the same time, the Tribunal assumed that the parties are free to define an "investment" in the way they wish. In the end, the Award examined the three criteria and ruled that the wheat sales satisfied none of them.'; cf., Dolzer and Schreurer (Chapter 1, fn. 123), 73–74.

TABLE 9 PRC BITS – objective criteria in the definition of investment

	Counterpart (*from 2003 on*)	Signed	In force	Express mention	Some specifications / reference	'In connection with eco activity'
88.	Germany	2003	2005	V	–	–
89.	Djibouti	2003	–	–	–	–
90.	Latvia	2004	2006	–	–	–
91.	Tunisia	2004	2006	–	–	–
92.	Finland	2004	2006	–	–	–
93.	Uganda	2004	–	–	–	–
94.	Benin	2004	–	–	–	–
95.	North Korea	2005	2005	–	–	–
96.	Equatorial Guinea	2005	2006	–	–	–
97.	Czech Rep.	2005	2006	–	–	V
98.	Madagascar	2005	2007	–	–	–
99.	Spain	2005	2008	–	–	–
100.	Portugal	2005	2008	–	–	–
101.	Belgium-Lux	2005	2009	–	–	
102.	Namibia	2005	–	–	V[124]	–
103.	Guinea	2005	–	–	–	–
104.	India	2006	2007	–	–	–
105.	Pakistan [FTA]	2006	2007	–	–	–
106.	Russia	2006	2009	–	–	–
107.	Vanuatu	2006	–	–	–	–
108.	Cuba	2007*	2007	–	–	–
109.	South Korea	2007	2007	–	V[125]	–
110.	France	2007	2010	–	–	–
111.	Costa Rica	2007	2016	–	–	–
112.	Seychelles	2007	–	–	–	–
113.	New Zealand [FTA]	2008	2008	–	–	–

124 The wording is original: "The term investment means property used by the investor of a Contracting Party in the territory of the other Contracting Part as long as the investment is made in accordance with the laws and regulations of the other Contracting Party and the investment is not speculative".

125 Lit.: 'every kind of asset used as investment'.

TABLE 9 PRC BITS – objective criteria in the definition of investment (*cont.*)

Counterpart (*from 2003 on*)		Signed	In force	Express mention	Some specifications / reference	'In connection with eco activity'
114.	Mexico	2008	2009	–	V[126]	–
115.	Colombia	2008	2013	–	V[127]	–
116.	Mali	2009	2009	–	–	–
117.	Malta	2009	2009	–	–	–
118.	ASEAN [CAIA/FTA]	2009	2010	–	–	–
119.	Peru [FTA]	2009	2010	–	–	–
120.	Switzerland	2009	2010	–	–	–
121.	Bahamas	2009	–	–	–	–
122.	Chad	2010	–	–	–[128]	–
123.	Libya	2010	–	–	–	–
124.	Uzbekistan	2011	2011	V[129]		
125.	DR Congo	2011	–	V[130]	–	–
126.	South Korea & Japan	2012	2014	V[131]	–	–
127.	Canada	2012	2014	V[132]	–	–
128.	Chile [SAI/FTA]	2012	2014	V[133]	–	–
129.	Tanzania	2013	2014	V[134]	–	–
130.	South Korea [FTA]	2015	2015	V[135]	–	–
131.	Australia [FTA]	2015	2015	V[136]	–	–
132.	Turkey	2015	–	–	–	V[137]

126 The definition features the 'exclusion' category (derived from the Canadian model).
127 Lit.: 'every kind of economic asset'; the definition also contains an 'exclusion' category (derived from the Canadian model).
128 The definition, nonetheless, refers to 'property' (as opposed to the more generic 'assets').
129 Objective criteria drawn from the US model.
130 Objective criteria drawn from the US model.
131 Objective criteria drawn from the US model.
132 Objective criteria drawn from the US model, mentioned in the definition of 'covered investment'.
133 Objective criteria drawn from the US model.
134 Objective criteria drawn from the US model.
135 Objective criteria drawn from the US model.
136 Objective criteria drawn from the US model.
137 Lit.: 'every kind of asset connected with business activities'.

3.2.6 *Indirect Investment*

The first explicit mention of 'indirect investments' in IIAs dates back to the 1967 Draft Convention on the Protection of Foreign Property – which, however, besides having never been adopted, has not been followed consistently by States in their practice.[138] The clause found its way into investment treaties only after the US adopted it in the 1992 model.[139] Nevertheless, it was a quite unique feature: *e.g.*, the German model BIT of 1991, as well as the British draft model of 1993, do not feature such wording. The situation progressively changed, as most European models adopted after year 2000,[140] as well as the US and Canadian models, expressly mention direct and indirect investments. The wording is significant because many investment disputes involve investments effected through subsidiaries (and not directly held by the national of the BIT party). BITs that expressly refer to indirect investments are thus potentially more protective of investors than those that do not.[141] Nevertheless, it remains a relatively uncommon feature in actual agreements in force.

Indeed, no Chinese model BIT refers to 'direct' and 'indirect' investments, nor do most actual stipulations. Exceptions are limited, even though some already happened in the early treaty practice (*e.g.*, 1983 BIT with Romania,[142] 1984 BIT with France,[143] 1988 BIT with Australia).[144] Subsequently, the 1997 China-Gabon BIT extends protection to '*every kind of assets or capital contribution invested directly or indirectly by investors*'.[145] A further six years had to lapse before a similar wording would resurface in a Chinese BIT: in 2003, with the renegotiation of the BIT with Germany, the Parties agreed to include the

138 See Art. 9 (Definitions); this notwithstanding, the Draft Convention is recognized to have '... played an important role in the development and formulation of subsequent treaties negotiated by OECD member states'; cf., *e.g.*, E Denza and S Brooks, 'Investment Protection Treaties: United Kingdom Experience' (1987) 36(4) *International and Comparative Law Quarterly* 910.

139 Art. 1.1.a., US model BIT.

140 *I.e.*, 2008 German model, 2006 British model, 2005 French model; the 2003 Italian model, however, does not.

141 Whether indirect investments are protected even absent such a clause is debated in the arbitral case-law: see the different views expressed, *e.g.*, in *Siemens A.G. v. The Argentine Republic*, Decision on Jurisdiction, Aug. 3rd, 2004, ICSID Case No. ARB/02/8 and *CMS Gas Transmission Co. v. Argentina*, Decision on Jurisdiction, June 17th, 2003, ICSID Case No. ARB/01/8, para. 48.

142 Chapter 1, fn. 103.

143 Art. 1.b of the 1984 China-France BIT provides coverage for '... autres formes de participation directes ou indirectes, même minoritaire, au société constituée sur le territoire de l'une des Parties'.

144 Art. 1.1.a. China-Australia BIT (1988).

145 Art. 1, China-Gabon BIT (1997).

catch-all locution, along with the *ad hoc* definition of 'indirect' investment'[146] (which, differently formulated, has been subsequently included in the German model as well).[147] After Gabon and Germany, China's next BITs expressly covering direct and indirect investments are the 2005 renegotiation with Portugal and the 2007 agreement with Seychelles. Interestingly, the 2005 renegotiation with Spain features, instead, the British-derived notion of 'ownership or control' (with 'control' at least partly reaching the extent of 'indirect investment').

Out of the four agreements just referred to, only the BIT with Germany and Seychelles provides for an express definition of what 'indirect investment' means (the latter features also an *ad hoc* definition of 'indirect control', at Art. 1.3). Amongst subsequent agreements, only the 2008 FTA with New Zealand does so. In a comparative treaty-making perspective, it is worth analyzing the links between the four agreements – which stress, once more, China's inclination for merging provisions from other treaties. Table 9, above, provides an illustration of this.

TABLE 10 Express mention to 'indirect investment' (selected IIAs)[148]

Ad 1.b to Art. 1 PRC-DE '03	Art. 1 PRC-ES '05	Art. 1 PRC-Seychelles '07	Art. 135 PRC-NZ FTA '08
"Invested indirectly" means invested by an investor of one CP through a company which is <u>fully or partially owned</u> by the investor and having its seat in the territory of the other CP.	1.1 [*idem PRC model '84*]	1.2 'Invested indirectly' includes: 1) invested by an investor of one CP through a company which is <u>fully or partially owned</u> by the investor and having its sear in the territory of the other CP, and	Investment means every kind of asset invested, directly or indirectly, by the investors of a Party in the territory of the other Party including, but not limited to, the following: [...]

146 *Ad* 1.b to Art. 1: '"Invested indirectly" means invested by an investor of one Contracting Party through a company which is fully or partially owned by the investor and having its seat in the territory of the other Contracting Party'.

147 Art. 1.1, final sentence: 'In the case of indirect investments, in principle only those indirect investments shall be covered which the investor realizes via a company situated in the other Contracting State'.

148 Text in the same color and/or style highlights identical parts.

TABLE 10 Express mention to 'indirect investment' (selected IIAs) (*cont.*)

Ad 1.b to Art. 1 PRC-DE '03	Art. 1 PRC-ES '05	Art. 1 PRC-Seychelles '07	Art. 135 PRC-NZ FTA '08
	1.2 Investment made **in the territory of one CP** by any company of that same CP which is actually owned or controlled **by investors of the other CP** shall likewise be considered as investment of investors of the latter CP if they have been made in accordance with the laws and regulation of the former CP.	2) **investments of legal persons of a third State which are** owned or controlled **by investor of one CP and which have been in the territory of the other CP** in accordance with the laws and regulations of the latter. **The relevant provisions of this agreement shall apply to such investments only when such third State has no right or abandons the right to claim compensation after the investments have been expropriated by the other CP.**[149]	Investment includes **investments of legal persons of a third country which are** owned or controlled **by investors of one Party and which have been made in territory of the other Party. The relevant provisions of this agreement shall apply to such investments only when such third country has no right or abandons the right to claim compensation after the investments have been expropriated by the other Party.**

China's attitude on the express mention of 'indirect investment' appears only partly altered more recently: despite the shift toward the North American model, and the numerous structure and content-related changes China brought into the 2012 stipulations with Canada, Chile, and Japan/Korea, none

149 The sentence is related to the finding of the International Court of Justice in the *Barcelona Traction* case (where it decided that the Belgian government was barred from exercising diplomatic protection for its citizens who owned the majority of the shares in a Canadian company against Spain; cf., *Case concerning the Barcelona Traction Light and Power Company Ltd* (Belgium v. Spain), Judgment [1970] ICJ Reports 3.

of these agreements features the words; nor do the BITs with Tanzania (2013) and Turkey (2015);[150] however, the 2015 IIAs with Korea and Australia employ the US model chapeau definition of investment *tel quel* (hence, including both indirect investment as well as ownership and control).

Along with that of many other States, China's reluctance to provide express coverage for indirect investments may be justified by the fact that the distinction between 'direct' and 'indirect' investment is not clear-cut among scholars.[151] As such, the exclusion of indirect investments clears the ground from additional controversy, in case of a dispute.

The table below illustrates how frequent is in the Chinese practice (starting from the 2003 BIT renegotiation with Germany) the express mention of 'indirect' investment, and/or investment under the 'control' of the investor in the definition of investment (thus affecting jurisdiction *ratione materiae*), and how often the treaty provides for a definition of 'indirect investment'. It is possible to see that only a handful of IIAs explicitly cover 'indirect investments'.[152] It is also worth noting, however, that since the 2007 renegotiation with Cuba, the specification regarding 'ownership or control' often found its way into the treaty, in the definition of investor. Overall, refining a previous doctrinal analysis, seeds of a trend may be distinguished out of the recent Chinese practice, in that BITs with importers of Chinese capital are more likely to expressly cover 'indirect investment'.[153] However, this finding is subject to several exceptions, thus not deemed capable of demonstrating a policy stance of China on the matter.

---

150 The China-Tanzania BIT, however, indirectly retains the 'ownership and control' criterion through the definition of 'enterprise'; the China-Turkey BIT, instead, specifically requires 'direct' ownership or control in the definition of 'investor'.

151 See Dolzer and Schreuer (Chapter 1, fn. 127), 60–65.

152 In addition to those mentioned, among the older generation agreements (*i.e.*, up to 1997–2000) it is possible to find an explicit mention of 'indirect investment', or some more articulated phrasing aimed at providing some additional coverage, in the BITs with Japan, Argentina, Estonia and Saudi Arabia.

153 Hadley (Chapter 1, fn. 107), 281, building on a distinction based on BITs concluded with 'democracies' and 'non-democracies', considered that '… Thus, it appears overall that BITs with developed democracies were more likely to contain the more protective "investment" provision; among developing countries, democracies were more likely than non-democracies to conclude BITs containing the more liberal provisions'. This distinction is not convincing, in light of the overall erratic inclusion of 'indirect investment' vis-à-vis China's economic transition from mostly capital importer to significant exporter.

TABLE 11 Investment indirect ownership and/or control in recent Chinese IIAs: presence and definition

Counterpart (*from 2003 on*)		Signed	In force	Investment			
				Indirect	Def.	Control	Def.
88.	Germany	2003	2005	V	V	–	–
…							
99.	Spain	2005	2008	–	–	V	–
100.	Portugal	2005	2008	V	–	–	–
…							
107.	Vanuatu	2006	–	–	–	–	–
108.	Cuba	2007*	2007	–	–	–	–
109.	South Korea	2007	2007	–	–	–	–
110.	France	2007	2010	–	–	–	–
111.	Costa Rica	2007	2016	–	–	–	–
112.	Seychelles	2007	–	V	V	V	V
113.	New Zealand [FTA]	2008	2008	V	–	V[154]	–
114.	Mexico	2008	2009	–	–	V	–
115.	Colombia	2008	2013	–	–	–	–
116.	Mali	2009	2009	–	–	–	–
117.	Malta	2009	2009	–	–	–	–
118.	ASEAN [CAIA/FTA]	2009	2010	–	–	–	–[155]
119.	Peru [FTA]	2009	2010	–	–	V	–
120.	Switzerland	2009	2010	–	–	–	–
121.	Bahamas	2009	–	–	–	–	–
122.	Chad	2010	–	–	–	V	–
123.	Libya	2010	–	–	–	–	–
124.	Uzbekistan	2011	2011	–	–	V	–
125.	DR Congo	2011	–	–	–	V	–
126.	South Korea & Japan	2012	2014	V	–	V	–

154 Peculiar is the distinction made at Art. 135 (definitions) for the definition of 'enterprise', where a private entity is more strictly defined (owned) that a governmental (owned or controlled); this definition seems somewhat inconsistent with the following definition of 'investment' proper, which more broadly includes 'owned or controlled' investments without distinction between public and private domains.

155 Footnote 9(b) to Art. 15 (denial of benefits) explicitly provides that "In the case of Indonesia, Myanmar, Philippines and Viet Nam, ownership and control shall be defined in its domestic laws and regulations."

TABLE 11 Investment indirect ownership and/or control in recent Chinese IIAs (*cont.*)

	Counterpart (*from 2003 on*)	Signed	In force	Investment			
				Indirect	Def.	Control	Def.
127.	Canada	2012	2014	V	–	V	–
128.	Chile [SAI/FTA]	2012	2014	–	–	V	–
129.	Tanzania	2013	2014	–	–	V	–
130.	South Korea [FTA]	2015	2015	V	–	V	–
131.	Australia [FTA]	2015	2015	V	–	V	–
132.	Turkey	2015	–	–	–	–	–

3.2.7 *The Chapeau: Contemporary Practice*

With reference to the earlier mentioned agreements signed between 2008 and 2009 in the Western Pacific area (*i.e.*, PRC-NZ FTA, AANZFTA, ACIA and CAIA), it may be noted how all keep the European chapeau 'investment means every kind of asset', and follow, for the most part, the order therein featured for the illustrative list of categories. None resorts to the so-called 'objective criteria', employed in the chapeau of the US model definition. All four agreements share, instead, the sentence opening the list of instances provided ('… including, but not limited to, the following'). Such wording is not featured in any model, and shows the cross-influences among the negotiating tables. As of the intertwine amongst the agreements, with regard to the explicit mention or coverage of 'direct and indirect' investments, 'owned or controlled' and *ratione legis* criteria, it is interesting to note the following:

- On the one side, China's literal reliance on the 2003 BIT with Germany for the stipulation with Western, liberal and market-economy New Zealand; thus, in the **China-NZ FTA**, China accepted the express mention of 'direct and indirect' investments (featured in both German and British models as well);
- On the other side, the preference of ASEAN, Australia and New Zealand for the British model – identically reproduced, in this respect, in both **ACIA** and **AANZFTA**; however, in both cases, the final wording, while retaining 'owned or controlled', curtails the UK model's express mention of 'direct and indirect' investments;
- Lastly, the cautiousness of ASEAN and China for either of the previous wording is manifest in that, in the **CAIA**, both 'owned or controlled' and

'directly and indirectly' criteria disappear, replaced with the *ratione legis* requirement.[156]

The above highlights the drift between two conceptually different stances toward investment policy. On the one side, ASEAN and China share concerns relatively to sovereign prerogatives; on the other, market economies tend to adopt a more liberal approach, with no additions to the kernel definition of investment.[157]

With regard to the 2012 BIT with Canada, a *prima facie* reading of the definition of investment may leave the impression that China embraced *in toto* the Canadian model, structure and wording. A second read, however, reveals once more China's insistence for an overall simplification of the fairly complex Canadian treaty machinery – also, through a number of insertions drawn from the US model (especially, with regard to the provision's content). What follows analyzes the contribution of the different sources that the Parties resorted to, and the original solutions ultimately agreed upon.

In this connection, it shall be preliminarily observed that, for the first time, China agreed to introduce the definition of 'covered investment' – so far, constantly neglected. It is possible to deduce Canada's insistence on keeping it: in the China-Chile SAI the definition has been – in accordance with the practice of both China and Chile – discarded from the final text. The wording is articulated, drawn only in part from Canada's template. Indeed, the final wording appears representing more of a compromise, than a synthesis.

The first part of the definition of covered investments – focusing on investments made before the entry into force of the BIT – is a repetition of the wording featured in the 2004 Canada model.[158] Subsequently, an alternative 'or' introduces the second part of the sentence, which covers '... an investment of an investor *admitted* in accordance with its laws and regulations thereafter ...'. The *ratione legis* requirement (*i.e.*, the express mandatory requirement of respect of domestic laws), typical of China, is here phrased through the past tense 'admitted', *in lieu* of the more usual 'made'. With regard to the illustrated debate over the arbitrators' review of the licitness of an investment as a jurisdictional requirement, the Parties seem here to have made clear their

156 Actually strengthened, with the introduction of the term 'policies' in addition to 'relevant laws and regulations'.

157 The only exception is the US model where, however, such additional wording is intended to provide guidance to the subsequent interpreter in case of dispute (as opposed to circumscribing tout-court the treaty coverage).

158 Canada's 2006 draft model includes in the definition the notion of ownership or control, absent in the 2004 model.

intention that the analysis shall be limited, at this stage, only to those laws relating to investment admission – as opposed to a generalized review of the investment's legality (including, *e.g.*, criminal law). As a result, in this part the provision, despite nominal *de minimis* departures, is equivalent to the 'application' provision of the Chinese model,[159] to which the substitution of 'made' with 'admitted' represents an improvement.

In the second – and last – part, the provision literally transplants the US model objective criteria for the qualification of an investment. By comparing this provision with that of the China-Chile SAI, it is possible to determine that this text has been seemingly insisted upon by China. It appears that, by shifting to the North American model, China opted for the insertion of such criteria: on the one hand, in fact, Canada does not contemplate them in either of its models, nor in any other stipulation to which it is a Party; on the other hand, the simultaneously negotiated SAI with Chile features those criteria as well (as all agreements concluded by Chile – except that with Canada!).[160] It may also be noted that China's reliance on Chile's extensive experience and network of FTAS with investment chapters, it also conforms to a quite constant trend in the Pacific – arguably in light of the trans-Pacific Partnership negotiations –,[161] as all stipulations of Chile in the area, as well as those of the US,[162] include these criteria. *A contrario*, as apparently Canada tended to discard the objective criteria from the stipulations to which it is party, it will be interesting to observe whether such inclusion in the China-Canada BIT will be maintained in subsequent stipulations – or included in a future official model BIT. In fact, as a case of 'reverse influence', the 2006 draft Canadian model BIT includes the objective criteria as well in the definition of covered investment.

The final wording of the provision constitutes a 'separated yet living together' affair, with the coexistence of two self-standing notions of covered investment, separated by the 'or' put in between them. The first reproduces the Canadian standard, while the second originally – and, so far, uniquely – combines the typical Chinese *ratione legis* requirement to the typical objective criteria featured in the US chapeau of the notion of investment (actually, *in lieu* of the

159 Art. 11 China model BIT (1997).

160 *I.e.*, the agreements with the US, Australia, Japan/Korea; the wording is always the same, drawn from the US model BIT.

161 For an analysis on the negotiations and the significance of that agreement, especially for the States in the region, see CL Lim, DK Elms and P Low (ed.), *The Trans-Pacific Partnership – A quest for a Twenty-First-Century Trade Agreement* (Cambridge University Press, 2012).

162 *E.g.*, KORUS, Art. 11.28.

chapeau, which disappears in the China-Canada BIT). What ultimately is left out of the US chapeau is the direct or indirect ownership or control criterion.

Being most of the relevant content subsumed under the definition of covered investment, that of investment per se does not contain, consequently, a chapeau – as it is the case with both Canadian models. Comparative Table 13 provides a visual support of the above illustration.

3.2.8 *The Asset-Based List: Model and Standard Practice*

Early investment treaties used not to focus much on the definition of investment: placed at about the end of the agreements (as all other definitions), it would feature no illustrative list (whether exhaustive or not) but something rather brief such as 'the term "investment" shall comprise all categories of assets'.[163] The situation changed in 1965, as the Germany-Iran BIT featured the first illustrative list – close to what is still the norm today.[164]

The Chinese, British and German model BIT share broad commonalities with regard to structure and wording, and their evolution, of the asset-based illustrative list (as shown earlier with Table 7) – similarities emphasized with the 1997 model (and the 2003 BIT with Germany).[165] The text of the list can be divided into the following four categories:

- **Words common to both German and British models, employed since the 1984 Chinese model**, such as:
  - Most of the definition of property rights (movable and immovable properties ... such as mortgages, pledges ...'),
  - The basic elements from the IP category (technical processes, know-how, goodwill),
  - Most of the concession category,
  - The 'change of form of investment' clause.

163 *E.g.*, Art. 8 Germany-Ethiopia BIT (1964); structure-wise, the 1967 OECD Draft Convention on the Protection of Foreign Property place as well the definitions around the end of the stipulation (Art. 9).

164 Art. 8 Germany-Iran BIT (1965).

165 As of the format, it follows the German path set with the 1959 BIT with Pakistan, which China chose since its first BIT with Sweden; the British model appears, instead, relying on the OECD Draft Convention on the Protection of Foreign Property; therefore, while the categories listed in the German model are also featured in the UK model BIT, since the *order* in which they are listed (especially in the 1984 Chinese model) is identical to the German practice, in Table 7 they are marked in red (*i.e.*, derived from the German model).

- **Words specific of the German model**, in particular:
  - The catch-all phrasing for contractual rights ('... performance having an economic value'),[166]
  - The more comprehensive list of elements featured in the IP category;
  - In the 2003 BIT Renegotiation: at letter *b*) (company participations), the substitution of the legal term 'participation' with the wider 'interest' (in the otherwise British-based definition 'any other kind of participation in companies');
- **Words specific of the British model**, most notably:
  - The catch-all formulation for property rights ('and other property rights'),[167]
  - In the concession category, the legal requirements 'conferred by law' and 'under contract', and the inclusion of 'cultivation'.

Thus, the technique of subsuming its own model text from the best practices of the time (*i.e.*, German and British) takes the form of a *bricolage*: wording and or/ definitions are chosen from the model deemed clearer on the point (*e.g.*, 'financial' *in lieu* of 'economic'; 'any other rights *in rem*' *in lieu* of 'any other property rights'). In this respect, it is significant that the replacements in favor of the British model made their way in the 2003 renegotiation with Germany, as opposed to *i*) sticking with the wording of the 1983 China-Germany BIT (already featuring a number of advanced elements subsequently made part of the 1997 model), or *ii*) rely on the German draft model (soon to become the 2005 official template).

Conversely, with regard to the wording specific of the Chinese model, it shall be noted that the *ratione personae, legis* and *loci* criteria made their way into the subsequent German practice, at times all of them (*e.g.*, BITs with USSR and Poland, of 1989; Brazil, 1995; Iran, 2002), at times only *personae* and *loci* (*e.g.*, China, 2003; Libya, 2004), at times only *legis* (*e.g.*, India, 1995; Indonesia, 2003; Yemen, 2005; Oman, 2007).[168] With the 2008 model BIT, Germany ultimately adopted in the model both *ratione personae* and *legis* in the chapeau of the definition of investment.

With regard to specific wording differences in the definition of investment between the Chinese and the major European models, it may be noted that:

- Under letter *a*) (property rights: '*movable and immovable property and other property rights such as mortgages, pledges and similar rights*'), the widening

166 As also in the 1992 US model BIT (Art. 1.a.iii), and differently from the British model: '... performance under contract having a financial value'.

167 As opposed to the German: '... any other right *in rem* ...'.

168 Nevertheless, most times Germany kept the simple 1991 model approach (*e.g.*, BITs with Guyana, 1994; Croatia, 1997; Gabon, 1998; Lebanon, 1999; Nigeria, 2000; Timor-Leste, 2005; Guinea, 2006); it appears, in this respect, that more articulated stipulations were reserved to counterparts with either a stronger negotiating position, or investment potential.

locution '*and similar rights*' is added; as such, however, it may seem redundant, as the sentence already includes the catch-all 'and other property rights' (and in fact it does not appear in any Chinese IIAs taken into account here);
- Under letter *c*) (contractual rights: '*claims to money or to any other performance having an economic value associated with an investment*'), the wording '*associated with an investment*' is added; despite limiting the scope of the provision, the addition clarifies the necessity of a connection of the claim with an investment activity: a simple claim to money, hence, may seemingly not be able to qualify as investment *per se*;
- Under letter *e*) (concessions: '*business concessions conferred by law or under contract permitted by law, including concessions to search for, cultivate, extract or exploit natural resources*'), note the additional '*permitted by the law*'; the repetition of the *ratione legis* requirement in this context – not featured in the German or British practice and models –, is common in Chinese BITs with both capital importing and exporting States, and has been perceived as '... demonstrat[ing] China's cautious stand towards business concessions to foreign companies';[169] since 1992, nevertheless, a similar formulation is featured in the 1992 US model BIT ('*any right conferred by law or contract, and any licenses and permits pursuant to law*'),[170] subsequently kept in the 2004 and 2012 models;[171]
- The 'change of form of investment' clause is followed, in the last sentence of the provision, by the addition '*... provided that such change is in accordance with the laws and regulations of the CP in whose territory the investment has been made*'; the rationale behind such specification is that the transformed investment, whilst enjoying the same treatment as the original investment, is subject to the same requirements and conditions upon which it was firstly approved;[172] as such, however, the clause is not featured in any IIAs under consideration.

China resisted alterations to its template list, with regard to both structure and content, also in the 2012 stipulations with Canada and Chile: this is visible in that the 'traditional' property rights category kept its position as first of the list, as in all European models (as opposed to the last, of the North American models).[173]

169 Gallagher and Shan, *Chinese Investment Treaties* (Chapter 1, fn. 63), 65.

170 Art. 1.a.v.

171 Art. 1, at let. *g*) of the definition of 'investment': 'licenses, authorizations, permits, and similar rights conferred pursuant to domestic law'.

172 Gallagher and Shan, *Chinese Investment Treaties* (Chapter 1, fn. 63), 70.

173 As defined by Dolzer and Stevens (Chapter 1, fn. 1), 27.

3.2.9 *Contemporary Practice*

Despite the undeniable ties of ACIA and AANZFTA with the US model, the definition of investment follows, in all agreements signed between 2008 and 2009 in the Western Pacific area here considered (*i.e.*, PRC-NZ FTA, AANZFTA, ACIA and CAIA), the European models – in terms of structure and most of the wording used. Notwithstanding the broad commonalities, however, differences among the provisions exist – and this highlights specific concerns of the relevant negotiating Parties. In fact, while *prima facie* the overall structure of the European models appears to be maintained in all four provisions, it may also be noted that the template elements and categories have been, progressively yet substantially, beefed up. Nevertheless, a quite clear distinction in this respect has to be drawn between, on the one side, the slightly earlier FTA with New Zealand – relying more consistently on China's latest model BIT (and that with Germany) – and, on the other side, the other three stipulations – whose general term of reference appears to be the British model.

The China-NZ FTA

The categories listed under letters *a*) to *e*) of the China-NZ FTA (*i.e.*, property rights, company participations, contractual rights, intellectual property rights, concessions) do not show particular innovations, by comparison with the China-Germany BIT. Among the minor changes (brought by concurrent negotiations – for China, of CAIA and, for New Zealand, of AANZFTA), it may be noted that, in the attempt to avoid subsequent broad interpretations, claims to money are expressly tied to 'contracts' (as in the other three agreements); such addition (drawn from the British model), coupled with the previous wording (drawn from the 1997 Chinese model), brings the final formulation to: '*claims to money or any other contractual performance having an economic value associated with an investment*'. A dual test is thus clearly established, as the claim has to:

- Arise out of a contract, and
- Flow from an investment.

Moreover, letters *f*) and *g*) appear quite innovative for the time, especially for China.

The first, moving from the US model, features, a 'list of covered liabilities' ('*bonds, including government issued bonds, debentures, loans and other forms of debt, and rights derived therefrom*') distinct from letter *b*) ('*shares, debentures, stock and any other kind of participation in companies*').[174] It appears that the Parties have tried, in the first place, to draw a clearer distinction between debts as investments and those resulting from normal trading activity (thus,

174 See letter *c*) US model.

excluded from the BIT protection). Secondly, the novel wording 'government issued bond' has been arguably introduced upon the insistence of China, and reflects concerns at the time over the macroeconomics of New Zealand.[175] As China braced to step into both the public and private economy of New Zealand, such a provision appears aimed at guaranteeing Chinese interests in the future.

As for letter *g*), its novelty consists in the fact that it features two catch-all locutions ('*any right conferred by law or under contract and any licenses and permits pursuant to law*'); the first, aiming at opening to no reservation categories *a*) to *d*); the second, targeting specifically category *e*). In such latter aspect, it may be noted that the wording appears to be borrowed from the US model (and in fact the provision is listed under the same letter *g*); nevertheless, the US model lacks a 'concession' category such as those featured in the European models). In terms of consistency of the wording employed, however, the result is not adamantine: the use of two different registries (*i.e.*, European and American), especially within the same norm, may cause confusion. The same, nevertheless, happens with ACIA and AANZFTA: both agreements feature an even closer wording to the US model, yet they maintain the European 'concession' category (let. *e*)), structure and (most) wording.

ACIA and AANZFTA

In connection with the analysis that follows on the list of investment instances featured in the CAIA (further below), three elements may be pointed out from the lists of ACIA and AANZFTA:

- Structural (*i.e.*, adoption of the roman numerals) and substantial (whether not literal at once) reliance on the British model (*i.e.*, *i*) property rights, *ii*) company participation, *iv*) claims to money and *vi*) concessions; plus the definition of 'return')
- Where departures from the British model have been adopted, both agreements share identical (or equivalent) structure and wording (*i.e.*, chapeau, *ii*) company participation, *iv*) contractual rights, *iii*) IP rights, *v*) and *vi*) concessions and permits)
- Increased reliance on the US model BIT, for clarifications or additions (*i.e.*, notion of 'covered investment', *ii*) company participations, *v*) permits)

---

175 In sum: gross external debt exceeds 150% of GDP, with one of the worse leverage ratios amongst OECD countries; government debt-over-GDP, despite still below 40%, doubled in three years and, as reported by the Ministry of the Treasury, corporate external debt exceeding 26% of GDP (more than double the OECD average); Source: Ministry of the Treasury of New Zealand, 'New Zealand's External Debt – An International Comparison' (2013) <http://www.treasury.govt.nz/economy/mei/jan13/03.htm> accessed 20 Nov. 2019.

CAIA

The list contained in the CAIA shows remarkable structural and linguistic similarities with ACIA and AANZFTA. This emphasizes how ACIA arguably served as template for the negotiations with China (as well as AANZFTA).[176] By the same token, the differences between CAIA and ACIA, especially when the latter shares identical wording with the AANZFTA, show either key aspects for China, or common understandings between China and ASEAN which could not be properly developed with full market economies – thus within the contexts of PRC-NZ FTA (in the case of China) or AANZFTA (in the case of ASEAN).

Moreover, China's conservative approach towards treaty innovations must be taken into account: modifications aimed at clarifying or simplifying the overall structure and language of the treaty are generally welcome, while those imposing (or implying) substantial changes (in either structure or language) encounter more resistance in finding their way into the final draft. Hence, China arguably insisted on 'purging' the ACIA-template of its US model-led innovations, and for the adoption instead of a structure more coherent with the Chinese (*i.e.*, European) model.

Consequently, China's disfavor for the notion of 'covered investment', nor the reinstatement of the *ratione legis* criterion at the very heart of the definition of investment (actually strengthened, with the addition of ACIA-derived 'policies') is not surprising. Unsurprising is also the preference for the British model wording for the categories 'property rights' and 'contractual rights' (respectively, *i*) and *v*)), as representing no substantial variation with respect to the Chinese model.

The introduction of the notion of 'juridical person' in the 'company participations' category (*ii*)), establishing a clearer civil-law legal standard (as opposed to the British model 'company') was, instead, accepted. Indeed, such wording was already present, *e.g.*, in the BIT with Germany (despite not referred to China);[177] in the same category, however, China refused to include the US model-derived 'bonds'.

Noteworthy, then, is the articulation of the 'IP rights' category, which features an unprecedented list of items.

In the 'concession' category, while resorting to the wording of its own 1997 model, China agreed to remove the 'permitted by law' locution (perhaps enfranchised by the presence of the *ratione legis* in the chapeau); also, those other US model-based specifications contained in both ACIA and AANZFTA (*i.e.*, turnkey, construction, management, production or revenue-sharing

176 Yen (fn. 37).

177 See the definition of investor for Germany at Art. 1 China-Germany BIT (2003).

contracts) have been discarded, as well as the earlier mentioned special 'liability list' category agreed in the PRC-NZ FTA.

China-Canada BIT

The first noteworthy aspect of the list of investment instances in the China-Canada BIT is that, following the Canadian model, this is *closed*.[178] Being this the sole exception to China's otherwise uniform policy, it may be concluded this aspect was due to the insistence of Canada. Indeed, the formula featured at let. *j*) (*i.e.*, '*any other tangible or intangible, moveable or immovable, property and related property right acquired or used for business purposes*'), drawn from the US model (and found also in the 2006 draft Canada model), may constitute a catch-all formula; however, the lack of any 'may include' locution preceding the list appears to impose, upon the interpreter, to verify whether the investment actually belongs to one of the categories listed, rather than eventually moving the analysis (whether treaty or doctrine-based) straight to the investment criteria. In this respect, the choice made in the China-Canada BIT may be considered a step towards a more orderly system.

Drawing from the draft 2006 Canadian model – in this respect, influenced by the US model, in both structure and wording –, the list of investment types in the China-Canada BIT follows the order therein set. Nevertheless, while let. *a*) ('an enterprise') is identically featured in all US and Canadian models, the text of let. *b*) is here literally drawn from the US model;[179] that of let. *c*), then, appears to be a mix of US and Canadian models: on the one side, it keeps the plural form of the terms as featured in the US model; on the other, it keeps loans in a separate category (let. *d*)), and closes with the Canadian locution 'of an enterprise'. With regard to the simplification that let. *c*) underwent with the 2006 draft Canadian model, it is arguably another case of 'reverse influence' the negotiations for the China-Canada BIT had on the Canada draft model. That this part of the Agreement was agreed upon at an early stage already (and anyway, before the elaboration of the draft model of 2006), and not renegotiated subsequently, appears in that let. *d*) reproduces the text of the 2004 model, elided of the exception therein featured for loans to a State enterprise.

Subsequently, letters *e*), *f*), *g*) and *i*) reproduce the simplified content of Canada's 2006 draft model. Letter *h*) (*i.e.*, interests in economic activities under contract, which ideally includes the 'concession' category of Chinese and

178 Canada 2004 model BIT has replaced the 1994 model's non exhaustive asset-based definition with a finite – yet more comprehensive – definition of investments, based on the definition provided in NAFTA Art. 1139.

179 Close, but not identical, to the Canadian model.

European models) as well mostly reproduces the content of either Canadian model, with one notable difference. In the part expressly dealing with 'concessions', the text bends back towards the typical wording of the Chinese model (*i.e.*, '... *concessions to search for and extract oil and other natural resources* ...').

Let. *j*) provides another instance of mutual influence between the draft Canadian models and the China-Canada BIT. The first part of the provision reproduces the content of let. *h*) of the US model; the last part, instead, draws partly from the 2004 model wording. This ultimately simpler result will be subsequently rephrased in the 2006 draft model – maintaining, nevertheless, equivalent meaning.

The China-Canada BIT follow closely the Canadian model by featuring as well the 'exclusion category' (*i.e.*, 'investment does not mean') – entirely absent in the US models. The content of let. *k*) ('claims to money that arises solely from') thus reproduces that featured in the Canadian models, with the sole simplification of the elimination, at sub-para. *i*) ('commercial contracts for the sale of goods or services'), of the British-derived repetition of the agent of such action (*i.e.*, '... by a national or enterprise in the territory of a Party to an enterprise in the territory of the other Party ...'), indeed redundant.

China-Chile SAI

By comparison with the China-Canada BIT, the SAI retains the non-exhaustive character of the list of investment instances (by way of the 1984 Chinese model wording: '... *in particular, though not exclusively, includes:* ...').

In more detail:

- Let. *a*) (property rights) is literally and entirely drawn from let. *H*) of the US model;
- In let. *b*) (company participation), the original wording of the 1997 Chinese model has been restored (with the only substitution of the word 'enterprise' in lieu 'companies');
- Let. *c*) (contractual rights) features again the 1997 Chinese model wording; however, this is the only instance where part of the language employed in the BIT with Canada survived: to the provision is appended a footnote, whose text is extracted from Art. (V)(iii) of Canada's 2004 model (which is, curiously discarded from the China-Canada BIT);[180]
- Let. *d*) (IP rights) follows the US model, with the simple mention of 'intellectual property rights'; it is interesting to note, in this respect, China's abandonment of the comprehensiveness of the German model (culminated

180 Which is, in turn, equivalent to that featured in Art. 14.5 (Non-conforming measures) of the US model.

in the articulated definition featured in the 2003 China-Germany BIT); such new simple definition is found to be part of both:
- The trend of simplification China generally favors, and
- The progressive reliance, where possible, to external agreements where certain definitions or norms are already established, and to which the parties to the agreements are also Party to.[181]

As such, the goal appears to be to avoid double-standards and inconsistent interpretations (as the different wording expressly contained in a BIT *vis-à-vis*, for instance, the TRIPS Agreement, may be understood as sovereign *lex specialis* choice to include or exclude certain elements from the category);
- Let. *e*) (concessions) discards the North American formulation – arguably too distant from the Chinese tradition; the definition shows a limited *labor limae* on the 1994 China-Chile BIT wording, here enriched with some innovations introduced with the 1997 Chinese model – without, however, the otherwise redundant 'permitted by the law' (as already featured in the chapeau) and the adjective 'business' in the locution 'business concessions';
- In let. *f*), arguably drawing from the experience with Canada, China agreed to keep in a separate category debt instruments not constituting participations in companies: 'bonds, loans and other debt instruments'; the enumeration is equivalent and almost identical to the US model (which, however, features 'debentures', here instead listed under the 'company participation' category, at let. *b*));[182]
- Let. *g*) (futures, options and other derivatives) represents a novelty for China; the category, not featured in the China-Canada BIT (nor expressly featured in either Canadian model), is literally drawn from the US model BIT;[183]
- The list ends with an exclusion, as the Parties agreed expressly not to consider as investments court orders or judgments; that exception, featured already in the Chile-US FTA (and kept by Chile in the 2008 Chile-Australia FTA), is drawn from the US model;[184] as such, it seems a novelty welcome to China (it is not contained in the China-Canada BIT);

181 In this respect, for instance, Art. 8.5 SAI makes reference to the TRIPS Agreement (and, consequently, to all sources and agreements therein featured).

182 Art. 1, notion of investment, let. *c*) US model BIT.

183 Art. 1, notion of investment, let. *d*) US model BIT.

184 See Chapter 10, Art. 10.27 Chile-US FTA; Chapter 10, Art. 10.1 Chile-Australia FTA (which features a list of definitions identical to the Chile-US FTA; while both chapters are broadly based on the US model, there are a number of minor differences which, looking at Chile's treaty negotiations in the Pacific, may be attributed this latter); Art. 1, notion of investment, footnote 3 to let. *g*) (concessions) US model BIT.

– Lastly, it may be noted that the clause 'change of form of the investment', derived in this form from the British model and typical of both Chinese and European models, is here not reproduced.

Comparative Table 14, below, provides for a visual support of the above illustration.

TABLE 12 Investment definition in 2008–2009 Asia-Pacific IIA

	Art. 1 US '04	Art. 135 PRC-NZ FTA '08	Art. 4 ACIA '09	Art. 21 AANZFTA '09	Art. 1 CAIA '09
Covered investment	'covered investment' means, with respect to a Party, an investment in its territory of an investor of the other Party in existence as of the date of entry into force of this Treaty or established, acquired, or expanded thereafter.	–	4.a 'covered investment' means, with respect to a Member State, an investment in its territory of an investor of any other Member State in existence as of the date of entry into force of this Agreement or established, acquired or expanded thereafter, and has been admitted according to its laws, regulations, and national policies, and where applicable, specifically approved in writing by the competent authority of a Member State;	2.a covered investment means with respect to a Party, an investment in its territory of an investor of another Party, in existence as of the date of entry into force of this Agreement or established, acquired or expanded thereafter, and which, where applicable, has been admitted by the host Party, subject to its relevant laws, regulations and policies;	–

TABLE 12 Investment definition in 2008-2009 Asia-Pacific IIA (*cont.*)

	Art. 1 US '04	Art. 135 PRC-NZ FTA '08	Art. 4 ACIA '09	Art. 21 AANZFTA '09	Art. 1 CAIA '09
Chapeau	'investment' means every asset that an investor owns or controls, directly or indirectly, that has the characteristics of an investment, including such characteristics as the commitment of capital or other resources, the expectation of gain or profit, or the assumption of risk. Forms that an investment may take include:	Investment means every kind of asset invested, **directly or indirectly**, by the investors of a Party in the territory of the other Party **including, but not limited to, the following**: *[*as in PRC-DE*, except bold]	4.c 'investment' means every kind of asset, **owned or controlled**, by an investor, **including but not limited to the following:**	2.c [idem ACIA]	1.d 'investment' means every kind of asset invested by the investors of a Party in accordance with the relevant laws, regulations and policies of another Party in the territory of the latter **including, but not limited to, the following**: *[as in *PRC model '84*, except 'policies' and bold]
Property rights	(a) an enterprise; (h) other tangible or intangible, **movable** or **immovable property**, and related **property rights, such as** leases, **mortgages**, liens, and **pledges.**	*(a) [idem as PRC '84 model*, '97 and PRC-DE]	(i) [idem UK model]	(i) [idem UK model]	(i) [idem UK model]

TABLE 12 Investment definition in 2008-2009 Asia-Pacific IIA (*cont.*)

	Art. 1 US '04	Art. 135 PRC-NZ FTA '08	Art. 4 ACIA '09	Art. 21 AANZFTA '09	Art. 1 CAIA '09
Company participation	(b) shares, stock, and other forms of equity participation in an enterprise;	(b) [*idem PRC '97 model*] *[*and as in PRC-DE, with 'participation' in lieu of 'interest'*]	(ii) shares, stocks, **bonds** and debentures and any other forms of participation in a **juridical person** and rights or interest derived therefrom;	(ii) [**idem** ACIA, without 'or interest']	(ii) shares, stocks and **debentures** of **juridical persons** or interests in the property of such juridical persons;
Contractual rights	–	(c) claims to money or to any other contractual performance having an economic value **associated with an investment**; *[*as in PRC '97 model* and PRC-DE, plus 'contractual'] (g) [part] any right conferred by law or under contract [...]	**(iv)** claims to money or to any contractual performance related to a business and having financial value; [fn3] [fn3*] For greater certainty, investment does not mean claims to money that arise solely from: (a) commercial contracts for sale of goods or services; or (b) the extension of credit in connection with such commercial contracts. * [*Drawn from the Canada model, featured in PRC-CA BIT as well*]	**(iv) [idem** ACIA**]**	(v) [idem UK model]

TABLE 12 Investment definition in 2008-2009 Asia-Pacific IIA (*cont.*)

	Art. 1 US '04	Art. 135 PRC-NZ FTA '08	Art. 4 ACIA '09	Art. 21 AANZFTA '09	Art. 1 CAIA '09
IP rights	(f) **intellectual property rights**	(d) [*idem PRC-DE*]	**(iii) intellectual property rights which are** conferred **pursuant to the laws and regulations of each MS;**	**(iii) intellectual property rights which are** recognized **pursuant to the laws and regulations of each Party** and goodwill;	**(iii) intellectual property rights,** including rights with respect to copyrights, patents and **utility models**, industrial designs, trademarks and service marks, geographical indications, layout designs of integrated circuits, trade names, trade secrets, technical processes, know-how and goodwill; *[*based on PRC-DE*, without 'business secret' but with 'utility models']

TABLE 12 Investment definition in 2008-2009 Asia-Pacific IIA (*cont.*)

	Art. 1 US '04	Art. 135 PRC-NZ FTA '08	Art. 4 ACIA '09	Art. 21 AANZFTA '09	Art. 1 CAIA '09
Concessions	(e) turnkey, construction, management, production, **concession,** revenue-sharing, and other similar contracts;	(e) concessions conferred by law or **under contract permitted** by law, including concessions to search for, **cultivate, extract** or exploit natural resources; *[*as PRC '97 model* and PRC-DE, but missing 'business']	**(vi)** business concessions required to conduct economic activities and having financial value conferred by law **or under a contract,** including any concessions to search, **cultivate, extract** or exploit natural resources.	**(vi) [idem ACIA]**	(iv) **business** concessions conferred by law, **or under contract,** including concessions to search for, **cultivate, extract,** or exploit natural resources; *[*as PRC '97 model*, but missing 'permitted by law']
	(g) licenses, authorizations, permits, and similar rights conferred pursuant to domestic law;	(g) [part] ... any licences and permits pursuant to law;	(v) rights under contracts, including turnkey, construction, management, production or revenue-sharing contracts;	(v) [idem ACIA]	–
Debt instruments [and derivatives]	(c) bonds, debentures, other debt instruments, and loans (d) futures, options, and other derivatives;	(f) bonds, including government issued bonds, debentures, loans and other forms of debt, and rights derived therefrom;	–	–	–

TABLE 12 Investment definition in 2008-2009 Asia-Pacific IIA (*cont.*)

	Art. 1 US '04	Art. 135 PRC-NZ FTA '08	Art. 4 ACIA '09	Art. 21 AANZFTA '09	Art. 1 CAIA '09
Change of form	–	[*idem PRC-DE*] *[as in ***PRC '97 model***, first sent.]	*Any alteration of the form in which assets are invested* **or reinvested** *shall not affect their classification as investment;* *[as in *PRC-DE*, plus 'or reinvested']	[...] [**idem** CAIA]	[...] *any alteration of the form in which assets are invested* **or reinvested** *shall not affect their* character *as investments;*
Reinvested returns	–	–	–	[...] [**idem** CAIA]	**For the purpose of the definition of investment in this Sub-para., returns that are invested should be treated as investments [...]**
Returns as investment	–	–	The term 'investment' also includes amounts yielded by investments, in particular, profits, interest, capital gains, dividend, royalties and fees.	–	–

TABLE 13 China-Canada BIT – definition of investment

	Art. 1 US model '04/'12	Art. 1 Canada model '04	Art. 1 Canada draft model '06	Art. 1 PRC-CA '12
Covered investment	"covered investment" means, with respect to a Party, an investment in its territory of an investor of the other Party in existence as of the date of entry into force of this Treaty or established, acquired, or expanded thereafter.	Covered investment means, with respect to a Party, an investment in its territory of an investor of the other Party existing on the date of entry into force of this *Agreement, as well as investments made or* acquired thereafter;	"covered investment" means, with respect to a Party, an investment in its territory that is *owned or controlled, directlyorindirectly,*[185] by an investor of the other Party existing on the date of entry into force of this *Agreement, as well as an investment made or* acquired thereafter;	"covered investment" means, with respect to a CP, an investment in its territory of an investor of the other CP existing on the date of entry into force of this *Agreement* or an investment of an investor *admitted* in accordance with its laws and regulations thereafter, and which involves the commitment of capital or other resources, the expectation of gain or profit, or the assumption of risk;
	"investment" means	investment means:	"investment" means:	1. "investment" means:
Chapeau	every asset that an investor *owns or controls, directly or indirectly*, that has the characteristics of an investment, including such characteristics as the commitment of capital or other resources, the expectation of gain or profit, or the assumption of risk. Forms that an investment may take include:	–	–	–

185 The insertion – featuring a wording drawn from the chapeau of the UK model, and equivalent to that featured in the chapeau of the US model – finds nevertheless an original placement in the draft model, in the definition of 'covered investment'.

TABLE 13 China-Canada BIT – definition of investment (*cont.*)

	Art. 1 US model '04/'12	Art. 1 Canada model '04	Art. 1 Canada draft model '06	Art. 1 PRC-CA '12
Company participation	(a) an enterprise;	(I) an enterprise;	(a) an enterprise;	(a) an enterprise;
	(b) shares, stock, and other forms of equity participation in an enterprise;	(II) an equity security of an enterprise;	(b) a share, stock or other form of equity participation in an enterprise;	(b) shares, stocks and other forms of equity participation in an enterprise;
	(c) bonds, debentures, other debt instruments, and loans;	(III) a debt security *of an enterprise* (i) where the enterprise is an affiliate of the investor, or (ii) where the original maturity of the debt security is at least three years, but does not include a debt security, regardless of original maturity, of a state enterprise;	(c) a bond, debenture or other debt instrument *of an enterprise*;	(c) bonds, debentures, and other debt instruments *of an enterprise*;
	(d) futures, options, and other derivatives;	(IV) *a loan to an enterprise (i) where the enterprise is an affiliate of the investor, or (ii) where the original maturity of the loan is at least three years,* but does not include a loan, regardless of original maturity, to a state enterprise;	(*d*) *a loan to an enterprise*;	(*d*) *a loan to an enterprise (i) where the enterprise is an affiliate of the investor, or (ii) where the original maturity of the loan is at least three years;*

TABLE 13 China-Canada BIT – definition of investment (*cont.*)

Art. 1 US model '04/'12	Art. 1 Canada model '04	Art. 1 Canada draft model '06	Art. 1 PRC-CA '12
	(V) (i) *notwithstanding subparagraph* (III) *and* (IV) *above, a loan to or debt security issued by a financial institution is an investment only where the loan or debt security is treated as regulatory capital by the Party in whose territory the financial institution is located*, and (ii) a loan granted by or debt security owned by a financial institution, other than a loan to or debt security of a financial institution referred to in (i), is not an investment; for greater certainty: (iii) a loan to, or debt security issued by, a Party or a state enterprise thereof is not an investment; and (iv) a loan granted by or debt security owned by a cross-border financial service provider, other than a loan	(*e*) *notwithstanding subparagraphs* (*c*) *and* (*d*) *above, a loan to or debt security issued by a financial institution is an investment only where the loan or debt security is treated as regulatory capital by the Party in whose territory the financial institution is located;*	(*e*) *notwithstanding sub-paragraphs* (*c*) *and* (*d*) *above, a loan to or debt security issued by a financial institution is an investment only where the loan or debt security is treated as regulatory capital by the CP in whose territory the financial institution is located;*

TABLE 13 China-Canada BIT – definition of investment (*cont.*)

	Art. 1 US model '04/'12	Art. 1 Canada model '04	Art. 1 Canada draft model '06	Art. 1 PRC-CA '12
		to or debt security issued by a financial institution, is an investment if such loan or debt security meets the criteria for investments set out elsewhere in this Article;		
		(VI) *an interest in an enterprise that entitles the owner to share in income or profits of the enterprise*;	(*f*) *an interest in an enterprise that entitles the owner to share in income or profits of the enterprise;*	(*f*) *an interest in an enterprise that entitles the owner to share in the income or profits of the enterprise*;
		(VII) *an interest in an enterprise that entitles the owner to share in the assets of that enterprise on dissolution*, other than a debt security or a loan excluded from subparagraphs (III) (IV) or (V);	(*g*) *an interest in an enterprise that entitles the owner to share in the assets of that enterprise on dissolution;*	(*g*) *an interest in an enterprise that entitles the owner to share in the assets of that enterprise on dissolution;*
Concessions	(e) **turnkey, construction,** management, production, **concession,** revenue-sharing, and other similar contracts;	(IX) *interests arising from the commitment of capital or other resources in the territory of a Party to economic activity in such territory, such as under*	(*h*) an *interest arising from the commitment of capital or other resources in the territory of a Party to economic activity in that territory, such as under*:	(*h*) *interests arising from the commitment of capital or other resources in the territory of a CP to economic activity in such territory, such as under*

TABLE 13 China-Canada BIT – definition of investment (*cont.*)

	Art. 1 US model '04/'12	Art. 1 Canada model '04	Art. 1 Canada draft model '06	Art. 1 PRC-CA '12
	(g) licenses, authorizations, permits, and similar rights conferred pursuant to domestic law; and	(*i*) *contracts involving the presence of an investor's property in the territory of the Party, including turnkey or construction contracts, or concessions, or*	(*i*) a *contract involving the presence of an investor's property in the territory of the Party, including a turnkey or construction contract, or a concession, or*	(*i*) *contracts involving the presence of an investor's property in the territory of the CP, including turnkey or construction contracts or concessions* to search for and ***extract*** oil and other natural resources, *or*
		(*ii*) *contracts where remuneration depends substantially on the production, revenues or profits of an enterprise;*	(*ii*) a *contract where remuneration depends substantially on the production, revenues or profits of an enterprise;*	(*ii*) *contracts where remuneration depends substantially on the production, revenue or profits of an enterprise;*
IP rights	(f) intellectual property rights;	_186	(*i*) intellectual property rights;	(*i*) intellectual property rights;
Property rights	(h) other tangible or intangible, movable or immovable property, and related property rights, such as leases, mortgages, liens, and pledges.	(VIII) real estate or other property, tangible or intangible, *acquired* in the expectation *or used for* the purpose	(*j*) any other tangible or intangible, moveable or immovable, property and related property rights	(*j*) *any* other tangible or intangible, moveable or immovable, property and related property rights *acquired*

186 Contained only in the list of definitions: 'Intellectual property rights means copyright and related rights, trademark rights, rights in geographical indications, rights in industrial designs, patent rights, rights in layout designs of integrated circuits, rights in relation to protection of undisclosed information, and plant breeders' rights'.

TABLE 13 China-Canada BIT – definition of investment (*cont.*)

	Art. 1 US model '04/'12	Art. 1 Canada model '04	Art. 1 Canada draft model '06	Art. 1 PRC-CA '12
		of economic benefit or other *business purposes*;	*acquired* in the expectation of *or used for* the *purpose* of economic benefit or other *business*	*or used for business purposes;*
Exclusions	–	*but investment does not mean,*	*but "investment" does not mean:*	*but "investment" does not mean:*
		(x) c*laims to money that arise solely from*	(*k*) *a claim to money that arises solely from:*	(*k*) *claims to money that arise solely from*
		(*i*) *commercial contracts for the sale of goods or services* by a national or enterprise in the territory of a Party to an enterprise in the territory of the other Party, or	(*i*) a *commercial contract for the sale of a good or service* by a national or enterprise in the territory of a Party to an enterprise in the territory of the other Party, or	(*i*) *commercial contracts for the sale of goods or services,* or
		(*ii*) *the extension of credit in connection with a commercial transaction, such as trade financing, other than a loan covered by subparagraphs* (IV) or (V); and	(*ii*) *the extension of credit in connection with a commercial transaction, such as trade financing;* or	(*ii*) *the extension of credit in connection with a commercial transaction, such as trade financing, other than a loan covered by sub-paragraph* (d); or
	–	(XI) *any other claims to money, that do not involve the kinds of interests set out in subparagraphs* (I) through (IX);	(*l*) *any other claim to money, that does not involve the kinds of interests set out in subparagraphs* (*a*) *to* (*j*);	(*l*) *any other claims to money, that do not involve the kinds of interests set out in sub-paragraphs* (*a*) *to* (*i*);

TABLE 14 China-Chile SAI – definition of investment

	Art. 1.1 PRC '97	Art. 1 US model '04/'12	Art. 1 CCSAI '12
Covered investment	–	"covered investment" means, with respect to a Party, an investment in its territory of an investor of the other Party in existence as of the date of entry into force of this Treaty or established, acquired, or expanded thereafter.	–
Chapeau	1.1 The term 'investment' means every kind of asset invested by investors of one CP in accordance with the laws and regulations of the other CP in the territory of the Latter, and in particular, though not exclusively, includes:	"investment" means every asset that an investor owns or controls, directly or indirectly, that has the characteristics of an investment, including such characteristics as the commitment of capital or other resources, the expectation of gain or profit, or the assumption of risk. Forms that an investment may take include:	investment means every kind of asset that an investor owns or controls, that has the characteristics of an investment, including such characteristics as the commitment of capital or other resources, the expectation of gain or profit, or the assumption of risk, invested by investors of one Party in accordance with the laws and regulations of the other Party in the territory of the latter, and in particular, though not exclusively, includes:
Property rights	(a) movable and immovable property and other property rights such as mortgages, pledges and similar rights;	(h) other tangible or intangible, movable or immovable property, and related property rights, such as leases, mortgages, liens, and pledges.	(a) tangible or intangible, movable, immovable property and related property rights such as mortgages, liens, leases and pledges;
Company participation	(b) shares, ***debentures***, stock and any other kind of participation in companies;	(a) an enterprise; (b) **shares, stock, and other forms of equity participation in an** enterprise;	(b) shares, ***debentures***, stock and any other kind of participation in enterprises; *[*as in PRC '97 model, with 'enterprises' in lieu of 'companies'*]

TABLE 14 China-Chile SAI – definition of investment (*cont.*)

	Art. 1.1 PRC '97	Art. 1 US model '04/'12	Art. 1 CCSAI '12
Contractual rights	(c) claims to money or to any other performance having an economic value *associated with an investment;*	–	(c) [*idem PRC '97 model*] [fn.1]; [*fn.1**] For greater certainty, investment does not include loans issued by one Party to the other Party. *[*Extracted from para. (V)(iii) Canada model*; *similar to Non-Conforming Measure Art. 14.5 US model*]
IP rights	(d) *intellectual property rights, in particular* copyrights, *patents, trademarks, trade-names, technical process,* know-how and *good-will;*	(f) intellectual property rights;	(d) **intellectual property rights;**
Concessions	(e) *business* concessions conferred by law *or under contract permitted by law,* including concessions to search for, *cultivate, extract* or exploit natural resources.	(e) turnkey, construction, management, production, concession, revenue-sharing, and other similar contracts; (g) licenses, authorizations, permits, and similar rights conferred pursuant to domestic law;	(e) concessions conferred by law *or under contract,* including concessions to search for, *cultivate, extract* or exploit natural resources; *[*as in PRC '97 model, without 'business' and 'permitted by law'*]
Debt instruments	['debentures' in (b)]	(c) bonds, debentures, other debt instruments, and loans;	(f) **bonds, loans**, and **other debt instruments**
Derivatives	–	(d) futures, options, and other derivatives	(g) futures, options, and other derivatives;
Exceptions	–	–	**but investment does not mean an order or judgment entered in a judicial or administrative action;** *[*idem fn.3 to cat.(g) US model*]

TABLE 14 China-Chile SAI – definition of investment (*cont.*)

	Art. 1.1 PRC '97	Art. 1 US model '04/'12	Art. 1 CCSAI '12
Change of form clause	*Any change in the form in which assets are invested does not affect their character as investments provided that such change is in accordance with the laws and regulations of the CP in whose territory the investment has been made.*	–	–

4 *Returns*

The definition of returns in the 1997 Chinese model reads as follows:

> *The term 'returns' means the amount yielded from investments, including profits, capital gains, royalties, fees and other legitimate income.*

The definition of returns in China's investment treaties and models follows a curious evolutionary path: the wording of the first Chinese stipulation, back in 1982 with Sweden, is already identical to the 1997 model. Sweden, which by the time of the conclusion had already signed 7 BITs,[187] never before defined 'returns' (nor it did for a while after the conclusion of the BIT with China).[188] It can be thus inferred that the presence of the definition is owed to China. Table 14, below, shows the broad commonality with the British practice at the time.

TABLE 15 Chinese model BITs – returns

Art. 1.3 China model '84 and '89	Art. 1.3 China model '97
The term 'returns' means the amount yielded by investments, such as profits, dividends, interests, royalties or other legitimate income.	The term 'returns' means the amount yielded from investments, including profits, **capital gains**, royalties, **fees** and other legitimate income.

187 With Ivory Coast (1965), Madagascar (1966), Senegal (1967), Egypt and Yugoslavia (1978), Malaysia (1979) and Pakistan (1981).

188 The almost contemporary BIT with Yemen (1983) makes use of the standard British formula; the subsequent BITs with Tunisia (1985) and Hungary (1987) do not feature a definition for returns.

TABLE 16 Returns – definition in PRC, UK, DE model BITs, plus PRC-DE BIT

Art. 1.3 PRC '84 & '89	Art. 1.3 PRC '97 (& '82 PRC-Sweden)	Art. 1(b) UK '06[189]	Art. 1.2 DE '08	Art. 1.3 PRC-DE '03
1.3 The term **'returns' means the amount yielded by investments,** such as profits, dividends, interests, royalties or other legitimate income.	1.3 The term 'returns' means the amount yielded *from* investments, including profits, dividends, interests, capital gains, royalties, **fees** and other legitimate income.	1(b) **'returns' means the amounts yielded by an investment** and in particular, though not exclusively, includes **profit, interest,** capital gains, **dividends, royalties and fees;**	1.2 The term **'returns' means the amounts yielded by** an **investment** for a definite period, such as profit, dividends, interest, royalties **or fees;**	1.3 [*idem as PRC '97 model*]
			2.4 **Returns from an investment, as well as returns from rseinvested returns, shall enjoy the same protection as the original investment.**	*Ad* Art. 1, let. C: **Returns from the investment and from reinvestments shall enjoy the same protection as the investment.**

The 1983 China-Germany BIT provides for a significantly simpler definition:

> *The term 'returns' means the amounts yielded by an investment for a definite period, such as profit, dividends, interest and other legitimate income.*[190]

It is also worth noting that the Chinese list of instances of all its models features the rather generic wording 'and other legitimate income' – which, back then,

189 The definition is unchanged since the first BIT with Egypt, in 1975.

190 Art. 1.3 of the 1983 China-Germany BIT. Note that 'for a definite period' is a typical German expression – surviving today in the 2008 model – which, however, has been used by China only with Germany.

was typical of the German practice; Germany, nevertheless, has discarded this formulation since its 1991 model, substituting it with the more punctual 'royalties or fees' (already found in the British practice).[191]

With regard to more recent practice, China-NZ FTA, ACIA, CAIA and AANZFTA, follow the German model.[192] CAIA and AANZFTA actually share the same wording, expressly protecting also 'reinvested returns' (in the ACIA, instead, ASEAN has opted, drawing from the British definition of return, for the express inclusion of the concept of 'return' into that of investment).

D Conclusion

Differently from Western States, China's rationale for the early adoption of a negotiating template for investment treaties descends from the distribution of power at domestic level more than a desire for strategic negotiating advantages, or to spread certain approaches or definitions in the field of international investment law. In fact, if between 1984 and 2000 China's models have often become the final text *tel quel*, it is because of the limited negotiating powers granted to Chinese negotiators. Indeed, anything more-than-cosmetic departures from the template required approval at the highest level – namely, the State Council. The significant delays in BIT negotiations that this 'triangulation' caused has arguably pushed several counterparts to accept the Chinese template as such – or, in any event, to reduce negotiations for alterations to a minimum.

With regard to the structure and content of Chinese models, the analysis detailed in this Chapter highlighted the ties these have to the British and German templates. For each provision, China has flexibly employed these latter, even merging their wording, based on a criterion privileging simplicity and in an attempt to minimize unclear expressions (potentially leading to subsequent broad or unexpected interpretations).[193] As a result, China has often resorted to a 'collage' technique: less clear terms or definitions in one reference template have been replaced with that of the other. When necessary, the

191 The German list of instances regularly used at the time (*e.g.*, the 1981 BIT with Somalia, 1982 BIT with Lesotho and the 1983 BIT with Panama, all listing '... profit, dividends, interest, licence or other fees') was ultimately not successful (especially in its mention of 'licences').

192 For all agreements, featured in the last sentence of the definition of investment: Art. 135 China-NZ FTA, Art. 4 ACIA, Art. 1 CAIA, Art. 2.c Chapter 11 AANZFTA.

193 In this respect, China seemingly pays attention to limiting the space for arbitral tribunals to broadly interpret BIT provisions.

result was then 'colored' with the addition of Chinese core interests, such as the *ratione legis* requirement in the definition of investment. In sum, it can be said that Chinese templates move from international best practices and then 'retro-fit' these to meet China's core interest and concerns at the time.

This conclusion appears quite readily from the detailed analysis carried out of China's templates and treaty practice with regard to the preamble, scope of application, and definition of investment, especially in relation to the *ratione legis* condition and the list of instances therein contained.

CHAPTER 3

Analytical Review of China's Treaty Practice and Key Protection Standards

A Defining the Research Perimeter and the Relevant Comparators

Since signing the first BIT, in 1982 (with Sweden), and adopting its first model BIT, in 1984, China's foreign investment protection program has developed consistently, in both quantitative and qualitative terms.

Quantitatively speaking, today the overall number of IIAs China concluded stands at 154, including bilateral, trilateral,[1] multilateral,[2] and supplementary[3] investment agreements, plus investment chapters of comprehensive FTAs.[4] The Chinese network is thus the world's largest – Germany standing at 133 BITs (the negotiations for further investment agreements having shifted to EU-level, and none of these agreements having entered into force yet).

Qualitatively speaking, however, an assessment of China's vast network, especially in light of the evolution of the formulation of some clauses, requires an accurate review in order to produce an analysis useful to treaty making and treaty practice considerations (*e.g.*, for investment arbitration). The analysis carried out in this Chapter builds on the data summary placed at the end of each section. These summaries are, in turn, based on the dedicated analytical comparative tables that follow each of them.

Firstly, out of the 154 individuated IIAs, 20 are not in force. An IIA signed yet not in force is taken into account in this study as long as not superseded by subsequent agreements that are also signed yet not in force (*e.g.*, Congo, Brunei). Being the former unlikely to enter in force at any stage, its value in terms of treaty practice or trend is limited, and it is thus discarded.

Secondly, there is the case of BIT renegotiations. This is a significant phenomenon for China, as since the turn of the millennium it engaged in updating several investment agreements with key partners (the UK and Italy being notable exceptions). This is the case of 14 new IIAs, whose older versions have

1 *I.e.*, the Trilateral Investment Agreement with Japan and South Korea (2012).
2 *E.g.*, the China-ASEAN Agreement on Investment (2009).
3 *E.g.*, the China-Chile Supplementary Agreement on Investments (2012).
4 *E.g.*, the China-New Zealand FTA (2008).

© KONINKLIJKE BRILL NV, LEIDEN, 2021 | DOI:10.1163/9789004443938_005

been expressly terminated. The terminated BITs are thus taken out from the survey lot, in order to better represent the evolution of China's treaty practice.

Thirdly, 12 BITs, while not expressly terminated, have been superseded by subsequent agreements (*i.e.*, comprehensive investment chapters in new FTAs).[5] For the same reason already mentioned (*i.e.*, of more properly representing the evolution of China's treaty practice), these older BITs, even if still in force, are discarded from the survey. This is not the case, however, when the concurrently existing IIAs between the parties are recent (*e.g.*, the three concurrent regimes between China and South Korea).[6]

Fourthly, 3 agreements are not available neither publicly nor upon request to MOFCOM: this is the case of Moldova (1992), Turkmenistan (1992), and Cameroon (1997). *Force majeure*, these agreements are not part of the survey.

In light of the above, the Chinese IIAs in force, whose text is available, not superseded by subsequent stipulations and offer access to ISDS totals 101. Adding the IIAs signed yet not in force (that meet the criterion mentioned above), the overall number of Chinese investment regimes taken into account in this analysis is of 120 (unless otherwise indicated).

The following sections analyzes each key investment protection clause (ISDS, expropriation, MFN, NT, FET, FPS, and PAD) in all treaties in the individuated pool, by contrasting these with the equivalent provisions in the Chinese models, as well as the principal European (*i.e.*, German, British, Dutch, French, Italian) and North American (US and Canadian) models.

B ISDS Clauses in Chinese IIAs

1 *Access to ISDS: The Significant Impact of Limited Consent to Arbitration*

Within a pool of 120 IIAs, a treaty practice analysis that aims to be useful also in the context of investment arbitration must consider the type of access an IIA offers to ISDS. As it is the case for many States (especially developing), a significant divide in the Chinese practice emerges in this respect. As illustrated, in both 1984 and 1989 BIT models China's consent to ISDS was limited to *ad hoc* arbitration on the amount of compensation due to expropriation. This is reflected

5 On the case of 'serious vertical treaty overlaps' created by the practice of not expressly terminating or phasing out earlier agreements, see J Huang, Procedural Models to Upgrade BITs: China's Experience, in Leiden Journal of International Law (2017), 1–23, at 2–3.

6 *I.e.*, 2007 China-Korea BIT, 2012 China-Japan-Korea TIA, 2015 China-Korea FTA.

in 60 BITs in force (50% of 120).[7] In the other half of the pool, conversely, and beside two recent cases featuring a complex set of limitations and exceptions (Turkey 2015 and Australia 2015), China offers unrestricted access to ISDS.

As illustrated, the Chinese policy regarding access to ISDS officially changed with the adoption of the 1997 model BIT and the conclusion of the first two ISDS-unrestricted stipulations (South Africa 1997 and Barbados 1998). The policy change, however, was only implemented coherently from year 2000 onward, as in two BITs concluded in 1999 (Qatar and Bahrain) consent to ISDS is still limited.

2 *Express Exclusion of the MFN Clause from Covering ISDS*

As known, since the 2001 *Maffezini* award the MFN clause has been the subject of an intense doctrinal debate over the extent of its application to procedural aspects (in addition to substantive protections).[8] This 'expansive reading', grounded on the IIAs' 'effective interpretation', is meeting increasing resistance from States, as many newly signed agreements expressly exclude such an extension.

China expressly barred expansive interpretations of the MFN clause for the first time in the investment chapter of the 2008 FTA with Pakistan. That this is a matter of concern appears evident in that in 13 of the 20 IIAs concluded thereafter (65% of cases) the express exclusion is featured, and it has become constant (100%) in the last 9 IIAs, signed between 2011–2015.

3 *Length of Mandatory Consultations*

Mandatory consultations between the investor and the host State prior to resorting to ISDS is a typical preliminary dispute-defusing mechanism of IIAs. The treaty practice is quite uniform in relation to this so-called 'cooling off' period: the German, French, Italian, US, and Canadian models all mandate for six months,[9] with only the British requiring three.[10] Starkly different is the Dutch approach, which does not feature this requirement at all.[11] At the opposite side of the spectrum, certain Latin American States, especially in their past practice, used to require up to eighteen months.

---

7 The issue is developed in detail, including a review of all publicly available case-law on the matter, in GM Vaccaro-Incisa, 'Arbitration clauses limited to compensation due to expropriation' (Chapter 1, fn. 165).

8 *Maffezini v. Spain*, Decision of the Tribunal on Objections to Jurisdiction, Jan. 25th, 2000, ICSID Case No. ARB/97/7.

9 Art. 10.2 German model BIT (2008), Art. 7.2 French model BIT (2006), Art. X.3, Italian model BIT (2003), Art. 24.3 US model (2004), Art. 26.1.b Canadian model BIT (2004).

10 Art. 8 UK model BIT (2006).

11 Art. 9 Dutch model BIT (2004).

China's practice is here virtually uniform and coinciding with any Chinese model BIT, as in **97** cases (81% of 120 IIAs) the length of mandatory consultations is fixed at six months. Shorter periods have been granted in most cases in recent Asia-Pacific agreements with developed States (Japan, South Korea, Australia). A group of **9** BITs from the late '80s and early '90s with former CIS or socialist States sets no specific duration. Other periods (either shorter or longer) have been agreed upon exceptionally (in total, **14** IIAs).

4 *Mandatory Prior Recourse to Domestic Court Proceedings*

Out of the pool of 120 IIAs of this survey, China **never** imposes any mandatory prior resort to domestic courts (coherently with the models and practice of all comparators here taken into account, and as opposed instead to the relatively common practice in the '90s of certain South American States).

Chinese investors are, instead, subject to this condition in the case of the 2009 China-Malta BIT (the condition is non-reciprocal), with China accepting in this respect Malta's not particularly advanced BIT practice.

5 *Mandatory Prior Recourse to Domestic Administrative Review*

The requirement that investors go through a domestic 'administrative review procedure' prior to initiating arbitration appeared in the Chinese investment treaty practice with the adoption of the third model BIT (1997), where China officially granted on a standard basis unrestricted access to ISDS. This means, firstly, that the **58** older agreements based on the first two Chinese model BITs (1984 and 1989), limiting ISDS access to disputes relating to the amount of compensation due to expropriation, do not feature the requirement. Conversely, out of the subsequent 62 IIAs, 60 feature the requirement, which has thus become a distinctive trait of China's investment treaty practice. The following elaborates on this specific feature.

Firstly, in the vast majority of cases, the 'prior administrative review' procedure is framed in general – thus, potentially reciprocal – terms, and not as a burden imposed only on foreign investors in China. While the provision is typical of China's investment treaty policy, and is thus *de facto* aimed at foreign investments in China, the abstract terms employed imply that China is prepared to accept that the treaty counterpart may put in place an equivalent mechanism.

Secondly, the prior administrative review procedure seemingly an essential condition for China to conclude an IIA granting unrestricted access to ISDS,[12]

12 Gallagher correctly notes that, quite exceptionally, the 2012 TIA (at Art. 15.7) does not make the requirement mandatory, but only subject to the host State request. The wording change is, however, so far isolated and, for practical purposes, perhaps only of limited

the negotiation bargain of the other party shifts on the actual length of the mandatory review itself. The more time granted to the Chinese administrative authorities, the longer this additional 'cooling off' period weighs on the investor's ability to initiate arbitration. Here, out of the 60 IIAs featuring the requirement, 39 adhere to the 1997 model, which poses no temporal limits to the duration of the review (66% of cases, including agreements signed as recently as 2013). Only in 17 cases (29%), all after 2003, China agreed to expressly indicate a term (of six, four, or three months). The insistence of China on this element is, therefore, manifest. Such an insistence on the domestic review seems, however, of a different rationale than that of some States, especially in Latin America. In these latter, resort to arbitration is 'stalled' by mandatorily requiring up to 18 months of preliminary domestic courts review (timeframe *prima facie* insufficient to comprise all judicial review stages, thus arguably intended to grant the host State more time for possible extra-judicial settlements). Conversely, the Chinese law reforming the administrative review procedure mandates that local administrative courts must conclude reconsideration procedures within four months, independently from the nationality of the claimant. In this respect, the IIA requirement reflects the domestic legal framework, which already features a clear time-limit. While of course domestic laws may be changed, the current system already provides for a maximum timeframe also for foreign investors, even in those cases the relevant IIA indicates a longer window, or no term at all.[13] As such, the policy seems corresponding to a concrete institutional will to remedy or reform the domestic act possibly in breach of IIA obligations (as opposed to a more political will to buy time for negotiations).

Third, and last, the 2 exceptions. As mentioned, out of 62 IIAs granting unrestricted access to ISDS, 60 require prior recourse to the local administrative review procedure. The agreements with Nigeria (2001) and Australia (2015), however, do not contain such reference. In the latter case, this can be explained by the temporary and currently limited scope of the investment regime established with the China-Australia FTA (a review of the chapter is supposedly undergoing already).[14] The case of Nigeria, instead, could be explained first by the fact that, at the time of the conclusion of the agreement, Chinese negotiators

relevance, as it merely changes the factors order: from domestic review – dispute notification, to dispute notification – dispute review. N Gallagher, 'China's BIT's and Arbitration Practice: Progress and Problems', in W Shan (ed.), *China and International Investment Law* (Brill Nijhoff, 2014) 180–214, at 201.

13 It is not certain that the same result could be reached through the NT or MFN clauses, given their contested applicability with regard to dispute settlement.

14 Cf., Art. 9.9 China-Australia FTA.

were perhaps unconcerned with the possibility of Nigerian investment in China; secondly, the debate opened with *Maffezini* on the possibility that the MFN clause (let alone, the NT) could apply to dispute settlement had yet to see the light.

6 *Mandatory Treaty-Based Procedural Rules: Presence and Extent*

The dispute settlement mechanisms menu of Chinese IIAs has no doubt evolved over the time. This is reflected, in particular, in the contrast between, on the one side, the substantial group of mostly older treaties, following in this respect the first two Chinese BIT models (1984 and 1989), and on the other, the treaties concluded since the adoption of the third model (1997).

The former group comprises **64** IIAs (53% of 120), spanning from 1984 to 2007 – with, however, only 13 signed after year 2000 (all with States not particularly significant in terms of current or foreseeable investment flows). The dispute settlement regime of these IIAs is characterized by the fact of comprising in a single provision an essential yet complete treaty-based set of rules for *ad hoc* arbitral proceedings. In 13 cases (without any discernible geopolitical or economic pattern), the treaty additionally mandates for an external set of procedural rules, or offers a choice between two sets, that the arbitrators 'shall' adopt:[15] ICSID rules are here expressly indicated 9 times, UNCITRAL rules 6 times, and PCA arbitration rules once.

The second most significant group is that following China's 1997 model BIT. It comprises **42** IIAs (35% of 120), 33 of which signed after year 2000. Here, the policy is reversed, as the ISDS clause only indicates a menu of dispute settlement mechanisms, without additional treaty-based rules or indications.

Two other groups of treaties are noteworthy as, despite still limited in absolute numbers, represent a steady trend of the last decade. They comprise **14** IIAs (mostly, but not only, investment chapters of FTAs) concluded from 2008 onward. With reference to the analytical IIA practice of the US and Canada (as opposed to that more concise of European States), 10 of these IIAs are here considered as 'embryo North American' investment regimes, while other 4 are full 'North American'. In the 'embryo' cases, the IIAs expand the European single-provision ISDS template by adding several elements typical of the North American practice – nevertheless, containing the ISDS discipline in a single

15 The IIAs considered are only those where the wording is affirmative ('shall apply', 'shall determine by applying', '[shall be] established under', 'unless otherwise agreed upon', 'under the rules of', 'in accordance with', 'with reference to'), either jointly with additional treaty-based indications or as the procedural rules of the *ad hoc* arbitration altogether; IIAs where this is a mere possibility (*e.g.*, when arbitrators 'may refer', 'may take as guidance', or 'may take guidance from' the mentioned set) are not considered.

provision.[16] In the fully 'North American' cases, instead, the dispute settlement template changes entirely, and ISDS becomes a self-standing section made of several provisions (separated from substantive protections). It is not surprising that the complete template switch in this respect begun with two NAFTA parties (Mexico 2008 and Canada 2012) and two States that had already concluded analogous agreements with the US (Chile 2012 and Australia 2015). Like for other aspects, China's treaty practice arguably stems from a will to emulate the practice of the 'other superpower'.

7 *Dispute Settlement Mechanisms*

The attitude of States toward dispute settlement has evolved since the traditional birth year of investment treaties (1959). The goal for capital-exporting States being to offer adequate protection to their own investors abroad (back then, especially, State controlled or participated entities), coupled with the need to facilitate and attract foreign investments for capital-importing States, pushed for the inclusion of international arbitration, as a neutral forum where it is possible to claim for alleged breaches of the substantive protections the BIT offers, relatively quick. Such a development was later unofficially sanctioned in the *Maffezini* award (and the doctrinal approach that followed), with international arbitration recognized as the principal protection an IIA today has to offer to foreign investors.[17]

In their models, the comparators here considered all share one institution and/or set of arbitration rules: ICSID. In the case of the Dutch and French models, ICSID arbitration is actually the only dispute settlement mechanism provided. The German, British, Italian, US, and Canadian models all allow for UNCITRAL arbitration as well. The first two, in addition, feature ICC arbitration. In further addition, Germany is open to arbitration at the LCIA. Only the Italian model, instead, expressly contemplate domestic courts.

Throughout the Chinese investment treaty models and practice, the first and foremost dispute settlement mechanism is the domestic court. All models explicitly and invariably mention domestic courts as first option, and so do the vast majority of China's IIAs: 102 out of 120 (85%). In other 5 treaties (four with developed States, plus Cuba), all concluded after 2000, the domestic courts reference, absent from the ISDS menu, is either implicit or placed somewhere

16 *E.g.*, New Zealand (2008), ASEAN (2009), South Korea (2015).

17 See *Maffezini v. Spain*, fn. 8, at para. 54: '... the Tribunal considers that there are good reasons to conclude that *today* dispute settlement arrangements are inextricably related to the protection of foreign investors ...' [emphasis added].

else.[18] Therefore, in 107 cases out of 120 treaties (89%), domestic courts are envisaged in Chinese IIAs. The 13 exceptions that do not contain a reference to domestic courts are all old-style BITs signed between 1985–1995, where ISDS is restricted to disputes relating to the amount of compensation due to expropriation.

With regard to dispute settlement mechanisms alternative to domestic courts, the most common choice in Chinese practice is ICSID arbitration, featured in 69 cases (57% of 120), 53 of which allowing for arbitration of 'any dispute'. It is noteworthy that ICSID is indicated in 13 BITs where arbitration is limited to expropriatory compensation disputes (all treaties signed between 1988–1999, all with not significant capital-exporters, at the time at least), several of those pre-dating China's accession to ICSID itself (in 1993).

UNCITRAL arbitration is a less common and more recent choice in Chinese practice, being expressly indicated only in 37 IIAs (30% of 120), 32 instances of which since year 2000.

To date, the Chinese investment treaty network does not feature other options.

8 *Fork in the Road and Parallel Proceedings*

European investment treaty models are all silent on the aspect of parallel proceedings, and do not contain any provision specifically addressing the so-called 'fork in the road'.[19] Conversely, the North American models and typical practice require that the investor submit '... written waivers of any right to initiate or continue before any administrative tribunal or court ... any proceeding ...'[20]

With regard to the relationship between court proceedings and arbitration, the Chinese investment treaty practice lacks the otherwise usual relative uniformity it displays in the other aspects of the ISDS clause. China's concern with the fork in the road and the possibility of parallel proceedings seems nonetheless undeniable, as all its models touch upon the issue, and the aspect is

18 *E.g.*, in the 2003 China-Germany BIT, Addendum 6 to Art. 9 provides: 'With respect to investments in [China] an investor of [Germany] may submit a dispute for arbitration under the following conditions only: ... (c) in case the issue has been brought to a Chinese court, it can be withdrawn by the investor according to Chinese law.'

19 Beside the cases of the French and Dutch models, which only provide for ICSID arbitration, the German, British, and Italian are silent as well on the point. The latter case is peculiar, as it expressly features the possibility of resorting to domestic courts in the dispute settlement menu – hence, an argument can be made as of implicit admission of parallel proceeding (domestic courts and international arbitration).

20 See Art. 26.2.b.ii US model (2004), and Art. 26.2.e Canada model (2004).

regulated to at least some extent in 102 IIAs (85% of 120). The more fragmented practice notwithstanding, it is possible to discern a certain trend, next to the general policy choice not favoring parallel proceedings in the vast majority of cases.

Firstly, the 1984 and 1989 templates, which mandate for the finality of the domestic court choice (whenever made by the investor), are followed, either textually or anyway materially, in **45** IIAs (44% of 102) concluded between 1985 and 2009. Notably, all contracting parties to these agreements are neither large States, nor key capital exporters.

The second group of IIA by size is in line with the 1997 model: **32** agreements (31% of 102) establish that 'any choice', once made, is final. Of these, 30 have been concluded after year 2000.

Therefore, while the template wording is not ultimately employed as such is the majority of cases, 75% of the Chinese treaty practice that regulates the relationship between domestic court proceedings and international arbitration is anyway in line with the material choice of a Chinese model BIT. This relative adherence is significant.

Two other groups of treaties are worth mentioning. In the first, the finality of the choice, while not expressly mentioned in the treaty, is anyway inferable through the overall wording of the ISDS clause, as the investor's 'choice' is between options clearly separated by an 'or', or expressly indicated as 'alternative'. This is the case of **11** IIAs, mostly old generation BITs or with States with limited exchange of investment flows.

The second and last group comprises **12** IIAs, all signed after year 2000, where the right to initiate arbitration is expressly subject to withdrawal from any domestic court proceedings possibly already in place or, in another case (Australia 2015), to the waiver of the right to initiate court proceedings.[21]

In general, BITs concluded before year 2000 impose on the investor to make a choice with final character (especially where the forum chosen first are domestic courts). From 2001 on, IIAs often grant the investor the possibility to withdraw the claim from domestic court and initiate arbitration.

21 In this treaty featured as standalone condition. The wording is otherwise also featured in three other recent IIAs, where it is nevertheless materially absorbed by the prior express finality of 'any choice'.

ISDS Clauses in Chinese IIAs – Data Summary

Total Number of Negotiated IIAs: 154[22]

- BITS:[23] 146
- Investment chapters of FTAs and FTA-related investment agreements: 8[24]

of which:

Signed yet not in Force: 20 (18)[25]

- Democratic Republic of the Congo (1997 and 2015),[26] Zambia (1996), Botswana (2000), Brunei (2000),[27] Jordan (2000), Sierra Leone (2001), Kenya (2001), Cote d'Ivoire (2002), Djibouti (2003), Uganda (2004), Benin (2004), Namibia (2005), Guinea (2005), Vanuatu (2006), Seychelles (2007), Bahamas (2009), Chad (2010), Libya (2010), Turkey (2015).

22 Source: author. The data contained in the UNCTAD / Investment Policy Hub database has been carefully scrutinized in order to focus only on the agreements actually creating a foreign investment protection regime. In combination with the data contained on the MOFCOM website, as well as the treaty texts not publicly available yet kindly disclosed by the Ministry to the author for this research, the data shown here is believed to be the most accurate and up to date on the Chinese IIA network.

23 Including the 2012 TIA with Japan and South Korea (which, besides the number of parties, is in essence a BIT).

24 Only those IIAs featuring a self-standing discipline are taken into account: 2006 China-Pakistan FTA, 2008 China-New Zealand FTA, 2009 China-Peru FTA, 2009 China-ASEAN AI, 2012 China-Canada BIT, 2012 China-Chile SAI, 2015 China-South Korea FTA, 2015 China-Australia FTA. Therefore, discarded are the agreements with Greater China regions (Hong Kong, Macao and Taiwan), Switzerland, Iceland, Costa Rica, Singapore, and, in general, all those not providing for a comprehensive investment protection regime with some form of ISDS.

25 The 1997 BIT with DRC and the 2000 BIT with Brunei are not expected to enter in force at any stage.

26 The 1997 China-DRC BIT never entered in force; while this agreement may be considered superseded by the 2015 renegotiation, not even this latter has yet entered in force. In accordance with the methodology used in this research, only the 2015 BIT is taken into account in analyzing the evolution of China's treaty practice.

27 In accordance with the methodology of this research, this agreement, never entered in force and superseded in its standards by the 2009 China-ASEAN Agreement, is not taken into account in the analysis of the evolution of the Chinese practice.

Renegotiated / Substituted and Expressly Terminated: 15

n.	*Party*	*1st IIA*	*Renegotiation*	*Note*
1.	Sweden	1982	2004	Addendum only introducing ISDS
2.	Germany	1983	2003	
3.	France	1984	2007	
4.	Belgium-Luxembourg	1984	2005	
5.	Finland	1984	2004	
6.	Netherlands	1985	2001	
7.	Switzerland	1986	2009	
8.	Russia	1990	2006	
9.	Czech Republic	1991	2005	
10.	Uzbekistan	1992	2011	
11.	Spain	1992	2005	
12.	Portugal	1992	2005	
13.	South Korea	1992	2007	
14.	Indonesia	1994	2009	China-ASEAN IA
15.	Nigeria	1997	2001	1st BIT never in force

Still in Force but Regime Superseded by Subsequent IIA: 12

n.	*Party*	*1st IIA*	*Subsequent IA*	*Note*
1.	Thailand	1985	2009	China-ASEAN IA
2.	Singapore	1985	2009	"
3.	Malaysia	1988	2009	"
4.	New Zealand	1988	2008	China-NZ FTA
5.	Japan	1988	2012	PRC-JP-SK TIA
6.	Pakistan	1989	2006	China-Pakistan FTA
7.	Philippines	1992	2009	China-ASEAN IA
8.	Vietnam	1992	2009	"

(cont.)

n.	*Party*	*1st IIA*	*Subsequent IA*	*Note*
9.	Chile	1994	2012	China-Chile SAI
10.	Peru	1994	2009	China-Peru FTA
11.	Cambodia	1996	2009	China-ASEAN IA
12.	Myanmar	2001	2009	"
*28	Australia	1988	2015	China-Australia FTA
	South Korea	2007	2012	PRC-JP-SK TIA
			2015	China-Korea FTA

In force but Text not Available: 3

- *Moldova (1992), Turkmenistan (1992), Cameroon (1997)*

IIA Text Available, in Force, Not Superseded, and with Access to ISDS: 101

Signed or in Force, Text Available, not Superseded and with Access to ISDS: 120 (122)[29]

NOTE: The analysis on China's IIA practice evolution here offered is based on this number, unless otherwise indicated.

28 In light of the specificities of the investment chapter of the 2015 China-Australia FTA, the 1988 BIT is still the only instrument for investors of either party to challenge expropriation. With regard to the series of agreements with South Korea (1992, 2007, 2012, 2015), the latter three are retained in the analysis of the evolution of China's practice in IIAs, in light of their recent stipulation.

29 The 1997 BIT with DRC and the 2000 BIT with Brunei, not expected to enter in force at any stage in light of the negotiation of a subsequent agreement (2015 China-DRC BIT and 2009 China-ASEAN IA), are excluded from the pool of IIAs of this research.

Of which:

Express ISDS Limitations to Cover IIA Substantive Protections: 60

- None: 60 (50%)
- Compensation due to expropriation only: 58 (48.5%)
  - First 51 BITs (including 1997 BIT with Sudan): no exception
  - First 59 BITs (including 1999 BITs with Bahrain and Qatar): 2 exceptions:
    - South Africa (1997) and Barbados (1998)
  - Restriction entirely halted thereafter
- Exclusion of admission,[30] umbrella clause, 'property and real rights upon the real estates': 1
  - Turkey (2015)
- NT only: 1
  - (*Australia 2015 FTA: temporary limitation ex Art. 9.9.3*)

Express Exclusion of MFN Operation Over ISDS: 13

- Practice started with the 2008 FTA with New Zealand
- Featured in 13 of the 20 IIAs (*i.e.*, 65%) signed between 2008 and 2015
  - No apparent policy discernible from the practice on insertion or exclusion
- Constant practice (100%) in the last 9 IIAs (signed between 2011–2015)

Length of Mandatory Consultations

- 3 months: 3
  - Australia (1988), Finland (2004), Sweden (2004)
- 4 months: 4
  - South Korea (2007), SK-JP (2012), South Korea (2015), Australia (2015)

30 Protection exceptionally agreed upon by China in the treaty, but reserved in case of dispute to evaluation by domestic courts.

- 5 months: **1**
  - Bahrain (1999)
- 6 months: **97** (81%) [*any PRC model*]
  - IIAs spanning 1984–2015
- More than 6 months: **1**
  - India (2006, where after 6 months of substantive consultations, the parties are called to find an agreement on a pre-listed forum before turning to international arbitration)
- 9 months: **2**
  - Colombia (2008), UK (1986, where the 6 months of substantive consultations are followed by 3 months of consultation on the arbitral forum)
- 12 months: **3**
  - Poland (1988), Turkey (1990), Syria (1996)
- No specific term indicated: **9**
  - Bulgaria (1989), Ghana (1989), Hungary (1991), Armenia (1992), Kazakhstan (1992), Kirgizstan (1992), Ukraine (1992), Belarus (1993), Tajikistan (1993)

Mandatory Domestic Proceedings: 1/120

- No: **119**
- Yes: **1**
  - Malta (2009; but only for PRC investment in Malta)

Mandatory Prior Domestic Administrative Review: 60/120

- No: **60** [*1984 and 1989 models*]
  - IIAs between 1985–2001
  - 58 IIAs ISDS limited to compensation due to expropriation
  - 2 IIAs unrestricted access to ISDS
    - Nigeria (2001), Australia (2015)
- Three months maximum: **12**
  - IIAs between 2003–2012
- Four months maximum: **5**
  - South Korea (2007), Mexico (2008), Canada (2012), SK-JP (2012), South Korea (2015)

- Six months maximum: **2**
  - Colombia (2008), Turkey (2015)
- Unlimited: **39** [*1997 model*]
  - IIAs between 1997–2013
- Unclear: **2**
  - Iran (2000), Latvia (2003)

Dispute Settlement Mechanisms

Ad hoc *arbitration treaty-based rules*

- Provision structure (and most or all content) as in *1984 and 1989 models:* **64** (53%)
  - IIAs between 1984–2007
  - Since 2000: 13 out of 59 IIAs (22%)
    - Iran (2000), Jordan (2000), Botswana (2000), Congo (2000), Nigeria (2001), Cyprus (2001), Mozambique (2001), Kenya (2001), Sierra Leone (2001), Cote d'Ivoire (2002), Djibouti (2003), North Korea (2005), Cuba (2007)
  - Mandatory reference to procedural rules: 13/64 (18%)
    - Norway (1984), Denmark (1985), Kuwait (1985), Sri Lanka (1986), Australia (1988), Bulgaria (1989), Papua NG (1991), Greece (1992), UAE (1993), Mauritius (1996), Qatar (1999), Cuba (2007)[31]
      - ICSID: 9
      - UNCITRAL: 6[32]
      - PCA: 1
- None: **42** (35%) [*1997 model*]
  - Since 2000: 33 (out of 59 IIAs concluded)
  - Before 2000: 9
    - UK (1986), Turkey (1990), Morocco (1995), Israel (1995), Lebanon (1996), Saudi Arabia (1996), Gabon (1997), Barbados (1998), Yemen (1998)

---

31 At first glance, the relative (and unprecedented, for China) complexity of Art. 9 of the 2007 Cuba BIT renegotiation makes the provision the very first instance of 'Embryo North American' ISDS China entertained. Nevertheless, it is here considered only as 'Treaty-based *ad hoc* procedure' in light of the imposed choice of procedural rules (even though via the possible alternative between given between UNCITRAL and PCA).

32 A choice among the mandatory procedural rules is given in Kuwait (1985; UNCITRAL or ICSID), UAE (1993; UNCITRAL or ICSID), Cuba (2007; UNCITRAL or PCA).

- Embryo North American model: 10/120 (8.5%)
  - New Zealand (2008), ASEAN (2009), Peru (2009), Chad (2010), DRC (2011), Uzbekistan (2011), SK-JP (2012), Tanzania (2013), South Korea (2015), Turkey (2015)
- North American model: 4/120 (3.5%)
  - Mexico (2008), Canada (2012), Chile (2012), Australia (2015)

Domestic courts: 107/120 (89%)

- Explicit mention: 102/120 [*any PRC model*] (85%)
- Implicit reference: 5
  - Germany (2003), Cuba (2007), New Zealand (2008), Canada (2012), Australia (2015)
- No reference: 13
  - IIAs between 1985–1995
  - All limited ISDS to compensation due to expropriation
  - 10 IIAs with ISDS treaty-based ad hoc procedure
    - Exceptions: UK (1986, UNCITRAL), Israel (1995, ICSID)

ICSID: 69/120 (57.5%)

- Any dispute: 53
- Compensation due to expropriation only: 13
  - All (at the time: 1988–1999) non-significant capital exporters
- NT only: 1
  - Australia (2015)
- FET and expropriation only: 1
  - Sweden (1982/2004)
- Other substantive limitations: 1
  - Turkey (2015)

UNCITRAL: 37/120

- IIAs between 1986–2015
- IIAs since 2000: 33
- Any dispute: 31
- Compensation due to expropriation only: 3
  - UK (1986), Turkey (1990), Lebanon (1996)
- NT only: 1
  - Australia (2015)
- FET and expropriation only: 1
  - Sweden (1982/2004)

- Other substantive limitations: 1
  - Turkey (2015)

•••

Fork in the Road & Parallel Proceedings: 102/120

- None: 18 (15%)

A) Express wording on any choice being 'final': 32 (33)[33] [*1997 model*]
  - Coupled with express waiver of right to initiate court proceedings (F): 3
    - Peru (2009), SK-JP (2012), SK (2015)
  - 30 IIAs after 2000
    - Exceptions: Argentina (1992), Uruguay (1993)

B) Express wording on finality of domestic court choice:[34] 45 (38%) [*1984 and 1989 models*]
  - IIAs between 1985–2009
  - All minor States and/or not significant capital exporters
  - With Malta (2009) the fork in the road is only for the China; Malta requires, instead, prior exhaustion of local remedies

C) ISDS mechanisms expressly listed as 'alternative': 1
  - Trinidad & Tobago (2002)

---

33 Art. 14.5 of the 2009 China-ASEAN IA establishes a dual regime: the investor choice is final for Indonesia, Philippines, Thailand, and Vietnam; for the other ASEAN members, and China, resort to international arbitration is subject to withdrawal of the claim from domestic courts. Because the majority of Parties have opted for the latter solution, the agreement is counted in the F) category.

34 Including 'provided that the investor has not submitted the dispute to a domestic court of that Contracting Party' or equivalent.

D) ISDS mechanisms implicitly alternative ('choice' of the investor between items separated by 'or'): **11**
   - IIAs between 1984–2006
     - Norway (1984), Italy (1984), Poland (1988), Greece (1992), Lithuania (1993), Morocco (1995), Gabon (1997), Yemen (1998), Cote d'Ivoire (2002), Madagascar (2005), India (2006)*

E) Arbitration subject to withdrawing from domestic courts: **12** (10)
     - Iran (2000), Netherlands (2001 only for PRC), Latvia (2004), Finland (2004), Sweden (2004/1982), Czech Republic (2005), Cuba (2007), New Zealand (2008), Mexico (2008), Switzerland (2009), some ASEAN States (2009),[35] Canada (2012; only for PRC).

F) Arbitration subject to waiver of right to initiate court proceedings: 4
   - Standalone requirement: **1**
     - Australia (2015)
   - Preceded by express finality of any choice (A): 3
     - Peru (2009), SK-JP (2012), SK (2015)

35 Within the 2009 China-ASEAN IA, this is the default choice, which applies however only to Brunei, Cambodia, China, Laos, Malaysia, Myanmar and Singapore.

TABLE 17 ISDS in Chinese IIAs[36]

Counterpart	Signed	In force	Cooling off	Limitation	Treaty-based ad-hoc proc.[38]	Treaty ref. to mandatory *ad hoc* arb. Proc. Rules[39]
PRC MODEL	1984		6	comp. exp.	V	–
Norway	1984	1985	6	comp. exp.	V	ICSID
Denmark	1985	1985	6	comp. exp.	V	ICSID
Austria	1985	1986	6	comp. exp.	V	ICSID
Kuwait	1985	1986	6	comp. exp.	V	UNCITRAL or ICSID
Italy	1985	1987	6	comp. exp.	V	–
UK	1986	1986	6+3	comp. exp. Comp. for losses[40]	–	–
Sri Lanka	1986	1987	6	comp. exp.	V	ICSID
Australia[41]	1988	1988	3	comp. exp.	V	ICSID
Poland	1988	1989	12	comp. exp.	V	–
PRC MODEL	1989		6	comp. exp	V	–
Ghana	1989	1990	–	comp. exp.	V	–
Bulgaria	1989	1994	–	comp. exp.	V	UNCITRAL

36 The table takes into account only those IIAs, signed or in force, which have not been superseded by subsequent IIAs and grant access to international arbitration for at least some classes of disputes (as indicated in the appropriate column).

37 Key: **A**) Express wording on any choice being 'final'; **B**) Express wording on finality of domestic court choice (including 'provided that the investor has not submitted the dispute to a domestic court of that Contracting Party' or equivalent); **C**) ISDS mechanisms expressly listed as 'alternative'; **D**) ISDS mechanisms implicitly alternative ('choice' or 'request' of the investor between items separated by 'or'); **E**) Arbitration subject to withdrawing from domestic courts; **F**) The investor is required to waive its right to initiate court proceedings.

38 Considered only when the provision sets a relatively complete set of rules (appointment, procedure, etc.).

I					
ICSID	UNCITRAL	Domestic courts	Prior review of PRC administ. courts (months)	Prior exhaustion of local remedies	Fork in the road & parallel proceedings[37]
–	–	V	–	–	B
–	–	V	–	–	D
–	–	V	–	–	B
–	–	–	–	–	–
–	–	V	–	–	–
–	–	V	–	–	D
–	V	–	–	–	–
–	–	V	–	–	B
V	–	V	–	–	–
–	–	V	–	–	D
–	–	V	–	–	B
–	–	–	–	–	–
–	–	–	–	–	–

39 Considered only when indicated through affirmative wording ('shall apply', 'shall determine by applying', '[shall be] established under', 'unless otherwise agreed upon', 'under the rules of', 'in accordance with', 'with reference to'), either jointly with additional treaty-based indications or as the procedural rules of the ad hoc arbitration altogether; not considered if mere possibility (*e.g.*, when arbitrators 'may refer', 'may take as guidance', or 'may take guidance from' the mentioned set).

40 Art. 7 (ISDS) only refers to 'amount of compensation', without expressly tying it to expropriation. Thus, as 'compensation' is also mentioned in Art. 4 (compensation for losses), consent for this class of disputes is deemed granted.

41 Considered because until the envisaged expansion of the investment regime in the 2015 China-Australia FTA, this is the only ISDS in place.

TABLE 17 ISDS in Chinese IIAs (*cont.*)

Counterpart	Signed	In force	Cooling off	Limitation	Treaty-based ad-hoc proc.	Treaty ref. to mandatory *ad hoc* arb. Proc. Rules
Turkey[42]	1990	1994	12	comp. exp.*[43]	–	–
Hungary	1991	1993	–	comp. exp.	V	–
Papua NG	1991	1993	6	comp. exp.	V	ICSID
Mongolia	1991	1993	6	comp. exp.	V	–
Greece	1992	1993	6	comp. exp.	V	UNCITRAL
Ukraine	1992	1993	–	comp. exp.	V	–
Argentina	1992	1994	6	comp. exp.*[44]	V	–
Kazakhstan	1992	1994	–	comp. exp.	V	–
Kyrgyzstan	1992	1995	–	[*comp. exp.*]*[45]	V	–
Armenia	1992	1995	–	comp. exp.	V	–
Philippines[46]	1992	1995	6	comp. exp.	V	–
Bolivia	1992	1996	6	comp. exp.	V	–
UAE	1993	1994	6	comp. exp.	V	UNCITRAL or ICSID
Tajikistan	1993	1994	–	comp. exp.	V	–
Croatia	1993	1994	6	comp. exp.	V	–
Estonia	1993	1994	6	comp. exp.	V	–
Lithuania	1993	1994	6	comp. exp.	V	–
Belarus	1993	1995	–	comp. exp.	V	–
Albania	1993	1995	6	comp. exp.	V	–
Georgia	1993	1995	6	comp. exp.	V	–

42 Taken into account as the 2015 China-Turkey BIT is not yet in force.

43 In terms of unrestricted access to arbitration, the second sentence of Art. VII.b is unclear: 'other disputes [than expropriation] … can be submitted to an international arbitral tribunal as stated above in accordance with the laws and regulations of the Contracting Party that is a party to the dispute.' The overall consistency, sense and context of the clause seems at odd with unrestricted access.

44 Art. 8.2 limits the investor's claim to amount of expropriation only with regard to China; Argentina accepts 'any disputes'.

I					
ICSID	UNCITRAL	Domestic courts	Prior review of PRC administ. courts (months)	Prior exhaustion of local remedies	Fork in the road & parallel proceedings
V	V	V	–	–	B
–	–	–	–	–	–
–	–	V	–	–	B
–	–	V	–	–	B
–	–	V	–	–	D
–	–	–	–	–	–
–	–	V	–	–	A
–	–	–	–	–	–
–	–	–	–	–	–
–	–	–	–	–	–
–	–	–	–	–	–
–	–	V	–	–	B
–	–	V	–	–	–
–	–	–	–	–	–
–	–	V	–	–	B
–	–	V	–	–	B
V	–	V	–	–	D
–	–	–	–	–	–
–	–	V	–	–	B
–	–	V	–	–	B

45 The Mandarin text here employs a character that *could* be interpreted as expropriation, but is different than that usually employed in this context. It could otherwise be translated as 'collection of funds' or even 'levy'. To solve the doubt, it is necessary to compare the Chinese with the Kirgiz version of the treaty.

46 Taken into account because, having the Philippines opted out the ISDS regime in the 2009 China-ASEAN IA, this is the only regime effectively in place between the parties.

TABLE 17 ISDS in Chinese IIAs (*cont.*)

Counterpart	Signed	In force	Cooling off	Limitation	Treaty-based ad-hoc proc.	Treaty ref. to mandatory *ad hoc* arb. Proc. Rules
Slovenia	1993	1995	6	comp. exp.	V	–
Uruguay	1993	1997	6	comp. exp.	V	–
Azerbaijan	1994	1995	6	comp. exp.	V	–
Egypt	1994	1996	6	comp. exp.	V	–
Jamaica	1994	1996	6	comp. exp.	V	–
Iceland	1994	1997	6	comp. exp.	V	–
Ecuador	1994	1997	6	comp. exp.	V	–
Oman	1995	1995	6	comp. exp.	V	–
Serbia	1995	1996	6	comp. exp.	V	–
Morocco	1995	1999	6	comp. exp.	–	–
Israel	1995	2009	6	comp. exp.	–	–
Bangladesh	1996	1997	6	comp. exp.	V	–
Lebanon	1996	1997	6	comp. exp.	–	–
Mauritius	1996	1997	6	comp. exp.	V	ICSID
Saudi Arabia	1996	1997	6	comp. exp.	–	–
Macedonia	1996	1997	6	comp. exp.	V	–
Zimbabwe	1996	1998	6	comp. exp.	V	–
Syria	1996	2001	12	comp. exp.	V	–
Algeria	1996	2003	6	comp. exp.	V	–
Zambia	1996	–	6	comp. exp.	V	–
PRC MODEL	1997		6	–	–	–
Sudan	1997	1998	6	comp. exp.	V	–
South Africa	1997	1998	6	–	V	–
Gabon	1997	2009	6	comp. exp.	–	–
Barbados	1998	1999	6	–	–	–
Ethiopia	1998	2000	6	comp. exp.	V	–
Cape Verde	1998	2001	6	comp. exp.	V	–

I ICSID	UNCITRAL	Domestic courts	Prior review of PRC administ. courts (months)	Prior exhaustion of local remedies	Fork in the road & parallel proceedings
–	–	V	–	–	B
–	–	V	–	–	A
–	–	V	–	–	B
–	–	V	–	–	B
–	–	V	–	–	B
V	–	V	–	–	B
–	–	V	–	–	B
–	–	V	–	–	B
V	–	V	–	–	B
V	–	V	–	–	D
V	–	–	–	–	–
–	–	V	–	–	B
–	V	V	–	–	B
–	–	V	–	–	B
V	–	V	–	–	-
V	–	V	–	–	B
–	–	V	–	–	B
–	–	V	–	–	B
–	–	V	–	–	B
–	–	V	–	–	B
V	–	V	Unlimited	–	A
–	–	V	–	–	B
–	–	V	Unlimited	–	B
V	–	V	–	–	D
V	V[47]	V	Unlimited	–	B
V	–	V	–	–	B
–	–	V	–	–	B

47 Notwithstanding para. 9, the last sentence of para. 2.b of Art. 10 is unclear as to the extent of the role of the ICSID Secretary General, as appointing authority within the UNCITRAL proceedings.

TABLE 17 ISDS in Chinese IIAs (*cont.*)

Counterpart	Signed	In force	Cooling off	Limitation	Treaty-based ad-hoc proc.	Treaty ref. to mandatory *ad hoc* arb. Proc. Rules
Yemen	1998	2002	6	comp. exp.	–	–
Qatar	1999	2000	6	comp. exp.	V	UNCITRAL
Bahrain	1999	2000	5	comp. exp.	V	–
Iran	2000	2005	6	–*48	V	–
Rep. of Congo	2000	2015	6	–	V	–
Botswana	2000	–	6	–	V	–
Jordan	2000	–	6	–	V	–
Cyprus	2001	2002	6	–	V	–
Mozambique	2001	2002	6	–	V	–
Netherlands	2001	2004	6	–	–	–
Nigeria	2001	2010	6	–	V	–
Sierra Leone	2001	–	6	–	V	–
Kenya	2001	–	6	–	V	–
Trinidad & Tobago	2002	2004	6	–	–	–
Bosnia	2002	2005	6	–	–	–
Cote d'Ivoire	2002	–	6	–	V	–
Guyana	2003	2004	6	–	–	–

48 Art. 12.2 features a potential limitation, as the investor '… may refer the dispute to the competent courts of the host contracting party *or with due regard to its own laws and regulations* to an arbitral tribunal …'

49 The clause at Art. 12.2, where the investor '… may refer the dispute to the competent courts of the host contracting party *or with due regard to its own laws and regulations* to an arbitral tribunal …', seemingly includes the Chinese administrative review procedure.

I					
ICSID	UNCITRAL	Domestic courts	Prior review of PRC administ. courts (months)	Prior exhaustion of local remedies	Fork in the road & parallel proceedings
V	–	V	–	–	D
–	–	V	–	–	B
V	–	V	–	–	B
–	–	V	[Unlimited]*[49]		E
V	–	V	Unlimited	–	B
V	–	V	Unlimited	–	B
V	V	V	Unlimited*[50]	–	B
V	–	V	Unlimited	–	B
V	–	V	Unlimited	–	B
V	V	V	Unlimited	–	E[51]
–	–	V	–	–	B
V	–	V	Unlimited	–	B
V	–	V	Unlimited	–	B
V	V	V	Unlimited	–	C
V	–	V	Unlimited	–	A
V	–	V	Unlimited	–	D
V	–	V	Unlimited	–	B

50 Equivocal format of Art. 10, where the Chinese administrative review procedure is tied only to para. 2.b (*ad hoc* arbitration), while arguably intended for the whole provision.

51 Only with reference to disputes with China; the limitation does not operate in the case of the Netherlands.

TABLE 17 ISDS in Chinese IIAs (*cont.*)

Counterpart	Signed	In force	Cooling off	Limitation	Treaty-based ad-hoc proc.	Treaty ref. to mandatory *ad hoc* arb. Proc. Rules
Germany	2003	2005	6	–	–	–
Djibouti	2003	–	6	–	V	–
Sweden	2004[54]	1982	3	–	–	–
Latvia	2004	2006	6	–	–	–
Tunisia	2004	2006	6	–	–	–
Finland	2004	2006	3	–	–	–
Uganda	2004	–	6	–	–	–
Benin	2004	–	6	–	–	–
North Korea	2005	2005	6	–	V	–
Equatorial Guinea	2005	2006	6	–	–	–
Czech Rep.	2005	2006	6	–	–	–
Madagascar	2005	2007	6	–	–	–
Spain	2005	2008	6	–	–	–
Portugal	2005	2008	6	–	–	–
Belgium-Lux	2005	2009	6	–	–	–
Namibia	2005	–	6	–	–	–
Guinea	2005	–	6	–	–	–
India	2006	2007	6+[57]	–	–	–
Pakistan [FTA]	2006	2007	6	–	–	–
Russia	2006	2009	6	–	–	–

52 Domestic courts are not mentioned in Art. 9 (ISDS), but *Ad.* 6 to Art. 9 refers to the possibility of parallel proceedings in China: 'With respect to investments in the [PRC] an investor … may submit a dispute for arbitration under the following conditions only: … (c) in case the issue has been brought to a Chinese court, it *can* be withdrawn by the investor according to Chinese law.'

53 *Ibid.*

54 In 2004 China and Sweden signed off an amendment to the 1982 BIT consisting of only one provision, introducing Art. 6 *bis* to in the treaty, hence the ISDS mechanism, before entirely absent. The rest of the BIT has been left untouched.

55 The administrative review procedure is referred to in the additional Protocol, where '… China *declares* that such a procedure will take a maximum period of three months.' Remarkable the difference with the

I ICSID	UNCITRAL	Domestic courts	Prior review of PRC administ. courts (months)	Prior exhaustion of local remedies	Fork in the road & parallel proceedings
V	–	implicit[52]	3	–	–[53]
V	–	V	Unlimited	–	B
V	V	V	3	–	E
V	–	V	3*[55]	–	E
V	–	V	3[56]	–	A
V	V	V	3	–	E
V	–	V	Unlimited	–	A
V	V	V	Unlimited	–	A
–	–	V	Unlimited	–	B
V	–	V	Unlimited	–	A
V	V	V	3	–	E
V	–	V	Unlimited	–	D
V	V	V	3	–	A
V	V	V	3	–	A
V	–	V	3	–	A
–	V	V	Unlimited	–	A
V	V	V	Unlimited	–	A
V	V	V	Unlimited	–	D*[58]
V	–	V	Unlimited	–	A
V	V	V	3	–	A

contemporary (and almost identical) BIT with Tunisia, where China '*guarantees*' an otherwise identical sentence.

56 The administrative review procedure is referred to in the additional Protocol, where '... China *guarantees* that such a procedure will take a maximum period of three months.' Remarkable the difference with the BIT with Latvia (*supra*), where China '*declares*' an otherwise identical sentence.

57 The procedure outlined in Art. 9 necessarily requires more than 6 months.

58 Possibly. According to the wording of Art. 9.3, if the disputing parties 'agree' to settle the dispute via 'judicial bodies', then arbitration seems precluded. However unlikely, in this case it seems that a fork in the road is in place. Conversely, if the parties do not agree to submit the dispute to judicial bodies (or conciliation fails) and the investor proceeds to arbitration, no explicit preclusion to subsequently resort to domestic courts is found.

TABLE 17 ISDS in Chinese IIAS (*cont.*)

Counterpart	Signed	In force	Cooling off	Limitation	Treaty-based ad-hoc proc.	Treaty ref. to mandatory *ad hoc* arb. Proc. Rules
Vanuatu	2006	–	6	–	–	–
Cuba	2007*[59]	2007	6	–	V	UNCITRAL or PCA
South Korea	2007	2007	4	–	–	–
France	2007	2010	6	–	–	–
Costa Rica	2007	2016	6	–	–	–
Seychelles	2007	–	6	–	–	–
New Zealand [FTA]	2008	2008	6	MFN on ISDS	Embryo North Am	–
Mexico	2008	2009	6	–	North Am.	–
Colombia	2008	2013	9	–	–	–
Mali	2009	2009	6	–	–	–
Malta	2009	2009	6	–	–	–
ASEAN [CAIA/ FTA]	2009	2010	6	MFN on ISDS & MFN in general*[60]	Embryo North Am	–
Peru [FTA]	2009	2010	6	MFN on ISDS	Embryo North Am	–
Switzerland	2009	2010	6	–	–	–
Bahamas	2009	–	6	–	–	–
Chad	2010	–	6	MFN on ISDS	Embryo North Am	–
Libya	2010	–	6	–	–	–

59 In reality, the Parties in 2007 signed an amendment to the 1995 BIT. The updates brought render, however, the resulting agreement more similar to a renegotiation.

60 Art. 14.1 punctually lists ISDS extent to disputes on NT, FET, expropriation, compensation for losses, transfers and, nominally, MFN; the latter is, however, severely limited (to the point of being potentially nullified) by the very formulation of the clause (Art. 5).

I ICSID	UNCITRAL	Domestic courts	Prior review of PRC administ. courts (months)	Prior exhaustion of local remedies	Fork in the road & parallel proceedings
V	–	V	Unlimited	–	A
–	–	implicit	Unlimited	–	E
V	V	V	4	–	A
V	V	V	Unlimited	–	A
V	–	V	Unlimited	–	A
V	–	V	Unlimited	–	A
V	V	implicit	3	–	E
V	V	V	4	–	E
V	–	V	6	–	A
V	V	V	Unlimited	–	A
V	V	V	Unlimited	V [only for Malta]	B* [for PRC only]
V	V	V	Unlimited	–	E, A*[61]
V	V	V	Unlimited	–	A, F
V	V	V	3	–	E
V	–	V	Unlimited	–	A
V	V	V	Unlimited	–	A
V	V	V	Unlimited	–	A

61 The standard set by Art. 14.5 requires the withdrawal from domestic court proceedings; however, for Indonesia, Philippines, Thailand, and Vietnam the choice is final.

TABLE 17 ISDS in Chinese IIAs (*cont.*)

Counterpart	Signed	In force	Cooling off	Limitation	Treaty-based ad-hoc proc.	Treaty ref. to mandatory *ad hoc* arb. Proc. Rules
Uzbekistan	2011	2011	6	MFN on ISDS	Embryo North Am	–
DR Congo	2011	–	6	MFN on ISDS	Embryo North Am.	–
South Korea & Japan	2012	2014	4	MFN on ISDS	Embryo North Am	–
Canada	2012	2014	6	MFN on ISDS	North Am.	–
Chile [SAI/FTA]	2012	2014	6	MFN on ISDS	North Am.	–
Tanzania	2013	2014	6	MFN on ISDS	Embryo North Am.	–
South Korea [FTA]	2015	2015	4	MFN on ISDS	Embryo North Am.	–
Australia [FTA]	2015	2015	4	NT only,[62] MFN on ISDS	North Am.	–
Turkey	2015	–	6	MFN on ISDS, admission, UC, 'property and real rights upon the real estates'[64]	Embryo North Am.	–

62 According to Art. 9.9.3, China and Australia are expected to expand the scope of ISDS within three years from the entry into force of the agreement.

63 Domestic courts are not explicitly mentioned in Art. 9.11 or 9.12. However, Art. 9.14 refers to the claimant's waiver of any right to '... initiate or continue before any administrative tribunal or court ... with respect to any measure or event alleged to constitute a breach ...' Thus, domestic courts may be assumed not to be precluded with respect to treaty claims.

64 Para. 4, originally formulated, carves out two exclusions from arbitration: '(a) only the disputes arising directly out of investment activities which have obtained necessary permission, if there is any permission

I ICSID	UNCITRAL	Domestic courts	Prior review of PRC administ. courts (months)	Prior exhaustion of local remedies	Fork in the road & parallel proceedings
V	V	V	Unlimited	–	A
V	V	V	Unlimited	–	A
V	V	V	4	–	A, F
V	V	implicit	4	–	E
V	V	V	3	–	A
V	V	V	Unlimited	–	A
V	V	V	4	–	A, F
V	V	implicit[63]	–	–	F
V	V	V	6[65]	–	A

requirement, in conformity with the relevant legislation of the hosting Contracting Party on foreign capital, and that effectively started shall be subject to the jurisdiction ...; (b) the disputes, related to the property and real rights upon the real estates are totally under the jurisdiction of the courts of the hosting Contracting Party and therefore shall not be submitted to jurisdiction ...'

65 The term of six months refers to mandatory negotiations and administrative review procedure jointly: 'If the dispute ... cannot be settled through negotiations or administrative review procedures ... within six (6) months following the date of the written notification ...'

C The Expropriation Clause in Chinese IIAs

1 *Introduction*

The general guarantee of non-expropriation and, in case, of adequate compensation, possibly represents the foundational protection in investment law. All investment treaties feature it, and so do all models. The specific wording employed to phrase the guarantee, or the very title of the relevant provision, say much already about the general approach of a State to foreign investments, as well as public international law (hence, of the State view on the relationship between expropriation and compensation). For instance, while the US model provision is labeled 'expropriation and compensation', echoed by the French 'dispossession and indemnification', the German model pragmatically labels the provision 'compensation in case of expropriation', focusing right away on the interest eventually at stake. The Dutch model, on its account, replaces the term 'expropriation' with the tentatively catch-all locution 'measures depriving ... of investments'. In any case, all templates outline conditions for which an expropriation may be deemed legitimate. The analysis that follows in this Section contrasts these approaches with the choices made by China throughout its models and practice.

From a structural point of view, since its first template, and differently than the other states considered, China seems having clearly listed the conditions under which lawful expropriation may occur:

- public interests;
- under domestic legal procedure;
- without discrimination;
- against compensation.

This list, preceded by the standard chapeau enshrining the general guarantee of non-expropriation, is then followed by a paragraph containing the expropriated assets' evaluation method, and any variation or part of the 'Hull rule' (which has seldom, and only recently, been used as such).

The expropriation clause in China's investment treaty practice is in several respects adherent to the relevant contemporary template text. Marginal variations (*i.e.*, that do not alter the substance of the disposition) are nevertheless not infrequent. Since the turn of the millennium, substantial variations from the model texts have become more common in certain aspects (*e.g.*, method for the calculation of compensation, interest parameters).

The analysis that follows draws from a **pool of 119 Chinese IIAs** out of 120 (the investment chapter of the 2015 China-Australia FTA does not contain for the time being an expropriation clause).

2 *Mention and Definition of 'Indirect Expropriation'*

With a dry standard wording *'Neither party shall expropriate, nationalize, or take other similar measures (hereinafter referred to as 'expropriation') ...'*, no Chinese template expressly mentions – let alone, features a definition of – indirect expropriation. The template choice is coherently followed in 109 IIAs (91% of 119). Since 2008, in connection with the evolution of the Chinese practice (relatively to its 1997 template), China accepted to insert the wording 'indirect expropriation' in 10 IIAs. Since 2011, this has become a constant practice, as the latest 8 IIAs, involving a variety of developed and developing States from different world regions, all mention indirect expropriation and, for the most part, feature a definition of it.

Except for the recent IIA with Turkey, the other 9 cases all define indirect expropriation. In 7 cases, China borrows from the German and British template wording (*'... measure the effects of which would be equivalent to expropriation or nationalization means indirect expropriation'*), while in other 2 (with Korea and Japan) the template seems the US model (where the word 'measure' is replaced with 'action', the rest of the wording being the same). The US influence is evident in the 3 IIAs with American States, plus Korea and Japan, where the text features the US model additional wording *'without formal transfer of same title or outright seizure'*.

All 10 IIAs feature, moreover, certain criteria for the determination of indirect expropriation. The practice is, however, quite varied. The IIAs with Canada (2012) and Chile (2012) transplant the US model text as such.[66] In the other IIAs, the mix of elements varies (see data and tables at the end of this Section). Nonetheless, all require, in a more or less detailed fashion, *i*) an economic impact of the adverse measure on the investment, *ii*) a reasonable weighing of the interference caused by the measure with the investor expectations, and *iii*) an excuse of legitimate regulatory concerns (*e.g.*, protection of public health).

3 *Protection of 'Portfolio Investment'*

The express protection from expropriation of indirect investment through the wording 'portfolio investment', absent from any template here considered, as well as from Chinese model texts, is quite rare in the latter's practice. Scattered throughout a considerable span of time (1985–2009), only 17 IIAs feature the wording, and all agreements are with the UK or former British colonies.

66 Cf., Annex B of the 2004 US model.

4 *Criteria for Lawful Expropriation*

4.1 Rationale of the Expropriation

As mentioned, China, as any State, offers the general guarantee of non-expropriation in its investment treaty models and practice – along a set of cumulative criteria for a legitimate exception to said general rule.

The primary rationale to justify an expropriation is, in the Chinese models, that of 'public interest'. The word 'interest' is that used in Dutch (and French) models and practice (the UK, the US and Italy preferring 'purpose', while Germany employs 'benefit'). The Chinese template choice is ultimately used in 78 IIAs (65% of 119), plus another 6 agreements (5%) where the term is enriched with some additional wording (see data and table below).

In 20 cases (17% of 119), however, China accepted the term 'purpose'; notably, 13 of these cases are IIAs concluded after 2000. Furthermore, a group of 10 IIAs (11% of 119) enrich the terms 'purpose' with additional wording – but all are concluded before 2000 (except for Seychelles 2007). The 2003 renegotiation with Germany resorts to the German model 'benefit', while the remaining 4 IIAs (all with minor capital importers/exporters) employ a variety of related expressions.

4.2 Expropriation's Rule of Law

Despite featured since the 1984 model, the express requirement that the expropriation be carried out 'in accordance with the law' (or any similar wording) is mentioned in 108 of the 119 IIAs under consideration (91%). It seems not possible to discern any specific policy criterion out of the 11 BITs that do not mention the requirement: the agreements span from 1985 to 2009, and are with different States in terms of economy or geography.

All Chinese models use the wording 'under domestic legal procedure'. Such wording is employed *tel quel* in 63 IIAs and, with very minor variations, in 66 cases overall (61% of 108). Related to this practice is the use of the simple 'legal procedure' (without the express mention of 'domestic'), to be found in a group of 13 IIAs that are however either dated or with small economies, or former Soviet States. Another group of 6 recent IIAs (concluded between 2008–2013) add, next to 'domestic legal procedure', the requirement of 'due process' – which possibly represent an evolution of the 1997 model wording. Overall, these groups bring the (relative) adherence to the Chinese model to 85 IIAs (79% of 108). The use of the expression 'domestic legal procedure' as such, indeed, seems declining: while kept in 33 IIAs since 2000 (57% out of 58 concluded), most of these treaties are with small economies (exceptions are the Netherlands 2001, Belgium-Luxembourg 2005, and Spain 2005).

In 7 IIAs (6.5% of 108), all with former British colonies, the expression 'domestic law' is used. The rest of the agreements (16 cases, or 15% of 108) resort for the most part to any equivalent combination or variation of the criteria of 'due process' and 'domestic law'. Combining these last two groups it is possible to conclude that in around 20% of cases the Chinese model pattern is not followed.

4.3 Prohibition of Discrimination

China accepted since its first model BIT that a lawful expropriation had to be carried out 'without discrimination'. Accordingly, the requirement is expressly mentioned (with a wording identical or equivalent to that of the models) in 110 IIAs (92% of 119).

No policy rationale seems to be found in the exclusion of the requirement in 9 IIAs: the agreements span from 1985 to 2003, include G7 economies (like Germany, the UK, and Italy) as well as much smaller and geographically dispersed States. In the case of the 2003 BIT renegotiation with Germany, China adapted to the latter's investment treaty policy (which expressly mentions the discrimination standard only with relation to the FET clause).[67]

5 *Compensation Characteristics*

5.1 Overarching Characterization of Compensation

In their investment treaty templates, some States tie an overarching characterization to the concept of compensation due to expropriation through certain adjectives ('just' for the Netherlands and Italy, 'prompt and adequate' for France, plus the well-known US 'Hull rule' of 'prompt, adequate and effective'). This characterization is of principle, and is other than the wording employed, *e.g.*, for the determination of the *quantum* and the moment of evaluation of the expropriated assets (see *ad hoc* subsections, below).

Differently than the States mentioned, China's templates, in line with the German and British models, do not characterize the term 'compensation' – and this is the case for 98 Chinese IIAs (82% of 119).

67 Such choice however tends to intertwine the expropriation clause (or any other) to the prohibition of discrimination as part of the FET standard: an allegedly discriminatory expropriation could *ipso jure* constitute a breach not only of the relevant standard, but also of the FET clause. The issue is debated in international investment arbitration, and several States have adjusted their investment treaty making policy *i*) narrowing down the wording of the FET clause, and/or *ii*) expressly excluding that a breach of any provision of the BIT automatically determines the breach of the FET standard; see the FET Section, below.

The remaining **21** IIAs resort to a variety of expressions, the most common being 'reasonable' (7 BITs, all before year 2000), 'fair' (5 BITs, all before year 2000), and 'adequate' (3 IIAs, all between 2005–2009). In this group, often the wording echoes that used for the FET standard (*e.g.*, 'fair', 'adequate', 'fair and reasonable', 'fair and equitable').

5.2 Timing of Payment of Compensation

International investment models and practice are nowadays uniform in expressly requiring that compensation due to expropriation shall be paid 'without delay' (only the Italian model partially weakens the locution by adding the adjective 'undue'). This requirement is other from that, possibly also present, mandating compensation to be 'prompt' (see *ad hoc* subsection).

With regard to China, all IIAs adhere to a model BIT choice: **36** follow the quite generous standard (in favor of the State, that is) of the 1984 model ('without unreasonable delay'), **30** the relatively more restrictive standard set in the 1989 model ('without undue delay'), and **53** the standard in accordance with contemporary international practice featured in the 1997 model ('without delay').

It is noteworthy that, while the 1997 model wording is employed over a time span relatively coherent with the model itself (from 1992 to nowadays), the standards of the 1984 and 1989 models have kept being used long after their official 'expiry' (respectively, until 2013 and 2005). No IIA with OECD or major economy, nevertheless, features the 'laxer' 1984 standard.

Exceptionally, in 4 cases (three of which, after 2000), China accepted to further restrict the standard by adding the express term 'prompt'.

5.3 Realizable Compensation

China's first two model BITs do not expressly grant that the compensation shall be 'realizable'. The specific policy choice to remain silent on the point reflected domestic monetary and currency exchange restrictions and controls in place until recently.[68] This template choice is followed in **56** Chinese IIAs, *i.e.*, 47% of the pool of 119 agreements under consideration (including recent agreements – up to 2009 – with relevant partners such as Switzerland, Peru and ASEAN).

With the 1997 model, China adopted the standard used by Germany and the UK (*i.e.*, that compensation shall be 'effectively realizable'). The more modern wording has been employed in **56** IIAs as well – mostly, from year 2000 on, but with several exceptions (15 BITs) since 1985.

68 However, also the Dutch and Italian BIT models do not expressly mention that the compensation be 'realizable'.

Therefore, in 112 IIAs (95% of 119) the agreements are coherent with China's model texts.

Lastly, the US-derived adjective 'fully' realizable has been used in 4 recent IIAs.

5.4 Convertible Compensation

The German, British, French, and US models do not expressly mention that compensation due to expropriation should be made in a 'convertible' currency. The Dutch and Italian model BITs, instead, do. It is plausible that the issue is connected to the 'international standing' of the currency of the State adopting the model (hence, the ease of its convertibility).

Accordingly, the evolution of China's position on the matter, as discernible from the model BITs, follows a 'reverse trend'. Quite possibly due to the past known (and, at the time, severe) convertibility limitations of the Chinese currency, the renminbi, the 1984 and 1989 model BITs expressly guarantee foreign investors that compensation shall be 'convertible' or 'in convertible currency'. In aligning with the British and German contemporary practice, however, the 1997 model eliminates such reference.

In practice, **54** Chinese IIAs (45% of 119), spanning between 1984 and 2013, are in line with the 1997 model, and do not mention the 'convertibility' requirement. In accordance with the first two models, instead, China bound itself to provide 'convertible' compensation in **65** IIAs (55% of 119) ranging from 1985 to 2015.

The actual model wording of 1984 or 1989 is employed in 36 of the 65 IIAs (55%), spanning from 1985 to 2009. Lastly, in 24 other IIAs, concluded for the most part before 1997, the obligation is strengthened as in 'freely convertible currency' (the only two modern agreements in this group are those with South Korea of 2015, and the 2012 TIA with South Korea and Japan).

5.5 Transferable Compensation

Related to concerns not too dissimilar from those just dealt with regard to 'convertibility', and tied to the perceived need especially by developing States to place controls on the financial flows in and out of the country, China explicitly accepted throughout its treaty models and practice that foreign investors' compensation due to expropriation shall be 'freely transferable'. This is the case for **105** IIAs (88% of 119).

With regard to the residual cases:

- **2** BITs simply mention 'transferable' (most notably, the 2001 renegotiation with the Netherlands, where the text follows the Dutch model choice);

- In other 4 BITs (3 of which, with Arab States), the promise is that the compensation will be 'allowed to be repatriated' (which may imply the need of a prior 'request', or anyway an administrative *iter* for expatriation of capital from the host State);
- In the remaining 8 BITs, all with non-key capital exporters and all concluded between 1996–2007 (thus falling in the 'transition period' of modernization of the Chinese investment treaty policy), the transferability requirement is not mentioned altogether.

6 *Evaluation of the Compensation Due to Expropriation*

6.1 Evaluation Method

On the method indicated – if any – in investment treaties to calculate the compensation owned to foreign investors due to expropriation, States have adopted different approaches in their templates over the time – and often departed from that choice in their practice.

China is no exception, as the preferred method to assess compensation is one of the aspects where models underwent subsequent adjustments, and the practice is, nevertheless, quite inconsistent from any template choice.

Firstly, 28 IIAs (24% of 119), all concluded between 1985–2005 with likely importers of Chinese capital, follow China's 1984 template (which in turn replicates Germany's standard) of not expressly indicating any method. Thus, these agreements simply state that compensation should be 'equivalent to the value of the expropriated investment'. Other 4 BITs (3 from the 1980s, plus Algeria 2003) feature an equivalent wording. In addition, 5 BITs (concluded between 1986 and 2003) do not even feature this phrase (most notably, the 2003 renegotiation with Germany). In all, however, the practice of not indicating an evaluation method, which ultimately comprises 37 Chinese BITs (31% of 119), seems ended, as since year 2000 only 7 agreements have adopted this approach, the last being in 2005 (BIT with Madagascar).

Chinese IIAs indicating an evaluation method are, thus, 82 (69% of out of 119 agreements). Three are the principal preferences: 'market value', 'fair market value', and 'generally recognized principles of valuation'.

The first group, relying essentially on the 'market value' parameter, consists of 25 IIAs (30% of 82), 14 of which (spanning from 1993 to 2015) make express, literal, and exclusive reference to the criterion. Six older BITs follow the articulated text of the 1989 Chinese model (the only one expressly mentioning 'market value' – whose determination, 'if not readily ascertainable', is then complemented with several subsidiary parameters). Lastly, with a wording somewhere in between the 1989 and 1997 models, 5 recent agreements subject the assessment of the market value 'in accordance with generally recognized principles of evaluation'.[69]

The second group consists of 20 Chinese IIAs adopting the US (and Italian) template 'fair market value'. The wording as such has been adopted 19 times in agreements concluded between 2001–2015 (33% of the 58 IIAs China concluded since year 2000). In three cases (with non-particularly significant partners), the text expressly mentions that the 'fair market value' has to be determined 'in accordance with generally recognized principles of evaluation'.[70]

Featuring a wording compatible with the concept of market value – even though without making an express reference to it – is, lastly, a third sizeable group of 18 IIAs concluded between 2000–2009 that refer exclusively to 'generally recognized principles of valuation'. Indeed, this is the standalone principle featured in China's 1997 model.

Another relatively sizeable group of 9 IIAs concluded between 1986 and 2007 resort to the French model 'real value' standard. This latter wording seems equivalent to 'actual value' employed in 5 older BITs with former Soviet Republics.

The influence of the British and Dutch model wording, *i.e.*, 'genuine value', is quite limited, as employed in only 3 cases (indeed, with former British colonies).

The residual 2 cases are dated BITs (Sweden 1982 and Argentina 1992) expressing an equivalent choice on the point (to place the investors in the *'same financial position as if the measure had not been taken'*).

In sum, it seems that since 2009 at least China has grown accustomed to the concept of '[fair] market value', even though exceptions are not infrequent even in recent treaties and, in all, a clear policy choice on the point may not yet have been determined.

6.2 *Dies a quo* for the Assessment of the *Quantum*

The moment in time when the evaluation of the expropriated asset is to take place may greatly impact the overall compensation assessment. Treaty models of key States vary on the point. For instance, with a view to better protect the

69 This is the wording adopted in China's 1997 model – without, however, the express reference to '[fair] market value'.

70 *Idem.*

investment's genuine value, the German,[71] British,[72] and Italian[73] models contemplate two alternative moments, *i.e.*, that of the 'actual expropriation' but also that of its 'public knowledge'. The UK model explicitly adds 'whichever is earlier'. The US model refers, instead, only to the moment 'immediately before the expropriation took place'. The French and Dutch models make no express reference to the evaluation moment.

While never silent on the point, China's model BITs evolved significantly. From the somewhat bureaucratic 1984 formulation referring only to the time of 'proclamation' of expropriation, the 1989 template adds the alternative moment of 'public knowledge', and the 1997 text specifies 'whichever is earlier' (meanwhile simplifying the overall phrasing of the clause).

On this aspect too, however, China's treaty practice retains a relatively modest adherence to the letter of its models – albeit remaining coherent with the conceptual substance therein expressed.

Out of the 118 IIAs providing at least one indication,[74] **76** (64%) refer to both expropriation and public knowledge. In this group, 36 agreements (47% of 76) reproduce the 1997 model. Except for the 2012 trilateral agreement with Japan and South Korea, all other IIAs in this group mention both criteria of actual expropriation or public knowledge in various fashions, but do not feature the British-derived locution 'whichever is earlier'. Another group of 13 BITs (17% of 76), 12 of which concluded prior to year 2000, echo more or less closely the 1989 morel wording – which, however, has never been adopted as such.

Reference only to 'expropriation' (hence, not expressly mentioning 'public knowledge') is the choice made in **35** IIAs (30% of 118). Of these, 26 (76% of 34), concluded up to 2001, reproduce the 1984 model wording ('at the time when expropriation is proclaimed'). The similar formulation 'immediately before expropriation' as been used in 5 IIAs, three of which in or after year 2000 (Iran 2000, Cyprus 2001, Peru 2009).

Aside **2** atypical choices not belonging to any category (Argentina 1992 and France 2007), the residual **5** IIAs (4% of 118) refer expressly to 'public knowledge' only. The agreements span through 1984–2001 and, besides those with Kenya and Mozambique (both of 2001), show no geographical or geopolitical connection.

71 '[I]mmediately before the date on which the actual or threatened expropriation … became publicly known'.

72 '[I]mmediately before the expropriation or before the impending expropriation became public knowledge, whichever is the earlier'.

73 '[I]mmediately prior to the moment in which the decision to nationalise or expropriate was announced or made public'.

74 The 1996 BITs with Mauritius does not feature any indication in this respect.

6.3 Interests

Investment treaty models vary with regard to the rate of calculation of interests accrued between the taking of the investment and the payment of compensation. The German model refers to 'usual bank interests', the British and Dutch to 'normal commercial rate' interests, the US model to a 'commercially reasonable rate', the French to the 'appropriate market rate', and the Italian to 'EURIBOR standards'.

Differently than the abovementioned models, in its early template and practice China did not make any reference to interests. Thus, the 1984 model, along with **42** IIAs (36% of 119), 93% of which concluded before year 2000, does not specify anything in this respect.

The remaining 76 IIAs (64% of 119) do mention the word 'interest' and most often specify a rate. The practice is, however, quite varied. The largest subgroup of this lot, with **23** IIAs (30% of 76) spanning through 1996–2012, follows the 1997 model wording, which draws from the British 'normal commercial rate'. Another **27** IIAs (36% of 76) decline the term 'commercial' in an assortment of similar choices: the US-derived 'reasonable commercial' (7), 'commercial' (6), 'current commercial' (6), 'prevailing commercial' (6), 'average commercial' (1), 'usual commercial' (1).

6 IIAs, with no apparent relation among them, simply provide 'interests'.

The remaining **20** IIAs (26% of 76, or 17% of 119) adopt an assortment of choices (including the 1989 model 'normal interest', employed three times) apparently agreed upon *ad hoc*.

With just 69 IIAs out of a total of 119 (thus, 58%) following any template choice, China's treaty practice with regard to the express inclusion of interests – and, in case, the rate –, is one of the least uniform aspect not only with regard to expropriation, but to the Chinese investment treaty practice as a whole.

7 *Right to Review*

In their treaty templates, States answer the question of the right of domestic review of the expropriation measure, and/or the quantification of the related compensation in two fashions. The German,[75] British,[76] American,[77] and

75 'The legality of any such expropriation, nationalization or other measure and the amount of compensation must be subject to review by due process of law.'

76 'The national or company affected shall have a right, under the law of the Contracting Party making the expropriation, to prompt review, by a judicial or other independent authority of that Party, of his or its case and of the valuation of his or its investment in accordance with the principles set out in this paragraph.'

77 'Each Party shall establish or maintain judicial, quasi-judicial, or administrative tribunals or procedures for the purpose of the prompt review and, where warranted, correction of

Italian[78] models expressly ensure that the expropriated investor maintains a right as such. The Dutch and French models, conversely, do not mention this aspect.

China's policy on the matter has evolved since year 2000. The majority of its treaty practice – *i.e.*, 80 IIAs (or 67% of 119) – reflects the choice of any Chinese template, which is not to make express mention of a 'right to review'. In the remaining 39 treaties (33% of 119), of which just over half are concluded after year 2000, an express reference, however, appears.

In general, the most comprehensive form of review granted in investment treaties is that expressly covering the 'case' as a whole as well as the 'amount' established as compensation by the host State. For China, this is the case in **19** IIAs (49% of 39), 14 of which concluded after year 2000. As most of these agreements are with common law jurisdictions, it is perhaps unsurprising that they are influenced by the British model.

In an equivalent fashion, other **6** BITs (spanning through 1985–2004) grant the review of the 'legality' of the expropriatory measure and the 'amount' of compensation. Notably, this is also the case of the 2003 China-Germany BIT.

Another small group of **6** mostly dated agreements is limited to grant an unspecified right to 'review'. Notably, this is the case also with the 2008 China-NZ FTA.

The remaining **8** IIAs offer a variety of solutions (*e.g.*, only 'legality', only 'case', only 'amount') which seem agreed upon *ad hoc*.

Lastly, it may be noted that in 23 cases (59% of 39), the review is assured to be 'prompt' (in the 2006 BIT with India, instead, the clause is phrased only as a 'best effort' commitment). Conversely, 14 IIAs show no qualification of sort in this regard.

Therefore, with respect to the 'right to review' of the expropriatory measure, it can be concluded that while a trend for its inclusion can be discerned, China is not showing yet a clear preference for its formulation.

---

final administrative actions regarding matters covered by this Treaty' (Art. 11 US model BIT, on Transparency).

78 'A national or company of either Contracting Party … shall enjoy the right of a prompt review by the appropriate judicial or administrative authorities of the other Contracting Party, in order to determine whether any such expropriation occurred and, if so, whether expropriation and any compensation thereof conform to the principles of international law, and in order to decide all other relevant matters.'

The Expropriation Clause in Chinese IIAs: Data Summary

Expropriation
119/120 IIAs[79]

Definition of 'Indirect Expropriation'

- No: **109** (91%) [*any PRC model*]
- Yes: 10
  - Colombia (2008), Chad (2010), Uzbekistan (2011), DRC (2011), SK-JP (2012), Canada (2012), Chile (2012), Tanzania (2013), South Korea (2015), Turkey (2015)
  - All between 2008–2015
  - Constant practice since 2011 → 8 IIAs
  - Wording:
    - Basic definition: *Measure the effects of which would be equivalent to expropriation or nationalization means indirect expropriation*: **9/10**
      - Turkey (2015) features only the determination criteria
      - JP-SK (2012) and South Korea (2015) instead of 'measure' use 'action'
    - Additional '... *without formal transfer of title or outright seizure'* (US model): **5/10**
      - Colombia (2008), Canada (2012), Chile (2012), JP-SK (2012), and South Korea (2015)
    - Determination criteria (floor, not ceiling; cf., US model):
      - **Economic** impact / effect / influence & **interference with expectation** clear / (obviously) reasonable / distinguishable / distinct / investment-backed: **10/10**
        - Colombia (2008) features these two only
      - **Discriminatory effect: 4/10**
        - Uzbekistan (2011), DRC (2011), Tanzania (2013), Turkey (2015)
      - **Character** of the measure: **2/10**
        - Canada (2012), Chile (2012)
      - **Character and objectives** / **purpose** of the measure (with or without 'proportionate'): **7/10**
    - **Legitimate regulatory excuse: 10/10**

Express protection of portfolio investment

- No: **102** [*any PRC model*]
- Yes: **17**

79 The China-Australia FTA (2015) does not contain an expropriation provision (yet).

  - IIAs between 1985–2009
  - IIAs since 2000: 6/58
  - UK & former colonies and/or common law countries: 10

Legitimacy Conditions

***Expropriation* rationale: 119/119**

- Public **interest**: 78 (65%) [*any PRC model*]
- Public 'interest+': **6** (5%)
  - Public and social interests: 3
    - Mongolia (1991), Argentina (1992), Albania (1993)
  - Public interest and national security: 2
    - Ghana (1989), Philippines (1992)
  - Public interest, security or national interest: 1
    - Belgium-Luxembourg (2005)
- Public **purpose:** 20 (17%)
  - 13 IIAs after 2000
- Public 'purpose+': **10** (11%)
  - *related to the internal needs of the Party*: 8
    - Denmark (1985), UK (1986), Iceland (1994), Oman (1995), Serbia (1995), Israel (1995), FYROM (1996), Seychelles (2007)
  - *in the national interest*: 1
    - Kuwait (1985)
  - *and security*: 1
    - Poland (1988)
- Public benefit: **2**
    - Kenya (2001), Germany (2003)
- Public purpose, public or social interests: **1**
    - Colombia (2008)
- Purpose authorized by the law: **1**
    - Sri Lanka (1986)
- Purpose which is in the public interest: **1**
    - Jordan (2000)

***Rule of law: 108/119* (*91%*)**

- Domestic legal procedure: **66** (61% of 108, 55% of 119)
  - Wording lit. as [*any PRC model*: 63]
  - IIAs between 1984–2010

  - Since 2000 used 33 times out of 58 IIAs concluded (57%), mostly with non-key capital exporters / developed States
    - Exceptions: Netherlands (2001), Belgium-Lux (2005), Spain (2005)
- Legal procedure: **13**
    - Austria (1985), Denmark (1985), Mongolia (1991), Ukraine (1992), Armenia (1992), Kyrgyzstan (1992), Kazakhstan (1992), Belarus (1993), Tajikistan (1993), Morocco (1995), Yemen (1998), Iran (2000)
  - *'proper legal procedure'* (*'dans le cadre d'une bonne administration de la justice'*): 1
    - Madagascar (2005)
- No express mention: **11**
  - IIAs between 1985–2009
  - No chronological, geographical or developmental pattern
- Domestic law: **7**
    - Kuwait (1985), Sri Lanka (1986), Australia (1988), UAE (1993), Zambia (1996), Trinidad & Tobago (2002), Guyana (2003), New Zealand (2008)
- Domestic legal procedure and due process: **6**
    - Colombia (2008), Chad (2010), DRC (2011), Uzbekistan (2011), Chile (2012), Tanzania (2013)
- Domestic due process of law: **5**
    - Lit.: Czech Rep. (2005), Canada (2012)
    - *Due process of national law*: Poland (1988), Estonia (1993), Mauritius (1996)
- Domestic law and international due process: **3**
    - South Korea (2007), SK-JP (2012), South Korea (2015)
- Due process: **2**
    - Mexico (2008), ASEAN (2009)
- In accordance with the law: **2**
    - Papua NG (1991), India (2006)
- Due process of law: **1**
    - Sweden (1982)
- Due process of law in accordance with domestic law: **1**
    - Greece (1992)
- Domestic laws and regulations: **1**
    - Turkey (2015)
- Lawfully: **1**
    - Seychelles (2007)

Non-Discriminatory Basis: **110/119**

- Express mention: **110** [*wording identical/equivalent to any PRC model*]
- No mention: **9**
  - No chronological, geographical or developmental pattern
    - Italy (1985), Austria (1985), UK (1986), Iceland (1994), Oman (1995), Serbia (1995), Macedonia (1996), Kenya (2001), Germany (2003)

Other

- No: **113**
- '*Contrary to any undertaking which the Contracting Party may have given*': **3**
  - Mauritius (1996), Netherlands (2001), New Zealand (2008)
- The measure is '*clear*': **1**
  - Greece (1992)

Compensation characteristics

Additional Overarching Characterization: **21/119**

- None: **98** [*any PRC model*]
- Reasonable: **7**
  - UK (1984), Australia (1988), Iceland (1994), Oman (1995), Serbia (1995), Israel (1995), FYROM (1997)
- Fair: **5**
  - Greece (1992), Uruguay (1993), Ecuador (1994), Mauritius (1996), Cape Verde (1998)
- Adequate: **3**
  - Madagascar (2005), Malta (2009), ASEAN (2009)
- Fair & reasonable: **2**
  - Kuwait (1985), Philippines (1992)
- Appropriate: **1**
  - Seychelles (2007)
- Fair & equitable: **1**
  - India (2006)
- Reasonable, effective & non-discriminatory: **1**
  - UAE (1993)
- Proper: **1**
  - Lithuania (1993)

Delay of Payment: 119/119

- 'Without delay': **53** [*1997 model*]
  - IIAs spanning from 1992 to 2015
  - Additional '*prompt*': 3
    - Uganda (2004), ASEAN (2009), Turkey (2015)
- 'Without *unreasonable* delay': **36** [*1984 model*]
  - IIAs spanning from 1986 to 2013
    - Not a single OECD member / major capital exporter
- 'Without *undue* delay': **30** [*1989 model*]
  - IIAs spanning from 1984 to 2005
  - Additional '*prompt*': 1
    - Yemen (1998)

Realizable: 62/119

- '*Effectively*' realizable: **56** [*1997 model*]
  - IIAs spanning 1985–2015
  - 15 BITs before 2000
- Not mentioned: **56** [*1984 & 1989 models*]
  - IIAs spanning 1985–2009
- '*Fully*' realizable: **4**
  - Jordan (2000), Finland (2004), Colombia (2008), Mexico (2008),
- Realizable: **1**
  - Norway (1984)
- '*Effective*' as in 'prompt and effective' locution (covering both realizable and convertible): **1**
  - Turkey (2015)

Convertible: 65/199

- Not mentioned: **54** (45% of 119) [*1997 model*]
  - IIAs spanning 1984–2013
- Convertible: **32** (49% of 65) [*1984 model*]
  - IIAs spanning 1985–2009
- Freely convertible currency: **14**
  - IIAs spanning 1993–2011
- Freely convertible: **10**
  - IIAs spanning 1985–2015
- Convertible currency: **5** [*1989 model*]
  - Greece (1992), Morocco (1995), Gabon (1997), Yemen (1998), Belgium-Luxemburg (2005)

- Effectively convertible: 1
    - Mali (2009)
- Freely usable currency: 2
    - ASEAN (2009), Chile (2012)
- '*Effective*' as in 'prompt and effective' locution (covering both realizable and convertible): 1
    - Turkey (2015)

Transferable: 111/119

- '*Freely*': 105 (88% of 119) [*any PRC model*]
  - IIAs spanning 1984–2015
- No mention: 8
  - IIAs spanning 1996–2007
  - Non-key States
    - Zambia (1996), South Africa (1997), Qatar (1999), Kenya (2001), Mozambique (2001), Finland (2004), Russia (2006), Seychelles (2007)
- 'Allowed to be repatriated': 4
    - Kuwait (1985), Slovenia (1993), UAE (1993), Oman (1995)
- Transferable: 2
  - Mauritius (1996), Netherlands (2001)

Compensation Evaluation

Method: 82/119 (69%)

- No indication: 37 (31% of 119)
  - No mention at all: 5
    - Sri Lanka (1986), Poland (1988), Papua NG (1991), Iran (2000), Germany (2003)
  - '*Equivalent to the value of the expropriated investment*': 28 [*1984 model*]
    - IIAs between 1985–2005
    - All capital importers
  - Wording equivalent to [*1984 model*: 4]
    - Norway (1985), Denmark (1985), Italy (1987), Algeria (2003)
  - Since 2000: 7 out of 58 IIAs (12%)
    - Iran (2000), Kenya (2001), Cyprus (2001), Nigeria (2001), Germany (2003), Madagascar (2005), Cuba (1995/2007)
- Market value: 25 (30% of 82)
  - As such: 14

    - IIAs between 1993–2015
    - Since 2000, 4 times out of 58 IIAs: Jordan (2000), Mozambique (2001), Switzerland (2009), Turkey (2015)
  - If market value not 'readily ascertainable', assessment in accordance with '*generally recognized principles of valuation and equitable principles taking into account the capital invested, depreciation, capital already repatriated, replacement value and other relevant factors*': 6 [*1989 model*]
    - Kuwait (1985), Australia (1988), Slovenia (1993), UAE (1993), Oman (1995), Barbados (1998)
  - *Market value in accordance with generally recognized principles of valuation*: 5
    - Guyana (2003), Tunisia (2004), Portugal (2005), Spain (2005), Russia (2006)
- Fair market value: 20
  - IIAs between 2001–2015
  - *In accordance with generally recognized principles of valuation*: 3
    - Finland (2004), Costa Rica (2007), Malta (2009)
  - '*Reasonable market value*': 1
    - Turkey (1990)
- '*Generally recognized principles of valuation*' 17 [*1997 model*]
  - IIAs between 2000–2009
  - Equivalent formulation – '*Generally accepted international methods*': 1
    - Greece (1992)
- Real value: 9
  - As such: 7
    - UK (1986), Kyrgyzstan (1992), Iceland (1994), Uganda (2004), Belgium-Lux (2005), Czech Rep. (2005), Seychelles (2007)
  - Real value '*in normal economic situation*': 2
    - Qatar (1999), France (2007)
- Actual value: 5
  - Ukraine (1992), Kazakhstan (1992), Armenia (1992), Tajikistan (1993), Belarus (1993)
- Genuine value: 3
    - Mauritius (1996), India (2006)
  - Taking into account also 'net asset value' and 'market value': 1
    - Zimbabwe (1996)
- '*Same financial position as if the measure had not been taken*': 2
    - Sweden (1982), Argentina (1992)

Moment: 118/119[80]

[*Two variables possibly referred to: expropriation and/or public knowledge*]

Expropriation and public knowledge: 76/118 (64%)

- *'Immediately before the expropriation is taken or the impending expropriation becomes public knowledge,* ***whichever is earlier****'* [*1997 model*]
  - Same (or quasi-identical)[81] wording: **36**
    - IIAs between 2000–2013: 36 (exception: Israel (1995))
  - Minor variations: **1**
    - Turkey (1990)
- 1997 model without 'whichever is earlier': **4**
    - Djibouti (2003), Guinea (2005), Equatorial Guinea (2005), Madagascar (2005)
- *'Immediately before the proclamation of the decision of expropriation or before the impending expropriation becomes public knowledge'* [*1989 model*]
  - Exact wording: 0
  - Minor variations: **13**
    - IIAs before 2000: 12 (exception: Czech Rep. (2005))
- Immediately before expropriation, without reflecting any change in value due to earlier public knowledge: **7**
    - Jordan (2000), Netherlands (2001), South Korea (2007), Mexico (2008), New Zealand (2008), ASEAN (2009), South Korea (2015)
- The day before expropriation or public knowledge: **7**
    - Armenia (1992), Kazakhstan (1992), Kyrgyzstan (1992), Belarus (1993), Tajikistan (1993), Morocco (1995), Belgium-Lux (2005)
- *'Immediately prior to the point of time when the decision for expropriation was announced or became publicly known'*: **4**
    - Kuwait (1985), UAE (1993), Slovenia (1993), Oman (1995)
- *'At the time when the expropriation was publicly announced or when the expropriation occurred, whichever is the earlier'*: **1**
    - SK-JP (2012)
- *'Before the expropriation was taken or became public knowledge'*: **1**
    - Turkey (2015)

80 The BIT with Mauritius (1996) does not feature this element.

81 Certain English official texts of BITs, especially with French speaking countries (*e.g.*, Sierra Leone, Cote d'Ivoire, Djibouti, Tunisia – but see, also, Bosnia) appear featuring a typo, in that 'whichever' is there replaced with the simple 'which'. 'Is taken' is replaced by 'takes place' in North Korea, 'was taken' in Switzerland, 'took place' in Chile, 'is made' in Botswana, and the verb is missing altogether in Canada. In Seychelles, 'expropriation' is called instead 'deprivation'.

- *'Immediately at the time of the expropriation taken place or known to the public'*: **1**
    - Gabon (1997)
- Prior to expropriation or public knowledge: **1**
    - Yemen (1998)

Expropriation only: 35/118 (30%)
- *'At the time when expropriation is proclaimed'* [*1984 model*]
  - Same wording: **26**
    - IIAs between 1988–2001
  - Expropriation 'declared': **2**
    - Italy (1985), Saudi Arabia (1996)
- Immediately before expropriation: **5**
    - Norway (1984), Sri Lanka (1986), Iran (2000), Cyprus (2001), Peru (2009)
- At the date of expropriation: **1**
    - Ukraine (1992)
- *'As if the expropriation had not taken place'*: **1**
    - Sweden (1982)

Public knowledge only: 5/118 (4%)
- Immediately before public knowledge: **5**
    - Austria (1985), Australia (1988), Lebanon (1996), Mozambique (2001), Kenya (2001)

Others: **2/118**
- Prior to any threat of expropriation: **1**
    - France (2007)
- *'As if the measure had not been taken'*: **1**
    - Argentina (1992)

***Interest rate until date of payment: 76/119* (64%)**
- No mention: **43** (36% of 119) [*1984 model*]
  - IIAs between 1985–2009
  - IIAs before 2000: 39 (93% of 42)
- *Normal commercial:* **23** (30% of 76) [*1997 model*]
  - IIAs between 1996–2012
  - IIAs wording exactly as 1997 model: 19 (all between 2001–2010)
- *Reasonable commercial*: **7**
    - Mexico (2008), Chad (2010), DRC (2011), Chile (2012), SK-JP (2012), Tanzania (2013), South Korea (2015)

- *Commercial*: 6
    - Jordan (2000), Finland (2004), Belgium-Lux (2005), Colombia (2008), Mali (2009), Uzbekistan (2011)
- *Current commercial*: 6
    - Barbados (1998), Congo (2000), Bosnia (2002), Madagascar (2005), Malta (2009), Libya (2010)
- Unqualified 'interests': 6
    - Norway (1984), Turkey (1990), Lithuania (1993), Cyprus (2001), Djibouti (2003), Costa Rica (2007)
- *Prevailing commercial*: 5
    - Netherlands (2001), Germany (2003), Czech Republic (2005), New Zealand (2008), ASEAN (2009)
- *LIBOR*: 4 (5)
    - Current: 2 (3)
        - UAE (1993; only if investment in USD), Oman (1995), Botswana (2000)
    - Six months: 1
        - Russia (2006)
    - Annual: 1
        - FYROM (1997)
- *Normal*: 3 [*1989 model*]
    - UK (1984), Iceland (1994), Serbia (1995)
- *Current*: 3 (2)
    - Kuwait (1985), UAE (1993; if investment not in USD), Slovenia (1993)
- *Provided by law*: 2
    - Israel (1995), Turkey (2015)
- *Appropriate*: 2
    - Denmark (1985), Greece (1992)
- *Usual bank*: 2
    - Lebanon (1996), Kenya (2001)
- *Fair and equitable*: 1
    - India (2006)
- *Average commercial*: 1
    - Guyana (2003)
- *Usual commercial*: 1
    - Zimbabwe (1996)
- *Normal market*: 1
    - Mozambique (2001)
- *Reasonable*: 1
    - Australia (1988)

- *Financial costs*: **1**
  - Iran (2000)
- *Market prevailing*: **1**
  - South Korea (2007)

Right to review

Review: 39/119 (33%)

- No mention: 80 (67%) [*any PRC model*]
  - Out of the 58 IIAs concluded since 2000, the 'right to review' is envisaged 22 times (56% of 39)
- 'Case' and 'amount': **19** (49% of 39)
  - IIAs between 1986–2015
  - IIAs from 2000: 14 (74% of 19)
  - Several common law jurisdictions, but not only
- 'Review': **6**
  - Poland (1988), Bulgaria (1989), Ghana (1989), Philippines (1992), Mozambique (2001), New Zealand (2008)
- 'Legality' and 'amount': **6**
  - Austria (1985), Denmark (1985), Lebanon (1996), Kenya (2001), Germany (2003), Tunisia (2004)
- 'Amount': **2**
  - Turkey (1990), Greece (1992)
- 'Amount', 'case' and 'payment': **2**
  - Portugal (2005), Spain (2005)
- 'Legality': **2**
  - Sri Lanka (1986), UAE (1993)
- 'Case': **1**
  - Norway (1984)
- 'Legality', 'process' and 'amount': **1**
  - Bosnia (2002)

Review characteristics: 39/39

- Prompt: **23** (59%)
  - Only as 'best effort': **1**
    - India (2006)
- None: **14** (36%)
- By due process of law in accordance with domestic legislation: **1**
  - Greece (1992)

TABLE 18 Expropriation characteristics in Chinese IIAs

Counterpart	Signed	In force	Clause format (list)	Ind. Exp. Def.	Rationale
PRC MODEL	1984		Yes (All)	–	public interest
Sweden	1982	1982	no	–	public interest
Norway	1984	1985	Yes (All) (purpose & rule of law same indent)	–	public purpose
Italy	1985	1987	no	–	public interest
Kuwait	1985	1986	no	–	public purpose in the national interest
Denmark	1985	1985	no	–	public purpose (related to Internal needs)
Austria	1985	1986	no	–	public purpose
UK	1986	1986	no	–	public purpose (related to Internal needs)
Sri Lanka	1986	1987	no	–	purpose authorized by law
Australia*	1988	1988	no	–	public purpose
Poland	1988	1989	no	–	public purpose and security
PRC MODEL	1989		Yes (All)	–	public interest
Ghana	1989	1990	Yes (rule of law non-discriminatory & compensation)	–	public interest and national security
Bulgaria	1989	1994	Yes (rule of law non-discriminatory & compensation)	–	public interest

Rule of Law	Non-discrimination	Other	Review (Legality / Amount / Case)	Review Carac.	Portfolio inv.
V (domestic legal procedure)	V	–	–	–	–
V (due process of law)	V	–	–	–	–
V (domestic legal procedure)*	V	–	V (case)	–	–
–	–	–	–	–	–
V (domestic law)	V	–	–	–	V
V (legal procedure)	V	–	V (legality/ amount)	–	V
V (legal procedure)	–	–	V (legality/ amount)	–	–
–	–	–	V (amount/ case)	prompt	V
V (domestic law)	V	–	V (legality)	–	V
V (domestic law)	V	–	–	–	–
V (due process of national law)	V	–	V	–	V
V (domestic legal procedure)	V	–	–	–	
V (domestic legal procedure)	V	–	V	–	–
V (domestic legal procedure)	V	–	V	–	–

TABLE 18 Expropriation characteristics in Chinese IIAs (*cont.*)

Counterpart	Signed	In force	Clause format (list)	Ind. Exp. Def.	Rationale
Turkey*	1990	1994	Yes (purpose rule of law & non-discriminatory) (purpose & rule of law same indent)	–	public purpose
Hungary	1991	1993	Yes (All)	–	public interest
Papua NG	1991	1993	Yes (All) (purpose & rule of law – non-discriminatory & compensation same indent)	–	public purpose
Mongolia	1991	1993	no	–	public and social interests
Bolivia	1992	1996	Yes (All)	–	public interest
Argentina	1992	1994	Yes (All)	–	public and social interests
Ukraine	1992	1993	no	–	public interest
Kazakhstan	1992	1994	no	–	public interest
Armenia	1992	1995	no	–	public interest
Kyrgyzstan	1992	1995	no	–	public interest
Philippines*	1992	1995		–	public interest and national security
Greece	1992	1993	Yes (All) (purpose & rule of law same indent)	–	public interest
Croatia	1993	1994	Yes (All)	–	public interest
Lithuania	1993	1994	Yes (All)	–	public interest
Georgia	1993	1995	Yes (All)	–	public interest
Slovenia	1993	1995	Yes (All)	–	public interest

Rule of Law	Non-discrimination	Other	Review (Legality / Amount / Case)	Review Carac.	Portfolio inv.
V (framework of its laws and regulations)	V	–	V (amount)	–	–
V (domestic legal procedure)	V	–	–	–	–
V (in accordance with the law)	V	–	–	–	–
V (legal procedure)	V	–	–	–	–
V (domestic legal procedure)	V	–	–	–	–
V (domestic legal procedure, due)	V	–	–	–	–
V (legal procedure)	V	–	–	–	–
V (legal procedure)	V	–	–	–	–
V (legal procedure)	V	–	–	–	–
V (legal procedure)	V	–	–	–	–
V (domestic legal procedure)	V	–	V	–	
V (due process of law in accordance with domestic law)	V	"measure is clear"	V (amount)	by due process of law in accordance with domestic legislation	–
V (domestic legal procedure)	V	–	–	–	–
V (domestic legal procedure)	V	–	–	–	–
V (domestic legal procedure)	V	–	–	–	–
V (domestic legal procedure)	V	–	–	–	–

TABLE 18 Expropriation characteristics in Chinese IIAs (*cont.*)

Counterpart	Signed	In force	Clause format (list)	Ind. Exp. Def.	Rationale
Uruguay	1993	1997	Yes (All)	–	public interest
Albania	1993	1995	Yes (All)	–	public and social interests
Estonia	1993	1994	Yes (All)	–	public interest
Tajikistan	1993	1994	no	–	public interest
Belarus	1993	1995	no	–	public interest
UAE	1993	1994	Yes (All)	–	public purpose
Azerbaijan	1994	1995	Yes (All)	–	public interest
Egypt	1994	1996	Yes (All)	–	public interest
Jamaica	1994	1996	Yes (All)	–	public interest
Ecuador	1994	1997	Yes (All)	–	public interest
Iceland	1994	1997	no	–	public purpose (related to Internal needs)
Oman	1995	1995	no	–	public purpose (related to Internal needs)
Serbia	1995	1996	no	–	public purpose (related to Internal needs)
Morocco	1995	1999	Yes (All)	–	public interest
Israel	1995	2009	no	–	public purpose (related to Internal needs)
Zambia	1996	–	Yes (All) (purpose & rule of law same indent)	–	public interest

Rule of Law	Non-discrimination	Other	Review (Legality / Amount / Case)	Review Carac.	Portfolio inv.
V (domestic legal procedure)	V	–	–	–	–
V (domestic legal procedure)	V	–	–	–	–
V (due process of national law)	V	–	–	–	–
V (legal procedure)	V	–	–	–	–
V (legal procedure)	V	–	–	–	–
V (domestic law, relevant)	V	–	V (legality)	prompt	V
V (domestic legal procedure)	V	–	–	–	–
V (domestic legal procedure)	V	–	–	–	–
V (domestic legal procedure)	V	–	–	–	–
V (domestic legal procedure)	V	–	–	–	–
–	–	–	V (amount/case)	prompt	–
–	–	–	–	–	V
–	–	–	–	–	–
V (legal procedure)	V	–	–	–	
–	V	–	V (amount/case)	prompt	V
V (domestic law)	V	–	–	–	–

TABLE 18 Expropriation characteristics in Chinese IIAs (*cont.*)

Counterpart	Signed	In force	Clause format (list)	Ind. Exp. Def.	Rationale
Bangladesh	1996	1997	Yes (All)	–	public interest
Zimbabwe	1996	1998	Yes (All)	–	public interest
Syria	1996	2001	Yes (All)	–	public interest
Algeria	1996	2003	Yes (All)	–	public interest
Saudi Arabia	1996	1997	Yes (All)	–	public interest
Mauritius	1996	1997	Yes (All) (purpose & rule of law same indent)	–	public interest
Lebanon	1996	1997	Yes (All)	–	public interest
Macedonia	1997	1997	no	–	public purpose (related to Internal needs)
Sudan	1997	1998	Yes (All)	–	public interest
Gabon	1997	2009	Yes (All)	–	public interest
PRC MODEL	1997		Yes (All)	–	public interest
South Africa	1997	1998	no	–	public purpose
Ethiopia	1998	2000	Yes (All)	–	public interest
Cape Verde	1998	2001	Yes (All)	–	public interest

Rule of Law	Non-discrimination	Other	Review (Legality / Amount / Case)	Review Carac.	Portfolio inv.
V (domestic legal procedure)	V	–	–	–	–
V (domestic legal procedure)	V	–	–	–	–
V (domestic legal procedure)	V	–	–	–	–
V (domestic legal procedure)	V	–	–	–	–
V (domestic legal procedure, local)	V	–	–	–	–
V (due process of national law)	V	"or contrary to any under-taking"	–	–	V
V (domestic legal procedure)	V	–	V (legality/ amount)	–	V
V (domestic legal procedure)	–	–	–	–	–
V (domestic legal procedure)	V	–	–	–	–
V (domestic legal procedure)	V	–	–	–	–
V (domestic legal procedure)	V	–	–	–	–
V (domestic legal procedure)	V	–	V (amount/case)	prompt	–
V (domestic legal procedure)	V	–	–	–	–
V (domestic legal procedure)	V	–	–	–	–

TABLE 18 Expropriation characteristics in Chinese IIAs (*cont.*)

Counterpart	Signed	In force	Clause format (list)	Ind. Exp. Def.	Rationale
Yemen	1998	2002	Yes (All)	–	public interest
Barbados	1998	1999	Yes (All)	–	public interest
Bahrain	1999	2000	Yes (rule of law non-discriminatory & compensation)	–	public interest
Qatar	1999	2000	Yes (All)	–	public interest
Botswana	2000	–	Yes (All)	–	public interest
Rep. of Congo	2000	2015	Yes (All)	–	public interest
Iran	2000	2005	no	–	public purpose
Jordan	2000	–	Yes (All)	–	purpose which is in the public interest
Sierra Leone	2001	–	Yes (All)	–	public interest
Cyprus	2001	2002	Yes (All)	–	public interest
Netherlands	2001	2004	Yes (All) (purpose & rule of law same indent)	–	public interest
Nigeria	2001	2010	Yes (All)	–	public interest
Mozambique	2001	2002	no	–	public purpose
Kenya	2001	–	no	–	public benefit
Cote d'Ivoire	2002	–	Yes (All)	–	public interest
Trinidad & Tobago	2002	2004	Yes (All)	–	public purpose

Rule of Law	Non-discrimination	Other	Review (Legality / Amount / Case)	Review Carac.	Portfolio inv.
V (legal procedure)	V	–	–	–	–
V (domestic legal procedure)	V	–	V (amount/case)	prompt	V
V (domestic legal procedure)	V	–	–	–	–
V (domestic legal procedure)	V	–	–	–	–
V (domestic legal procedure)	V	–	–	–	–
V (domestic legal procedure)	V	–	–	–	–
V (legal procedure)	V	–	–	–	–
V (domestic legal procedure)	V	–	V (amount/case)	prompt	–
V (domestic legal procedure)	V	–	–	–	–
V (domestic legal procedure)	V	–	–	–	–
V (domestic legal procedure)	V	"or contrary to any under-taking"	–	–	–
V (domestic legal procedure)	V	–	–	–	–
V (domestic legal procedure)	V	–	V	prompt	–
–	–	–	V (legality/ amount)	–	–
V (domestic legal procedure)	V	–	–	–	–
V (domestic law)	V	–	V (amount/case)	prompt	–

TABLE 18 Expropriation characteristics in Chinese IIAs (*cont.*)

Counterpart	Signed	In force	Clause format (list)	Ind. Exp. Def.	Rationale
Bosnia	2002	2005	Yes (All)	–	public interest
Djibouti	2003	–	Yes (All)	–	public interest
Guyana	2003	2004	Yes (All)	–	public purpose
Germany	2003	2005	no	–	public benefit
Uganda	2004	–	no	–	public interest
Benin	2004	–	Yes (All)	–	public interest
Latvia	2004	2006	Yes (All)	–	public interest
Finland	2004	2006	Yes (All)	–	public interest
Tunisia	2004	2006	Yes (All)	–	public interest
Belgium–Lux	2005	2009	Yes (rule of law non-discriminatory & compensation)	–	public interest, security or national interest
Guinea	2005	–	Yes (All)	–	public interest
North Korea	2005	2005	Yes (All)	–	public interest
Equatorial Guinea	2005	2006	Yes (All)	–	public interest
Madagascar	2005	2007	Yes (All) (purpose & rule of law same indent)	–	public interest
Namibia	2005	–	Yes (All)	–	public interest
Czech Rep.	2005	2006	Yes (rule of law non-discriminatory & compensation)	–	public purpose
Portugal	2005	2008	Yes (All)	–	public interest

Rule of Law	Non-discrimination	Other	Review (Legality / Amount / Case)	Review Carac.	Portfolio inv.
V (domestic legal procedure)	V	–	V (legality/amount/process)	prompt	–
V (domestic legal procedure)	V	–	–	–	–
V (domestic law)	V	–	V (amount/case)	prompt	–
–	–	–	V (legality/amount)	–	–
–	V	–	–	–	–
V (domestic legal procedure)	V	–	–	–	–
V (domestic legal procedure)	V	–	–	–	–
V (domestic legal procedure)	V	–	V (amount/case)	prompt	V
V (domestic legal procedure)	V	–	V (legality/amount)	–	–
V (domestic legal procedure)	V	–	–	–	–
V (domestic legal procedure)	V	–	–	–	–
V (domestic legal procedure)	V	–	–	–	–
V (domestic legal procedure)	V	–	–	–	–
V (legal procedure, proper)	V	–	–	–	–
V (domestic legal procedure)	V	–	V (amount/case)	–	–
V (domestic due process of law)	V	–	V (amount/case)	prompt	V
V (domestic legal procedure)	V	–	V (amount/case/payment)	prompt	–

TABLE 18 Expropriation characteristics in Chinese IIAs (*cont.*)

Counterpart	Signed	In force	Clause format (list)	Ind. Exp. Def.	Rationale
Spain	2005	2008	Yes (All)	–	public interest
Vanuatu	2006	–	Yes (All)	–	public interest
Pakistan [FTA]	2006	2007	Yes (All)	–	public interest
Russia	2006	2009	Yes (rule of law non-discriminatory & compensation)	–	public interest
India	2006	2007	no	–	public purpose
France	2007	2010	no	–	public interest
Cuba	2007	2007	Yes (All)	–	public interest
Costa Rica	2007	2016	Yes (All)	–	public interest
South Korea	2007	2007	Yes (All)	–	public interest
Seychelles	2007	–	no	–	public purpose (related to Internal needs)
Colombia	2008	2013	Yes (All)	V	public purpose, public or social interests
New Zealand [FTA]	2008	2008	Yes (All)	–	public purpose
Mexico	2008	2009	Yes (All)	–	public purpose
Malta	2009	2009	Yes (All)	–	public interest
Bahamas	2009	–	Yes (All)	–	public interest
Mali	2009	2009	Yes (All)	–	public interest

Rule of Law	Non-discrimination	Other	Review (Legality / Amount / Case)	Review Carac.	Portfolio inv.
V (domestic legal procedure)	V	–	V (amount/case/ payment)	prompt	–
V (domestic legal procedure)	V	–	–	–	–
V (domestic legal procedure)	V	–	–	–	–
V (domestic legal procedure)	V	–	–	–	–
V (in accordance with the law)	V	–	V (amount/ case)	prompt (best effort)	V
–	V	–	–	–	–
V (domestic legal procedure)	V	–	–	–	–
V (domestic legal procedure)	V	–	–	–	–
V (domestic law & int'l due process)	V	–	V (amount/case)	prompt	–
V (lawfully)	V	–	V (amount/case)	prompt	V
V (domestic legal procedure & due process)	V	–	–	–	–
V (domestic law)	V	"or contrary to any under-taking"	V	prompt	–
V (due process)	V	–	V (amount/case)	prompt	–
V (domestic legal procedure)	V	–	–	–	V
V (domestic legal procedure)	V	–	–	–	–
V (domestic legal procedure)	V	–	–	–	–

TABLE 18 Expropriation characteristics in Chinese IIAs (*cont.*)

Counterpart	Signed	In force	Clause format (list)	Ind. Exp. Def.	Rationale
Peru [FTA]	2009	2010	Yes (All)	–	public interest
ASEAN [CAIA/FTA]	2009	2010	Yes (All)	–	public purpose
Switzerland	2009	2010	no	–	public interest
Chad	2010	–	Yes (All)	V	public interest
Libya	2010	–	Yes (All)	–	public interest
Uzbekistan	2011	2011	Yes (All)	V	public interest
DR Congo	2011	–	Yes (All)	V	public interest
Chile [SAI/FTA]	2012	2014	Yes (All)	V	public interest
Canada	2012	2014	no	V	public purpose
South Korea & Japan	2012	2014	Yes (All)	V	public purpose
Tanzania	2013	2014	Yes (All)	V	public interest
Turkey	2015	–	no	V	public purpose
South Korea [FTA]	2015	2015	Yes (All)	V	public purpose
Australia [FTA]	2015	2015			

Rule of Law	Non-discrimination	Other	Review (Legality / Amount / Case)	Review Carac.	Portfolio inv.
V (domestic legal procedure)	V	–	–	–	–
V (due process)	V	–	–	–	–
–	V	–	V (amount/case)	prompt	V
V (domestic legal procedure & due process)	V	–	–	–	–
V (domestic legal procedure)	V	–	–	–	–
V (domestic legal procedure & due process)	V	–	–	–	–
V (domestic legal procedure & due process, relevant)	V	–	–	–	–
V (domestic legal procedure & due process)	V	–	–	–	–
V (domestic due process of law)	V	–	V (amount/case)	prompt	–
V (domestic law & int'l due process)	V	–	V (amount/case)	prompt	–
V (domestic legal procedure & due process, relevant)	V	–	–	–	–
V (domestic law & due process)	V	–	–	–	–
V (domestic law & int'l due process)	V	–	V (amount/case)	prompt	–

TABLE 19 Compensation due to expropriation: characteristics and criteria

Counterpart	Signed	In force	Overarch. characterization	Payment delay	Realizable
Sweden	1982	1982	–	model 1984	–
PRC MODEL	1984		–	unreasonable delay	–
Norway	1984	1985	–	model 1989	V
Italy	1985	1987	–	model 1989	–
Austria	1985	1986	–	model 1989	–
Kuwait	1985	1986	fair and reasonable	model 1989	–
Denmark	1985	1985	–	model 1989	V (effectively)
Sri Lanka	1986	1987	–	model 1984	V (effectively)
UK	1986	1986	reasonable	model 1989	V (effectively)
Poland	1988	1989	–	model 1984	–
Australia*	1988	1988	reasonable	model 1989	–
Ghana	1989	1990	–	model 1984	–
Bulgaria	1989	1994	–	model 1984	–

Convertible	Transferable	Eval. method	Eval. moment	Int. Rate	Inter. rate period
V (convertible)	freely	same financial position	as if measure had not been taken	–	–
V (convertible)	freely	NO / equivalent to the value of the expropriated investment	at the time when expropriation proclaimed	–	–
–	freely	model 1984, similar	expropriation, immediately before	unqualified 'interests'	until date of payment
V (convertible)	freely	model 1984, similar	model 1984, similar	–	–
V (convertible)	freely	model 1984, exact	public knowledge, immediately before	–	–
V (freely convertible)	allowed to be repatriated	market value, model 1989	expropriation or public knowledge, immediately prior to point of time	current %	until date of payment
–	freely	model 1984, similar	model 1989, similar	appropriate %	until date of payment
V (freely convertible)	freely	NO	expropriation, immediately before	–	–
–	freely	real value	model 1989, similar	normal %	until date of payment
V (convertible)	freely	NO	model 1984, exact	–	–
V (freely convertible)	freely	market value, model 1989	public knowledge, immediately before	reasonable %	from expropriation until date of payment
V (convertible)	freely	model 1984, exact	model 1984, exact	–	–
V (convertible)	freely	model 1984, exact	model 1984, exact	–	–

TABLE 19 Compensation due to expropriation: characteristics and criteria (*cont.*)

Counterpart	Signed	In force	Overarch. characterization	Payment delay	Realizable
PRC MODEL	1989		–	undue delay	–
*Turkey**	1990	1994	–	model 1989	V (effectively)
Hungary	1991	1993	–	model 1984	–
Mongolia	1991	1993	–	model 1984	–
Papua NG	1991	1993	–	model 1989	–
Argentina	1992	1994	–	model 1997	V (effectively)
Kyrgyzstan	1992	1995	–	model 1989	–
*Philippines**	1992	1995	fair and reasonable	model 1984	–
Bolivia	1992	1996	–	model 1984	–
Kazakhstan	1992	1994	–	model 1989	–
Armenia	1992	1995	–	model 1989	–
Ukraine	1992	1993	–	model 1989	–
Greece	1992	1993	fair	model 1997	–

Convertible	Transferable	Eval. method	Eval. moment	Int. Rate	Inter. rate period
V (*i.e.* convertible currency)	freely	MV / generally recognised princ. of valuation & equitable principles	immediately before expropriation decision proclaimed or before public knowledge	normal %	from expropriation until date of payment
–	freely	market value, reasonable	model 1997, similar	unqualified 'interests'	until date of payment
V (convertible)	freely	model 1984, exact	model 1984, exact	–	–
V (convertible)	freely	model 1984, exact	model 1984, exact	–	–
V (freely convertible)	freely	NO	model 1989, similar	–	–
–	freely	same financial position	as if measure had not been taken	–	–
V (convertible)	freely	real value	expropriation or public knowledge, day before	–	–
V (convertible)	freely	model 1984, exact	model 1984, exact	–	–
V (convertible)	freely	model 1984, exact	model 1984, exact	–	–
V (freely convertible)	freely	actual value	expropriation or public knowledge, day before	–	–
V (freely convertible)	freely	actual value	expropriation or public knowledge, day before	–	–
V (freely convertible)	freely	actual value	model 1984, similar	–	–
V (*i.e.* convertible currency)	freely	generally recognised principles of valuation*	model 1989, similar	appropriate %	until date of payment

TABLE 19 Compensation due to expropriation: characteristics and criteria (*cont.*)

Counterpart	Signed	In force	Overarch. characterization	Payment delay	Realizable
Belarus	1993	1995	–	model 1989	–
Uruguay	1993	1997	fair	model 1984	–
Albania	1993	1995	–	model 1984	–
Georgia	1993	1995	–	model 1984	–
Croatia	1993	1994	–	model 1984	–
Tajikistan	1993	1994	–	model 1989	–
Estonia	1993	1994	–	model 1984	–
Lithuania	1993	1994	proper	model 1984	–
UAE	1993	1994	reasonable, effective, non discriminatory	model 1989	–
Slovenia	1993	1995	–	model 1989	–
Ecuador	1994	1997	fair	model 1989	–
Azerbaijan	1994	1995	–	model 1984	–
Egypt	1994	1996	–	model 1984	–
Jamaica	1994	1996	–	model 1984	–

Convertible	Transferable	Eval. method	Eval. moment	Int. Rate	Inter. rate period
V (convertible)	freely	actual value	expropriation or public knowledge, day before	–	–
V (convertible)	freely	model 1984, exact	model 1984, exact	–	–
V (convertible)	freely	model 1984, exact	model 1984, exact	–	–
V (convertible)	freely	model 1984, exact	model 1984, exact	–	–
V (convertible)	freely	market value	model 1984, exact	–	–
V (freely convertible)	freely	actual value	expropriation or public knowledge, day before	–	–
V (*i.e.*, freely convertible currency)	freely	model 1984, exact	model 1984, exact	–	–
V (convertible)	freely	model 1984, exact	model 1989, similar	unqualified 'interests'	from expropriation
V (*i.e.*, freely convertible currency)	allowed to be repatriated	market value, model 1989	expropriation or public knowledge, immediately prior to point of time	current % / LIBOR if USD	from expropriation until date of payment
V (*i.e.*, freely convertible currency)	allowed to be repatriated	market value, model 1989	expropriation or public knowledge, immediately prior to point of time	current %	from expropriation until date of payment
V (convertible)	freely	model 1984, exact	model 1984, exact	–	–
V (convertible)	freely	model 1984, exact	model 1984, exact	–	–
V (convertible)	freely	model 1984, exact	model 1984, exact	–	–
V (convertible)	freely	model 1984, exact	model 1984, exact	–	–

TABLE 19 Compensation due to expropriation: characteristics and criteria (*cont.*)

Counterpart	Signed	In force	Overarch. characterization	Payment delay	Realizable
Iceland	1994	1997	reasonable	model 1989	V (effectively)
Morocco	1995	1999	–	model 1989	–
Oman	1995	1995	reasonable	model 1989	–
Serbia	1995	1996	reasonable	model 1989	V (effectively)
Israel	1995	2009	reasonable	model 1989	V (effectively)
Saudi Arabia	1996	1997	–	model 1989	–
Algeria	1996	2003	–	model 1984	–
Bangladesh	1996	1997	–	model 1984	–
Syria	1996	2001	–	model 1984	–
Zambia	1996	-	–	model 1997	V (effectively)
Zimbabwe	1996	1998	–	model 1997	V (effectively)
Lebanon	1996	1997	–	model 1997	V (effectively)
Mauritius	1996	1997	fair	model 1997	V (effectively)
Sudan	1997	1998	–	model 1984	–

Convertible	Transferable	Eval. method	Eval. moment	Int. Rate	Inter. rate period
–	freely	real value	model 1989, similar	normal %	until date of payment
V (*i.e.* convertible currency)	freely	market value	expropriation or public knowledge, day before	–	–
V (*i.e.*, freely convertible currency)	allowed to be repatriated	market value, model 1989	expropriation or public knowledge, immediately prior to point of time	LIBOR current	until date of payment
–	freely	market value	model 1989, similar	normal %	until date of payment
–	freely	market value	model 1997, exact	provided by law	until date of payment
–	freely	model 1984, exact	model 1984, similar	–	–
V (convertible)	freely	model 1984, similar	model 1984, exact	–	–
V (convertible)	freely	model 1984, exact	model 1984, exact	–	–
V (convertible)	freely	model 1984, exact	model 1984, exact	–	–
–	–	market value	model 1989, similar	normal commercial %	until date of payment
–	freely	genuine value (plus net asset value and market value)	model 1989, similar	usual commercial	until date of payment
–	freely	market value	public knowledge, immediately before	usual bank	until date of payment
V (*i.e.*, freely convertible currency)	V	genuine value	–	normal commercial %	until date of payment
V (convertible)	freely	model 1984, exact	model 1984, exact	–	–

TABLE 19 Compensation due to expropriation: characteristics and criteria (*cont.*)

Counterpart	Signed	In force	Overarch. characterization	Payment delay	Realizable
Gabon	1997	2009	–	model 1989	–
PRC MODEL	1997		–	delay	V (effectively)
FYROM	1997	1997	reasonable	model 1989	V (effectively)
South Africa	1997	1998	–	model 1997	V (effectively)
Cape Verde	1998	2001	fair	model 1984	–
Ethiopia	1998	2000	–	model 1984	–
Yemen	1998	2002	–	model 1989 (+ prompt)	–
Barbados	1998	1999	–	model 1984	V (effectively)
Qatar	1999	2000	–	model 1997	–
Bahrain	1999	2000	–	model 1984	–
Iran	2000	2005	–	model 1997	V (effectively)

Convertible	Transferable	Eval. method	Eval. moment	Int. Rate	Inter. rate period
V (*i.e.* convertible currency)	freely	model 1984, exact	expropriation or public knowledge, immediately at the time	–	–
–	freely	generally recognised principles of valuation	immediately before expropriation taken or public knowledge, whichever earlier	normal commercial %	from expropriation until date of payment
–	freely	market value	model 1989, similar	LIBOR annual	from expropriation until date of payment
–	–	market value	model 1989, similar	normal commercial %	until date of payment
V (convertible)	freely	model 1984, exact	model 1984, exact	–	–
V (convertible)	freely	model 1984, exact	model 1984, exact	–	–
V (*i.e.* convertible currency)	freely	market value	expropriation or public knowledge, prior to	–	–
–	freely	market value, model 1989	model 1989, similar	current commercial %	from expropriation until date of payment
–	–	real value (normal economic situation)	model 1984, exact	–	–
V (convertible)	freely	market value	model 1984, exact	–	–
–	freely	NO	expropriation, immediately before	financial costs*	from due date until payment

TABLE 19 Compensation due to expropriation: characteristics and criteria (*cont.*)

Counterpart	Signed	In force	Overarch. characterization	Payment delay	Realizable
Rep. of Congo	2000	2015	–	model 1997	V (effectively)
Botswana	2000	–	–	model 1997	V (effectively)
Jordan	2000	–	–	model 1997	V (fully)
Sierra Leone	2001	–	–	model 1997	V (effectively)
Cyprus	2001	2002	–	model 1984	–
Netherlands	2001	2004	–	model 1997	–
Kenya	2001	–	–	model 1997	–
Mozambique	2001	2002	–	model 1997	V (effectively)
Nigeria	2001	2010	–	model 1984	–
Cote d'Ivoire	2002	–	–	model 1997	V (effectively)

Convertible	Transferable	Eval. method	Eval. moment	Int. Rate	Inter. rate period
–	freely	model 1997, exact	model 1997, exact	current commercial %	from expropriation until date of payment
–	freely	model 1997, exact	model 1997, exact	LIBOR current %	from expropriation until date of payment
–	freely	market value	expropriation and no change for earlier public knowledge, immediately before	commercial %	from expropriation until date of payment
–	freely	model 1997, exact	model 1997, exact	normal commercial %	from expropriation until date of payment
V (convertible)	freely	model 1984, exact	expropriation, immediately before	unqualified 'interests'	from expropriation until date of payment
V (*i.e.*, freely convertible currency)	V	fair market value	expropriation and no change for earlier public knowledge, immediately before	prevailing commercial %	from expropriation until date of payment
–	–	model 1984, exact	public knowledge, immediately before	usual bank %	until date of payment
–	–	market value	public knowledge, immediately before	normal market %	until date of payment
V (convertible)	freely	model 1984, exact	model 1984, exact	normal commercial %	until date of payment
–	freely	model 1997, exact	model 1997, exact	normal commercial %	from expropriation until date of payment

TABLE 19 Compensation due to expropriation: characteristics and criteria (*cont.*)

Counterpart	Signed	In force	Overarch. characterization	Payment delay	Realizable
Bosnia	2002	2005	–	model 1997	V (effectively)
Trinidad & Tobago	2002	2004	–	model 1997	V (effectively)
Guyana	2003	2004	–	model 1997	V (effectively)
Djibouti	2003	–	–	model 1997	V (effectively)
Germany	2003	2005	–	model 1997	V (effectively)
Tunisia	2004	2006	–	model 1997	V (effectively)
Finland	2004	2006	–	model 1997	V (fully)
Uganda	2004	–	–	model 1997 (+ prompt)	V (effectively)

Convertible	Transferable	Eval. method	Eval. moment	Int. Rate	Inter. rate period
–	freely	model 1997, exact	model 1997, exact	current commercial %	from expropriation until date of payment
–	freely	model 1997, exact	model 1997, exact	normal commercial %	from expropriation until date of payment
–	freely	market value in accordance with generally recognised principles of valuation	model 1997, exact	average commercial %	from expropriation until date of payment
–	freely	model 1997, exact	model 1997, no 'whichever is earlier'	unqualified 'interests'	from expropriation until date of payment
–	freely	NO	model 1997, exact	prevailing commercial %	until date of payment
–	freely	market value in accordance with generally recognised principles of valuation	model 1997, exact	–	–
V (*i.e.*, freely convertible currency)	–	fair market value in accordance with generally recognised principles of valuation	model 1997, exact	commercial %	from expropriation until date of payment
–	freely	real value	model 1997, exact	normal commercial %	from expropriation until date of payment

TABLE 19 Compensation due to expropriation: characteristics and criteria (*cont.*)

Counterpart	Signed	In force	Overarch. characterization	Payment delay	Realizable
Latvia	2004	2006	–	model 1997	V (effectively)
Benin	2004	–	–	model 1997	V (effectively)
Madagascar	2005	2007	adequate	model 1989	–
Namibia	2005	–	–	model 1997	V (effectively)
North Korea	2005	2005	–	model 1997	V (effectively)
Portugal	2005	2008	–	model 1997	V (effectively)
Spain	2005	2008	–	model 1997	V (effectively)
Guinea	2005	–	–	model 1997	V (effectively)

Convertible	Transferable	Eval. method	Eval. moment	Int. Rate	Inter. rate period
–	freely	model 1997, exact	model 1997, exact	normal commercial %	from expropriation until date of payment
–	freely	model 1997, exact	model 1997, exact	normal commercial %	from expropriation until date of payment
–	freely	model 1984, exact	model 1997, no 'whichever is earlier'	current commercial %	from expropriation until date of payment
–	freely	model 1997, exact	model 1997, exact	normal commercial %	from expropriation until date of payment
–	freely	model 1997, exact	model 1997, exact	normal commercial %	from expropriation until date of payment
–	freely	market value in accordance with generally recognised principles of valuation	model 1997, exact	normal commercial %	from expropriation until date of payment
–	freely	market value in accordance with generally recognised principles of valuation	model 1997, exact	normal commercial %	from expropriation until date of payment
–	freely	model 1997, exact	model 1997, no 'whichever is earlier'	normal commercial %	from expropriation until date of payment

TABLE 19 Compensation due to expropriation: characteristics and criteria (*cont.*)

Counterpart	Signed	In force	Overarch. characterization	Payment delay	Realizable
Equatorial Guinea	2005	2006	–	model 1997	V (effectively)
Belgium-Lux	2005	2009	–	model 1989	–
Czech Rep.	2005	2006	–	model 1989	V (effectively)
Russia	2006	2009	–	model 1997	–
Vanuatu	2006	–	–	model 1997	V (effectively)
Pakistan [FTA]	2006	2007	–	model 1997	V (effectively)
India	2006	2007	fair and equitable	model 1984	V (effectively)
Cuba	2007	2007	–	model 1984	–

Convertible	Transferable	Eval. method	Eval. moment	Int. Rate	Inter. rate period
–	freely	model 1997, exact	model 1997, no 'whichever is earlier'	normal commercial %	from expropriation until date of payment
V (*i.e.* convertible currency)	freely	real value	expropriation or public knowledge, day before	commercial %	from expropriation until date of payment
V (*i.e.*, freely convertible currency)	freely	real value	model 1989, similar	prevailing commercial	until date of payment
V (*i.e.*, freely convertible currency)	–	market value in accordance with generally recognised principles of valuation	model 1997, exact	LIBOR 6 months	from expropriation until date of payment
–	freely	model 1997, exact	model 1997, exact	normal commercial %	from expropriation until date of payment
–	freely	model 1997, exact	model 1997, exact	normal commercial %	from expropriation until date of payment
–	freely	genuine value	model 1997, exact	fair and equitable %	until date of payment
V (convertible)	freely	model 1984, exact	model 1984, exact	–	–

TABLE 19 Compensation due to expropriation: characteristics and criteria (*cont.*)

Counterpart	Signed	In force	Overarch. characterization	Payment delay	Realizable
Costa Rica	2007	2016	–	model 1997	V (effectively)
South Korea	2007	2007	–	model 1997	V (effectively)
Seychelles	2007	–	appropriate	model 1984	V (effectively)
France	2007	2010	–	model 1997	V (effectively)
Mexico	2008	2009	–	model 1997	V (fully)
New Zealand [FTA]	2008	2008	–	model 1997	V (effectively)
Colombia	2008	2013	–	model 1997	V (fully)
Peru [FTA]	2009	2010	–	model 1984	–
Bahamas	2009	–	–	model 1997	V (effectively)

Convertible	Transferable	Eval. method	Eval. moment	Int. Rate	Inter. rate period
–	freely	fair market value in accordance with generally recognised principles of valuation	model 1997, exact	unqualified 'interests'	from expropriation until date of payment
V (*i.e.*, freely convertible currency)	freely	fair market value	expropriation and no change for earlier public knowledge, immediately before	market prevailing %	from expropriation until date of payment
–	–	real value	model 1997, exact	normal commercial %	until date of payment
–	freely	real value (normal economic situation)	expropriation, prior to any threat of	normal commercial %	until date of payment
–	freely	fair market value	expropriation and no change for earlier public knowledge, immediately before	reasonable commercial %	from expropriation until date of payment
V (*i.e.*, freely convertible currency)	freely	fair market value	expropriation and no change for earlier public knowledge, immediately before	prevailing commercial %	from expropriation until date of payment
V (*i.e.*, freely convertible currency)	freely	fair market value	model 1997, exact	commercial %	until date of payment
V (convertible)	freely	fair market value	expropriation, immediately before	–	–
–	freely	model 1997, exact	model 1997, exact	normal commercial %	**from expropriation until date of payment**

TABLE 19 Compensation due to expropriation: characteristics and criteria (*cont.*)

Counterpart	Signed	In force	Overarch. characterization	Payment delay	Realizable
Malta	2009	2009	adequate	model 1997	V (effectively)
Mali	2009	2009	–	model 1997	–
Switzerland	2009	2010	–	model 1997	–
ASEAN [CAIA/FTA]	2009	2010	adequate	model 1997 (+ prompt)	–
Libya	2010	–	–	model 1997	V (effectively)
Chad	2010	–	–	model 1984	V (effectively)
Uzbekistan	2011	2011	–	model 1984	V (effectively)
DR Congo	2011	–	–	model 1984	V (effectively)

Convertible	Transferable	Eval. method	Eval. moment	Int. Rate	Inter. rate period
–	freely	fair market value in accordance with generally recognised principles of valuation	model 1997, exact	current commercial %	from expropriation until date of payment
V (*i.e.*, effectively convertible)	freely	model 1997, exact	model 1997, exact	commercial %	from expropriation until date of payment
V (*i.e.*, freely convertible currency)	freely	market value	model 1997, exact	normal commercial %	from expropriation until date of payment
V (*i.e.*, freely usable currency)	freely	fair market value	expropriation and no change for earlier public knowledge, immediately before	prevailing commercial	until date of payment
–	freely	fair market value	model 1997, exact	current commercial %	from expropriation until date of payment
–	freely	fair market value	model 1997, exact	reasonable commercial %	until date of payment
–	freely	fair market value	model 1997, exact	commercial %	until date of payment
V (*i.e.*, freely convertible currency)	freely	fair market value	model 1997, exact	reasonable commercial %	until date of payment

TABLE 19 Compensation due to expropriation: characteristics and criteria (*cont.*)

Counterpart	Signed	In force	Overarch. characterization	Payment delay	Realizable
South Korea & Japan	2012	2014	–	model 1997	V (effectively)
Chile [SAI/FTA]	2012	2014	–	model 1997	V (effectively)
Canada	2012	2014	–	model 1997	V (effectively)
Tanzania	2013	2014	–	model 1984	V (effectively)
South Korea [FTA]	2015	2015	–	model 1997	V (effectively)
Turkey	2015	–	–	model 1997 (+ prompt)	V (prompt & effective comp.*)
Australia [FTA]	2015	2015			

Convertible	Transferable	Eval. method	Eval. moment	Int. Rate	Inter. rate period
V (freely convertible)	freely	fair market value	expropriation or public knowledge, whichever earlier	reasonable commercial %	from expropriation until date of payment
V (*i.e.*, freely usable currency)	freely	fair market value	model 1997, exact	reasonable commercial %	from expropriation until date of payment
–	freely	fair market value	model 1997, exact	normal commercial %	until date of payment
–	freely	fair market value	model 1997, exact	resaonable commercial %	until date of payment
V (freely convertible)	freely	fair market value	expropriation and no change for earlier public knowledge, immediately before	reasonable commercial %	from expropriation until date of payment
V (prompt & effective comp.*)	freely	market value	expropriation or public knowledge, before	provided by law	until date of payment

D The Most-Favored-Nation Clause in Chinese IIAs

1 *Introduction and Relevant Pool of Investment Agreements*

China extends the MFN guarantee throughout its three models and the 120 investment treaties here considered, with no exception. The stable framework of the clause in the Chinese practice can be inferred *inter alia* by the fact that in 91 cases (76% of 120) the provision is located in Art. 3, as per all Chinese (as well as German, British, Dutch, and Italian)[82] templates. The templates' structure and wording are as follows:

- 1984 model
  Art. 3.2: *The treatment and protection referred to in Paragraph 1 of this Article shall not be less favourable than that accorded to* ***investments*** *and activities associated with such investments of investors of a third State.*
- 1989 model
  Art. 3.1: *Neither contracting party shall, in its territory, subject* ***investments*** *or activities associated with investments of investors of the other contracting party to treatment less favourable than that accorded to investments or associated activities by investors of any third State.*
  Art. 3.2: *Neither contracting party shall, in its territory, subject* ***investors*** *of the other contracting party, as regards their management, maintenance, use, enjoyment or disposal of their investments or activities related with investments, to treatment less favourable than that which it accords co investors of any third State.*
- 1997 model
  Art. 3.3: *Neither Contracting Party shall subject* ***investments*** *and activities associated with such investments by the investors of the other Contracting Party to treatment less favorable than that accorded to the investments and associated activities by the investors of any third State.*

While the provision's basic formulation did not undergo overwhelming changes over the time, even relatively minor evolutions of wording and position in a treaty (*e.g.*, joint with or separate from NT and/or FET), when contrasted with regional and global trends in investment treaty making, are a reflection, or contribute revealing, changes (and rationale) of China's attitude towards specific aspects in international investment law.

The analysis that follows takes into account, therefore, the pool of 120 IIAs, comparing these as usual with the three Chinese models, as well as those of key European and North American States.

82 In the French and US models the MFN is located in Art. 4 (in the case of the US, as a standalone provision; in the French model, jointly with NT).

2 *Structure of the MFN Clause*

As illustrated with the NT analysis (see Section E), the position of the MFN clause in relation to the other basic standards of protection tends to vary in the treaty practice of the various States.[83] China here maintained a unique approach, to be found with the NT clause as well. The outcome between the two comparative analyses, however, may differ significantly, as in the case of MFN the pool of treaties scrutinized is almost double than with NT (120 v 67).

Under a structural point of view, in terms of positioning of the clause within the model treaties, China always devoted a specific paragraph to the MFN, within the 'treatment of investment' provision. However, the material position of the clause within the provision changed over the time. In the 1984 model, MFN followed FET; in the 1989 model, it opened instead the provision (to be then followed by FET and NT); in the 1997 model, the MFN is found after FET and NT.

The analysis that follows takes into account the structural relation of MFN with NT and FET. It does not, however, consider which clause comes first throughout the actual Chinese treaty practice.

The largest group of treaties, comprising **37** BITS (31% of 120 IIAS) spanning between 1985 and 1999, is based on the 1984 model and features the MFN clause in a dedicated paragraph in the same provision as FET and FPS.

In the second largest group, counting **30** IIAS (25%), the MFN is found in the same provision with FET and NT. Of these, in 24 cases (20% of 120), all between 2000 and 2009, the clause is framed in a separate paragraph, in accordance with the 1997 model, of which it replicates the wording as well.[84] Conversely, in 5 BITS of this group (between 1995–2001, all with minor investment partners), the MFN shares the same paragraph with FET and NT.

In a third group, comprising **26** agreements (22% of 120), the MFN is dedicated a standalone provision. This group is, however, divided in two subgroups: 13 BITS are dated agreements (1984–1996) which do not feature NT; the other 13 represent instead the most advanced practice (2008–2015), where structure and wording get closer to the North American template.

The fourth significant practice path, totalling **21** BITS (17,5% of 120), frames MFN and NT in the same provision. Even if this practice echoes the structural choice of the 1989 model, the latter wording is employed only in 4 cases, and

83 See Section E of this Chapter.

84 In Latvia (2004) and Finland (2004) the provision features a specific additional paragraph granting 'the most favorable' treatment between MFN and NT. The choice of words is specific, and different from the UK-derived 'whichever is more favorable' (accepted by China in only a handful of agreements).

the MFN maintains its own paragraph only in 15 cases.[85] In other 4 cases (notably, the Indian Ocean region, with Madagascar 2005, Seychelles 2007, and India 2007), MFN and NT are joined in the same paragraph (as per the British and German practice). The last two cases (Saudi Arabia 1996, and Turkey 2015) intertwine MFN and NT (*i.e.*, 'treatment accorded to ... its own investors or ... of any third State'), but split the treatment in two *ad hoc* paragraphs, one for 'investors' and the other for 'investments'.

In the residual 6 BITs the practice varies (see table at the end of this Section).

3 *Object of Coverage*

One aspect that is usually overlooked in both practice and academia is the actual object of the coverage of investment protection clauses. In the case of MFN, this usually includes investments and/or investors, but other elements may also be made explicit (*e.g.*, returns, activities related/associated by/of investors).[86] For the avoidance of doubt, the US, Canadian, and German models specify that the MFN guarantee (in the latter case, along with NT, as the two are intertwined) applies to both investors *and* investments,[87] by dedicating each a specific paragraph with identical or quasi-identical wording. The British model, in all equivalent, features two paragraphs as well (also intertwining MFN and NT), one for 'investments or returns' and the other for 'national or companies'. The Dutch model focuses only on 'investments', the Italian 'investments and income accruing to', and the French 'investors'.

The MFN clause contained in China's first model, of 1984, extends protection to 'investments and activities associated with such investments of investors'. In the 1989 model, the coverage is then split into two standalone paragraphs (as per the German model – but keeping MFN and NT separate), the first referring to 'investments or activities associated with investments of investors', and the second to 'investors'. The 1997 model, lastly, restores the wording of 1984 with an important distinction: like in the NT clause, now the locution refers to investments and activities associated 'by' investors (not 'of' investors). The template locution, unique among the models here surveyed, appears particularly liberal, as the formulation 'associated by' seemingly leaves

85 The BIT with Jordan (2001) features the same specific wording indicated in the earlier footnote; see *supra*.

86 Independently from (or redundantly with respect to) the treaty definition of 'investment'.

87 The US and Canadian models refer to 'covered investment'.

broad discretion to the investor in determining the 'accessory elements' of an investment (as opposed to leaving this aspect to the contract, or the State; cf., Morocco's definitory attempt in *Salini* – ultimately rejected, yet reflecting the possible State view on the point).

China's practice on the point, however, is quite fragmented. Over half of the agreements (69 out of 120, or 57,5%) extend coverage to investments and activities 'associated', 'in connection' or 'related'. In turn, 35 of these (34 of which concluded between 1988 and 1999) refer to 'investment *of* investors' (as per the 1984 model), while 31 (all concluded between 2000–2015) to 'investment *by* investors' (as per the 1997 model). The use of the actual wording of the two models is, however, more limited: the 1984 model is employed in 31 cases, while the 1997 in 21. This shows quite some flexibility on the point from China, as overall adherence to the wording of the models is well below 50% (to be precise, 43% of 120 IIAs).

In the second largest group, comprising 22 BITs (18% of 120) concluded between 1986 and 2012, the coverage is articulated in two separate paragraphs, encompassing an assortment of pairings ('investment' and 'activities associated'; 'investments' and 'investors and activities associated'; 'investments and returns' and 'investors'; 'investment' and 'investors'). It is noteworthy that the wording of the 1989 model, the only one splitting the coverage in two separate paragraphs ('investment or activities associated of investors' and 'investors'), has never been employed as such.

Less adherent to the models' structure and wording patterns, 11 mostly dated BITs (1984–2001) cover only 'investments', 9 recent IIAs (concluded between 2004–2015) 'investors and investments' (or vice-versa), and 5 (concluded between 2005–2007, with France and former colonies) employ the French model expression 'investors with respect to investments and associated activities'. Lastly, in 2 recent BITs the coverage is limited to 'investors' only (Namibia 2005, India 2006), while in other 2 recent BITs this is expanded to the seemingly catch-all 'investors, investments and associated activities' (South Korea 2007, New Zealand 2008). Combined, the weight of IIAs not related to any Chinese model amount to the 24% of the total practice.

Therefore, the object of coverage of the MFN clause seems to be one of the most flexible aspects throughout China's investment treaty practice. The 'relative flexibility' already visible in the first two decades has become a 'relative adherence' in the subsequent two (and, particularly, in the last one). As per the NT, the fragmented practice of major traditional players has no doubt contributed to the illustrated variety.

4 *Ambit of Coverage*

Similarly than with NT, most European models do not specify to what MFN protection extends to. This is the case of the German, Dutch, French and Italian models. The UK, however, followed by the US and Canada, seems to have paved the way to a more specific definition, by adding the list of activities that are expressly covered. For the UK the treatment not less favourable is '... as regards ... management, maintenance, use, enjoyment or disposal' of investments, which the US refined and expanded as 'acquisition, expansion, management, conduct, operation, and sale or other disposition', and Canada further expanded to include, notably, 'establishment'.[88]

While China's 1984 model, in accordance with most European models, does not provide a list of specifically covered activities, the 1989 model replicates the British list which, in 1997, is nevertheless removed from the new template.

In this respect, the Chinese practice is, overall, consistently bent toward not featuring the list of expressly covered activities. This is the case of **87** IIAs out of 120 (72,5%), 36 of which concluded from year 2000 onward (*i.e.*, 61% of 59 concluded since then). While the non-list practice seems to have ceased in 2010, it features significant partners such as the Netherlands, Spain, India, Russia, and France.

Out of the 33 IIAs that do offer a list of protected treatments, **15** are identical or based on the British model (hence, in line with the 1989 Chinese model). These BITs, that span from 1985 (Denmark) to 2009 (Switzerland), comprise a variety of unrelated counterparts, including 5 middle Eastern States, Germany, and Mexico. Lastly, 5 agreements feature one additional element (*e.g.*, 'operation', 'acquisition'), while two one less ('maintenance').

In **12** recent IIAs, concluded between 2004–2015, the MFN extends to 'establishment' or 'admission'.[89] Three of these agreements replicate the list provided in the Canadian model (Peru 2009, Canada 2012, Australia 2015). Peculiar is the 2015 BIT with Turkey, which, next to an otherwise unqualified plain definition, expressly features 'admission'.

A last group of **6** IIAs, four of which recent (Colombia 2008, Chad 2010, DRC 2011, Chile 2012), and two dated (Austria 1985 and FYROM 1997) contain lists combining in various ways elements that can be retrieved in the British and Canadian models.

---

88 For the different understanding between the UK and North American practice of the term 'disposal' and 'disposition', see Section E.5 of this Chapter.

89 The IIAs actually referring to establishment are 7: Finland (2004), Peru (2009), ASEAN (2009), Uzbekistan (2011), Canada (2012), Tanzania (2013), Australia (2015). While establishment is wider in scope than admission, express coverage of the latter represents a notable advancement on the part of China.

The current trend seems clear, as out of the latest 20 IIAs (hence, those concluded since 2008), only three contain a definition of the MFN clause that does not identify the ambit of coverage (Bahamas 2009, Mali 2009, Libya 2010). Therefore, as per the NT, while it appears that China has not yet settled on the specific elements to be included in the list, it seems quite settled that a list of terms is now included as part of the MFN clause.

5 *MFN Treatment Formulation (Positive, Negative, with Comparator)*

In investment treaties, the MFN clause is formulated as the commitment by which neither party shall 'subject to' or 'grant' investors and/or investments 'treatment less favourable' than that accorded to those from other nations. All European and North American templates move from this base formulation. This is refined, in the US and Canadian models, by a comparator (*e.g.*, 'in like circumstances'), which nowadays is often found in treaty practice.

Differently than in the case of NT, China's models and practice show in this respect a high degree of consistency. An overall number of **98** IIAs (over 80% of 120) make use of the simple 'less favorable' formulation, while **19** more recent treaties (16%), from 2007 onward, add a comparator. In 15 cases this is the North American 'in like circumstances'. Some earlier and exceptional formulations resort to the terms 'situation' or 'condition', *i.e.*, 'in like situations' (Turkey 1990), 'in a comparable condition' (Iran 2000), 'in similar conditions' (Cuba 2007), or 'in the same situation' (Chad 2010).

Residual, yet peculiar, is the case of other **3** BITs: two refer to treatment 'granted to the most-favored-nation' (France 2007, Seychelles 2007), and one to treatment 'at least equal' (Mali 2009).

6 *Exceptions to the MFN*

6.1 'Subject to Domestic Law'

As it will be illustrated, China's models, and a solid majority of its treaty practice, subject the NT clause to conformity with domestic laws and regulations.[90] However, if domestic legislation were allowed to differentiate treatment between foreign investors on the basis of their nationality, that would quite defeat the scope of a MFN clause. Where MFN is subject to such an overarching exception, this may be due to poor treaty drafting.

The general understanding of the scope of MFN seems to have been always clear to China, which, despite the illustrated 'conservative' approach to investment treaty law, in all its models never felt necessary to subject the clause to domestic legislation. In this respect, the model choice is virtually uniformly

90 See Section E of this Chapter.

put to practice, as among the 120 IIAs here under consideration, only 4 do not conform.

The BITs with Iran (2000) and Jordan (2001) seem indeed cases of poor drafting. In the latter case especially, the conceptual inconsistency is due to the use of two subsequent and identically worded paragraphs for NT and MFN.

Different is the case of the two BITs with Turkey (1990, still in force, and 2015, yet to enter in force). Even if located in different positions in the respective treaties, and resorting to partially different wording, in both cases the MFN clause is subject to domestic law only within an unusual *ad hoc* reference to admission of investments. Consequently, it seems that the treaty parties consciously chose (*rectius*, China accepted a specificity of Turkey's investment treaty practice) to decline extending possible privileges granted by domestic law to investors of third States.

6.2 Position

With the exception of the UK, European models feature, in the same provision where MFN and NT are located, general carve-outs from their operation, usually excluding privileges deriving from forms of economic integration (*i.e.*, the EU) and tax arrangements. The British model, on its part, features a more specific provision dedicated to exceptions,[91] while North American models offer a more articulated regime altogether (broken down in several provisions, general and *ad hoc*).[92]

Drawing from the continental European models and practice, in its 1984 model China established already, in the last paragraph of the same provision featuring MFN and FET, a general carve-out on '... *customs union, free trade zone, economic union, agreement relating to avoidance of double taxation or for facilitating frontier trade*'. The 1989 model features the same general exception, also at the end of the provision but this time referred to MFN and NT (having FET, FPS, and PAD been transfered to the earlier article). In the 1997 model, lastly, the general carve-out, whilst remaining substantially equivalent, is slightly rephrased and explicitly referred to MFN only (correctly, therefore, the exception does not operate with respect to FET and NT, also contained in the provision).

The Chinese treaty practice, even the most recent, is for the most part in line with the outlined model framework. The 92,5% of IIAs (111 out of 120) feature the general exception in the same provision where the MFN clause is located. A modest group of 7 BITs feature an *ad hoc* exception provision. Of these, four

91 Cf., Art. 7 UK model.

92 Cf., in general, Arts. 14–18 US model, and Arts. 9–10 Canadian model.

are concluded prior to year 2000, while the other three are the recent agreements with Mexico (2008), Canada (2012), and Chile (2012), all largely influenced by NAFTA's investment chapter as well as the Canadian model. Lastly, in **2** cases (ASEAN 2009 and Australia 2015) the general exception regime is contained both in the same and an *ad hoc* provision.

6.3 Wording of the MFN Exceptions (Relatively to PRC Models)

As mentioned, since its 1984 model China established, in the last paragraph of the same provision featuring MFN and FET, a general carve-out on '*... customs union, free trade zone, economic union, agreement relating to avoidance of double taxation or for facilitating frontier trade*'. It shall be noted that 'facilitating frontier trade' is an original and typical trait of the Chinese practice. The categories of the carve-out to the operation of the MFN regime have not changed throughout the templates – the 1997 model operating only marginal stylistic rearrangements.[93]

The analysis of the Chinese practice on the point shows a remarkable adherence to any model wording (79%), and an even more remarkable overall equivalency of general exceptions ultimately featured in the treaties (95%). More specifically, **46** BITS (38%), 45 of which concluded before year 2000, feature a wording identical, very similar or anyway compatible (*i.e.*, with a variance of maximum one category among those mentioned above) with the 1984–1989 models (employed *tel quel* in 30 agreements). The 1997 model is the reference for **49** BITS (41%), its wording employed as such in 17 cases. Other **19** IIAS (16%), whilst employing a wording different from any model, feature anyway the same classes of exceptions. It shall be noted that, in these three groups, the Chinese distinctive exception on 'small-scale frontier trade' is at variance with the treaty templates in 28 cases (25% of the 114 IIAS referred to in this paragraph), thus repeatedly not finding its way in the final treaty.

Lastly, in **6** IIAS both wording and exceptions ultimately used are different from the Chinese models. These are the dated BITS with Sweden (1984) and Denmark (1985), and the recent IIAS with New Zealand (2008), ASEAN (2009), Canada (2012), and Australia (2015).

93 Cf., Art. 3.4 China model BIT (1997): The provisions of Paragraphs 3 of this Article shall not be construed so as to oblige one Contracting Party to extend to the investors of the other Contracting Party the benefit of any treatment, preference or privilege by virtue of:
(a) any customs union, free trade zone, economic union and any international agreement resulting in such unions, or similar institutions;
(b) any international agreement or arrangement relating wholly or mainly to taxation;
(c) any arrangements for facilitating small scale frontier trade in border areas.

In sum, with respect to the adherence to the model wording of the general exceptions to the operation of the MFN, it emerges that, whilst China feels no longer bound by the model wording, it still maintains the established exceptions featured in European models, plus its own on 'small-scale border trade' whenever possible.

6.4 Investment Agreements Featuring Ad Hoc Exceptions to MFN

An overall limited number of IIAs concluded by China, mostly recent or very recent, contemplate *ad hoc* exceptions to the MFN regime in specific circumstances. Differently than in the case of the NT, this type of exclusions can also to be found in the investment treaty practice of other States, with formulations that, if not standard, often echo each other.

Out of the 15 IIAs contemplating *ad hoc* exceptions to the MFN principle, 12 are concluded after year 2000. The three earlier agreements – the BITs with Argentina (1992), Lebanon (1996), and South Africa (1997) – all contain exceptions tailored to cater to specific needs of China's treaty counterpart.

Anyone agreement can contain one or several of these *ad hoc* exceptions to MFN, making classification a complex affair. Indeed, *ad hoc* exceptions tend to be crafted on the necessities of the parties to the agreement, hence the ensuing panoply of results and choices. The following focuses on those that are most frequently found (for the entire list, see the scheme at the end of this Section).

The most common exception, found in six IIAs and carving out an entire economic sector, is 'fisheries and maritime matters'. Similarly, 'aviation' is excluded four times.

Another relatively common exception, found in four agreements – although formulated each time differently –, is that relating to certain domestic developmental needs. In this sense, Lebanon (1996) carves out '*individual investment projects from Arab countries for development purposes*'; South Africa (1997), financial advantages for '*development finance institutions for development assistance through non-profit*'; Guyana (2003), '*special incentives for the growth of local industries*'; and Peru (2009), disadvantaged minorities.

Four agreements exclude the operation of MFN where preferential treatment is granted on the basis of prior international agreements. This is the case of New Zealand (2008), ASEAN (2009), Canada (2012), and Chile (2012).

The rest of cases represents an assortment of choices, often extending to NT as well.

However, out of the last 20 IIAs, *i.e.*, those concluded since 2008, 12 do not contemplate *ad hoc* carve-outs to the MFN principles. This shows that, while China is by this time prepared to negotiate this type of exception (a necessity, in the face of negotiations with, *e.g.*, the US and the EU), it is in general satisfied with general model-based carve-outs, as reflected in the vast majority of its practice.

7 *Non-Conforming Measures*

Like the case of NT, in investment law non-conforming measures have been firstly developed in the context of NAFTA,[94] subsequently systematized in the North American models since the turn of the millennium.[95] This exceptional regime allows an IIA contracting State to maintain, continue, and amend measures which, already in place at the time of the entry into force of the IIA, would otherwise constitute a breach of treaty guarantees.

As for the case of general exceptions to both NT and MFN, in the context of non-conforming measures as well to maintain a discriminatory favor toward investors of a third State (as opposed to potentially reasonable concerns for domestic investors or nationals, like in the case of NT) is hardly compatible with the essence of the MFN principle. As such, the measure *institutionalizes discrimination* between foreign investors.

The normalizing factor of such discrimination, hence the difference – thus, its logic – with respect to general and permanent exceptions, is that non-conforming measures often find a temporal limit in what is known as the 'roll-back effort', by which the parties to the treaty commit to take 'all appropriate steps to progressively remove all the nonconforming measures'.[96] While it is ultimately up to the parties to bring an end to these exceptions, the roll-back promise highlights the fact that these exceptions are supposed to be transitional.

Accordingly, in the Chinese practice, the IIAs featuring non-conforming measures with respect to MFN are only **13** – all included in the larger group of 19 IIAs allowing for non-conforming measures with respect to NT (see the subsequent Section). Thus, in all cases were non-conforming measures are extended to MFN, this happens because the text of the treaty joins the exception with respect to both MFN and NT. These 13 IIAs have been concluded between 2001 and 2012, all of them with European or Western States, plus India and ASEAN.

Therefore, reiterating, *in abstracto*, the general consideration that exceptions provided by non-conforming measures are well-suited to China's overall conservative investment treaty policy, it is difficult to determine if, at this stage, this has become a standard feature of its treaty practice – let alone, with respect to MFN, as seen conceptually more problematic than with NT.

---

94 See NAFTA Art. 1108 (Reservations and Exceptions).

95 Cf., Art. 14 US model (2004) and Art. 9 Canada model (2004).

96 *E.g.*, Art. 3.3 China-Czech Republic BIT (2005), Art. 3.3 China-Japan-Korea TIT (2012).

The Most-Favored-Nation Clause in Chinese IIAs: Data Summary

MFN
120/120 IIAS

Contained in Art. 3: 91 (76% of 120) [any PRC model]

Structure of the Provision

- Together with FET, FPS & NT: **4**
  - Dedicated para.: 1
    - Slovenia (1993)
  - Para shared with NT: 3
    - South Africa (1997), Netherlands (2001), Switzerland (2009)
- Together with FET & FPS: **37** (31%)
  - Dedicated para.: 37
  - IIAs between 1985–1999
  - Wording identical / minor variations to *1984 model*: 35
- Together with FET & NT: **30** (25%)
  - Dedicated para. [*1997 model*]: 24 (20% of 120)
    - IIAs between 2000–2009
    - In Latvia (2004) and Finland (2004): specific additional para granting '*the most favorable*' treatment between MFN and NT[97]
  - Dedicated para. / no model wording: 1
    - Namibia (2005)
  - Para shared with FET & NT: 5
    - Morocco (1995), Gabon (1997), Yemen (1998), Iran (2000),[98] Cyprus (2001)
- Together with FET: **2**
  - Dedicated para: 2
    - Sweden (1984), Tunisia (2004)
- Together with NT: **21** (17,5%)
  - Dedicated para. / no model wording: 11 (10)
    - IIAs between 2002–2008
    - In Jordan (2001): specific additional para granting '*the most favorable*' treatment between MFN and NT

97 The wording is specific and different from the UK-derived 'whichever is more favorable' (accepted by China in only a handful of agreements).

98 The FET formulation here is specific, as refers to 'full legal protection and fair treatment'.

- Dedicated para. / [*1989 model*]: 4
    - UK (1986), Iceland (1994), Serbia (1995), Macedonia (1997)
- Para shared with NT: 4 (5)
    - Syria (1996),[99] Bosnia (2002),[100] Madagascar (2005), India (2006), Seychelles (2007)
- MFN split in two paras (investors and investments): 2
    - Saudi Arabia (1996), Turkey (2015)

- Standalone provision **26** (22%)
    - 13 IIAs (between 1984–1996) do not offer NT
    - 13 IIAs (between 2008–2015) feature a truly standalone MFN provision

Object of Coverage

- Investors: **2**
    - Namibia (2005)[101]
    - Plus 'returns'
        - India (2006)[102]
- Investors with respect to investments and associated activities: **5**
    - Equatorial Guinea (2005),[103] Guinea (2005), Madagascar (2005), Seychelles (2007), France (2007)
- Investors, investments and associated activities: **2**
    - South Korea (2007), New Zealand (2008)
- Investors and investments (*and vice versa*): **9** (7,5% of 120)
    - Tunisia (2004), ASEAN (2009), Chad (2010), Uzbekistan (2011), DR Congo (2011), SK-JP (2012), Tanzania (2013)
    - With the specification 'covered' investments: **2**
        - South Korea (2015), Australia (2015)
- Investments (with or without 'of'/'by' investors): **11** (9% of 120)
    - Sweden (1984), Norway (1984), Papua NG (1991), Croatia (1993), Finland (2004), Colombia (2008).

99 The MFN clause is featured in Art. 1 protocol (which complements Art. 3 of the BIT); NT treatment is granted, however, only by Syria, while China's treatment is only on a MFN basis.

100 The provision features a paragraph where the MFN is associated with the NT, plus a subsequent *ad hoc* MFN paragraph; the content is, however, equivalent but differently worded, thus redundant and possible source of confusion.

101 The coverage is tighter than the more usual 'activities associated', as it specifically provides for 'treatment afforded … to an investor … directly related to the investment'.

102 Unclear wording: investors 'including in respect of returns'.

103 The wording is here slightly different and potentially broader: 'investors with respect to investments, returns and business activities in connection with investments'.

  - 'and'/'or' returns: 4
    - Sri Lanka (1986), Serbia (1995), Mauritius (1996), Mozambique (2001)
  - Investments *'in a comparable situation'*: 1
    - Iran (2000)
- Investments and activities 'associated' / 'in connection' / 'related': **69** (57,5% of 120)
  - As such: 3
    - Turkey (1990), Kyrgyzstan (1992), Cuba (2007)
  - '... *with investments **of** investors of either* CP': 35 (51% of 69)
    - IIAs between 1988–1999: 34
      - Exception: BLEU (2005)
    - Identical (or very minor variations) to [*1984 model*]: 31
  - '... *with investments **by** investors of either* CP': 31 (45% of 69)
    - IIAs between 2000–2015: 29
    - exceptions: Algeria (1996), South Africa (1997)
    - Identical (or very minor variations) to [*1997 model*]: 21
    - With the addition of 'returns': 3
      - Jordan (2001), Trinidad & Tobago (2002), Guyana (2003)
- Separate paras. (*e.g.*, 'investment' and 'activities associated'; 'investments' and 'investors & activities associated'; 'investments & returns' and 'investors'; 'investment' and 'investors'): 22 (18%)
  - IIAs between 1986–2012 (but only 7 since 2000)
  - '*investment or activities associated of investors*' and '*investors*' [*1989 model*]: 0

Specifically covered activities / ambit of coverage: 33/120 (27,5%)

- No: 87 (72,5%) [*1984 and 1997 models*]
  - IIAs between 1982–2010
  - 36 IIAs since 2000
    - Including Netherlands (2001), Spain (2005), India (2006), Russia (2006), France (2007)
- *'Management, maintenance, use, enjoyment or disposal'*: **15** (45% of 33) [*1989 model*][104]
  - IIAs between 1985–1996: 8 (53% of 15)

104 Formulation identical to the UK model: 'management, maintenance, use, enjoyment or disposal'.

- Exactly as *1989 model*: 8 (53% of 15)
  - Denmark (1985), Kuwait (1985), UK (1986), Oman (1995), Israel (1995), Germany (2003), Czech Rep. (2005), Switzerland (2009)
- One additional element: 5
  - '*operation*': Trinidad & Tobago (2002), Guyana (2003), Mexico (2008)
  - '*acquisition*': UAE (1993)
  - '*means to assure BIT rights*': Saudi Arabia (1996)
- One less element (no '*maintenance*'): 2
  - Iceland (1993), Malta (2009)

- Other combinations of elements from the UK and Canada models:[105] 6
  - Austria (1985), FYROM (1997), Colombia (2008), Chad (2010), DR Congo (2011), Chile (2012)
- Covering as well/only 'establishment'/'admission': **12** (36% of 33)
  - IIAs between 2004–2015
    - Finland (2004), South Korea (2007),[106] New Zealand (2008), ASEAN (2009),[107] Peru (2009), Uzbekistan (2011), Canada (2012), SK-JP (2012),[108] Tanzania (2013), South Korea (2015),[109] Australia (2015), Turkey (2015)
  - Only 'admission': 1
    - Turkey (2015)
  - Exactly as in Canada model:[110] 3
    - Peru (2009), Canada (2012), Australia (2015)

105 Including definitions with two or more different elements from the Chinese / British model.

106 The provision mentions 'investment and business activities including admission'. 'Investment activities' are earlier specifically defined through a combination of elements drawing from the UK and Canada models.

107 Featuring both 'establishment' and 'admission', in a uniquely rich wording: 'establishment, acquisition, admission, expansion, management, maintenance, use, conduct, sale, operation and other forms of disposal'.

108 The provision mentions 'investment activities including admission'. 'Investment activities' are earlier specifically defined through a combination of elements drawing from the UK and Canada models.

109 The provision mentions 'investment activities including admission'. 'Investment activities' are earlier specifically defined through a combination of elements drawing from the UK and Canada models.

110 *I.e.*, 'Establishment, acquisition, expansion, management, conduct, operation, sale and other disposition'. The US adopted an identical wording with the 2012 BIT model.

Treatment Formulation

- Treatment '*not less favorable*' as such: **63** (52,5%) [*1984 model*]
  - IIAs between 1982–2009
  - IIAs since 2000: 15
- Treatment not less favorable + comparator: **19** (16%)
  - '*in like circumstances*': 15 (79% of 19)
    - IIAs between 2007–2015
  - '*in a comparable situation*': 1
    - Iran (2000)
  - '*in like situations*': 1
    - Turkey (1990)
  - '*in similar conditions*': 1
    - Cuba (2007)
  - '*in the same situation*'
    - Chad (2010)
- Treatment '*less favorable*': **35** (29%) [*1989 and 1997 models*]
  - IIAs between 1984–2010
  - IIAs since 2000: 23
- Treatment '*granted to the most-favored-nation*': **2**
  - Seychelles (2007), France (2007)
- Treatment '*at least equal*': **1**
  - Mali (2009)

***Clause 'subject to domestic law': 4/120* (3%)**

- As such: 2
  - Iran (2000), Jordan (2001)
- Limited to admission: 2
  - Turkey (1990), Turkey (2015)

Position of general exceptions to MFN

- Same provision: 111 (92,5% of 120) [*any PRC model*]
- *Ad hoc* provision: 7
  - Sri Lanka (1986), UAE (1993), Israel (1995), Mauritius (1996), Mexico (2008), Chile (2012), Canada (2012)

- Same & *ad hoc* provision: 2
  - ASEAN (2009), Australia (2015)

In-clause Exceptions to MFN (Relatively to PRC Models)

- Wording identical or very similar to *1984–1989 model*: **46** (38%)
  - Identical: 30
  - IIAs prior to 2000: 45
    - exception: Peru (2009)
  - One less element: 9
    - No 'frontier trade': 8
  - One additional element: 1
    - Papua NG (1991): '*movement of capital*'
- Wording identical or very similar to *1997 model*: **49** (41%)
  - Identical: 17
    - IIAs between 2000–2011: 16
  - exception: South Africa (1997)
  - Additional 'domestic taxation matters': 7
    - UK (1984), Iceland (1994), Israel (1995), Cyprus (2001), Mozambique (2001), Spain (2005), Mexico (2008)
  - No 'frontier trade': 10
    - IIA between 1988–2008
- Different from any PRC models but equivalent: **19** (16%)
  - IIAs between 1990–2015
  - IIAs since 2000: 12 (63% of 19)
  - One less element: 11
    - No 'frontier trade': 10
  - Additional 'domestic taxation matters': 1
    - Seychelles (2007)
- Different wording & exceptions: **6**
  - Sweden (1984), Denmark (1985), New Zealand (2008), ASEAN (2009), Canada (2012), Australia (2015)

Ad hoc *exceptions to MFN (i.e., not contemplated in PRC models): 15/120 (12,5%)*[111]

- IIAs since 2000: 12
  - Exceptions: Argentina (1992), Lebanon (1996), South Africa (1997)
- Types of *ad hoc* exceptions:
  - '*Fisheries and maritime matters*': 6
    - New Zealand (2008), Canada (2012), Chile (2012), SK-JP (2012), Australia (2015), South Korea (2015)
  - Domestic development carve-outs: 4
    - '*Individual investment projects from Arab countries for development purposes*'
      - Lebanon (1996)
    - Financial advantages for '*Development finance institutions for development assistance through non-profit*'
      - South Africa (1997)
    - Special incentives for the growth of local industries
      - Guyana (2003)
    - Disadvantaged minorities
      - Peru (2009)
  - Control or nationality limitations on State enterprises: 1
    - Canada (2012)
  - Acquisition of land property: 1
    - JP-SK (2012)
  - Preferential treatment on the basis of prior international agreements: 4
    - New Zealand (2008), ASEAN (2009), Canada (2012), Chile (2012)
  - Other forms of economic integration than those contemplated in PRC models: 4
    - Russia (2006),[112] New Zealand (2008), ASEAN (2009), Canada (2012)

---

111 These exceptions may be found jointly with the MFN or in *ad hoc* provisions (usually, on 'exceptions'). Only exceptions that are specifically referred to the MFN treatment are taken into account (thus, not the exceptions to the investment agreement or chapter as a whole).

112 Specific clause, protecting the bond between former USSR republics and carving out '… agreements between the Russian Federation and the states, which had earlier formed part of the Union of Soviet Socialist Republics, related to the investment in term of this Agreement'.

- '*Aviation*': 4
  - Chile (2012), SK-JP (2012), Australia (2015), South Korea (2015)
- '*Subsidies and grants*': 2
  - Canada (2012), Chile (2012)
- *Future* better treatment accorded to investors from third States: 1 (2)
  - Argentina (1992),[113] ASEAN (2009)[114]
- '*Procurement*': 1
  - Canada (2012)
- Preferential treatment due to IP international agreements: 2
  - Canada (2012), Chile (2012)
- Cultural industries: 1
  - Peru (2009)
- Cultural and linguistic diversity: 1
  - France (2007)
- Essential security interests in time of war and public order: 1
  - Finland (2004)
- [*temporary limitation*]: Any items in negative lists in any international agreement to which the contracting party is party to: 1
  - Australia (2015)
- Reference to preferential treatment granted with the respective FTAs with Peru: 1
  - Canada (2012)

Non-Conforming Measures: 13/120 (11%)

- Netherlands (2001), Bosnia (2002), Germany (2003), Finland (2004), Czech Rep. (2005), Portugal (2005), Spain (2005), Belgium-Lux (2005), India (2006), ASEAN (2009), Switzerland (2009), Canada (2012), Australia (2012)

113 Limited to 'concessional financing' pursuant to the treaty between Argentina and Spain of 1968.

114 Seemingly on an *ad hoc* basis (*i.e.*, investment contracts).

TABLE 20 MFN in Chinese IIAS

Counterpart	Signed	In force	Art.	Structure	Object of coverage	Expressly covered activities
Sweden	1982	1982	2	= art. FET / ≠ §	investments by investors	–
Norway	1984	1985	4	indep.	investments of nationals or companies	–
PRC MODEL	1984		3	= art. FET FPS / ≠ § [1984 model]	investments and activities associated of investors [1984 model]	–
Austria	1985	1986	3	indep.	(§) investments by nationals or companies (§) activities associated by nationals or companies	maintenance, use and disposal ('in particular')
Denmark	1985	1985	3	= art. FET FPS / ≠ §	(§) investments made by nationals or companies or returns (§) nationals or companies	management, maintenance, use, enjoyment or disposal
Italy	1985	1987	3	indep.	(§) investments and returns of investors (§) investors	–
Kuwait	1985	1986	3	indep.	(§) investments made by nationals or companies or returns (§) nationals or companies	management, maintenance, use, enjoyment or disposal
Sri Lanka	1986	1987	4	indep.	investments of investors + returns	–

Treatment formulation	Subject to domestic law	Position MFN exceptions	In-clause exceptions to MFN (v PRC models)	Other *ad hoc* exceptions	Non-conforming measures
not less favourable	–	= art.	≠ any model (FTA/CU; treatment pursuant to prior int'l ags.)	–	–
less favorable	–	= art.	model 1984–9, equivalent	–	–
not less favorable	–	= art.	customs union, free trade zone, economic union, double taxation, frontier trade	–	–
less favorable	–	= art.	model 1984–9, equivalent	–	–
less favorable	–	= art.	≠ any model (taxation only)	–	–
not less favorable	–	= art.	model 1984–9, exact	–	–
not less favorable	–	= art.	model 1984–9, equivalent – (frontier trade)	–	–
less favorable	–	≠ art.	model 1984–9, equivalent – (frontier trade)	–	–

TABLE 20 MFN in Chinese IIAs (*cont.*)

Counterpart	Signed	In force	Art.	Structure	Object of coverage	Expressly covered activities
UK	1986	1986	3	= art. NT / ≠ § / [1989 model]	(§) investments or returns of nationals or companies (§) nationals or companies	management, maintenance, use, enjoyment or disposal
*Australia**	1988	1988	3	= art. FET FPS / ≠ §	investments and activities associated of investors	–
Poland	1988	1989	3	= art. FET FPS / ≠ § / [model 1984]	investments and activities associated of investors	–
Bulgaria	1989	1994	3	= art. FET FPS / ≠ § / [model 1984]	investments and activities associated of investors	–
Ghana	1989	1990	3	= art. FET FPS / ≠ § / [model 1984]	investments and activities associated of investors	–
PRC MODEL	1989		3	= art. NT / ≠ § / [1989 model]	(§) investments or activities associated of investors (§) investors [1989 model]	management, maintenance, use, enjoyment or disposal
*Turkey**	1990	1994	2	indep.	investments and activities associated	–
Hungary	1991	1993	3	= art. FET FPS / ≠ § / [model 1984]	investments and activities associated of investors	–
Mongolia	1991	1993	3	= art. FET FPS / ≠ § / [model 1984] *	investments and activities associated of investors	–

Treatment formulation	Subject to domestic law	Position MFN exceptions	In-clause exceptions to MFN (v PRC models)	Other *ad hoc* exceptions	Non-conforming measures
less favorable	–	= art.	model 1997, equivalent + (domestic taxation)	–	–
not less favorable	–	= art.	model 1997, equivalent – (frontier trade)	–	–
not less favorable	–	= art.	model 1997, equivalent	–	–
not less favorable	–	= art.	model 1984–9, exact	–	–
not less favorable	–	= art.	model 1984–9, exact	–	–
less favorable	–	= art.	[idem 1984 model]	–	–
not less favorable in like situations	V (on admission)	= art.	≠ any model but equivalent – (taxation) – (frontier trade)	–	–
not less favorable	–	= art.	model 1984–9, exact	–	–
not less favorable	–	= art.	model 1984–9, exact	–	–

TABLE 20 MFN in Chinese IIAS (*cont.*)

Counterpart	Signed	In force	Art.	Structure	Object of coverage	Expressly covered activities
Papua NG	1991	1993	3	indep.	investments by nationals or companies	–
Argentina	1992	1994	3	= art. FET FPS / ≠ § / [model 1984]	investments and activities associated of investors	–
Armenia	1992	1995	3	= art. FET FPS / ≠ § / [model 1984]	investments and activities associated of investors	–
Bolivia	1992	1996	3	= art. FET FPS / ≠ § / [model 1984]	investments and activities associated of investors	–
Greece	1992	1993	3	indep.	(§) investments owned wholly or partially by investors (§) activities associated	–
Kazakhstan	1992	1994	3	= art. FET FPS / ≠ § / [model 1984]	investments and activities associated of investors	–
Kyrgyzstan	1992	1995	3	= art. FET FPS / ≠ § / [model 1984]	investments and activities associated	–
*Philippines**	1992	1995	3	= art. FET FPS / ≠ § / [model 1984]	investments and activities associated of investors	–

Treatment formulation	Subject to domestic law	Position MFN exceptions	In-clause exceptions to MFN (v PRC models)	Other *ad hoc* exceptions	Non-conforming measures
less favorable	–	= art.	model 1984–9, equivalent + (movement of capital) – (frontier trade)	–	–
not less favorable	–	= art.	model 1984–9, exact	Financing ag. w/ ES	–
not less favorable	–	= art.	≠ any model but equivalent	–	–
not less favorable	–	= art.	model 1984–9, exact	–	–
less favorable	–	= art.	≠ any model but equivalent – (frontier trade)	–	–
not less favorable	–	= art.	≠ any model but equivalent	–	–
not less favorable	–	= art.	model 1997, equivalent	–	–
not less favorable	–	= art.	model 1984–9, equivalent	–	–

TABLE 20 MFN in Chinese IIAs (*cont.*)

Counterpart	Signed	In force	Art.	Structure	Object of coverage	Expressly covered activities
Ukraine	1992	1993	3	= art. FET FPS / ≠ § / [model 1984]	investments and activities associated of investors	–
Albania	1993	1995	3	= art. FET FPS / ≠ § / [model 1984]	investments and activities associated of investors	–
Belarus	1993	1995	3	indep.	(§) investors (§) investments and activities associated of investors	–
Croatia	1993	1994	3	= art. FET FPS / ≠ § / [model 1984]	investments of investors	–
Estonia	1993	1994	3	= art. FET FPS / ≠ § / [model 1984]	investments and activities associated of investors	–
Georgia	1993	1995	3	= art. FET FPS / ≠ § / [model 1984]	investments and activities associated of investors	–
Lithuania	1993	1994	3	= art. FET FPS / ≠ § / [model 1984]	investments and activities associated of investors	–
Slovenia	1993	1995	3	= art. FET FPS NT / ≠ §	investments and activities associated of investors	–

Treatment formulation	Subject to domestic law	Position MFN exceptions	In-clause exceptions to MFN (v PRC models)	Other *ad hoc* exceptions	Non-conforming measures
not less favorable	–	= art.	model 1997, equivalent	–	–
not less favorable	–	= art.	model 1984–9, exact	–	–
not less favorable	–	= art.	model 1984–9, equivalent	–	–
not less favorable	–	= art.	model 1984–9, exact	–	–
not less favorable	–	= art.	model 1984–9, exact	–	–
not less favorable	–	= art.	model 1984–9, exact	–	–
not less favorable	–	= art.	model 1984–9, exact	–	–
not less favorable	–	= art.	model 1984–9, exact	–	–

TABLE 20 MFN in Chinese IIAs (*cont.*)

Counterpart	Signed	In force	Art.	Structure	Object of coverage	Expressly covered activities
Tajikistan	1993	1994	3	= art. FET FPS / ≠ § / [model 1984]	investments and activities associated of investors	–
UAE	1993	1994	3	indep.	(§) investments and returns of investors (§) investors	management, maintenance, use, enjoyment, acquisition or disposal
Uruguay	1993	1997	3	= art. FET FPS / ≠ § / [model 1984]	investments and activities associated of investors	–
Azerbaijan	1994	1995	3	= art. FET FPS / ≠ § / [model 1984]	investments and activities associated of investors	–
Ecuador	1994	1997	3	= art. FET FPS / ≠ § / [model 1984]	investments and activities associated of investors	–
Egypt	1994	1996	3	= art. FET FPS * / ≠ § / [model 1984] / whichever more favorable § **	investments and activities associated of investors	–
Iceland	1994	1997	3	= art. NT / ≠ § / [1989 model]	(§) investments or returns of investors (§) investors	management, use, enjoyment or disposal

Treatment formulation	Subject to domestic law	Position MFN exceptions	In-clause exceptions to MFN (v PRC models)	Other *ad hoc* exceptions	Non-conforming measures
not less favorable	–	= art.	model 1984–9, equivalent	–	–
not less favorable	–	≠ art.	model 1984–9, equivalent – (frontier trade)	–	–
not less favorable	–	= art.	model 1984–9, equivalent – (frontier trade)	–	–
not less favorable	–	= art.	model 1984–9, exact	–	–
not less favorable	–	= art.	model 1984–9, exact	–	–
not less favorable	–	= art.	model 1984–9, exact	–	–
less favorable	–	= art.	model 1997, equivalent + (domestic taxation)	–	–

TABLE 20 MFN in Chinese IIAS (*cont.*)

Counterpart	Signed	In force	Art.	Structure	Object of coverage	Expressly covered activities
Jamaica	1994	1996	3	= art. FET FPS / ≠ § / [model 1984]	investments and activities associated of investors	–
Israel	1995	2009	3	indep.	(§) investments or returns of investors (§) investors	management, maintenance, use, enjoyment or disposal
Morocco	1995	1999	3	= art. FET NT / = §	(§) investments (§) investors on activities associated	–
Oman	1995	1995	3	indep.	(§) investments and returns of investors (§) investors on investment and activities associated	management, maintenance, use, enjoyment or disposal
Serbia	1995	1996	3	= art. NT / ≠ § / [1989 model]	investments of investors + returns	–
Algeria	1996	2003	3	= art. FET FPS / ≠ § / [model 1984]	investments and activities associated by investors	–
Bangladesh	1996	1997	3	= art. FET FPS / ≠ § / [model 1984]	investments and activities associated of investors	–
Lebanon	1996	1997	3	= art. FET FPS / ≠ § / [model 1984]	investments and activities associated of investors	–

Treatment formulation	Subject to domestic law	Position MFN exceptions	In-clause exceptions to MFN (v PRC models)	Other *ad hoc* exceptions	Non-conforming measures
not less favorable	–	= art.	model 1984–9, equivalent	–	–
less favorable	–	≠ art.	model 1997, equivalent + (domestic taxation) – (frontier trade)	–	–
not less favorable	–	= art.	model 1984–9, equivalent – (frontier trade)	–	–
not less favorable	–	= art.	model 1984–9, equivalent	–	–
less favorable	–	= art.	model 1997, equivalent	–	–
not less favorable	–	= art.	model 1984–9, exact	–	–
not less favorable	–	= art.	model 1984–9, exact	–	–
not less favorable	–	= art.	≠ any model but equivalent	Arab investors privilege	–

TABLE 20 MFN in Chinese IIAs (*cont.*)

Counterpart	Signed	In force	Art.	Structure	Object of coverage	Expressly covered activities
Mauritius	1996	1997	4	indep.	investments of nationals and companies + returns	–
Saudi Arabia	1996	1997	3	= art. NT / ≠ § (2 paras)	(§) investments and returns of investors (§) activities associated	management, maintenance, use, enjoyment, disposal or means to assure BIT rights
Syria	1996	2001	1 protocol	= art. NT / = § *	investments and activities associated of investors	–
Zambia	1996	–	3	= art. FET FPS / ≠ § / [model 1984]	investments and activities associated of investors	–
Zimbabwe	1996	1998	3	= art. FET FPS / ≠ § / [model 1984]	investments and activities associated of investors	–
Gabon	1997	2009	3	= art. FET NT / = §	(§) investments (§) investment-related activities	–
Macedonia	1997	1997	3	= art. NT / ≠ § / [1989 model]	(§) investments or returns of investors (§) investors	management, use, enjoyment, disposal, extension, liquidation
PRC MODEL	1997		3	= art. FET NT / ≠ § / [model 1997]	investments and activities associated by investors [1997 model]	–

Treatment formulation	Subject to domestic law	Position MFN exceptions	In-clause exceptions to MFN (v PRC models)	Other *ad hoc* exceptions	Non-conforming measures
less favorable	–	≠ art.	model 1997, equivalent	–	–
not less favorable	–	= art.	model 1984–9, equivalent	–	–
not less favorable	–	= art.	model 1984–9, exact	–	–
not less favorable	–	= art.	model 1984–9, exact	–	–
not less favorable	–	= art.	model 1984–9, exact	–	–
not less favorable	–	= art.	model 1984–9, equivalent – (frontier trade)	–	–
less favorable	–	= art.	model 1984–9, exact	–	–
less favorable	–	= art.	(a) customs union, free trade zone, economic union and related or agreements (b) taxation (c) small scale frontier trade	–	–

TABLE 20 MFN in Chinese IIAs (*cont.*)

Counterpart	Signed	In force	Art.	Structure	Object of coverage	Expressly covered activities
South Africa	1997	1998	3	= art. FET FPS NT / = § NT	investments and activities associated by investors	–
Sudan	1997	1998	3	= art. FET FPS / ≠ § / [model 1984]	investments and activities associated of investors	–
Barbados	1998	1999	3	= art. FET FPS / ≠ § / [model 1984]	investments and activities associated of investors	–
Cape Verde	1998	2001	3	= art. FET FPS / ≠ § / [model 1984]	investments and activities associated of investors	–
Ethiopia	1998	2000	3	= art. FET FPS / ≠ § / [model 1984]	investments and activities associated of investors	–
Yemen	1998	2002	3	= art. FET NT / = §	(§) investments (§) investors on activities associated	–
Bahrain	1999	2000	3	= art. FET FPS / ≠ § / [model 1984]	investments and activities associated of investors	–

Treatment formulation	Subject to domestic law	Position MFN exceptions	In-clause exceptions to MFN (v PRC models)	Other *ad hoc* exceptions	Non-conforming measures
not less favorable	–	= art.	model 1997, exact	"Development finance institutions for development assistance through non-profit"	–
not less favorable	–	= art.	model 1984–9, exact	–	–
not less favorable	–	= art.	model 1984–9, exact	–	–
not less favorable	–	= art.	model 1984–9, exact	–	–
not less favorable	–	= art.	model 1984–9, exact	–	–
not less favorable	–	= art.	model 1984–9, equivalent – (frontier trade)	–	–
not less favorable	–	= art.	model 1984–9, exact	–	–

TABLE 20 MFN in Chinese IIAs (*cont.*)

Counterpart	Signed	In force	Art.	Structure	Object of coverage	Expressly covered activities
Qatar	1999	2000	3	= art. FET FPS / ≠ § / [model 1984]	investments and activities associated of investors	–
Botswana	2000	–	3	= art. FET NT / ≠ § / [model 1997]	investments and activities associated by investors	–
Iran	2000	2005	4	= art. FET NT / = §	investments of investors ('in a comparable situation')	–
Rep. of Congo	2000	2015	3	= art. FET NT / ≠ § / [model 1997]	investments and activities associated by investors	–
Netherlands	2001	2004	3	= art. FET FPS NT / = § NT	investments and activities associated by investors	–
Cyprus	2001	2002	3	= art. FET NT / = §	investments and activities associated by investors	–
Jordan	2001	–	4	= art. NT / ≠ § / whichever more favourable §	investments and activities associated by investors + returns	–
Kenya	2001	–	3	= art. FET NT / ≠ § / [model 1997]	investments and activities associated by investors	–

Treatment formulation	Subject to domestic law	Position MFN exceptions	In-clause exceptions to MFN (v PRC models)	Other *ad hoc* exceptions	Non-conforming measures
not less favorable	–	= art.	model 1984–9, exact	–	–
less favorable	–	= art.	model 1997, equivalent	–	–
not less favorable ('in a comparable situation')	V	= art.	≠ any model but equivalent – (frontier trade)	–	–
not less favorable	–	= art.	model 1997, exact	–	–
not less favorable	–	= art.	model 1997, equivalent	–	V
not less favorable	–	= art.	model 1997, equivalent + (domestic taxation) – (frontier trade)	–	–
not less favorable	V	= art.	model 1997, equivalent – (frontier trade)	–	–
less favorable	–	= art.	model 1997, equivalent	–	–

TABLE 20 MFN in Chinese IIAs (*cont.*)

Counterpart	Signed	In force	Art.	Structure	Object of coverage	Expressly covered activities
Mozambique	2001	2002	3	= art. FET NT / ≠ § / [model 1997]	investments by investors + returns	–
Nigeria	2001	2010	3	= art. FET NT / ≠ § / [model 1997]	investments and activities associated by investors	–
Sierra Leone	2001	–	3	= art. FET NT / ≠ § / [model 1997]	investments and activities associated by investors	–
Bosnia	2002	2005	3	= art. NT / = & ≠ §	investments and activities associated by investors	–
Cote d'Ivoire	2002	–	3	= art. FET NT / ≠ § / [model 1997]	investments and activities associated by investors	–
Trinidad & Tobago	2002	2004	4	= art. NT / ≠ §	investments and activities associated by investors + returns	operation, management, maintenance, use, enjoyment, or disposal (def. 'activities associated')
Germany	2003	2005	3	= art. FET NT / ≠ § / [model 1997]	investments and activities associated by investors	management, maintenance, use, enjoyment or disposal
Djibouti	2003	–	3	= art. FET NT / ≠ § / [model 1997]	investments and activities associated by investors	–

Treatment formulation	Subject to domestic law	Position MFN exceptions	In-clause exceptions to MFN (v PRC models)	Other *ad hoc* exceptions	Non-conforming measures
less favorable	–	= art.	model 1997, equivalent + (domestic taxation)	–	–
not less favorable	–	= art.	model 1997, equivalent – (frontier trade)	–	–
less favorable	–	= art.	model 1997, equivalent	–	–
not less favorable	–	= art.	model 1997, equivalent	–	V
less favorable	–	= art.	model 1997, equivalent	–	–
less favorable	–	= art.	≠ any model but equivalent – (frontier trade)	–	–
less favorable	–	= art.	model 1997, equivalent – (frontier trade)	–	V
less favorable	–	= art.	model 1997, equivalent	–	–

TABLE 20 MFN in Chinese IIAs (*cont.*)

Counterpart	Signed	In force	Art.	Structure	Object of coverage	Expressly covered activities
Guyana	2003	2004	3	= art. NT / ≠ §	investments and activities associated by investors + returns	operation, management, maintenance, use, enjoyment, or disposal (def. 'activities associated')
Finland	2004	2006	3	= art. FET NT / ≠ § / [model 1997] / whichever more favourable §	investments by investors	establishment, acquisition, operation, management, maintenance, use, enjoyment, expansion, sale or other disposal
Benin	2004	–	3	= art. NT / ≠ §	investments and activities associated by investors	–
Latvia	2004	2006	3	= art. FET NT / ≠ § / [model 1997] / whichever more favourable §	investments and activities associated by investors	–
Tunisia	2004	2006	3	= art. FET / ≠ §	investors and investments	–
Uganda	2004	–	3	= art. FET NT / ≠ § / [model 1997]	investments and activities associated by investors	–
Belgium-Lux	2005	2009	3	= art. NT / ≠ §	investments and activities associated of investors	–

Treatment formulation	Subject to domestic law	Position MFN exceptions	In-clause exceptions to MFN (v PRC models)	Other *ad hoc* exceptions	Non-conforming measures
less favorable	–	= art.	≠ any model but equivalent – (frontier trade)	Special incentives for growth of local industries	–
not less favorable	–	= art.	model 1997, equivalent	essential security interests in time of war; public order	V
less favorable	–	= art.	model 1997, equivalent	–	–
less favorable	–	= art.	model 1997, exact	–	–
not less favorable	–	= art.	model 1997, equivalent	–	–
less favorable	–	= art.	≠ any model but equivalent – (frontier trade)	–	–
less favorable	–	= art.	model 1997, exact	–	V

TABLE 20 MFN in Chinese IIAs (*cont.*)

Counterpart	Signed	In force	Art.	Structure	Object of coverage	Expressly covered activities
Czech Rep.	2005	2006	3	= art. NT / ≠ §	(§) investments and returns of investors (§) investors	management, maintenance, use, enjoyment or disposal
Portugal	2005	2008	3	= art. FET NT / ≠ § / [model 1997]	investments and activities associated by investors	–
Spain	2005	2008	3	= art. FET NT / ≠ § / [model 1997]	investments and activities associated by investors	–
Equatorial Guinea	2005	2006	3	= art. FET NT / ≠ § / [model 1997]	investors with respect to investments, returns and business activities in connection	–
Guinea	2005	–	3	= art. NT / ≠ §	investors with respect to investments and associated activities	–
Madagascar	2005	2007	4	= art. NT / = §	investors with respect to investments and associated activities	–
Namibia	2005	–	3	= art. FET NT / ≠ §	investors (treatment "directly related to investment")	–
North Korea	2005	2005	3	= art. FET NT / ≠ § / [model 1997]	investments and activities associated by investors	–
India	2006	2007	4	= art. NT / = §	investors "including in respect of returns"	–

Treatment formulation	Subject to domestic law	Position MFN exceptions	In-clause exceptions to MFN (v PRC models)	Other *ad hoc* exceptions	Non-conforming measures
not less favorable	–	= art.	≠ any model but equivalent	–	V
less favorable	–	= art.	model 1997, equivalent	–	V
less favorable	–	= art.	model 1997, equivalent + (domestic taxation)	–	V
not less favorable	–	= art.	model 1997, exact	–	–
not less favorable	–	= art.	model 1997, exact	–	–
not less favorable	–	= art.	≠ any model but equivalent – (frontier trade)	–	–
not less favorable	–	= art.	model 1997, exact	–	–
less favorable	–	= art.	model 1997, equivalent – (frontier trade)	–	–
not less favorable	–	= art.	≠ any model but equivalent – (frontier trade)	–	V

TABLE 20 MFN in Chinese IIAs (*cont.*)

Counterpart	Signed	In force	Art.	Structure	Object of coverage	Expressly covered activities
Pakistan [FTA]	2006	2007	48	= art. FET NT / ≠ § / [model 1997]	investments and activities associated by investors	–
Russia	2006	2009	3	= art. FET NT / ≠ § / [model 1997]	investments and activities associated by investors	–
Vanuatu	2006	–	3	= art. FET NT / ≠ § / [model 1997]	investments and activities associated by investors	–
South Korea	2007	2007	3	= art. NT / ≠ §	investors, investments and activities associated by investors	admission, expansion, operation, management, maintenance, use, enjoyment, and sale or other disposal (def. 'investment and business activities')
Costa Rica	2007	2016	3	= art. FET NT / ≠ § / [model 1997]	investments and activities associated by investors	–
France	2007	2010	4	= art. NT / ≠ §	investors with respect to investments and associated activities	–
Seychelles	2007	–	5	= art. NT / = §	investors with respect to investments and associated activities	–

Treatment formulation	Subject to domestic law	Position MFN exceptions	In-clause exceptions to MFN (v PRC models)	Other *ad hoc* exceptions	Non-conforming measures
less favorable	–	= art.	model 1997, exact	–	–
less favorable	–	= art.	model 1997, equivalent – (frontier trade)	CIS investments	–
less favorable	–	= art.	model 1997, exact	–	–
not less favorable in like circumstances	–	= art.	model 1997, exact	–	(only NT)
less favorable	–	= art.	model 1997, exact	–	–
treatment granted to MFN	–	= art.	≠ any model but equivalent – (frontier trade)	preservation of cultural and linguistic diversity	–
treatment granted to MFN	–	= art.	≠ any model but equivalent + (domestic taxation) – (frontier trade)	–	–

TABLE 20 MFN in Chinese IIAs (*cont.*)

Counterpart	Signed	In force	Art.	Structure	Object of coverage	Expressly covered activities
Cuba	2007*	2007	3	= art. FET FPS / ≠ § / [model 1984]	investments and activities associated *	–
New Zealand [FTA]	2008	2008	139	indep.	investors, investments and activities associated by investors	admission, expansion, management, conduct, operation, maintenance, use, enjoyment and disposal
Colombia	2008	2013	3	= art. NT / ≠ §	investments of investors	operation, management, use, enjoyment, or disposal
Mexico	2008	2009	4	indep.	(§) investors (§) investments of investors	operation, management, maintenance, use, enjoyment or disposal (§=§)
ASEAN [CAIA/ FTA]	2009	2010	5	indep.	investors and investments	establishment, acquisition, admission, expansion, management, maintenance, use, conduct, sale, operation and other forms of disposal
Switzerland	2009	2010	4	= art. FET FPS NT / = § NT	(§) investments or returns of investors (§) investors	management, maintenance, use, enjoyment or disposal

Treatment formulation	Subject to domestic law	Position MFN exceptions	In-clause exceptions to MFN (v PRC models)	Other *ad hoc* exceptions	Non-conforming measures
not less favorable in similar conditions	–	= art.	model 1984–9, exact	–	–
not less favorable in like circumstances	–	= art.	≠ any model	fisheries and maritime matters; treatment pursuant to prior int'l ag.; agreements on trade and economic integration	– (only NT)
not less favorable in like circumstances	–	= art.	model 1997, equivalent – (frontier trade)	–	–
not less favorable in like circumstances	–	≠ art.	model 1997, equivalent + (domestic taxation) – (frontier trade) *	–	–
not less favorable in like circumstances	–	= & ≠ art.	≠ any model	future better treatment to third States; inter–ASEAN privilege; treatment pursuant to prior int'l ags.	V
not less favorable	–	= art.	≠ any model but equivalent – (frontier trade)	–	V

TABLE 20 MFN in Chinese IIAs (*cont.*)

Counterpart	Signed	In force	Art.	Structure	Object of coverage	Expressly covered activities
Peru [FTA]	2009	2010	131	indep.	(§) investors (§) investments of investors	establishment, acquisition, expansion, management, conduct, operation, sale and other disposition (§=§)
Bahamas	2009	–	3	= art. FET NT / ≠ § / [model 1997]	investments and activities associated by investors	–
Mali	2009	2009	3	= art. FET NT / ≠ § / [model 1997]	investments and activities associated by investors	–
Malta	2009	2009	3	= art. FET NT / ≠ § / [model 1997]	investments and activities associated by investors	management, use, enjoyment or disposal
Chad	2010	–	5	indep.	investors and investments	operation, management, maintenance, use, enjoyment, sale or disposal
Libya	2010	–	3	= art. FET NT / ≠ § / [model 1997]	investments and activities associated by investors	–
DR Congo	2011	–	5	indep.	investors and investments	operation, management, maintenance, use, enjoyment, sale or disposal

Treatment formulation	Subject to domestic law	Position MFN exceptions	In-clause exceptions to MFN (v PRC models)	Other *ad hoc* exceptions	Non-conforming measures
not less favorable in like circumstances	–	= art.	model 1984–9, exact	disadvantaged minorities, cultural industries	– (only NT)
less favorable	–	= art.	model 1997, exact	–	–
at least equal	–	= art.	model 1997, exact	–	–
less favorable	–	= art.	≠ any model but equivalent	–	–
not less favorable in the same situation	–	= art.	model 1997, exact	–	–
less favorable	–	= art.	model 1997, exact	–	–
not less favorable in like circumstances	–	= art.	model 1997, exact	–	–

TABLE 20 MFN in Chinese IIAS (*cont.*)

Counterpart	Signed	In force	Art.	Structure	Object of coverage	Expressly covered activities
Uzbekistan	2011	2011	4	indep.	investors and investments	establishment, acquisition, expansion, management, maintenance, use, enjoyment, sale or disposal
Canada	2012	2014	5	indep.	(§) investors (§) covered investments	establishment, acquisition, expansion, management, conduct, operation, sale and other disposition (§=§)
South Korea & Japan	2012	2014	4	indep.	investors and investments	admission + management, conduct, operation, maintenance, use, enjoyment and sale or other disposition (def. 'investment activities')

Treatment formulation	Subject to domestic law	Position MFN exceptions	In-clause exceptions to MFN (v PRC models)	Other *ad hoc* exceptions	Non-conforming measures
not less favorable in like circumstances	–	= art.	model 1997, exact	–	–
not less favorable in like circumstances	–	≠ art.	≠ any model	FTA/CU; fisheries and maritime matters; treatment pursuant to pre-1994 int'l ags.; State enterprises control or nationality limitations; ref. to CA–Peru & PRC–Peru FTA; IP rights int'l ag. Prevail; procurement; subsidies / grants.	V
not less favorable in like circumstances	–	= art.	≠ any model but equivalent	aviation, fishery and maritime matters; acquisition of land property	– (only NT)

TABLE 20 MFN in Chinese IIAS (*cont.*)

Counterpart	Signed	In force	Art.	Structure	Object of coverage	Expressly covered activities
Chile [SAI/ FTA]	2012	2014	5	indep.	(§) investors (§) investments of investors	management, conduct, operation, sale or other disposition (§=§)
Tanzania	2013	2014	4	indep.	investors and investments	establishment, acquisition, expansion, operation, management, maintenance, use, enjoyment, sale or disposition
Australia [FTA]	2015	2015	4	indep.	investors and investments (covered)	establishment, acquisition, expansion, management, conduct, operation, sale and other disposition

Treatment formulation	Subject to domestic law	Position MFN exceptions	In-clause exceptions to MFN (v PRC models)	Other *ad hoc* exceptions	Non-conforming measures
not less favorable in like circumstances	–	≠ art.	≠ any model but equivalent	aviation, fishery, and maritime matters; subsidies/grants; IP rights int'l ag. prevail; treatment pursuant to prior int'l ag.; Chile national debt	–
not less favorable in like circumstances	–	= art.	model 1997, equivalent	–	–
not less favorable in like circumstances	–	= & ≠ art.	≠ any model	aviation, fishery, and maritime matters; PRC (temporary): any item in any negative list in any IA; AUS: sectors & activities in Annex III;	V

TABLE 20 MFN in Chinese IIAS (*cont.*)

Counterpart	Signed	In force	Art.	Structure	Object of coverage	Expressly covered activities
South Korea [FTA]	2015	2015	12.4	indep.	investors and investments (covered)	admission + management, conduct, operation, maintenance, use, enjoyment and sale or other disposition (def. 'investment activities')
Turkey	2015	–	4	= art. NT / ≠ § (2 paras)	investments and activities associated by investors	admission

Treatment formulation	Subject to domestic law	Position MFN exceptions	In-clause exceptions to MFN (v PRC models)	Other *ad hoc* exceptions	Non-conforming measures
not less favorable in like circumstances	–	= art.	model 1997, equivalent – (taxation)	aviation, fishery, and maritime matters; info /statistical needs	– (only NT)
not less favorable in like circumstances	V (on admission)	= art.	≠ any model but equivalent	–	– (only NT)

E The National Treatment Clause in Chinese IIAs

1 *Introduction and Relevant Pool of Treaties*

Reflecting the particularly cautious approach ensuing from opening up, in the early '80s, to investors coming from different political and legal systems, China has long refrained to embrace the National Treatment (NT) standard in its treaty practice. Accordingly, the 1984 model does not mention the clause. After a 'best effort' transition reflected in a modest number of agreements following the 1989 model, the NT protection, at last featured in the 1997 model, has become part of China's standard treaty practice from year 2000 on (the last agreements not featuring a NT clause are the 1999 BITs with Qatar and Bahrain). Pivotal agreements include:

- The 1986 BIT with the UK, the first featuring a NT clause in the 'best effort' form (subsequently introduced in the 1989 model);
- The 1995 BIT with Morocco, the first including a full NT clause – subject, however, to 'domestic laws and regulations' (as per the standard formulation of the 1997 model);
- The 2001 BITs with the Netherlands and Cyprus, the firsts featuring an unrestricted NT guarantee.

While the clause has ultimately become part of China's standard investment treaty practice, it shall be noted that even today, whenever possible, preference is to expressly make it 'subject to domestic laws and regulations'.

In sum, because of its prolonged rejection of this type of protection, the NT clause is featured only in 68 IIAs out of the pool of 120 here examined, and actually granted by China in 67.[115] Of these, 57 (85% of 67) have been concluded after year 2000. Overall, NT is included in just over half of China's investment treaties (to be precise, 56%).

The analysis that follows, therefore, moves from a **pool of 67 IIAs**, and the only two Chinese models (1989 and 1997) that feature the standard.

2 *Type of NT Clause*

Because of the cautiousness and the policy evolution just referred to, the first NT clauses China accepted to commit to (and that are still in force) offer a mostly symbolic protection. Hence, in the 5 agreements with the UK (1986), Iceland (1994), and the former Jugoslav republics of Slovenia (1993), Serbia

115 In the 1996 China-Syria BIT, Syria offers NT, while China does not. For the purposes of this analysis, focusing on China's treaty practice, this BIT is thus not considered in the pool of IIAs featuring a NT clause.

(1995), and Macedonia (1997), all in line with the 1989 Chinese template, not only the clause is termed as a 'best effort' standard, but such an effort is additionally 'subject to domestic laws'.

In 40 IIAs concluded between 1995 and 2013 (35 of which, since year 2000), or 60% of the pool of 67 agreements featuring the NT, the clause is 'without prejudice to its laws and regulations' (which is the wording of the 1997 model, followed *tel quel* in 32 agreements), or equivalent formulations.

In the remaining 22 cases (33% of 67), all signed from 2001 onward, China accepted an unrestricted NT clause. The absence of limitations in the definition does not exclude that these find nevertheless space in subsequent provisions featuring general or *ad hoc* exclusions (which indeed is the case in several of the most recent treaties; see below).

Hence, against a relatively modest overall adherence throughout China's treaty practice to either the 1989 or 1997 model clause (54% of treaties), it may be concluded that, today, China either follows the 1997 model or accepts a nominally unrestricted definition of the standard of protection (provided that specific limitations are then featured in other provisions of the agreement).

3 *Structure of the NT Clause*

In their investment treaty models, States differ in terms of where they locate the NT clause – in particular, in relation to the other basic standards of protection: FET, FPS, PAD, and MFN. Germany and the UK place NT in the same provision with MFN, intertwining the two ('*treatment accorded to investments of its own investors or … of any third State*'), while FET, FPS and PAD are gathered in a separate (and preceding) 'admission and protection' provision.[116] France and Italy are, in this respect, equivalent.[117] The Netherlands intertwine NT and MFN as well, however within a catch-all provision containing, in the preceding paragraph, FET, FPS, and PAD.[118] The US and Canada, instead, make of the NT clause a standalone provision.[119]

In its 1997 model, China has taken a unique stance in terms of structure. In fact, NT, FET, and MFN, while under the same provision (labeled 'treatment of investment'), are featured each in a dedicated paragraph, leaving FPS and

116 Cf., Art. 2 and Art. 3, German model BIT (2008) and same provisions in the UK model BIT (2006).

117 Arts. II or III of the Italian model (2003) do not expressly mention FPS. In the French model (2006), FET is featured in a standalone provision (without admission, nor FPS), while the treaty does not mention PAD at all; cf., Art. 3–5.

118 Cf., Art. 3 of the Dutch model BIT (2003).

119 Cf., Art. 3 of the US (2004) or Canadian (2004) models.

PAD (each with its own paragraph as well) in the preceding provision (labeled 'promotion and protection of investments').[120] This specific differentiation, present in a considerable number of agreements, is believed to underscore the different legal cultures and nuances in the understanding, in China and in the West, of the terms 'promotion', 'protection', and 'treatment'.

Probably reflecting the adjustment each time needed, during negotiations, over a relatively marginal aspect such as the position of a clause (as opposed to its actual formulation), China's 1997 model has been adhered to only in **22** IIAs (*i.e.*, 33% of 67), signed between 2000–2010. In **29** cases overall (43%), nevertheless, the NT clause is featured in the same provision with MFN and FET (hence, compatibly with the Chinese model). In other **20** cases (30%), NT is framed with MFN (but not FET), however only in 5 agreements China accepted the Anglo-German 'intertwining' earlier mentioned. In the last significant group, comprising **13** recent agreements (19%) signed between 2008–2015, China aligned to the North American practice of featuring the NT clause in a standalone provision. The latter seems to have become standard practice as, since 2010, only one IIA (with Turkey) does not follow this pattern. Lastly, with 5 counterparts with no apparent connection among themselves, all substantive treatments (FET, FPS, PAD, NT, and MFN), are gathered in a single provision (as per the Dutch model – and indeed one of these agreement is the BIT with the Netherlands).

4 *Object of Coverage of the Clause*

One aspect that is usually overlooked in both practice and academia is the actual object of coverage of investment protection clauses. In the case of NT, this usually includes investments and/or investors, but other elements may also be made explicit (*e.g.*, returns, activities related/associated by/of investors).[121] For the avoidance of doubt, the US, Canadian, and German practice specifies that the NT guarantee (in the latter case, along with MFN, as the two are there intertwined) applies to both investors *and* investments,[122] by dedicating to each a specific paragraph with identical or quasi-identical wording. The British model, in all equivalent, features two paragraphs as well (also intertwining NT and MFN), one for 'investments or returns' and the other for

120 Cf., Art. 2 and Art. 3 Chinese model (1997).

121 Independently from (or redundantly with respect to) the treaty definition of 'investment'.

122 The US and Canadian models refer to 'covered investment'.

'national or companies'. The Dutch model focuses only on 'investments', the Italian on 'investments and income accruing to', and the French on 'investors'.

The Chinese 1989 model focuses on 'investments', upon which the 1997 model expands to include '*activities associated with such investments by the investors*'. The locution, used for the MFN as well and unique among the models here surveyed, appears particularly liberal, as the formulation 'associated by' seemingly leaves broad discretion to the investor in determining the 'accessory elements' of an investment (as opposed to leaving this aspect to the contract, or the State; cf., Morocco's definitory attempt in *Salini* – ultimately rejected, yet reflecting the possible State view on the point).[123]

In practice, 39 IIAs out of the 67 featuring the NT clause (hence, 58%) follow a Chinese model: 9 the 1989 model, and 30 the 1997 model. Of this latter group, 29 are IIAs concluded from year 2000 on.

In 17 cases (25%), mostly modern IIAs from 2005 on, investors *and* investments are expressly covered, 9 times each in a dedicated paragraph, and 8 times jointly in the same paragraph.

The last significant group, composed of 5 treaties (7,5%) signed between 2005–2007, follows the French model (indeed, these agreements are with France and 4 former French colonies).

Thus, next to a relevant adherence to the Chinese model, from 2005 on the Chinese practice shows considerable flexibility, possibly facilitated by the fact that models and practice of traditional major players on the point is quite fragmented.

5 *Ambit of Coverage of the Clause*

European models *en bloc* do not specify to what exactly the protection granted via NT extends to. Since NAFTA and the subsequent 2004 models, instead, Canada and the US refined the definition, specifying the protection extends '*with respect to establishment, acquisition, expansion, management, conduct, operation and sale or other disposition*'. The locution echoes the earlier British formulation for the coverage of PAD ('*management, maintenance, use, enjoyment or disposal*'), and has triggered quite a jigsaw of terms employed in the subsequent State practice over substantive protections, between the British understanding of 'disposal' (*i.e.*, giving up the investment – hence the position of the term as last one in the list), and the broader meaning of the term

123 See para. 46, *Salini Costruttori S.p.A. and Italstrade S.p.A. v. Kingdom of Morocco*, ICSID Case No. ARB/00/4.

'disposition' in the North American models and practice. The latter term, with reference to 'things', does indeed include 'to dispose of', but is more commonly understood as 'to arrange'. In this sense, the position as last of the list of the terms in the US model, in the form 'or other disposition', seems meant to be a catch-all locution aimed at including any action with regard to the investment the investor might want to take (as opposed to being limited to any form of giving up the investment).

The premise is necessary as, while the Chinese model follows the European States (*i.e.*, does not refine the definition) in 69% of the cases (46 treaties out of 67), in the remaining 31% the distinction between the two terms (or lack thereof) had quite a significant impact on the Chinese practice. In 7 cases, all from 2002 on, the British model, or modest variations of it, has been followed. In other 14 (21%), however, the lists of protected actions are all at least partly different, mixing elements of the various models and practices, without a single discernible model of reference. Of course, the flexibility to accept this panoply of variants finds place over the last 15 years, at a time when China's practice has become less bound to its own model (as the State Council relaxed its scrutiny, all the while granting more autonomy to negotiators).[124]

Only two BITS (with Libya and Turkey), out of 14 concluded to date since 2009, do not expressly list the ambit of coverage with respect to NT. Therefore, while it appears that China has not yet settled on which terms to include in the list, it seems quite settled that a list of terms is now employed to define the ambit of coverage of the NT clause.

6 *NT Treatment Formulation* (*Positive, Negative, with Comparator*)

In investment treaties, the NT guarantee may be formulated in a positive ('same as accorded') or negative ('not less favorable') fashion. In the latter case, the formulation can be refined by a comparator (*e.g.*, 'in like circumstances'). For instance, all European models resort to the negative formulation, which the North American ones, drawing from NAFTA, enrich with the comparator 'in like circumstances'.

While this aspect may seem a nicety of limited use in an arbitral context, the distinction holds value in the framework of a study of the vast and articulated treaty practice of a major source as well as destination of foreign investment. This is especially so when, as it happens, China – for a while and on this aspect as well – maintained specific policy traits in this respect.

124 See Chapter 2, Section A.

In an original fashion, the 1989 model framed its best effort clause as treatment 'the same as accorded to its own investors'. The wording thus appears in five agreements that follow the 1989 model *in toto* (three with former Yugoslav republics in the mid-90s, plus UK 1986 and Iceland 1994), plus one where the guarantee is full yet 'subject to domestic laws' (Congo 2000). These **6** agreements constitute the 9% of the 67 featuring a NT clause.

With the 1997 model, instead, China adopted the European standard. This found application in **43** agreements (64% of 67), spanning between 1995 and 2010. It is noteworthy that, before year 2000, the model wording as such is employed in only five agreements, all with Mideastern or African States. This *inter alia* confirms that the actual practice of the model has taken place from year 2000.

The introduction of a comparator appears for the first time in the Chinese practice with the 2000 BIT with Iran – where the wording adopted is, however, atypical ('in a comparable situation'). The North American wording 'in like circumstances' began being accepted by the China in 2007, and since 2010 has become an unexcepted practice. Overall, NT clauses featuring a comparator are **16** (24% of 67).

7 *Exceptions to the NT*

7.1 Position

With the exception of the UK, European models feature, in the provision where the NT and MFN guarantees are jointly located, a carve out from their operation, usually excluding privileges deriving from forms of economic integration (*i.e.*, the EU) and bilateral tax arrangements. The British model, on its part, features a more specific provision dedicated to exceptions,[125] while North American models offer a more articulated regime altogether (broken down in several provisions, general and *ad hoc*).[126]

Drawing from the continental European models and practice, in its 1989 template China established a general carve out to MFN and NT, in the last paragraph of the same provision where they are located. There, China added an original case, aiming at preserving privileges established to 'facilitating frontier trade'.

In the 1997 model, China expressly – and correctly – excluded from the general carve out the NT clause (which, with reference to exceptions referring only to international agreements, can hardly include NT cases).

---

125 Cf., Art. 7 UK model.

126 Cf., in general, Arts. 14–18 US model, and Arts. 9–10 Canadian model.

The Chinese practice can be thus summarized as follows: **24** IIAs (hence, 36% of 67 agreements), including the agreements that follow the 1997 model, do not contain express exceptions to NT. Therefore, 43 IIAs feature exceptions, general or *ad hoc*. Of these, in **37** IIAs (86% of 43) exceptions are general and listed in the same provision where NT is located. In the remaining **6** cases, NT exceptions are listed in an *ad hoc* provision (or in several provisions dealing with exceptions). The most recent treaties, concluded from 2008 on, fall in this latter category.

7.2 Wording of NT Exceptions (Relatively to Chinese Models)

As found, 43 Chinese IIAs out of the 67 featuring the NT guarantee comprise exceptions to it as well, general or *ad hoc*. Therefore, an exception regime to NT is present in 64% of cases.

China's 1989 model features three categories of exceptions to the operation of both NT and MFN: *i*) customs union, free trade zone, and economic union; *ii*) avoidance of double taxation; and *iii*) facilitating frontier trade. As such, the model found application in **2** BITs in the second half of the '90s.

As noted, the 1997 model, while refining the wording of the earlier template, maintains the three exception categories but correctly refers them to MFN only. In practice, however, China often resorted to formulations whose wording is identical, equivalent or compatible with that featured in the 1997 model, albeit maintaining a joint reference to NT and MFN.

Therefore, while identical wording as in the 1997 model has been extended to NT only in two early cases (South Africa 1997 and Congo 2000), quasi-identical wording featuring identical exceptions appears in 11 IIAs, and other compatible formulations (*i.e.*, equivalent wording and a variance of maximum one category of exceptions relatively to the model) in another 10 IIAs. In all, identical-to-compatible reference to the 1997 model wording may be found in **23** IIAs out of 43 (53%).

Albeit displaying a different wording than any model, another significant group of 10 IIAs (23%) features anyway an equivalent content in terms of NT exceptions (with a variance of maximum one category). In 9 of these agreements, however, the 'frontier trade' exception (typically Chinese) has been ultimately discarded.

No model is instead the template of the exception regime contained in 8 recent IIAs, 6 of which concluded from 2012 on.

7.3 Relation between NT and MFN Exceptions (within the Same IIA)

The relation between NT and MFN exceptions is another way to look at the structure and evolution of the exception regime to their operation.

In this respect, the Chinese practice is quite uniform: in **32** cases of out of 43 (74%), NT and MFN share both provision and exception regime. While majoritarian, this practice seems nevertheless terminated, as the last agreements following it are of 2009 (BITs with Malta and Switzerland).

In **3** cases, still in the context of a shared exception regime, one exception specifically applies to MFN but not to NT: that is the case of 'frontier trade facilitations' (Czech Republic 2005 and Turkey 2015) and, seemingly, economic integration (France 2007).[127]

In other **3** IIAs, NT and MFN share an *ad hoc* exception regime located in another provision(s): this is the case of the agreements with Canada (2012), Chile (2012) and Australia (2015).

Only **5** IIAs (12% of 43) contemplate a different regime of exceptions altogether for NT and MFN respectively: this is the case of Madagascar (2005), Peru (2009), South Korea-Japan (2012), Tanzania (2013), and South Korea (2015).

China seems thus in a 'state of flux' with regard to how to frame the regime of exceptions to the NT, and the relationship of the latter regime with that for MFN. While a change from the relatively steady previous practice (up to 2009) is evident, a new trend is not clearly discernible at this time.

7.4 Investment Agreements Featuring Ad Hoc Exceptions to NT

A limited number of recent Chinese IIAs contemplate exceptions specifically excluding NT operation in certain circumstances. Differently than in the case of MFN, however, and reflecting how the NT guarantee impacts on domestic sensitive areas and concerns, *ad hoc* exceptions vary considerably from treaty to treaty. The impact of these exceptions, in materially reducing the level of protection of foreign investment, varies as well. In fact, *ad hoc* exceptions to NT seem often tied to cultural and historical values, minimum developmental needs, or human rights-oriented concerns. In this respect, it seems also that, in most cases, the carveouts are introduced upon request of China's treaty counterparts.

Out of the **11** IIAs featuring this type of exclusions in the Chinese practice, 10 are concluded from 2003 on. The only earlier agreement is the 1997 BIT with South Africa, which excludes NT operation if a breach determined by domestic laws is 'aimed to remedy past discriminatory practices'.[128] Guyana (2003)

127 The text of Art. 4, at paragraph 4, seems attached and continuing the previous paragraph 3, devoted to the MFN clause, and excluding economic integration privileges only against the MFN (*'ce traitement'* seemingly referred only to MFN). The subsequent paragraph 5, instead, by expressly referring the fiscal and tax carve outs to the overall provision (*'les dispositions du present article'*) includes paragraph 1, featuring the NT clause.

128 Art. 3.3 China-South Africa BIT (1997).

and Tanzania (2013) carve out incentives to support the development of local entrepreneurship or industries.[129] Peru (2009) wishes to maintain special treatments for disadvantaged minorities.[130] France (2007) aims at preserving cultural and linguistic diversity.[131] More formalistic, and drawn from the US model, are the exclusions in the IA with Japan and South Korea (2012), as well as in the FTA with South Korea (2015), carving out 'special formalities not impacting investments' and 'information and statistical needs'.[132]

Potentially more disruptive (if relatively unsurprising) is, next to Finland (2004) exclusion of 'essential security interest in time of war' along the vague 'public order',[133] the carve out of 'cross-border capital transactions in exceptional circumstances' of the Japan-South Korea BIT (2012).[134] Drawn from the North American models are the exceptions for 'subsidies and grants' and 'government procurement' with Canada (2012) and South Korea (2015).[135] Noteworthy are, also, Canada's concern for 'control or nationality limitations' of State enterprises,[136] and Chile (2012) 'public debt'.[137] Australia (2015) carves out entire sectors (listed in a separate annex).[138] Peculiar is, lastly, the cross-exclusion that China and Canada make with reference to their respective FTA with Peru.[139]

As mentioned, the recent practice to introduce exceptions to the NT regime seems due to several factors. Firstly, China's progressive alignment with the US models and practice. Hence, the increased sensitivity of China's treaty counterpart about the potential pervasiveness of Chinese investment.

---

129 Art. 3.6 China-Guyana BIT (2003); Art. 3.2 China-Tanzania BIT (2013).

130 Art. 129.3 China-Peru FTA (2009).

131 Art. 4.6 China-France BIT (2007).

132 Art. 16.1 China-Japan-South Korea IA (2012) and Art. 12.13 China-South Korea FTA (2015); cf., Art. 1111 NAFTA (1994) and Art. 15 US model (2004).

133 Art. 3.6 China-Finland BIT (2004).

134 Art. 19 China-Japan-South Korea IA (2012).

135 Art. 8.5 China-Canada BIT (2012) and Art. 12.5.6 China-South Korea FTA (2015); cf., Art. 14 US model (2004) and Art. 9 Canada model (2004).

136 Art. 8.2.a.ii China-Canada BIT (2012).

137 Annex C China-Chile SAI (2012).

138 Schedule of Non-Conforming Measures, Annex III, Section B China-Australia FTA (2015).

139 Annex B.8, China-Canada BIT (2012).

8 *Non-Conforming Measures*

Typical of the North American practice,[140] the regime of non-conforming measures allows a contracting State to maintain, continue, and amend measures which, already existing at the time of the entry into force of the IIA, would otherwise constitute a breach of the NT guarantee. While this exceptional regime is not limited to NT (as it may also exclude MFN and other guarantees), this is its key ambit of application, as it *institutionalizes* a discrimination in favor of domestic investors, or to protect nationals, also with respect to potential or perceived back-lashes due to foreign investment.

In the Chinese practice, **19** IIAs concluded from 2001 onward feature a non-conforming measure regime. This represents 28% of the 67 IIAs featuring a NT clause, and 32% of the 59 agreements concluded since year 2000.

While, *in abstracto*, it is possible to say that the general exception provided by a non-conforming measure regime is well-suited to China's overall conservative investment treaty policy, it is difficult to determine if, at this stage, this has become a standard feature of its treaty practice. Looking at the last 20 agreements concluded, in fact, only 9 feature it.

140 Cf., Art. 14 US model (2004) and Art. 9 Canada model (2004).

The National Treatment clause in Chinese IIAs: Data Summary

NT
67/120 IIAS

Presence

- No: **53** (52) (45%) [*1984 model*]
  - IIAs between 1984–1999: 51
    - Exception: Tunisia (2004)
- Yes: **67** (68)[141] (56%)
  - IIAs since 2000: 57 (85%)
    - Exceptions: UK (1986), Slovenia (1993), Iceland (1994), Serbia (1995), Morocco (1996), Saudi Arabia (1996), FYROM (1997), South Africa (1997), Gabon (1997), Yemen (1998)

Type

- Best effort & subject to domestic laws: **5** (7% of 67) [*1989 model*]
  - UK (1986), Slovenia (1993), Iceland (1994), Serbia (1995), FYROM (1997)
- Subject to / in accordance with / without prejudice to domestic laws and regulations: **40** (60% of 67)
  - IIAs between 1995–2013
  - IIAs since 2000: 35
  - As in *1997 model* (*'without prejudice to its laws and regulations'*): 32 (47% of 67)
  - *'subject to its laws'* (no 'regulations'): 1
    - Mali (2009)
- Full: **22** (33% of 67)
  - IIAs between 2001–2015

Structure of the Clause

- Together with MFN: **20** (30% of 67)
  - Same para: 5
    - Bosnia (2002), Czech Rep. (2005), Madagascar (2005), India (2006), Seychelles (2007)

141 In the 1996 China-Syria BIT, Syria offers NT, while China does not. For the purposes of this analysis, focusing on China's treaty practice, this BIT is thus not considered in the pool of IIAs featuring a NT clause.

  - Dedicated para.: 15
    - As in *1989 model*: 4
- Together with MFN & FET: **29** (43% of 67)
  - As in the *1997 model*: 22
    - IIAs between 2000–2010
- Together with MFN, FET & FPS: 5
  - Slovenia (1993), South Africa (1997), Iran (2000), Netherlands (2001), Switzerland (2009)
- Independent clause: **13** (19% of 67)
  - IIAs between 2008–2015

Object of Coverage

- Investors: 6
  - As such: 1
    - Namibia (2005)
  - With respect to investments and activities related / in connection: 5
    - Guinea (2005), Equatorial Guinea (2005), Madagascar (2005), Seychelles (2007), France (2007)
- Investments: 44 (66% of 67)
  - Investments of investors: **9** (13% of 67) [*1989 model*]
    - UK (1986), Slovenia (1993), Iceland (1994), Serbia (1995), Saudi Arabia (1996), FYROM (1997), Iran (2000), India (2006), Colombia (2008)
  - Investment by investors: 2
    - Mozambique (2001), Finland (2004)
  - Investments and activities associated by investors: **30** (45% of 67) [*1997 model*]
    - IIAs between 2000–2015: 29 (exception: South Africa (1997))
  - Investments and activities associated **of** investors: 1
    - Belgium-Lux (2005)
  - Investment and activities associated / related **by** investors: 1
    - Mali (2009)
  - *Ad hoc* para for 'investment-related activities': 1
    - Gabon (1997)
- Investors & investments: **17** (25% of 67)
  - Same para: 8
    - South Korea (2007), ASEAN (2009), Chad (2010), Uzbekistan (2011), DRC (2011), SK & JP (2012), Tanzania (2013), South Korea (2015)

- Separate paras (investments (with/without 'returns') / investors): 9
  - Morocco (1995), Yemen (1998), Czech Rep. (2005), Mexico (2008), Peru (2009), Switzerland (2009), Canada (2012), Chile (2012), Australia (2015)

Ambit of Coverage: 21/67 (31%)

- No: **46** (69% of 67) [*any PRC model*]
- Yes: IIAs between 2002–2015
- Management, maintenance, use, enjoyment or disposal:[142] 7
  - As such: 3
    - Germany (2003), Czech Rep. (2005), Switzerland (2009)
  - One additional element: 3
    - '*operation*': Trinidad & Tobago (2002), Guyana (2003), Chile (2012)
  - One less element: 1
    - '*maintenance*': Colombia (2008)
- Other (richer) combinations: **14** (21%)

Treatment Formulation: 67/67

- '*Not less favorable*' as such: **43** (64%) [*1997 model*]
  - IIAs between 1995–2010
  - IIAs before 2000: 5
    - Morocco (1995), Saudi Arabia (1996), Gabon (1997), South Africa (1997), Yemen (1998)
- '*Not less favorable*' + comparator: **16** (24%)
  - '*in like circumstances*': 14
    - IIAs between 2007–2015
  - '*in a comparable situation*': 1
    - Iran (2000)
  - '*in similar conditions*': 1
    - Chad (2010)
- Same as accorded: **6** (9%) [*1989 model*]
  - UK (1986), Slovenia (1993), Iceland (1994), Serbia (1995), FYROM (1997), Rep. of Congo (2000)
- At least equal: **1**
  - Mali (2010)

142 Formulation identical to the UK model: 'management, maintenance, use, enjoyment or disposal'.

- Same or similar: 1
  - Namibia (2005)

Position of Exceptions to NT*: 43/67* **(***64%***)**

- No NT-specific exceptions: 24 (36%) [*1997 model*]
  - IIAs between 1993–2011
  - BITs before year 2000: 4
    - Slovenia (1993), Morocco (1995), Gabon (1997), Yemen (1998)
- Same provision: 37 (86% of 43)
  - IIAs between 1986–2016
  - IIAs since year 2000: 31
- *Ad hoc* provision: 6
  - Mexico (2008), Chile (2012), Canada (2012), SK-JP (2012), Australia (2015), South Korea (2015)

Wording of Exceptions to NT **(***Relatively to PRC Models***)***: 43/67*

- Wording as in *1997 model* on MFN: **23** (53% of 43)
  - Exact: 2
    - South Africa (1997), Rep. of Congo (2000)
  - Equivalent: 11
    - IIAs between 1995–2008
  - +/– 1 exception: 10
    - Without 'frontier trade': 6
    - Plus 'domestic taxation': 6
- Different than any model but equivalent content: 10 (23% of 43)
  - Malta (2009)
  - No 'frontier trade': 8
    - Trinidad & Tobago (2002), Guyana (2003), Uganda (2004), Czech Rep. (2005), India (2006), France (2007), Switzerland (2009), Turkey (2015)
  - No 'frontier trade', plus 'domestic taxation'
    - Seychelles (2007)
- Different than any model: 8
  - Madagascar (2005), Peru (2009), Canada (2012), Chile (2012), SK-JP (2012), Tanzania (2013), South Korea (2015), Australia (2015)
- Wording as in *1984–9 models* on MFN: 2
  - Saudi Arabia (1996), FYROM (1997)

Exceptions NT *v* MFN *(within same* IIA*): 43/67*

- Same provision and content as MFN: **32/43** (74%)
  - IIAs between 1986–2009
- One less element: **3**
  - No 'frontier trade': 2
    - Czech Rep. (2005), Turkey (2015)
  - No CU/FTA: 1
    - France (2007)[143]
- Different provision and content: **5** (12% of 43)
    - Madagascar (2005), Peru (2009), SK-JP (2012), Tanzania (2013), South Korea (2015)
- *Ad hoc* exception provision shared with MFN: **3**
    - Canada (2012), Chile (2012), Australia (2015)

Ad hoc *Exceptions to* NT*: 11/67*

- IIAs since 2003: 10
  - Exception: South Africa (1997)
- Types of *ad hoc* exceptions:
  - Specific sectors (listed in Annex III)
    - Australia (2015)
  - Subsidies & grants
    - Canada (2012); South Korea (2015)
  - Incentives to support the development of local entrepreneurship / industries
    - Guyana (2003), Tanzania (2013)
  - State enterprises (control or nationality limitations); cross-reference to exceptions in Canada-Peru and China-Peru FTAs; regulations of IP rights in other international agreements; government procurement
    - Canada (2012)
  - National debt
    - Chile (2012)

143 The text of Art. 4, at paragraph 4, seems attached and continuing the previous paragraph 3, devoted to the MFN clause, and excluding economic integration privileges only against the MFN (*'ce traitement'* seemingly referred only to MFN). The subsequent paragraph 5, instead, by expressly referring the fiscal and tax carve out to the overall provision (*'les dispositions du present article'*) includes paragraph 1, featuring the NT clause.

- Cross-border capital transactions in exceptional circumstances
  - SK-JP (2012):
- Special formalities not impacting investments
  - SK-JP (2012), South Korea (2015)
- Special treatments for disadvantaged minorities
  - Peru (2009)
- Preservation of cultural and linguistic diversity
  - France (2007)
- Essential security interest in time of war; public order
  - Finland (2004)
- Domestic laws to remedy past discriminatory practices
  - South Africa (1997)
- Information and statistical needs
  - South Korea (2015)

Non-Conforming Measures: 19/67 (*28%*)

- IIAs spanning 2001–2015
- Out of 59 IIAs concluded since year 2000: 32%

TABLE 21 NT in Chinese IIAs

Counterpart	Signed	In force	Presence & overarching limitations	Structure	Object of coverage	Expressly covered activities
Sweden	1982	1982	–	–	–	–
PRC MODEL	1989		to the extent possible + in accordance with the stipulations of laws and regulations	= art. MFN / ≠ §	investments of investors	–
PRC MODEL	1984		–	–	–	–
Norway	1984	1985	–	–	–	–
Kuwait	1985	1986	–	–	–	–
Italy	1985	1987	–	–	–	–
Denmark	1985	1985	–	–	–	–
Austria	1985	1986	–	–	–	–
UK	1986	1986	1989 model	= art. MFN / ≠ § / [1989 model]	investments of nationals or companies	–
Sri Lanka	1986	1987	–	–	–	–
Poland	1988	1989	–	–	–	–
*Australia**	1988	1988	–	–	–	–
Ghana	1989	1990	–	–	–	–
Bulgaria	1989	1994	–	–	–	–
*Turkey**	1990	1994	–	–	–	–
Papua NG	1991	1993	–	–	–	–
Mongolia	1991	1993	–	–	–	–
Hungary	1991	1993	–	–	–	–
Ukraine	1992	1993	–	–	–	–
*Philippines**	1992	1995	–	–	–	–
Kyrgyzstan	1992	1995	–	–	–	–
Kazakhstan	1992	1994	–	–	–	–
Greece	1992	1993	–	–	–	–

Treatment formulation	Position NT exceptions	Exceptions = MFN	Wording of exceptions to NT (v PRC models)	Non-conforming measures	Other *ad hoc* exceptions
–	–	–	–	–	–
same as accorded	–	–	wording as model 1984 on MFN	–	–
–	–	–	–	–	–
–	–	–	–	–	–
–	–	–	–	–	–
–	–	–	–	–	–
–	–	–	–	–	–
–	–	–	–	–	–
same as accorded	= art.	=	wording model 1997 on MFN, equivalent + (domestic taxation)	–	–
–	–	–	–	–	–
–	–	–	–	–	–
–	–	–	–	–	–
–	–	–	–	–	–
–	–	–	–	–	–
–	–	–	–	–	–
–	–	–	–	–	–
–	–	–	–	–	–
–	–	–	–	–	–
–	–	–	–	–	–
–	–	–	–	–	–
–	–	–	–	–	–
–	–	–	–	–	–
–	–	–	–	–	–

TABLE 21 NT in Chinese IIAs (*cont.*)

Counterpart	Signed	In force	Presence & overarching limitations	Structure	Object of coverage	Expressly covered activities
Armenia	1992	1995	–	–	–	–
Argentina	1992	1994	–	–	–	–
Bolivia	1992	1996	–	–	–	–
Slovenia	1993	1995	1989 model	= art. FET FPS MFN / ≠ §	investments of investors	–
UAE	1993	1994	–	–	–	–
Tajikistan	1993	1994	–	–	–	–
Lithuania	1993	1994	–	–	–	–
Georgia	1993	1995	–	–	–	–
Estonia	1993	1994	–	–	–	–
Croatia	1993	1994	–	–	–	–
Belarus	1993	1995	–	–	–	–
Albania	1993	1995	–	–	–	–
Uruguay	1993	1997	–	–	–	–
Iceland	1994	1997	1989 model	= art. MFN / ≠ § / [1989 model]	investments of investors	–
Jamaica	1994	1996	–	–	–	–
Egypt	1994	1996	–	–	–	–
Ecuador	1994	1997	–	–	–	–
Azerbaijan	1994	1995	–	–	–	–
Serbia	1995	1996	1989 model	= art. MFN / ≠ § / [1989 model]	investments of investors	–
Morocco	1995	1999	in accordance with its laws and regulations	= art. FET MFN / = §	(§) investments (§) investors on activities associated	–
Oman	1995	1995	–	–	–	–
Israel	1995	2009	–	–	–	–

Treatment formulation	Position NT exceptions	Exceptions = MFN	Wording of exceptions to NT (v PRC models)	Non-conforming measures	Other *ad hoc* exceptions
–	–	–	–	–	–
–	–	–	–	–	–
–	–	–	–	–	–
same as accorded	no ad hoc NT exceptions	/	/	–	–
–	–	–	–	–	–
–	–	–	–	–	–
–	–	–	–	–	–
–	–	–	–	–	–
–	–	–	–	–	–
–	–	–	–	–	–
–	–	–	–	–	–
–	–	–	–	–	–
–	–	–	–	–	–
same as accorded	= art.	=	wording model 1997 on MFN, equivalent + (domestic taxation) *	–	–
–	–	–	–	–	–
–	–	–	–	–	–
–	–	–	–	–	–
–	–	–	–	–	–
same as accorded	= art.	=	wording model 1997 on MFN, equivalent	–	–
not less favourable	no ad hoc NT exceptions	/	/	–	–
–	–	–	–	–	–
–	–	–	–	–	–

TABLE 21 NT in Chinese IIAs (*cont.*)

Counterpart	Signed	In force	Presence & overarching limitations	Structure	Object of coverage	Expressly covered activities
Saudi Arabia	1996	1997	subject to its laws and regulations	= art. MFN / ≠ §	investments of investors (and returns)	–
Zimbabwe	1996	1998	–	–	–	–
Zambia	1996	–	–	–	–	–
Mauritius	1996	1997	–	–	–	–
Lebanon	1996	1997	–	–	–	–
Bangladesh	1996	1997	–	–	–	–
Algeria	1996	2003	–	–	–	–
Syria	1996	2001	– (China) / full (Syria)	= art. MFN / ≠ § *	investments and activities associated of investors	–
South Africa	1997	1998	without prejudice to its laws and regulations	= art. FET FPS MFN / = § MFN	investments and activities associated by investors	–
FYROM	1997	1997	1989 model	= art. MFN / ≠ § / [1989 model]	investments of investors	–
Gabon	1997	2009	subject to its laws and regulations	= art. FET MFN / = §	(§) investments (§) investment–related activities	–
PRC MODEL		1997	without prejudice to its laws and regulations	= art. FET MFN / ≠ § / [model 1997]	investments and activities associated by investors	–
Sudan	1997	1998	–	–	–	–

Treatment formulation	Position NT exceptions	Exceptions = MFN	Wording of exceptions to NT (v PRC models)	Non-conforming measures	Other *ad hoc* exceptions
not less favourable	= art.	=	wording model 1984–9 on MFN, equivalent	–	–
–	–	–	–	–	–
–	–	–	–	–	–
–	–	–	–	–	–
–	–	–	–	–	–
–	–	–	–	–	–
–	–	–	–	–	–
not less favourable	–	–	–	–	–
not less favourable	= art.	=	wording model 1997 on MFN, exact	–	domestic laws to remedy past discrimina-tory practices
same as accorded	= art.	=	wording model 1984–9 on MFN, exact	–	–
not less favourable	no ad hoc NT exceptions	/	/	–	–
not less favourable	no ad hoc NT exceptions	/	/	–	–
–	–	–	–	–	–

TABLE 21 NT in Chinese IIAs (*cont.*)

Counterpart	Signed	In force	Presence & overarching limitations	Structure	Object of coverage	Expressly covered activities
Yemen	1998	2002	in accordance with its laws and regulations	= art. FET MFN / = §	(§) investments (§) investors on activities associated	–
Ethiopia	1998	2000	–	–	–	–
Cape Verde	1998	2001	–	–	–	–
Barbados	1998	1999	–	–	–	–
Qatar	1999	2000	–	–	–	–
Bahrain	1999	2000	–	–	–	–
Rep. of Congo	2000	2015	subject to its laws and regulations	= art. FET MFN / ≠ § / [model 1997]	investments and activities associated by investors	–
Jordan	2000	–	without prejudice to its laws and regulations	= art. MFN / ≠ § / whichever more favourable (§)	investments and activities associated by investors (+ returns)	–
Botswana	2000	–	without prejudice to its laws and regulations	= art. FET MFN / ≠ § / [model 1997]	investments and activities associated by investors	–
Iran	2000	2005	in accordance with its laws and regulations	= art. FET FPS MFN / = §	investments of investors ('in a comparable situation')	–
Netherlands	2001	2004	full	= art. FET FPS MFN / ≠ §	investments and activities associated by investors	–

Treatment formulation	Position NT exceptions	Exceptions = MFN	Wording of exceptions to NT (v PRC models)	Non-conforming measures	Other *ad hoc* exceptions
not less favourable	no ad hoc NT exceptions	/	/	–	–
–	–	–	–	–	–
–	–	–	–	–	–
–	–	–	–	–	–
–	–	–	–	–	–
–	–	–	–	–	–
same as accorded	= art.	=	wording model 1997 on MFN, exact	–	–
not less favourable	= art.	=	wording model 1997 on MFN, equivalent – (frontier trade)	–	–
not less favourable	= art.	=	wording model 1997 on MFN, equivalent	–	–
not less favor-able ('in a comparable situation')	no ad hoc NT exceptions	/	/	–	–
not less favourable	= art.	=	wording model 1997 on MFN, equivalent	V	–

TABLE 21 NT in Chinese IIAs (*cont.*)

Counterpart	Signed	In force	Presence & overarching limitations	Structure	Object of coverage	Expressly covered activities
Cyprus	2001	2002	full	= art. FET MFN / = §	investments and activities associated by investors	–
Mozambique	2001	2002	without prejudice to its laws and regulations	= art. FET MFN / ≠ § / [model 1997]	investments by investors (and returns)	–
Nigeria	2001	2010	without prejudice to its laws and regulations	= art. FET MFN / ≠ § / [model 1997]	investments and activities associated by investors	–
Sierra Leone	2001	–	without prejudice to its laws and regulations	= art. FET MFN / ≠ § / [model 1997]	investments and activities associated by investors	–
Kenya	2001	–	without prejudice to its laws and regulations	= art. FET MFN / ≠ § / [model 1997]	investments and activities associated by investors	–
Bosnia	2002	2005	full	= art. MFN / = §	investments and activities associated by investors	–
Cote d'Ivoire	2002	–	without prejudice to its laws and regulations	= art. FET MFN / ≠ § / [model 1997]	investments and activities associated by investors	–

Treatment formulation	Position NT exceptions	Exceptions = MFN	Wording of exceptions to NT (v PRC models)	Non-conforming measures	Other *ad hoc* exceptions
not less favourable	= art.	=	wording model 1997 on MFN, equivalent + (domestic taxation) – (frontier trade)	–	–
not less favourable	= art.	=	wording model 1997 on MFN, equivalent + (domestic taxation)	–	–
not less favourable	= art.	=	wording model 1997 on MFN, equivalent – (frontier trade)	–	–
not less favourable	= art.	=	wording model 1997 on MFN, equivalent	–	–
not less favourable	= art.	=	wording model 1997 on MFN, equivalent	–	–
not less favourable	= art.	=	wording model 1997 on MFN, equivalent	V	–
not less favourable	= art.	=	wording model 1997 on MFN, equivalent	–	–

TABLE 21 NT in Chinese IIAs (*cont.*)

Counterpart	Signed	In force	Presence & overarching limitations	Structure	Object of coverage	Expressly covered activities
Trinidad & Tobago	2002	2004	without prejudice to its laws and regulations	= art. MFN / ≠ §	investments and activities associated by investors (+ returns)	operation, management, maintenance, use, enjoyment, or disposal (def. 'activities associated')
Germany	2003	2005	full	= art. FET MFN / ≠ § / [model 1997]	investments and activities associated by investors	management, maintenance, use, enjoyment or disposal
Guyana	2003	2004	without prejudice to its laws and regulations	= art. MFN / ≠ §	investments and activities associated by investors (+ returns)	operation, management, maintenance, use, enjoyment, or disposal (def. 'activities associated')
Djibouti	2003	–	without prejudice to its laws and regulations	= art. FET MFN / ≠ § / [model 1997]	investments and activities associated by investors	–

Treatment formulation	Position NT exceptions	Exceptions = MFN	Wording of exceptions to NT (v PRC models)	Non-conforming measures	Other *ad hoc* exceptions
not less favourable	= art.	=	≠ any model but equivalent – (frontier trade)	–	–
not less favourable	= art.	=	wording model 1997 on MFN, equivalent – (frontier trade)	V	–
not less favourable	= art.	=	≠ any model but equivalent – (frontier trade)	–	Special incentives for growth of local industries
not less favourable	= art.	=	wording model 1997 on MFN, equivalent	–	–

TABLE 21 NT in Chinese IIAs (*cont.*)

Counterpart	Signed	In force	Presence & overarching limitations	Structure	Object of coverage	Expressly covered activities
Finland	2004	2006	full	= art. FET MFN / ≠ § / whichever more favourable (§)	investments by investors	operation, management, maintenance, use, enjoyment, expansion, sale or disposal (≠ MFN)
Uganda	2004	–	without prejudice to its laws and regulations	= art. FET MFN / ≠ § / [model 1997]	investments and activities associated by investors	–
Latvia	2004	2006	without prejudice to its laws and regulations	= art. FET MFN / ≠ § / whichever more favourable (§)	investments and activities [associated] by investors	–
Benin	2004	–	without prejudice to its laws and regulations	= art. MFN / ≠ §	investments and activities associated by investors	–
Tunisia	2004	2006	–	–	–	–
Czech Rep.	2005	2006	full	= art. MFN / = §	(§) investments and returns (§) investors	management, maintenance, use, enjoyment or disposal
Spain	2005	2008	full	= art. FET MFN / ≠ § / [model 1997]	investments and activities associated by investors	–

Treatment formulation	Position NT exceptions	Exceptions = MFN	Wording of exceptions to NT (v PRC models)	Non-conforming measures	Other *ad hoc* exceptions
not less favourable	= art.	=	wording model 1997 on MFN, equivalent	V	essential security interests in time of war; public order
not less favourable	= art.	= (?)	≠ any model but equivalent – (frontier trade)	–	–
not less favourable	no ad hoc NT exceptions	/	/	–	–
not less favourable	no ad hoc NT exceptions	/	/	–	–
–	–	–	–	–	–
not less favourable	= art.	= – (frontier trade)	≠ any model but equivalent – (frontier trade)	V	–
not less favourable	= art.	=	wording model 1997 on MFN, equivalent + (domestic taxation)	V	–

TABLE 21 NT in Chinese IIAs (*cont.*)

Counterpart	Signed	In force	Presence & overarching limitations	Structure	Object of coverage	Expressly covered activities
Portugal	2005	2008	full	= art. FET MFN / ≠ § / [model 1997]	investments and activities associated by investors	–
Belgium-Lux	2005	2009	full	= art. MFN / ≠ §	investments and activities associated of investors	–
Madagascar	2005	2007	in accordance with its laws and regulations	= art. MFN / = §	investors with respect to investments and activities in connection	–
North Korea	2005	2005	without prejudice to its laws and regulations	= art. FET MFN / ≠ § / [model 1997]	investments and activities associated by investors	–
Guinea	2005	2006	without prejudice to its laws and regulations	= art. MFN / ≠ §	investors in relation to investment and investment–related activities	–
Equatorial Guinea	2005	2006	full	= art. FET MFN / ≠ § / [model 1997]	investors with respect to investments, returns and business activities in connection	–

Treatment formulation	Position NT exceptions	Exceptions = MFN	Wording of exceptions to NT (v PRC models)	Non-conforming measures	Other *ad hoc* exceptions
not less favourable	= art.	=	wording model 1997 on MFN, equivalent	V	–
not less favourable	no ad hoc NT exceptions	/	/	V	–
not less favourable	= art.	≠ (only tax)	≠ any model (tax only)	–	–
not less favourable	= art.	=	wording model 1997 on MFN, equivalent – (frontier trade)	–	–
not less favourable	no ad hoc NT exceptions	/	/	–	–
not less favourable	no ad hoc NT exceptions	/	/	–	–

TABLE 21 NT in Chinese IIAs (*cont.*)

Counterpart	Signed	In force	Presence & overarching limitations	Structure	Object of coverage	Expressly covered activities
Namibia	2005	–	without prejudice to its laws and regulations	= art. FET MFN / ≠ §	investors	–
India	2006	2007	full	= art. MFN / = §	investments of investors	–
Vanuatu	2006	–	without prejudice to its laws and regulations	= art. FET MFN / ≠ § / [model 1997]	investments and activities associated by investors	–
Russia	2006	2009	without prejudice to its laws and regulations	= art. FET MFN / ≠ § / [model 1997]	investments and activities associated by investors	–
Pakistan [FTA]	2006	2007	without prejudice to its laws and regulations	= art. FET MFN / ≠ § / [model 1997]	investments and activities associated by investors	–
South Korea	2007	2007	full	= art. MFN / ≠ §	investors and investments	expansion, operation, management, maintenance, use, enjoyment, and sale or other disposal (def. 'investment and business activities')

Treatment formulation	Position NT exceptions	Exceptions = MFN	Wording of exceptions to NT (v PRC models)	Non-conforming measures	Other *ad hoc* exceptions
same or similar	no ad hoc NT exceptions	/	/	–	–
not less favourable	= art.	=	≠ any model but equivalent – (frontier trade)	V	–
not less favourable	no ad hoc NT exceptions	/	/	–	–
not less favourable	no ad hoc NT exceptions	/	/	–	–
not less favourable	no ad hoc NT exceptions	/	/	–	–
not less favourable in like circum-stances	no ad hoc NT exceptions	/	/	V	–

TABLE 21 NT in Chinese IIAS (*cont.*)

Counterpart	Signed	In force	Presence & overarching limitations	Structure	Object of coverage	Expressly covered activities
France	2007	2010	without prejudice to its laws and regulations	= art. MFN / ≠ §	investors with respect to investments and associated activities	–
Seychelles	2007	–	full	= art. MFN / = §	investors with respect to investments and associated activities	–
Costa Rica	2007	2016	without prejudice to its laws and regulations	= art. FET MFN / ≠ § / [model 1997]	investments and activities associated by investors	–
Cuba	2007	2007	–	–	–	–
New Zealand [FTA]	2008	2008	full	indep.	investments and activities associated by investors	management, conduct, operation, maintenance, use, enjoyment or disposal
Colombia	2008	2013	without prejudice to its laws and regulations at the time the investment is made	= art. MFN / ≠ §	investments of investors	operation, management, use, enjoyment or disposal

Treatment formulation	Position NT exceptions	Exceptions = MFN	Wording of exceptions to NT (v PRC models)	Non-conforming measures	Other *ad hoc* exceptions
not less favourable	= art.	= – (eco integration) ?	≠ any model but equivalent – (frontier trade)	–	preservation of cultural and linguistic diversity
not less favourable	= art.	=	≠ any model but equivalent + (domestic taxation) – (frontier trade)	–	–
not less favourable	no ad hoc NT exceptions	/	/	–	–
–	–	–	–	–	–
not less favourable in like circumstances	no ad hoc NT exceptions	/	/	V	–
not less favourable in like circumstances	= art.	=	wording model 1997 on MFN, equivalent	–	–

TABLE 21 NT in Chinese IIAs (*cont.*)

Counterpart	Signed	In force	Presence & overarching limitations	Structure	Object of coverage	Expressly covered activities
Mexico	2008	2009	without prejudice to its laws and regulations at the time the investment is made	indep.	(§) investors (§) investments	operation, management, maintenance, use, enjoyment or other disposal
Peru [FTA]	2009	2010	full	indep.	(§) investors (§) investments	management, conduct, operation, sale or other disposition
Switzerland	2009	2010	full	= art. FET FPS MFN / = §	(§) investments or returns of investors (§) investors	management, maintenance, use, enjoyment or disposal
ASEAN [CAIA/ FTA]	2009	2010	full	indep.	investors and investments	management, conduct, operation, maintenance, use, sale, liquidation or other forms of disposal
Malta	2009	2009	without prejudice to its laws and regulations	= art. FET MFN / ≠ § / [model 1997	investments and activities associated by investors	–

Treatment formulation	Position NT exceptions	Exceptions = MFN	Wording of exceptions to NT (v PRC models)	Non-conforming measures	Other *ad hoc* exceptions
not less favourable in like circumstances	≠ art.	=	wording model 1997 on MFN, equivalent + (domestic taxation) – (frontier trade) *	–	–
not less favourable	= art.	≠	≠ any model	V	disadvantaged minorities
not less favourable	= art.	=	≠ any model but equivalent – (frontier trade)	V	–
not less favourable in like circumstances	no ad hoc NT exceptions	/	/	V	–
not less favourable	= art.	=	≠ any model but equivalent	–	–

TABLE 21 NT in Chinese IIAs (*cont.*)

Counterpart	Signed	In force	Presence & overarching limitations	Structure	Object of coverage	Expressly covered activities
Mali	2009	2009	subject to its laws	= art. FET MFN / ≠ § / [model 1997]	investments and invest-ment–related activities by investors	–
Bahamas	2009	–	without prejudice to its laws and regulations	= art. FET MFN / ≠ § / [model 1997]	investments and activities associated by investors	–
Libya	2010	–	without prejudice to its laws and regulations	= art. FET MFN / ≠ § / [model 1997]	investments and activities associated by investors	–
Chad	2010	–	without prejudice to its laws and regulations	indep.	investors and investments	operation, management, maintenance, use, enjoy-ment, sale or disposal
Uzbekistan	2011	2011	without prejudice to its laws and regulations	indep.	investors and investments ('associated')	management, conduct, maintenance, use, enjoy-ment, sale or disposal
DR Congo	2011	–	without prejudice to its laws and regulations	indep.	investors and investments ('associated')	management, conduct, maintenance, use, enjoy-ment, sale or disposal

Treatment formulation	Position NT exceptions	Exceptions = MFN	Wording of exceptions to NT (v PRC models)	Non-conforming measures	Other *ad hoc* exceptions
at least equal	no ad hoc NT exceptions	/	/	–	–
not less favourable	no ad hoc NT exceptions	/	/	–	–
not less favourable	no ad hoc NT exceptions	/	/	–	–
not less favourable in similar conditions	no ad hoc NT exceptions	/	/	–	–
not less favourable in like circumstances	no ad hoc NT exceptions	/	/	–	–
not less favourable in like circumstances	no ad hoc NT exceptions	/	/	–	–

TABLE 21 NT in Chinese IIAs (*cont.*)

Counterpart	Signed	In force	Presence & overarching limitations	Structure	Object of coverage	Expressly covered activities
Canada	2012	2014	full	indep.	(§) investors (§) investments ('covered')	expansion, management, conduct, operation and sale or other disposition
South Korea & Japan	2012	2014	full	indep.	investors and investments	management, conduct, operation, maintenance, use, enjoyment and sale or other disposition (def. 'investment activities')
Chile [SAI/ FTA]	2012	2014	without prejudice to its laws and regulations at the time the investment is made	indep.	(§) investors (§) investments of investors	operation, management, maintenance, use, enjoyment, or disposal

Treatment formulation	Position NT exceptions	Exceptions = MFN	Wording of exceptions to NT (v PRC models)	Non-conforming measures	Other *ad hoc* exceptions
not less favourable in like circumstances	≠ art.	shared ad hoc NT	≠ any model	V	State enterprises control or nationality limitations; ref. to CA–Peru & PRC–Peru FTA; IP rights int'l ag. prevail; procurement; subsidies/grants.
not less favourable in like circumstances	≠ art.	≠	≠ any model	V	cross–border capital transactions in serious/exceptional circumstances; special formalities not impacting investments
not less favourable in like circumstances	≠ art. (Annex C)	shared ad hoc NT	≠ any model	–	Chile national debt

TABLE 21 NT in Chinese IIAs (*cont.*)

Counterpart	Signed	In force	Presence & overarching limitations	Structure	Object of coverage	Expressly covered activities
Tanzania	2013	2014	without prejudice to its laws and regulations	indep.	investors and investments (associated)	operation, management, maintenance, use, enjoyment, sale or disposition
South Korea [FTA]	2015	2015	full	indep.	investors and investments ('covered')	management, conduct, operation, maintenance, use, enjoyment and sale or other disposition (def. 'investment activities')
Australia [FTA]	2015	2015	full	indep.	(§) investors (§) investments ('covered')	expansion, management, conduct, operation, sale or other disposition *PRC (AUS + establishment, acquisition)
Turkey	2015	–	full	= art. MFN / ≠ §	investments and activities associated by investors	–

Treatment formulation	Position NT exceptions	Exceptions = MFN	Wording of exceptions to NT (v PRC models)	Non-conforming measures	Other *ad hoc* exceptions
not less favourable in like circumstances	= art.	≠	≠ any model	–	incentives / preferences to develop local entrepreneurship
not less favourable in like circumstances	≠ art.	≠	≠ any model	V	subsidies/ grants; special formalities not impacting investments; info /statistical needs
not less favourable in like circumstances	≠ art.	shared ad hoc NT	≠ any model	V	AUS: sectors & activities in Annex III
not less favourable in like circumstances	= art.	= – (frontier trade)	≠ any model but equivalent – (frontier trade)	V	–

F Fair and Equitable Treatment, Full Protection and Security, and Prohibition of Arbitrary or Discriminatory Treatment in Chinese IIAs

1 *Introduction and Relevant Pool of Investment Agreements*

Since its first model BIT, China committed to grant 'fair and equitable treatment' (FET) and 'protection' (FPS)[144] to foreign 'investments and activities associated with investment of investors'.[145] The model, however, fell short of contemplating a general prohibition of arbitrary or discriminatory treatment (PAD; or, as noted, a NT clause). In 1989, the model evolved as to expressly cover FET 'at all times', and upgraded the earlier 'protection' to 'constant protection and security'; moreover, it committed China '*... without prejudice to its laws and regulations,* [*not to*] *in any way impair by unreasonable or discriminatory measures the management, maintenance, use, enjoyment or disposal of investments*'. The 1997 model confirms the 1989 wording, with some minor variations.

Similarly to the wording, the actual position in the treaty of the protection standards here under scrutiny (FET, FPS, PAD) underwent substantial variations as well, throughout models and actual practice alike.

Out of the 120 Chinese IIAs analyzed, the 1993 BITs with Belarus and the 2015 IIAs with Australia do not feature any of these protections. Thus, the analysis that follows moves from a **pool of 118 Chinese IIAs.**

2 *Location of FET and FPS in Chinese IIAs*

As noted, the protection offered in the 1984 model (which lacked PAD and NT) was more limited than that granted in the subsequent templates. Consequently, FET and FPS clauses are the two protections featured on a standard basis throughout China's investment treaty models and practice. In light of the continued presence of these two standards, hence their potential significance in the context of analyzing the progression of China's treaty policy, this section and the following focus on the evolution of their location in the treaty, structure of the provisions, and key wording.

144 In this section, the acronym FPS is used to indicate the general commitment toward the physical protection of investments/investors, not only in case of the actual formulation as 'full protection and security'. Thus, unless otherwise indicated, variations are also included as, *e.g.*, 'protection', 'full protection, 'protection and security', 'constant protection and security'. When the distinction is relevant, it is indicated.

145 Art. 3 China 1984 model BIT.

In the models and practice of several key States, FET and FPS are frequently put side-by side.[146] The first Chinese model (which lacked both PAD and NT) featured FET and FPS together with MFN.[147] In 1989, FET and FPS stood together, but were moved in the preceding 'promotion and protection' provision.[148] Lastly, with the 1997 model the two standards split: FPS stayed with PAD under the promotion and protection provision, while FET was joined to MFN and NT.[149]

China's treaty practice shows a significant, yet not absolute, adherence to any model. Next to 8 IIAs that do not mention FPS altogether (in seven cases, recent arrangements: India, Seychelles, Madagascar, Namibia, Equatorial Guinea, and Cyprus), 37 IIAs (31%) concluded between 1985 and 2000 follow the 1984 model (in 35 cases, exactly so), as FPS and FET are featured in the MFN provision. In 29 cases (25%) the standards are instead both included in the 'promotion and protection' provision, in accordance with the 1989 model (which is followed exactly in 24 IIAS). In other 29 treaties (25%), FET and FPS are split in different provisions in line with the structural choice of the 1997 model (in 22 cases, *tel quel*). Out of the remaining 15 cases, 6 recent agreements feature a standalone FET and FPS provision, while the North American choice of listing the standards under the MST is followed in other 4 recent cases with significant partners (Mexico, Canada, Chile, South Korea).

Perhaps perfunctorily inspired by the German model,[150] occasional redundancies, such as featuring twice (possibly, with different wording) FET and/or FPS in different provisions (*e.g.*, Lebanon, Cape Verde, Djibouti), find a full double repetition in the 1994 BIT with Egypt.

---

146 *E.g.*, the German and UK models (respectively in the 'admission and protection' and 'promotion and protection' provision); also, the US and Canada models (in both cases, in the MST provision, identically worded). In the Dutch model the two standards are in the same paragraph, but in different sentences. In the French model FPS opens the expropriation provision. The Italian model does not feature the FPS clause.

147 Art. 3.1 China 1984 model BIT.

148 Art. 2.2 China 1989 model BIT.

149 Art. 2.2 and Art. 3.1 China 1997 model BIT.

150 Cf., the redundancy in the German model BIT (2008), with FET and 'full protection' granted in Art. 2 (admission and protection) and the standalone FPS granted in the chapeau of Art. 4 (expropriation).

3 *Structure and Key Wording of FET and FPS Relatively to Chinese Models*

In the investment treaty models and practice of the key States here considered, FET and FPS standards are formulated as such,[151] with only occasional minor variations.[152]

As mentioned in the introduction, since its first model BIT China grants FET, which since the second model it expressly offers 'at all times' (drawing from the British and Italian standard). The FPS protection, not featured in the first template, has become part of China's policy since the second (formulated as 'constant protection and security'), and kept it as such in the third as well.

In this respect, combined adherence to any model in the treaty practice is just over 66%. The largest group, comprising 35 BITs (or 30% of 118 agreements) spanning between 1989–1999, either replicate or are equivalent to the 1984 model. While no agreement features the exact structure or choice of word of the 1989 model, equivalent formulations can be found in 18 BITs (15%) concluded across the entire Chinese treaty practice (even though the majority is dated). The 1997 model BIT formulation has been used *tel quel* in 19 agreements, and has been the basis in 25 IIAs overall (21%), spanning between 1994–2010.

The largest group of treaties, however, does not follow any template structure: this is the case for 40 agreements (34%) spanning throughout the entire Chinese practice – even though roughly half of these have been concluded after year 2000.

In sum, in this aspect of the Chinese practice, overall adherence to any template, despite significant (78 IIAs, two-thirds of the overall pool of 118) is among the lowest of all characteristics analyzed up to now. This may be due to several factors, including, *e.g.*, *i*) the fact that Chinese formulations are different from those widely accepted internationally; *ii*) the perception of compatibility between formulations internationally accepted and those featured in the Chinese templates; and *iii*) China's gradual disengagement from model formulations since year 2000.

The following sections dissect the Chinese practice with regard to FET, FPS and PAD standards.

4 *FET Formulation in Chinese IIAs*

As mentioned, since the inception of its foreign investment protection program, China offers FET as such (*i.e.*, 'fair and equitable treatment'). The

151 See German, UK, US, and Canadian model BITs.

152 The Dutch model specifies that FPS is 'physical'. The French model defines FPS are 'complete protection and safety'. The Italian model rephrases FET as 'just and fair' treatment.

wording is identical in the models and practice of almost all States here under consideration.[153]

Consequently, it is no surprise that in 105 IIAs (89% of 118) the standard is formulated as such as well.

In this group, while texts up to 2008 fell short of providing further indications, with the turn to more complex arrangements and increased reference to the North American templates, China began including an actual definition of FET. This new trend seems now to have become the 'new normal', in two variants. A group of six IIAs (New Zealand, Colombia, Peru, Chad, DRC, South Korea), in fact, contain an open-ended non-exhaustive definition of FET that replicates, or draws significantly from, the US model: '… *includ[ing] the prohibition against denial of justice in criminal, civil, or administrative proceedings …*'[154] Concurrently, other four IIAs (ASEAN, Uzbekistan, Tanzania, Turkey) feature similar (when not outright identical) definitions which are, however, closed (*i.e.*, the verb 'include' is replaced by 'require' or 'mean'). The verb change entails a quite noticeable difference *inter alia* in terms of standard of proof for a FET violation to be found (notwithstanding that such difference can be possibly overcome via MFN).

With regard to the remaining treaties, i.e. those not featuring the FET locution as such, a group of 6 BITs (five of which from the early 90s' with former Soviet States) refers only to 'fair'. The remaining 7 BITs, all dated as well, hinge, instead, on the sole 'equitable' (in the cases of Italy and Denmark, coupled with 'reasonable').

It has been noted earlier that, since the adoption of the second model, China expressly offers FET 'at all times'. The locution, drawn from the British and Italian models, has been adopted in 50 IIAs (42% of 118), 35 of which since year 2000 (almost 60% of the 59 IIAs concluded since then). However, this element, while frequent in the last two decades, seems never having been considered essential – indeed, 68 Chinese IIAs (58% of 118), spanning from 1982 to 2015, do not contain it.

Therefore, while it can be concluded for China's association to the ongoing international trend in investment treaty practice to clarify the meaning of FET (probably reacting to expansive arbitral interpretations on the point), the current practice is less clear in terms of making such definitory attempt as exhaustive or open to additional meanings. On the other hand, while ready to offer FET expressly 'at all times', China seems to consider this element dispensable.

---

153 Only the Italian model differs; there, FET is phrased as 'just and fair' treatment.

154 Art. 2 China-Colombia BIT (2008).

5 *Object of Coverage of the FET Clause*

In all investment treaty models of the key States here considered, the object of FET protection is 'investments'. The German model provision expressly adds '*returns from an investment, as well as returns from reinvested returns, shall enjoy the same protection as the original investment*'.[155] With regard to the relation between 'investments' and 'investors', the German and French models connects the terms by employing, respectively, the preposition 'by' and the locution 'made by', arguably requiring or anyway implying an active role of investors in connection with the investment. The British, Dutch and Italian models rely instead to the more generic 'of' (hence, 'investments of investors'). The US and Canadian models employ the concept of 'covered investments' (which, in turn, refers to 'investment of an investor').

On the one hand, China's 1984 template speaks of 'investments and activities associated of investors', which evolved into 'investments made by investors' in 1989, and in 'investments of investors' in 1997. Hence, looking at the models' sequence, a path toward definitory simplification seems discernible.

On the other hand, the Chinese treaty practice may be mostly comprised in two macro-categories:

- The first, encompassing **72** IIAs (61% of 118), refers to 'investments' – 47 cases of which are 'of investors', in line with the 1997 model, while 4 'made by investors', as per the 1989 model.
- The second, a batch of **39** IIAs (33%), refers to a practice, seemingly ceased in 2001, referring to investments and activities 'associated', 'in connection' or 'related' to these. Most treaties in this group (33) replicate the earlier recalled wording of the 1984 model.
- Lastly, a small group of **4** recent BITs expressly refers to both investors and investments, while the remaining **3** BITs (not recent and unrelated among themselves) refer to 'investors'.

To conclude, in this respect, the choices made by China in its treaty practice over the last decade (hence, the 20 IIAs concluded since 2008) either replicate or are compatible with the latest model choice ('investments of investors'), or explicitly extend protection to include 'investors' as well.

6 *Additional Elements Directly Affecting FET Scope and Coverage*

Among the investment treaty models here under consideration of States other than China, only the North Americans additionally provide that FET (and FPS)

155 This does not exclude that other models, such as the British, expressly include returns and other elements in the very definition of 'investment'.

'*do not require treatment in addition to or beyond*' the '*customary international law minimum standard of treatment of aliens*'.[156]

As illustrated, no Chinese model adds elements to the FET clause, and only a handful of recent IIAs feature a definition of FET. The foregoing does not exclude, however, that in 22 treaties the FET clause is escorted by an assortment of additional specifications that directly affect its scope and coverage. In 19 cases, these are agreements concluded since the turn of the millennium.

The 3 earlier exceptions, with unrelated parties (Morocco, Gabon, Yemen) all share the same additional phrasing expressly confirming that FET shall not be *less* than treatment granted on a MFN or NT basis. This commitment (present also in the 2005 BIT with the Czech Republic) is noteworthy, as it runs quite contrarywise to more recent formulations by which a breach of any other BIT provision (such as MFN or NT) does not automatically entail a breach of FET as well (see next section). In the case of Yemen, also, investors are barred to claim FET breaches out of measures adopted to maintain public order.

Other formulations are more conservative. The 2 BITs with Chad and DRC mandate concisely that FET cannot imply anything *more* than NT. Potentially even stricter, with respect to the relationship between FET, NT and MFN, is the approach adopted in 3 other BITs with unrelated parties (Jordan, Vanuatu, Chad), where FET application is expressly subject to domestic laws.

More generously, other 8 IIAs mandate for FET treatment in accordance with principles of international law. In the 2012 trilateral agreement with Japan and South-Korea, this generosity is somewhat mitigated by the convoluted wording: '*reasonable and appropriate standard of treatment accorded in accordance with generally accepted rules of international law*'.[157] This phrasing seems reflecting China's cautiousness towards the potentially different understanding of conducts and principles of law domestically vis-à-vis internationally. Always in connection with international standards, but in a more decidedly conservative fashion, are the 6 agreements that rely on the North American template – (i.e., FET cannot be interpreted as anything more than the customary international law understanding of minimum standard of treatment of aliens). It is no surprise that the IIAs with Mexico and Canada (along Chile, South Korea, Peru and Colombia) are comprised in this group.

In conclusion, taking into account the 20 IIAs concluded over the last decade, it seems that China is still testing whether to include and, in case, how to frame, additional wording directly affecting scope and coverage of the FET clause: only half of the treaties contain some, and the terms employed still vary considerably.

---

156 See the MST section, below.

157 Art. 5.1, China-Japan-South Korea TIA.

7 *FPS Formulation in Chinese IIAs*

When it comes to the nowadays fairly common standard of 'full protection and security', States tend to offer relatively equivalent solutions with, however, varied wording and location of the protection in the treaty. The Anglo-Saxon tradition (UK, US and Canada) grants FPS as such (the former, in the 'promotion and protection' provision, the latter two in the MST article). Germany and the Netherlands, instead, commit twice: the former offers 'full protection' in the 'admission and protection' article, then FPS in the chapeau of the expropriation provision; the latter grants 'protection' subject to domestic laws in the 'admission and protection' provision, while 'full physical security and protection' in the 'treatment' article. And while the French model offers 'complete protection and safety' only in the chapeau of the expropriation article, the Italian model does not feature a specific protection clause.

Over the time, China upgraded its standard offer from the 'protection' contained in the 'treatment' provision (1984) to the 'constant protection and security' contained in the 'promotion and protection' article (1989 and 1997).

Next to a group of 10 BITs (8,5% of 118), dated as well as recent, with unrelated, non-Western counterparts, that do not mention the FPS standard altogether, the Chinese treaty practice in the remaining 108 IIAs can be gathered in the following three main groups.

The first group pivots on the sole 'protection' standard, thus is compatible with China's 1984 template. It comprises **39** BITs (36% of 108), 37 of which, concluded between 1984 and 1999, show no variations with respect to the 1984 model. Only the BITs with Italy (1985) and Nigeria (2001) enrich the word with an adjective (respectively, 'adequate' and 'continuous').

In the second group, comprising **27** BITs (25% of 108), the standard offered is that of 'protection and security'. As such, it is employed only in one case (Denmark 1985). Conversely, adhering to the 1989 and 1997 template, 24 of these stipulations, concluded between 1992 and 2010, resort to the wording 'constant protection and security' – which becomes 'most constant' in case of the UK (1986) and repeat the FET additional assurance 'at all times' with Australia (1988).

The third significant group, consisting of **35** IIAs (32%), is that where the protection is granted with actual FPS standard formulation. As such, it is found in 23 IIAs spanning from 1989 (BIT with Bulgaria) to 2012 (TIA with Japan and South Korea).

Within this latter group, and beside four minor variations, the practice from 2008, similarly to the FET clause, shows that China now is willing to include a definition of FPS. This is the case of 8 IIAs, only the latest of which (South

Korea 2015) replicates the US model, thus accepting the reference to customary international law.[158] In fact, after two warm-up stipulations on the point (New Zealand 2008, ASEAN 2009) offering only 'measures reasonably necessary', in the subsequent five cases (Chad 2010, DRC 2011, Uzbekistan 2011, Tanzania 2013, Turkey 2015) the FPS is originally redefined as the commitment of the Parties to '*... take reasonable and necessary police measures when performing the duty of ensuring investment protection and security*'. It will be interesting to see whether China's practice will evolve in the sense of accepting the US clause or maintain, instead, the original definition developed through the 7 IIAs just mentioned. Also, as the more moderate definitions have been agreed upon either with equally conservative and/or less strong negotiating power counterparts, it is also possible that China maintains a dual treaty policy on the point.

Conversely, particularly extensive is the standard granted in the 3 BITs with Yemen (1998), Benin (2004), and Uganda (2004), calling for 'full and complete protection and safety' – standard that it can be assumed China insisted upon in light of prospective investments there.

The remaining 4 BITs provide for 'full protection' (Austria 1985, Russia 2006), 'full and adequate protection' (Gabon 1997), and the peculiar 'full legal protection' (Iran 2000).

8 *Object and Coverage of the FPS Clause*

Since in most cases FET and FPS guarantees, whatever the specific wording, are placed one next to other, it is normal that they share the same object – *i.e.*, 'investments of investors' for the British, Dutch, American and Canadian models;[159] 'investments by investors' in the German model; and 'investments made by investors' in the French model (the Italian model does not feature FPS). The clause template object remains the same also where FET and FPS are split in different provisions, or the FPS is repeated somewhere else in the treaty (as per the German and Dutch models). From the foregoing, it can be concluded that, in general, for the FET and FPS object of coverage to differ is an unusual choice, one that can be assumed either to a specific will of the parties, or to a treaty drafting blur (due to, *e.g.*, cross model-wording mergers).

Chinese models are no exceptions to this treaty drafting principle as, there too, the FPS object of coverage follows that of FET – which, as illustrated

158 Art. 5.2.b US model (2004): 'Full protection and security' requires each Party to provide the level of police protection required under customary international law.

159 In the case of the American and Canadian model, this is via the definition of 'covered investments'.

earlier, shifted over the time from 'investment and activities associated of investors' (1984), to 'investment made by investors' (1989), to 'investments of investors' (1997).

Accordingly, in the Chinese practice as well the two guarantees share or have identical object of coverage in 98 out of the lot of 108 IIAs under consideration (91%). Thus, the analysis carried out on the point for FET applies here as well.

The following focuses on the 10 exceptions. Preliminarily, these can be found across the Chinese practice, as they comprise treaties concluded between 1985 and 2009. Their overall modest number, as well as the chronological inconsistency, let infer that these instances seem not attributable to China.

In three BITs (Italy 1985, Finland 2004, and Malta 2009), as the object of coverage between FET and FPS features only minor variations, the protection offered could be considered equivalent.

In four cases, however, the FPS formulation could be interpreted as narrower than the FET: in the BIT with the United Arab Emirates (1993), FET covers investments *and* returns, while FPS only investments; in the BITs with Uganda (2004) and Mali (2009), FET covers investments *of* investors, while FPS investments *made by* investors; lastly, the FET clause in the BIT with Russia (2006) covers investments *made by investors and associated activities*, while the FPS covers only investment *of* investors.

In two cases, conversely, it is the scope of FPS to appear broader than FET: in the BIT with Belgium-Luxemburg (2005), FET covers investments *made by* investors, while FPS the more generic investments *of* investors; the BIT with Austria (1985) extends FET coverage to investments, while FPS to investments, *returns and reinvestments*.

More articulated is the case of the BIT with Yemen (1998), where the clauses cover two different subjects altogether: 'investors' for FET, and 'investments, returns and reinvestments' for FPS.

The 10 illustrated exceptions aside, the Chinese practice is consistent with its own models and the international practice, in not dissociating the object of coverage of FET and FPS.

9 Ad hoc *Limitations to the FPS Clause*

A more entangled aspect is that relating to specific limitations introduced in the investment treaty to the coverage of the FPS clause. Among the models of key States here considered, this is only, and partly, the case with the Netherlands, where the first mention of 'protection' is framed as a duty '*within the framework of its laws and regulations, [to] promote economic cooperation through the protection*'.[160] Looking exclusively at this wording, it could be concluded that protection not only is subject to domestic laws, but also granted only to investments actually enhancing the economic cooperation between the State parties to the BIT.

While the Chinese templates do not feature any specific limitations to FPS, in practice this is the case in 20 IIAs (18,5% of 108), 15 of which concluded after year 2000. Preliminarily, the relationship between limitations in FET and FPS shall be outlined. Indeed, while in 9 cases these are exactly the same, in other 8 structure and wording exclude, more or less explicitly, that FET limitations apply to FPS as well. Interesting is also the case of 5 IIAs, where FPS is subject to specific limitations, while FET none at all.

To limit FPS coverage is a sensitive affair, and this is shown also by the fact that exceptions vary significantly among the remaining 11 IIAs that do not equate FET and FPS exclusions. Thus, two more dated BITs (Morocco 1995 and Yemen 1998) exclude measures taken to maintain public order, and other two (Vanuatu 2006 and Russia 2006) subject FPS operation to domestic laws. Less palpable is the required accordance of FPS obligations 'with the BIT' (Sri Lanka 1986), or that with 'relevant international agreements' (UAE 1993). Drawn from the North American standard is the requirement that FPS does not require treatment in excess of MST of aliens (Tanzania 2013). A sort of transitional wording is found with Colombia (2008) and Peru (2009), where the international MST parameter, though still expressly mentioned, is somewhat frustrated by the additional specification that anyway FPS does not provide more than NT. Lastly, the shorter yet ultimately equivalently narrow wording in Chad (2010) and Uzbekistan (2011) solely provides that FPS shall not exceed NT.

In conclusion, while the Chinese practice as a whole shows no discomfort in including a form of FPS in investment treaties, it does not usually include *ad hoc* exceptions to it. The practice of the last 20 IIAs (hence, from 2008) is, in this respect, quite inconsistent: in between 11 IIAs that feature an assortment of limitations to FPS (shared or not with FET), 9 IIAs do not – and exclusion does not seem to depend from any specific characteristics of the treaty counterpart. Noticeably, the North American models, which with respect to other aspects and clauses are gaining traction in China's practice as well, are not followed here – possibly due to China's resistance to terms whose interpretation

160 See Art. 2 Dutch model (2004). The limitation could be anyway overcome by the additional mention, in the following Art. 3, of the duty to 'full physical security and protection'.

is tied to international standards (such as the MST), hence their perceived unpredictable interpretation in the context of investment arbitration. On the other hand, the very considerable flow of Chinese investment in States whose political and social stability is vulnerable adds perhaps to the jigsaw of choices so far made, as the otherwise conservative Chinese policy finds here a limit in the interest to preserve intact a guarantee presiding its investment abroad. Thus, it seems that China is still testing opportunity, value and extent of the scope of limiting a protection, the FPS, that it has always been keen to offer (and is now quite interested to receive).

10 *Prohibition of Arbitrary or Discriminatory Treatment (PAD) in Chinese IIAs*

Several investment treaty models expressly feature, in the 'admission and protection' or in the 'treatment' provision, a general commitment of States not to 'impair' with certain measures investments and/or investors. This section analyzes how the protection is worded and those adjectives attached to the term 'measures' whose application would result in illegitimate ill-treatment. In the German model, these are 'arbitrary or discriminatory'. The UK and Dutch templates refer to 'unreasonable or discriminatory'. The Italian 'unjustified or discriminatory'. Conversely, the French, US and Canadian templates do not contain a commitment phrased as such. Canada, however, specifies that the 'general exceptions' regime does not operate in case of measures 'applied in a manner that would constitute arbitrary or unjustifiable discrimination',[161] while the US points out in various provisions that exceptions need be 'non-discriminatory'.[162] All templates (but the French) thus share in some form a general prohibition of discriminatory measures or treatment against foreign investments that goes beyond NT and MFN.

China evolved its template offer from not featuring any form of PAD such as those outlined (1984 model), to the British-derived 'unreasonable or discriminatory' standard (1989 and 1997 models). In practice, however, the number of IIAs adhering to the first model, or anyway not featuring PAD, is conspicuous: 57 treaties, or 48% of the pool of 118 here considered, spanning from 1982 to 2015, 17 of which concluded after year 2000 (hence, 29% of the 59 IIAs since then), with all sorts of counterparts.

Among the remaining 61 IIAs (52% of 118), the most common wording, chosen 55 times (90% of 61), is that of the 1989 and 1997 Chinese model. In 4 cases

161 Art. 10 Canada model BIT (2004).

162 *E.g.*, Arts. 5.4, 7.4., 20.2.a.

the German-derived wording prevailed (BITs with Saudi Arabia 1996, Jordan 2000, Germany 2003, and Portugal 2005), while the Italian-derived wording figures in 1 BIT (Morocco 1995). A dated treaty mentions only 'discriminatory' (Austria 1985).

Out of the last 20 IIAs concluded (hence, since 2008), 10 do not contemplate PAD. Among these there are treaties with States with which China has significant investment flows such as, *e.g.*, Mexico (2008), Peru (2009), ASEAN (2009), Canada (2012) and Chile (2012). This seems at least in part due to the progressive shift toward the North American templates.

Looking at the treaty practice on the point, both as a whole and focusing on the last decade, it can be concluded that China does not consider PAD an essential element.

11 *PAD Object and Coverage*

The object of coverage of the PAD clause – the identification of which may impact scope and extent of the protection itself – is usually 'investors' and/or 'investments'. The templates here considered adopt different solutions: the German model specifically refers to 'activity of investors ... with regard to investments', the British model focuses instead on 'investments of investors', while the Dutch template covers 'investors'. The Italian and Canadian models make an express reference to both.

The 1989 Chinese model follows the British approach; the 1997 model, however, while still focusing on 'investments', use the pronoun 'by', hence referring to 'investments by investors' (which, as seen, reflects a possibly more restrictive intent). It is interesting to note that, in both cases, this choice resulted in differentiating the scope of PAD from FET (narrower in 1989, with 'investments made by investors', and broader in 1997, with 'investments of investors'). Given the switch of terms, however, it is difficult to determine, just by analyzing the evolution of the treaty model language, whether the potential impact of these changes has been actually intended (and understood) as such.

The Chinese practice offers the following picture. In **16** cases out of the 61 that feature PAD (hence, 26%), the object of coverage is the same as that of FET. Despite the majority of these treaties are concluded after year 2000, some instances are more dated. Out of the 45 cases that use a different wording to refer to the object of PAD, **26** (thus, over half the cases) feature minor variations that seemingly do not impact the extent of the protection – which, consequently, may be deemed equivalent to FET. In **12** cases, scattered throughout the Chinese practice, however, the extent of PAD could be understood as narrower than that of FET: here, certain elements (reinvestments, returns) are expressly mentioned only in FET; in other cases, PAD employs the locution 'made by investors' as opposed to FET's 'of investors'. Conversely, 4 IIAs seemingly feature a broader object: for instance, in the FTA with South Korea (2015), FET focuses on 'investments' only, while PAD refers to 'investors *or* investments'.

Peculiar is the case of 3 IIAs where FET and PAD could be understood as having different coverage altogether: the BITs with Yemen (1998) and Guinea (2005) expressly refer FET to 'investors' but PAD to 'investments'; in the BIT with Russia (2006), FET covers 'investments made by investors and associated activities', while PAD focuses on 'activities in connection with investments'.

In those cases where the outlined variations in the investment treaty in English language (whether authoritative, as most of the time is, or not), seemingly lead to differentiated coverage between clauses, it seems no doubt appropriate to operate a linguistic comparison with the language employed in the (authoritative) Mandarin text, focusing on both the relevant IIA and equivalent texts.

From the textual analysis carried out, in light of the fact that FET and PAD have identical or anyway equivalent object of coverage in 42 cases out of 61 (thus, 69%), it could seem *prima facie* plausible to conclude for China's preference to maintain uniformity of coverage between the two clauses. However, in this specific respect it is necessary also to take into account that such apparent preference for uniformity is not reflected in the Chinese templates, which offer, conversely, a rather contradictory picture – let alone the fact that the 1989 model formulation has been *in concreto* used only once (Israel 1995).

12 *PAD Ambit of Coverage*

When featured, the PAD clause is usually accompanied by a list of terms that define its ambit of coverage, which usually mirrors that provided for NT (and, even if less commonly, MFN). The German and British models, while sharing all elements of this list ('*management, maintenance, use, enjoyment or disposal*') differ in that the latter's list is exhaustive, while the former is left open (*i.e.*, introduced by a 'such as'). The Dutch and Italian models, both of which feature a closed list that builds on the mentioned elements as well, respectively add 'operation' and 'transformation'.

The Chinese 1989 and 1997 models are aligned, in this respect, to the British template.

With regard to the treaty practice, preliminarily it shall be noted that 60 out of 61 IIAs do feature any such list (the only exception being Austria 1985), and that 57 of these (*i.e.*, 90% of 60 IIAs) are in all or mostly compatible with the Chinese template. In fact, in 45 cases the model wording is replicated as such.

Three BITs feature one less element (respectively, 'disposal', 'maintenance', and 'management'), while seven agreements one additional element (which in three cases is 'acquisition', in two 'expansion', once 'extension' and once 'local content, technology transfer or export performance requirements').[163] Lastly, more marked are the differences in the case of Russia (2006), where only two elements made it in the list (*'management and disposal'*), and South Korea (2015), where PAD ambit is specifically limited (*'losses due to war, revolt, insurrection, riot, or other civil strife'* and *'performance requirements on export or transfer of technology'*).[164]

Differently than in the earlier section, in this respect China's practice shows a very significant adherence to its own templates (entirely drawn, as seen, from the British model).

13 *Relationship between PAD and Domestic Laws*

There are several logical and legal arguments that militate against the insertion of a *ratione legis* limitation in the scope of PAD. Indeed, none of the template comparators here used subjects the clause to domestic laws. The one point that may root in favor, although of a non-purely legal nature, is that of restating a 'conservative' policy framework by which the international legal dimension of the BIT is filtered through the lens of the domestic legal system, hence (tentatively) subject to the interpretation given by its courts.

Perhaps unsurprisingly, the 1997 model retains the 1989 template wording where China offers PAD 'without prejudice to its laws and regulations'.

China's treaty practice shows a significant adherence to the model choice, as 44 IIAs out of the 61 that feature PAD (*i.e.*, 72%) maintain a connection with domestic laws, in most cases employing the actual model wording (35 IIAs, or 80% of 44), and in other 7 resorting to equivalent formulations. Particularly conservative appears the BIT with Saudi Arabia (1996), which stresses the importance of the domestic legal framework with the wording *'without prejudice to its laws and regulations **in any way**'*.

The IIAs not featuring a PAD's *ratione legis* condition are 17 (28% of 61 IIAs) and, while as a whole are scattered across a lapse of time that goes between 1996 and 2015, 15 of these have been concluded after year 2000. In another perspective, out of the latest 20 IIAs China negotiated, on top of the 10 that do not feature a PAD clause at all (see earlier section), another 4 do not feature

163 This latter case is with the 2007 South Korea BIT.

164 See Art. 12.5.4 and Art. 12.7.2 SK-China FTA (2015).

the domestic laws limitation. Combining these two elements may support the conclusion that China's conservative concern on the point is gradually fading.

14 *MST in Chinese Treaty Practice*

The use of the concept of MST in investment law is a typical feature of the North American practice since NAFTA.[165] However, due to perceived erratic interpretations by arbitral tribunals,[166] in 2001 the NAFTA parties issued a 'joint interpretive statement' that aimed at clarifying the relationship between customary international law and the concepts of MST, FET and FPS.[167] While the statement did not eliminate all interpretive issues, it brought sufficient clarity to the extent that the clause is nowadays often included in investment treaties.

The Chinese investment treaty models, along with the Europeans and the vast majority of IIAs in general, do not feature MST. However, in a selection of 7 treaties concluded since 2008, China accepted its inclusion. Notably, the counterparts of this IIAs all already had solid relations at all levels with the US, and have long been accustomed to the latter's treaty standards. Thus, the 'pilot' case was the BIT with a NAFTA party, Mexico (2008), shortly followed by Colombia (2008) and Peru (2009), and then South Korea-Japan (2012), Chile (2012), Canada (2012) and South Korea (2015).

Interestingly, in the latest agreement (South Korea 2015) the parties have innovatively refined their understanding of MST in that, next to the traditional elements and definitions in the provision drawn from the US model, a dedicated annex provides for a definition of the standard itself, as '*refer[ring] to all customary international law principles that protect the economic rights and interests of aliens*'.[168]

Overall, however, the presence of the clause is still too sporadic to determine whether it will become a standard feature of the Chinese investment treaty practice. The only element that seems fairly established is that China is open to consider the inclusion of this standard (and overcome its otherwise usually tepid relation with potentially ambiguous notions such as 'customary international law' to determine the content of economic obligations) with

165 Art. 1105.

166 With FET either considered as standalone principle of customary international law or part of MST (and to which extent).

167 The Joint Interpretive Statement can be found at the following link (the relevant part is Section B): https://ustr.gov/about-us/policy-offices/press-office/press-releases/archives/2001/july/joint-statement-nafta-free-trade-commission-.

168 See Annex 12-A, China-South Korea FTA (2015).

counterparts that are already accustomed to North American standards and practice.

15 Ad hoc *Express General Exclusions from Operation of FET, FPS, and PAD in China's Investment Treaty Practice*

With regard to general exceptions limiting wholesale the operation of the protection clauses here being analyzed, whether contained in the same protection provisions or in separate *ad hoc* provisions, the international practice of reference is relatively varied, even though common ground seems to limit such restrictions to specific areas. For instance, the British model features no exceptions altogether,[169] the German model only excludes taxation agreements,[170] the Dutch model economic integration processes (as it does not separate the general limitations to MFN from all other protections as well).[171]

The Chinese practice is quite varied on the point. Out of the pool of 108 agreements that features at least FET and FPS (as per the 1984 model, which does not include PAD), **44** (41%) do not contemplate any general exclusions of specific areas such as those mentioned, hence reflecting the policy choice made in the 1989 and 1997 models. Conversely, **64** IIAs (59%) do. The following analysis focuses on this latter group, moving from the general exceptions applied to MFN and with reference to their extension to FET, FPS and PAD.

In **49** BITs (77% of 64), the general exclusions are simply shared with MFN. In 39 of these cases, spanning between 1985 and 2001, these reflect China's 1984 model wording and structure (where, lacking PAD, MFN exclusions are shared with FET and FPS). The other 10 cases are instead agreements all concluded between 2000–2005 that feature only FET (hence, without FPS or PAD).

Responding to certain arbitral case-law, another recent batch of **13** IIAs, signed between 2008–2015, clarifies that a breach of a BIT protection does not entail *ipso facto* a breach of due treatment. In this respect, building from two warm-up stipulations expressly disassociating BIT breaches solely from FET breaches (New Zealand 2008 and ASEAN 2009), the other eleven cases expressly expand the exclusion to FPS (and PAD, where present, or MST,

169 The Italian and French models, perhaps due to their more limited protection range (as illustrated, the former does not expressly include FPS, the latter PAD) feature no limitations as such either.

170 Art. 2.3 German model BIT (2008), with reference to Art. 7.3.

171 Art. 3.3 Dutch model BIT (2004), which operates on paras. 1 and 2, hence all BIT basic protections (FET, PAD, FPS, NT and MFN).

where the notion is employed).[172] The 2 residual cases (Czech Republic and Madagascar, both of 2005) feature *ad hoc* choices (the former styled from the German model, the latter based on the concept of public order).

Overall, focusing on the last 20 IIAs (hence, agreements concluded from 2008 onward), the only general exception to these protections that appears, and it does so in 13 cases (65% of 20), is the latter illustrated (the remaining 7 cases do not feature any). This confirms, in this respect, China's comfort for the North American practice on the point, while however not necessarily showing yet a definite treaty-making policy choice.

172 See, *e.g.*, Art. 5.2 ('MST') of China-Mexico BIT (2008): 'A determination that there has been a breach of another provision of this Agreement, or of a separate international agreement, does not establish that there has been a breach of this Article'; see also Art. 2.4.b ('promotion, admission and protection of investments') of China-Colombia BIT (2008), Art. 6.3 ('MST') of China-Chile SAI (2012), and Art. 5 ('FET') of China-Tanzania BIT (2013).

FET, FPS, and PAD in Chinese IIAs: Data Summary

FET, FPS, MST, and PAD

118/120 IIAs[173]

Structure of the Provision (FET & FPS)[174]

- Only FET (no FPS): 8
  - In promotion & protection provision: 3
    - Kuwait (1985), India (2006), Seychelles (2007)
  - Standalone FET provision: 1
    - Madagascar (2005)
  - Same art. MFN & NT: 1
    - Cyprus (2001)
  - Same art. MFN: 1
    - Namibia (2005)
  - Double (redundant) FET (with discr. provision and with MFN & NT): 1
    - Equatorial Guinea (2005)
  - Mention in preamble: 1
    - Turkey (1990)
- Same art. MFN: 37 (31%)
  - FET & FPS in same para: 35 [*1984 model*]
    - BITs between 1985–2000
  - FET & FPS in separate paras: 2
    - Sweden (1982), Australia (1988)
- Same art. MFN & NT: 4
  - FET & FPS in same para: 3
    - Syria (1996),[175] Netherlands (2001), Switzerland (2009)
  - FET & FPS in different paras: 1
    - Slovenia (1993)

173 The BIT with Belarus (1993) and the IIA with Australia (2015) do not feature any of these protections.

174 In light of the four variables taken into account (FET, FPS, MST, discrimination), the data on the structure of the provision move from the position of FET & FPS, to relate / locate the others.

175 Art. 3 of the China-Syria BIT (1996) features only FET and FPS; the addendum to the provision, however, extend these treatments on a NT and MFN basis. In this sense, the provision features all treatments together, while FET and FPS are in a portion of the provision separate from NT and MFN.

- Same art. MST (FET & FPS in same para): **4**
  - Mexico (2008), Canada (2012), Chile (2012), South Korea (2015)
- FET *ad hoc* provision (including FPS): **6** (7)[176]
  - New Zealand (2008), Peru (2009),[177] Chad (2010), DRC (2011), Uzbekistan (2011), Tanzania (2013)
- In promotion & protection provision: **29** (25%)
  - FET & FPS in same para: 24 [*1989 model*]
    - IIAs between 1986–2015
  - FET & FPS in separate paras: 5
    - Austria (1985), Jordan (2000), Benin (2004), Belgium-Lux (2005), Guinea (2005)
- Split: **29** (25%)
  - FET separate / FPS with expropriation: 2
    - As such: 1
      - France (2007)
    - FET with promotion: 1
      - Italy (1985)
  - FET with MFN / FPS with discrimination: 2 (0)[178]
    - Lebanon (1996), Cape Verde (1998)
  - FET with MFN & NT / FPS with discrimination: 22 [*1997 model*]
    - FET always in stand-alone para
    - IIAs between 2000–2010
  - FET with MFN & NT / FPS in prot. art.: 2 (1)
    - Djibouti (2003),[179] Russia (2006)
  - FET & discrimination / FPS & expropriation: 1
    - Saudi Arabia (1996)
- Full repetition (redundancy): **1**
  - FET & FPS in prot. art. (w/ discr.) *and* in art. MFN
    - Egypt (1994)

---

176 Madagascar features a standalone FET provision which, however, does not include FPS (hence, it is listed in the earlier category).

177 In Peru the article is expressly labelled FET and FPS.

178 In both cases, the FPS protection is repeated both in art. 2 and art. 3; this redundancy makes the BITs qualify also for the earlier category 'same with MFN' (neither agreement featuring NT).

179 The FTS is repeated in the protection provision as well as in that featuring MFN and NT; this redundancy makes the agreement qualify for the earlier category 'same with MFN & NT' as well.

FET & FPS: *Structure and Key Wording* (*Relatively to PRC Models*)

- Unrelated to any model: 40 (34%)
  - IIAs between 1982–2015
  - IIA since 2000: 27 (46% of 59 IIAs)
- Based on the *1984 model*: 35 (30%)
  - BITs between 1989–1999
  - Exactly as 1984 model: 24
  - Minor variations, equivalent formulations: 11
    - Equivalent variations: 10
    - Improvements ('at all times', actual FPS): 1
      - Bulgaria (1989)
- Based on the *1989 model*: 18 (19) (15%)
  - IIAs between 1986–2015
  - IIAs since 2000: 6
  - Exactly as 1989 model: 0
- Based on the *1997 model*: 25 (21%)
  - IIAs between 1994–2010
  - IIAs since 2000: 23
    - Exceptions: Egypt (1994), Cape Verde (1998)
  - Exactly as in 1997 model: 19 (17)[180]
  - Minor variation, equivalent formulations: 6
    - Egypt (2004),[181] Nigeria (2001), Uganda (2004), Vanuatu (2006), Malta (2009), Mali (2009)

FET *Formulation*

- Equitable: 5
  - Poland (1988), Ghana (1989), Hungary (1991), Philippines (1992), Bahrain (1999)
- Equitable & reasonable: 2
  - Italy (1985), Denmark (1985)

180 The BIT with Cape Verde (1998) features two definitions drawing from two different models: in one, FPS and PAD follow literally the 1997 model, in the other, FET and FPS are phrased exactly as in the 1984 model. Despite the clear redundancy, the BIT, on a MFN basis, is listed in the category using the more modern standard (*i.e.*, 1997). Roughly the same is for the BIT with Djibouti (2003), where the standards phrased exactly as in the 1997 model are then repeated through a wording similar to that of the 1989 model.

181 The BIT with Egypt, redundantly, features two definitions: one exactly replicating the wording of China's 1984 model, the other similar and anyway equivalent to the 1997 model. Here as well, the treaty is listed in the more modern/favorable standard formulation category.

- Fair: 6
  - Armenia (1992), Kazakhstan (1992), Kyrgyzstan (1992), Ukraine (1992), Tajikistan (1993), Iran (2000)
- FET: 105 (89%)
  - As such (no definition): 94 [*any PRC model*]
    - IIAs between 1982–2012
  - Closed definition: 4
    - '*denial of justice & obvious discriminatory or arbitrary measures*': 2
      - Tanzania (2013), Turkey (2015)
    - '***willful** denial of justice & obvious discriminatory or arbitrary measures*': 1
      - Uzbekistan (2011)
    - '*obligation not to deny justice in any legal or administrative proceedings*': 1
      - ASEAN (2009)
  - Open-ended definition: 6[182]
    - New Zealand (2008), Colombia (2008), Peru (2009), Chad (2010),[183] DRC (2011),[184] South Korea (2015)
  - FET '–': 1
    - '*desirable*': Turkey (1990)

FET Coverage

- Investors: 3
  - As such: 2
    - Yemen (1998), Guinea (2005)
  - '*and investment related activities*': 1
    - Kirgizstan (1992)
- Investments: 72 (61%)
  - As such: 4
    - Norway (1984), Italy (1985), Austria (1985), Turkey (1990)
  - '*Approved*': 2
    - Sri Lanka (1986), Mauritius (1996)

---

182 Here, a similar or identical wording to that employed in other IIAs to provide for an exhaustive close definition of FET is used, instead, with the broader opening 'including' (hence, '… including denial of justice, etc.'). This formulation leaves, consequently, the definition of FET open to additional meanings.

183 Same wording than the BIT with Uzbekistan, but in lieu of the closed 'requires' the definition is introduced by the open 'includes'.

184 *Idem.*

- *'Covered'*: 4
  - Canada (2012), Chile (2012), South Korea (2015)
  - Plus *'returns'*: 1
    - Morocco (1995)[185]
- Of investors: **47**
  - As such: 38 (37)[186] [*1997 model*]
  - Plus *'returns'*: 9[187]
    - IIAs between 1985–2009
- Of nationals or companies: 4
  - Denmark (1985), UK (1986), PNG (1991), Madagascar (2005).
- By investors: 11
  - As such: 6
    - Sweden (1982), Saudi Arabia (1996), Botswana (2000), Congo (2000), Finland (2004), Namibia (2005)
  - Plus *'returns'*: 1
    - Greece (1992)
  - *'made by investors'* [*1989 model*]: 4
    - Israel (1995), Belgium-Lux (2005), France (2007), Seychelles (2007)
- *'and associated investments'*: 3

- Investors & investments: **4**
  - As such: 1
    - Chad (2010),
  - *'and associated investment'*: 3
    DRC (2011), Uzbekistan (2011), Tanzania (2013)
- Investments and activities associated / related / in connection: **39** (33%)
  - As such: 3
    - Australia (1988), Armenia (1992), Tajikistan (1993)
  - By investors: 2
    - Argentina (1992), Algeria (1996)
  - Made by investors: 1
    - Russia (2006)[188]

---

185 The text expressly mentions 'reinvestments' as well.

186 As noted, featuring Egypt two redundant definitions of FET, the one here taken into account is the more modern, based on the 1997 model (discarding instead that drawing on the 1984 model).

187 Gabon (1997) expressly mentions 'reinvestments' as well.

188 The wording here is 'made by investors' (as per the 1989 model); however, as also the broader 'activities in connection' are mentioned, the agreements is deemed to fall into this category.

- Of investors: 33 [*1984 model*]
  - BITs between 1988–2001
  - Plus '*returns*': Mongolia (1991)

FET Granted Expressly 'At All Times'

- Yes: 50/118 (42%) [*1989 & 1997 models*]
  - IIAs between 1985–2015
  - IIAs since 2000: 35 (70% of 50; 59% of 59)
- No: 68 (58%) [*1984 model*]
  - IIAs between 1982–2015
  - IIAs sine 2000: 23 (34% of 68; 39% of 59)

Other Express FET Specifications: 22/118 (19%)

- None: 96 (81%) [*any PRC model*]
- IIAs between 1995–2015
- IIAs since 2000: 19 (86% of 22)
  - Exceptions: 3
    - Morocco (1995), Gabon (1997), Yemen (1998)
- Subject to domestic law / in accordance with domestic laws & regulations: 3
  - Jordan (2000), Vanuatu (2006), Chad (2010)[189]
- No less than MFN or NT: 4
  - Morocco (1995), Gabon (1997), Yemen (1998), Czech Republic (2005)
- No more than NT: 2
  - Chad (2010), DRC (2011)
- No more than customary international law understanding of minimum standard of treatment: 6
  - Mexico (2008), Colombia (2008), Peru (2009), Canada (2012), Chile (2012), South Korea (2015)
- In accordance with principles of international law: 8
  - Jordan (2000),[190] Madagascar (2005), Seychelles (2007), Costa Rica (2007),[191] France (2007),[192] New Zealand (2008),[193] Turkey (2015)

---

189 The text expressly includes also 'general legal principles'.

190 Of a potentially limiting significantly the impact of the standard are the following words in the provision: 'recognized by both parties'.

191 Potentially limiting the subsequent wording: 'universally accepted'.

192 With possibly very modest impact is the attached wording 'generally recognized'.

193 Unusual wording of the provision: 'in accordance with commonly accepted rules of international law'.

    - No more than '*reasonable and appropriate standard of treatment accorded in accordance with generally accepted rules of international law*': SK-JP (2012)
- '*Except measures necessary to maintain public order*': 1
    - Yemen (1998)

Protection and Security: Formulation: 108/118 (91,5%)

- No mention: 10 (8,5%)
    - Sweden (1982), Kuwait (1985), Turkey (1990), Oman (1993), Cyprus (2001), Madagascar (2005), Namibia (2005), Equatorial Guinea (2005), India (2006), Seychelles (2007)
- IIAs between 1984–2015
    - IIAs out of 59 concluded since 2000: 53 (90%; 49% of 108)
- Protection: **39** (36% of 108)
    - As such: 37 [*1984 model*]
        - BITs between 1984–1999
    - *Adequate*: 1
        - Italy (1985)
    - *Continuous*: 1
        - Nigeria (2001)
- Protection & security: **27** (25%)
    - As such: 1
        - Denmark (1985)
    - *At all times*: 1
        - Australia (1988)
    - *Constant*: 24 [*1989 and 1997 models*]
        - IIAs between 1992–2010
    - Most constant: 1
        - UK (1986)
- Full protection: **3**
    - As such: 2
        - Austria (1985), Russia (2006)
    - '*and adequate*': 1
        - Gabon (1997)
- Full & complete protection & safety: **3**
    - Yemen (1998), Benin (2004), Uganda (2004)
- FPS: **35** (32%)
    - As such: 23 (64% of 36)
        - IIAs between 1989–2012

        - 1st instance with Bulgaria (1989)
      - IIAs since 2000: 13
    - *'and constant'*: 1
      - South Korea (2007)
    - *'most constant'*: 1
      - Egypt (1994),
    - *'and comprehensive'*: 2
      - Guinea (2005), France (2007)
    - *Ad hoc* definition: 8
      - Customary international law level of police protection: 1
        - South Korea (2015)
      - Measures reasonably necessary: 2
        - New Zealand (2008), ASEAN (2009)
      - Reasonable & necessary police measures: 5
        - Chad (2010), DRC (2011), Uzbekistan (2011), Tanzania (2013), Turkey (2015)
- Full legal protection: 1
  - Iran (2000)

***FPS* ad hoc *Coverage* (*v.* *FET*): *10/108* (9%)**

- No (same as FET): 98 (91%) [*any PRC model*]
- Yes: 10
  - IIAs between 1985–2009
  - IIAs before 2000: 4
- Different but equivalent: 3
  - FET investments of investors v FPS investments
    - Malta (2009)
  - FET investments v FPS investments by national or companies
    - Italy (1985)
  - FET investments by investors v FPS investments of investors
    - Finland (2004)
- Potentially narrower: 4
  - FET investments & returns v FPS investments
    - UAE (1993)
  - FET investments of investors v FPS investments made by investors
    - Uganda (2004), Mali (2009)
  - FET investments made by investors & associated activities v FPS investments of investors
    - Russia (2006)

- Potentially broader: 2
  - FET investments made by investors v FPS investment of investors
    - Belgium-Lux (2005)
  - FET investments v FPS investments, returns & reinvestments
    - Austria (1985)
- Potentially different: 1
  - FET investors v FPS investments, returns & reinvestments
    - Yemen (1998)

FPS Limitations: 20/108 (18,5%)

- No: 88 (81,5%) [*any PRC model*]
- Yes: 20
  - IIAs between 1986–2015
  - IIAs after year 2000: 15
- FET limitations not applied to FPS as well: 8
- Limitations to FPS only (no specifications in FET): 5
- Same as FET: 9
- *Ad hoc*: 11
  - Public order: 2
    - Morocco (1995), Yemen (1998)
  - In accordance with domestic laws: 2
    - Vanuatu (2006), Russia (2006)
  - In accordance with the BIT: 1
    - Sri Lanka (1986)
  - In accordance with relevant international agreements: 1
    - UAE (1993)
  - No more than MST in customary international law: 1
    - Tanzania (2013)
  - No more than MST in customary international law and anyway no more than NT: 2
    - Colombia (2008), Peru (2009)
  - No more than NT: 2
    - Chad (2010), Uzbekistan (2011)

General Prohibition of Arbitrary or Discriminatory Treatment (PAD): 61/118 (52%)

- No: 57 (55)[194] (48%) [*1984 model*]
  - IIAs between 1982–2015
  - IIAs since 2000: 17 (29% of 59)
- '*Unreasonable or discriminatory measures*': 55 [*1989 and 1997 models*]
  - '*at all times*': 1
    - Australia (1988)
- '*Arbitrary or discriminatory measures*': 4
    - Saudi Arabia (1996), Jordan (2000), Germany (2003), Portugal (2005)
- '*Unjustified or discriminatory*': 1
    - Morocco (1995)
- '*Discriminatory*': 1
    - Austria (1985)

PAD Object of Coverage (v FET): 45/61 (74%)

- No (same as FET): 16 (18)[195] (26% of 61)
    - IIAs between 1985–2009
    - IIAs since 2000: 11
- Different but equivalent: 26 (58% of 45)
  - FET investments of investors v PD investments: 4
    - Denmark (1985), FYROM (1997), Colombia (2008), Turkey (2015)
  - FET investment of investors v PD investments by investors: 19 [*1997 model*]
  - FET investments by investors v PD investments of investors: 2
    - Saudi Arabia (1996), Namibia (2005)
  - FET investments by investors v PD investments made by investors: 1
    - Finland (2004)
- Potentially narrower: 12 (27%)
  - FET investments of investors, returns & reinvestments v PD investments: 1
    - Gabon (1997)
  - FET investments & returns v PD investments: 5

194 The BITs with Madagascar (2005) and Seychelles (2007) do not feature a general prohibition of arbitrary or discriminatory treatment (PAD); however, in the context of FET protection, they specifically forbid '*ipso facto or ipso jure*' discrimination on *investment-related purchases*. Lacking a proper PAD, these agreements are counted amongst those that do not contemplate it altogether.

195 See previous footnote.

- Kuwait (1985), Oman (1995), Mozambique (2001), Trinidad & Tobago (2002), Switzerland (2009)
- FET investment & activities associated v PD investments: 5
  - Argentina (1992), Egypt (1994), South Africa (1997), Cape Verde (1998), Cyprus (2001)
- FET investments & activities associated v PD investments made by investors: 1
  - Lebanon (1996)
- Potentially broader: **4**
  - FET investments v PD investors or investments: 1
    - South Korea (2015)
  - FET investments & returns v PD investments or rights: 2
    - PNG (1991),[196] UAE (1993)
  - FET investments made by investors v PD investments of investors: 1 [*1989 model*]
    - Israel (1995)
- Potentially different: **3**
  - FET investments made by investors & associated activities v PD activities in connection with investments: 1
    - Russia (2006)
  - FET investors v PD investments: 2
    - Yemen (1998), Guinea (2005)

PAD: Express Ambit of Coverage: 60/61 (98%)

- No: 1
  - Austria (1985)
- '*management, maintenance, use, enjoyment and disposal*': **57** (90% of 60)
  - As such: **45** [*1989 model*]
    - IIAs between 1985–2015
    - IIAs since 2000: 31 (69% of 45)
  - One less element: 3
    - Disposal: 1
      - Saudi Arabia (1996)
    - Maintenance: 1
      - Malta (2009)
    - Management: 1
      - Namibia (2005)

196 The text here refers to 'rights related'.

- One additional element: 7
  - *Acquisition*: 3
    - PNG (1991), UAE (1993), Lebanon (1996)
  - *Expansion*: 2
    - Cyprus (2001), Bosnia (2002)
  - *Extension*: 1
    - Switzerland (2009)
  - '*Local content, technology transfer or export performance requirements*': 1
    - South Korea (2007)
- Two additional elements: 2
  - Expansion, sale: 1
    - Finland (2004)
  - Extension, liquidation: 1
    - FYROM (1997)
- More than two additional elements: **1**
  - '*development*, management, maintenance, use, enjoyment, *expansion, sale* and *liquidation*'
    - Jordan (2000)
- More than two elements less: **1**
  - '*management and disposal*'
    - Russia (2006)
- Different formulations altogether: **1**
  - losses due to war, revolt, insurrection, riot, or other civil strife; performance requirements on export or transfer of technology
    - South Korea (2015)

PAD: Domestic Law Safeguard: 44/61 (72%)

- No: 17 (28%)
  - IIAs between 1996–2015
  - IIAs since 2000: 15
    - Exceptions: Lebanon (1996), South Africa (1997)
- '*Without prejudice to its laws and regulations*': **43**
  - As such: 35 (81% of 43) [*1989 and 1997 models*]
  - Equivalent formulations:[197] 7
  - Plus '*in any way*': 1
    - Saudi Arabia (1996)

---

197 *I.e.*, 'without prejudice to its laws', 'subject to its laws and regulations', and 'subject to its laws'.

- Without prejudice to the legislation on joint ventures: 1
  - Austria (1985)

MST: 7/108 (6,5%)

- As per the North American practice: 7
  - As such: 6
    - Mexico (2008), Colombia (2008), Peru (2009), SK-JP (2012), Chile (2012), Canada (2012)
  - Plus a definition: 1
    - South Korea (2015)

Exclusions: 64/108 (59%)

- No: 44 (41%) [*1989 and 1997 models*][198]
- Same as MFN: 49 (77% of 64)
  - For all (FET / FPS /discrimination):[199] 39 [*1984 model*]
    - BITs between 1985–2001
  - For FET only: 10
    - BITs between 2000–2005
- Breach of BIT not automatically also:
  - Breach of FET: 2
    - New Zealand (2008), ASEAN (2009)[200]
  - Breach of standards of treatments (FET / FPS / discr.):[201] 11
    - IIAs between 2008–2015
- FET excepted on public order, public health, morality, environment: 1
  - Madagascar (2005)
- PAD excepted v NT for subsidies/grants in case of war, revolt, insurrection, riot, or other civil strife: 1
  - South Korea (2015)
- All excluded from international tax arrangements: 1
  - Czech Republic (2005)

---

198 In the 1989 model, FET, FPS and PAD are placed in Art. 2, while the general exception contained in Art. 3 covers only the protection therein featured (*i.e.*, MFN and NT); in the 1997 model, while the FET is located in the same provision as MFN and NT, the operation of the general exclusion expressly focuses on MFN only.

199 Any combination; *e.g.*, China's 1984 model does not feature PAD at all.

200 The provision expressly includes FPS as well.

201 Including MST, where employed.

TABLE 22 FET, FPS, MST and PAD in Chinese IIAs

Counterpart	Signed	In force	Location & relationship FET & FPS	Structure and key wording FET & FPS v PRC models	MST	FET formulation	FET object of coverage	FET at all times	FET other
Sweden	Tabl	1982	= art. MFN / FET & FPS in ≠ §	≠	–	FET	investments by investors	–	–
PRC MODEL		1984	= art. MFN / FET & FPS in = §	3.1 – investment and activities associated of investors shall be accorded FET and shall enjoy protection	–	FET	investments & activities associated of investors	–	–
PRC MODEL		1989	prot. art. / FET & FPS in = §	2.2 – investments made by investors shall **at all times** be accorded FET and shall enjoy **constant** protection **and security**	–	FET	investments made by investors	V	–
PRC MODEL		1997	split: art. 2 = FPS & disc. / art. 3 = FET with MFN & NT (FET in ≠ §)	2.2 – investments of investors shall enjoy constant protection and security / 3.1 – investment of investors shall all the time be accorded FET	–	FET	investments of investors	V	–

Protection formulation	Protection object of coverage	Protection limitations	Discrimination prohibition	Object of coverage	Expressly covered activities	Subject to laws	Express exclusions / other
–	/	/	–	/	/	/	–
protection	= FET [1984 model]	–	–	/	/	/	= MFN
protection & security – constant	= FET [1989 model]	–	unreasonable or discriminatory measures	investments of investors	management, maintenance, use, enjoyment or disposal	without prejudice to its laws & regulations	–
[1989 model]	= FET [1997 model]	–	[1989 model]	investments by investors	[1989 model]	[1989 model]	–

TABLE 22 FET, FPS, MST and PAD in Chinese IIAs (*cont.*)

Counterpart	Signed	In force	Location & relationship FET & FPS	Structure and key wording FET & FPS v PRC models	MST	FET formulation	FET object of coverage	FET at all times	FET other
Norway	1984	1985	prot. art. / FET & FPS in = §	≠	–	FET	investments	–	–
Italy	1985	1987	split: art. 1 = FET & prom / art. 4 = FPS & exp.	≠	–	equitable and reasonable	investments	–	–
Kuwait	1985	1986	prot. art. / no FPS	≠	–	FET	investments of investors + returns	V	–
Austria	1985	1986	prot. art. / FET & FPS in ≠ §	≠	–	FET	investments	V	–
Denmark	1985	1985	= art. MFN / FET & FPS in = §	≠	–	equitable and reasonable	investments of nationals or companies	V	–
Sri Lanka	1986	1987	prot. art. / FET & FPS = §	≠	–	FET	investments ('approved')	–	–
UK	1986	1986	prot. art. / FET & FPS in = §	1989 model, similar	–	FET	investments of nationals or companies	V	–
*Australia**	1988	1988	= art. MFN / FET & FPS in ≠ §	≠	–	FET	investments & activities associated	V	–
Poland	1988	1989	= art. MFN / FET & FPS in = §	1984 model, similar	–	equitable	investments & activities associated of investors	–	–

Protection formulation	Protection object of coverage	Protection limitations	Discrimination prohibition	Object of coverage	Expressly covered activities	Subject to laws	Express exclusions / other
protection	= FET	–	–	/	/	/	–
protection – adequate	investments by nationals or companies	–	–	/	/	/	–
–	/	/	[1989 model]	investments of investors	[1989 model]	subject to its laws & regulations	–
protection – full	investments, returns, and reinvestments	–	discriminatory	= FET	–	without prejudice to the legislation on joint ventures	–
protection & security	= FET	–	[1989 model]	investments	[1989 model]	without prejudice to its laws & regulations	= MFN
protection	= FET	in accordance with BIT	–	/	/	/	–
protection & security – most constant	= FET	–	[1989 model]	= FET	[1989 model]	without prejudice to its laws & regulations	–
protection & security – at all times	= FET	–	[1989 model] + at all times	= FET	[1989 model]	without prejudice to its laws	–
protection	= FET	–	–	/	/	/	= MFN

TABLE 22 FET, FPS, MST and PAD in Chinese IIAS (*cont.*)

Counterpart	Signed	In force	Location & relationship FET & FPS	Structure and key wording FET & FPS v PRC models	MST	FET formulation	FET object of coverage	FET at all times	FET other
Bulgaria	1989	1994	= art. MFN / FET & FPS in = §	1984 model (advanced)	–	FET	investments & activities associated of investors	V	–
Ghana	1989	1990	= art. MFN / FET & FPS in = §	1984 model, exact	–	equitable	investments & activities associated of investors	–	–
Turkey	1990	1994	preamble / no FPS	≠	–	FET 'desirable'	investments	–	–
Papua NG	1991	1993	prot. art. / FET & FPS in = §	1989 model, similar	–	FET	investments of nationals or companies	V	–
Hungary	1991	1993	= art. MFN / FET & FPS in = §	1984 model, similar	–	equitable	investments & activities associated of investors	–	–
Mongolia	1991	1993	= art. MFN / FET & FPS in = §	1984 model, exact	–	FET	investments & activities associated of investors + returns	–	–
Greece	1992	1993	prot. art. / FET & FPS in = §	1989 model, similar	–	FET	investments by investors + returns	V	–
Argentina	1992	1994	= art. MFN / FET & FPS in = §	1989 model, similar	–	FET	investments & activities associated by investors	V	–
Armenia	1992	1995	= art. MFN / FET & FPS in = §	1984 model, similar	–	fair	investments & activities associated	–	–

Protection formulation	Protection object of coverage	Protection limitations	Discrimination prohibition	Object of coverage	Expressly covered activities	Subject to laws	Express exclusions / other
FPS	= FET	–	–	/	/	/	= MFN
protection	= FET	–	–	/	/	/	= MFN
–	/	/	–	/	/	/	–
FPS	= FET	–	[1989 model]	investments or rights related	manage-ment, main-tenance, use, enjoyment, acquisition or disposal	subject to its laws & regulations	–
protection	= FET	–	–	/	/	/	= MFN
protection	= FET	–	–	/	/	/	= MFN
FPS	= FET	–	–	/	/	/	–
protection & security – constant	= FET	–	[1989 model]	investments	[1989 model]	without prejudice to its laws & regulations	–
protection	= FET	–	–	/	/	/	= MFN

TABLE 22 FET, FPS, MST and PAD in Chinese IIAs (*cont.*)

Counterpart	Signed	In force	Location & relationship FET & FPS	Structure and key wording FET & FPS v PRC models	MST	FET formulation	FET object of coverage	FET at all times	FET other
*Philippines**	1992	1995	= art. MFN / FET & FPS in = §	1984 model, similar	–	equitable	investments & activities associated of investors	–	–
Kazakhstan	1992	1994	= art. MFN / FET & FPS in = §	1984 model, similar	–	fair	investments & activities associated of investors	–	–
Bolivia	1992	1996	= art. MFN / FET & FPS in = §	1984 model, exact	–	FET	investments & activities associated of investors	–	–
Ukraine	1992	1993	= art. MFN / FET & FPS in = §	1984 model, similar	–	fair	investments & activities associated of investors	–	–
Kyrgyzstan	1992	1995	= art. MFN / FET & FPS in = §	1984 model, similar	–	fair	investors and investment–related activities	–	–
Belarus	1993	1995	/	/	/	/	/	/	/
UAE	1993	1994	prot. art. / FET & FPS in = § + FPS indep.	≠	–	FET	investments of investors + returns	V	–
Tajikistan	1993	1994	= art. MFN / FET & FPS in = §	1984 model, similar	–	fair	investments & activities associated	–	–
Albania	1993	1995	= art. MFN / FET & FPS in = §	1984 model, exact	–	FET	investments & activities associated of investors	–	–
Croatia	1993	1994	= art. MFN / FET & FPS in = §	1984 model, exact	–	FET	investments & activities associated of investors	–	–

Protection formulation	Protection object of coverage	Protection limitations	Discrimination prohibition	Object of coverage	Expressly covered activities	Subject to laws	Express exclusions / other
protection	= FET	–	–	/	/	/	= MFN
protection	= FET	–	–	/	/	/	= MFN
protection	= FET	–	–	/	/	/	= MFN
protection	= FET	–	–	/	/	/	= MFN
protection	= FET	–	–	/	/	/	= MFN
/	/	/	/	/	/	/	/
FPS	investments	consistent with relevant int. ags.	[1989 model]	investments or rights	management, maintenance, use, enjoyment, acquisition or disposal	subject to its laws & regulations	–
protection	= FET	–	–	/	/	/	= MFN
protection	= FET	–	–	/	/	/	= MFN
protection	= FET	–	–	/	/	/	= MFN

TABLE 22 FET, FPS, MST and PAD in Chinese IIAs (*cont.*)

Counterpart	Signed	In force	Location & relationship FET & FPS	Structure and key wording FET & FPS v PRC models	MST	FET formulation	FET object of coverage	FET at all times	FET other
Estonia	1993	1994	= art. MFN / FET & FPS in = §	1984 model, exact	–	FET	investments & activities associated of investors	–	–
Georgia	1993	1995	= art. MFN / FET & FPS in = §	1984 model, exact	–	FET	investments & activities associated of investors	–	–
Lithuania	1993	1994	= art. MFN / FET & FPS in = §	1984 model, exact	–	FET	investments & activities associated of investors	–	–
Uruguay	1993	1997	= art. MFN / FET & FPS in = §	1984 model, exact	–	FET	investments & activities associated of investors	–	–
Slovenia	1993	1995	= art. MFN & NT / FET & FPS ≠ §	1984 model, exact	–	FET	investments & activities associated of investors	–	–
Iceland	1994	1997	prot. art. / FET & FPS in = §	1989 model, similar	–	FET	investments of investors	V	–
Ecuador	1994	1997	= art. MFN / FET & FPS in = §	1984 model, exact	–	FET	investments & activities associated of investors	–	–
Jamaica	1994	1996	= art. MFN / FET & FPS in = §	1984 model, exact	–	FET	investments & activities associated of investors	–	–
Azerbaijan	1994	1995	= art. MFN / FET & FPS in = §	1984 model, exact	–	FET	investments & activities associated of investors	–	–

Protection formulation	Protection object of coverage	Protection limitations	Discrimination prohibition	Object of coverage	Expressly covered activities	Subject to laws	Express exclusions / other
protection	= FET	–	–	/	/	/	= MFN
protection	= FET	–	–	/	/	/	= MFN
protection	= FET	–	–	/	/	/	= MFN
protection	= FET	–	–	/	/	/	= MFN
protection	= FET	= FET	–	/	/	/	= MFN
FPS	= FET	–	[1989 model]	= FET	[1989 model]	without prejudice to its laws & regulations	–
protection	= FET	–	–	/	/	/	= MFN
protection	= FET	–	–	/	/	/	= MFN
protection	= FET	–	–	/	/	/	= MFN

TABLE 22 FET, FPS, MST and PAD in Chinese IIAs (*cont.*)

Counterpart	Signed	In force	Location & relationship FET & FPS	Structure and key wording FET & FPS v PRC models	MST	FET formulation	FET object of coverage	FET at all times	FET other
Egypt	1994	1996	full double (!): FET & FPS in prot. art. (w/ discr.) + in = art. MFN / in boht: FET & FPS in = §	1997 model, similar + 1984 model, exact	–	FET	investments of investors + investments & associated activities of investors	V	–
Serbia	1995	1996	prot. art. / FET & FPS in = §	1989 model, similar	–	FET	investments of investors	V	–
Oman	1995	1995	prot. art. / FET & FPS in = §	1989 model, similar	–	FET	investments of investors + returns	V	–
Morocco	1995	1999	prot. art. / FET & FPS in = §	1989 model, similar	–	FET	investments made by investors + returns & reinvestments	–	not less than MFN or NT
Israel	1995	2009	prot. art. / FET & FPS in = §	1989 model, similar	–	FET	investments made by investors	–	–
Lebanon	1996	1997	split & double (!): art. 2 FPS & disc. / art. 3 FET & FPS in = art. MFN (& = §)	1984 model, exact (art. 3) / ≠ (art. 2)	–	FET	investments & activities associated of investors	–	–
Bangladesh	1996	1997	= art. MFN / FET & FPS in = §	1984 model, exact	–	FET	investments & activities associated of investors	–	–
Mauritius	1996	1997	prot. art. / FET & FPS in = §	≠	–	FET	investments ('approved')	–	–

Protection formulation	Protection object of coverage	Protection limitations	Discrimination prohibition	Object of coverage	Expressly covered activities	Subject to laws	Express exclusions / other
protection & security – most constant	= FET	–	[1989 model]	investments of investors	[1989 model]	without prejudice to its laws & regulations	= MFN
FPS	= FET	–	–	/	/	/	–
–	/	/	[1989 model]	investments of investors	[1989 model]	subject to its laws & regulations	–
FPS	= FET	public order	unjustified or discriminatory	= FET	[1989 model]	without prejudice to its laws & regulations	–
FPS	= FET	–	[1989 model]	investments of investors	[1989 model]	without prejudice to its laws & regulations	–
protection	=FET (art. 3) / investment made by investors (art. 2)	–	[1989 model]	investments made by investors	management, maintenance, use, enjoyment, extension, sale or liquidation	–	–
protection	= FET	–	–	/	/	/	–
protection	= FET	–	–	/	/	/	–

TABLE 22 FET, FPS, MST and PAD in Chinese IIAs (*cont.*)

Counterpart	Signed	In force	Location & relationship FET & FPS	Structure and key wording FET & FPS v PRC models	MST	FET formulation	FET object of coverage	FET at all times	FET other
Saudi Arabia	1996	1997	split: art. 2 = FET & disc. / art. 4 = FPS & exp.	≠	–	FET	investments by investors	–	–
Syria	1996	2001	= art. MFN & NT / FET & FPS = § *	1984 model, exact	–	FET	investments & activities associated of investors	–	–
Algeria	1996	2003	= art. MFN / FET & FPS in = §	1984 model, similar	–	FET	investments & activities associated by investors	–	–
Zambia	1996	–	= art. MFN / FET & FPS in = §	1984 model, exact	–	FET	investments & activities associated of investors	–	–
Zimbabwe	1996	1998	= art. MFN / FET & FPS in = §	1984 model, exact	–	FET	investments & activities associated of investors	–	–
Gabon	1997	2009	prot. art. / FET & FPS in = §	1989 model, similar	–	FET	investments of investors + returns & reinvestments	–	no less than MFN or NT
Macedonia	1997	1997	prot. art. / FET & FPS in = §	1989 model, similar	–	FET	investments of investors	V	–
South Africa	1997	1998	= art. MFN / FET & FPS in = §	1984 model, exact	–	FET	investments & activities associated of investors	–	–
Sudan	1997	1998	= art. MFN / FET & FPS in = §	1984 model, exact	–	FET	investments & activities associated of investors	–	–

Protection formulation	Protection object of coverage	Protection limitations	Discrimination prohibition	Object of coverage	Expressly covered activities	Subject to laws	Express exclusions / other
FPS	= FET	–	arbitrary or discriminatory	investments of investors	[1989 model] – disposal	without prejudice to its laws & regulations in any way	–
protection	= FET	–	–	/	/	/	= MFN
protection	= FET	–	–	/	/	/	= MFN
protection	= FET	–	–	/	/	/	= MFN
protection	= FET	–	–	/	/	/	= MFN
protection – full & adequate	= FET	–	[1989 model]	investments	[1989 model]	without prejudice to its laws & regulations	–
FPS	= FET	–	[1989 model]	investments	[1989 model] + extension, liquidation	without prejudice to its laws & regulations	–
protection	= FET	–	[1989 model]	investments	[1989 model]	–	= MFN
protection	= FET	–	–	/	/	/	= MFN

TABLE 22 FET, FPS, MST and PAD in Chinese IIAs (*cont.*)

Counterpart	Signed	In force	Location & relationship FET & FPS	Structure and key wording FET & FPS v PRC models	MST	FET formulation	FET object of coverage	FET at all times	FET other
Yemen	1998	2002	prot. art. / FET & FPS in = §	≠	–	FET	investors	–	no less than MFN or NT; public order exception
Barbados	1998	1999	= art. MFN / FET & FPS in = §	1984 model, exact	–	FET	investments & activities associated of investors	–	–
Ethiopia	1998	2000	= art. MFN / FET & FPS in = §	1984 model, exact	–	FET	investments & activities associated of investors	–	–
Cape Verde	1998	2001	split & double (!): art. 2 = FPS & disc. / art. 3 = FET & FPS = art. MFN (& = §)	1997 model, exact (FPS & disc.) + 1984 model, exact (FET & FPS)	–	FET	investments & activities associated of investors	–	–
Bahrain	1999	2000	= art. MFN / FET & FPS in = §	1984 model, similar	–	equitable	investments & activities associated of investors	–	–
Qatar	1999	2000	= art. MFN / FET & FPS in = §	1984 model, exact	–	FET	investments & activities associated of investors	–	–
Jordan	2000	–	prot. art. / FET & FPS ≠ §	≠	–	FET	investments of investors + returns	–	in accordance with IL princ. recognized by both parties

Protection formulation	Protection object of coverage	Protection limitations	Discrimination prohibition	Object of coverage	Expressly covered activities	Subject to laws	Express exclusions / other
protection & safety – full & complete	investments, returns, and reinvestments	public order	[1989 model]	investments	[1989 model]	without prejudice to its laws & regulations	–
protection	= FET	–	–	/	/	/	= MFN
protection	= FET	–	–	/	/	/	= MFN
protection & security – constant	= FET [1997 model] + [1984 model]	–	[1989 model]	investments	[1989 model]	without prejudice to its laws & regulations	= MFN
protection	= FET	–	–	/	/	/	= MFN
protection	= FET	–	–	/	/	/	= MFN
FPS	= FET	–	arbitrary or discriminatory	= FET	development, management, maintenance, use, enjoyment, expansion, sale and liquidation	–	–

TABLE 22 FET, FPS, MST and PAD in Chinese IIAS (*cont.*)

Counterpart	Signed	In force	Location & relationship FET & FPS	Structure and key wording FET & FPS v PRC models	MST	FET formulation	FET object of coverage	FET at all times	FET other
Iran	2000	2005	= art. MFN / FET & FPS = §	≠	–	fair	investments of investors	–	in accordance with laws & regulations
Rep. of Congo	2000	2015	split: art. 2 = FPS & disc. / art. 3 = FET with MFN & NT (FET in ≠ §)	1997 model, exact	–	FET	investments by investors	V	–
Botswana	2000	–	split: art. 2 = FPS & disc. / art. 3 = FET with MFN & NT (FET in ≠ §)	1997 model, exact	–	FET	investments by investors	V	–
Cyprus	2001	2002	= art. MFN & NT / no FPS	≠	–	FET	investments & activities associated of investors	V	–
Mozambique	2001	2002	split: art. 2 = FPS & disc. / art. 3 = FET with MFN & NT (FET in ≠ §)	1997 model, exact	–	FET	investments of investors + returns	V	–
Netherlands	2001	2004	= art. MFN & NT / FET & FPS = §	1989 model, similar	–	FET	investments of investors	V	–
Nigeria	2001	2010	split: art. 2 = FPS & disc. / art. 3 = FET with MFN & NT (FET in ≠ §)	1997 model, similar	–	FET	investments of investors	V	–

Protection formulation	Protection object of coverage	Protection limitations	Discrimination prohibition	Object of coverage	Expressly covered activities	Subject to laws	Express exclusions / other
protection – full legal	= FET	= FET	–	/	/	/	= MFN
protection & security – constant	= FET	–	[1989 model]	= FET	[1989 model]	subject to its laws	= MFN only for FET
protection & security – constant	= FET	–	[1989 model]	= FET	[1989 model]	without prejudice to its laws & regulations	= MFN only for FET
–	/	/	[1989 model]	investments by investors	[1989 model] + expansion	–	–
protection & security – constant	= FET	–	[1989 model]	investments by investors	[1989 model]	without prejudice to its laws & regulations	–
protection & security – constant	= FET	–	[1989 model]	investments by investors	[1989 model]	–	= MFN
protection – continuous	= FET	–	[1989 model]	investments by investors	[1989 model]	subject to its laws & regulations	= MFN only for FET

TABLE 22 FET, FPS, MST and PAD in Chinese IIAs (*cont.*)

Counterpart	Signed	In force	Location & relationship FET & FPS	Structure and key wording FET & FPS v PRC models	MST	FET formulation	FET object of coverage	FET at all times	FET other
Kenya	2001	–	split: art. 2 = FPS & disc. / art. 3 = FET with MFN & NT (FET in ≠ §)	1997 model, exact	–	FET	investments of investors	V	–
Sierra Leone	2001	–	split: art. 2 = FPS & disc. / art. 3 = FET with MFN & NT (FET in ≠ §)	1997 model, exact	–	FET	investments of investors	V	–
Bosnia	2002	2005	prot. art. / FET & FPS = §	1989 model, similar	–	FET	investments of investors	V	–
Trinidad & Tobago	2002	2004	prot. art. / FET & FPS = §	1989, similar	–	FET	investments of investors + returns	–	–
Cote d'Ivoire	2002	–	split: art. 2 = FPS & disc. / art. 3 = FET with MFN & NT (FET in ≠ §)	1997 model, exact	–	FET	investments of investors	V	–
Guyana	2003	2004	prot. art. / FET & FPS = §	1989 model, similar	–	FET	investments of investors	–	–
Germany	2003	2005	split: art. 2 = FPS & disc. / art. 3 = FET with MFN & NT (FET in ≠ §)	1997 model, exact	–	FET	investments of investors	V	–

Protection formulation	Protection object of coverage	Protection limitations	Discrimination prohibition	Object of coverage	Expressly covered activities	Subject to laws	Express exclusions / other
protection & security – constant	= FET	–	[1989 model]	investments by investors	[1989 model]	without prejudice to its laws & regulations	= MFN only for FET
protection & security – constant	= FET	–	[1989 model]	investments by investors	[1989 model]	without prejudice to its laws & regulations	= MFN only for FET
FPS	= FET	–	[1989 model]	= FET	[1989 model] + expansion	–	–
FPS	= FET	–	[1989 model]	investments by investors	[1989 model]	without prejudice to its laws & regulations	–
protection & security – constant	= FET	–	[1989 model]	= FET	[1989 model]	without prejudice to its laws & regulations	= MFN only for FET
FPS	= FET	–	[1989 model]	investments by investors	[1989 model]	without prejudice to its laws & regulations	–
protection & security – constant	= FET	–	arbitrary or discriminatory	investments by investors	[1989 model]	–	= MFN only for FET

TABLE 22 FET, FPS, MST and PAD in Chinese IIAs (*cont.*)

Counterpart	Signed	In force	Location & relationship FET & FPS	Structure and key wording FET & FPS v PRC models	MST	FET formulation	FET object of coverage	FET at all times	FET other
Djibouti	2003	–	split & double (!): art. 2: FET & FPS in prot. art. = § / art. 3 FET with MFN & NT (FET in ≠ §)	1989 model, similar + 1997 model, exact	–	FET	investments of investors	V	–
Tunisia	2004	2006	split: art. 2 = FPS & disc. / art. 3 = FET with MFN & NT (FET in ≠ §)	1997 model, exact	–	FET	investments of investors	V	–
Benin	2004	–	prot. art. / FET & FPS ≠ §	≠	–	FET	investments of investors	V	–
Latvia	2004	2006	split: art. 2 = FPS & disc. / art. 3 = FET with MFN & NT (FET in ≠ §)	1997 model, exact	–	FET	investments of investors	V	–
Uganda	2004	–	split: art. 2 = FPS & disc. / art. 3 = FET with MFN & NT (FET in ≠ §)	1997 model, similar	–	FET	investments of investors	V	–
Finland	2004	2006	split: art. 2 = FPS & disc. / art. 3 = FET with MFN & NT (FET in ≠ §)	1997 model, exact	–	FET	investments by investors	V	–

Protection formulation	Protection object of coverage	Protection limitations	Discrimination prohibition	Object of coverage	Expressly covered activities	Subject to laws	Express exclusions / other
protection & security – constant	= FET	–	[1989 model]	investments by investors	[1989 model]	without prejudice to its laws & regulations	= MFN only for FET
FPS	= FET	–	[1989 model]	= FET	[1989 model]	–	–
protection & safety – full & complete	= FET	–	[1989 model]	investments by investors	[1989 model]	without prejudice to its laws & regulations	–
protection & security – constant	= FET	–	[1989 model]	investments by investors	[1989 model]	without prejudice to its laws & regulations	–
protection & safety – full & complete	invest-ments made by investors	–	[1989 model]	investments by investors	[1989 model]	without prejudice to its laws & regulations	= MFN
protection & security – constant	invest-ments of investors	–	[1989 model]	investments made by investors	[1989 model] + expansion, sale	–	= MFN only for FET

TABLE 22 FET, FPS, MST and PAD in Chinese IIAs (*cont.*)

Counterpart	Signed	In force	Location & relationship FET & FPS	Structure and key wording FET & FPS v PRC models	MST	FET formulation	FET object of coverage	FET at all times	FET other
Spain	2005	2008	split: art. 2 = FPS & disc. / art. 3 = FET with MFN & NT (FET in ≠ §)	1997 model, exact	–	FET	investments of investors	V	–
Portugal	2005	2008	split: art. 2 = FPS & disc. / art. 3 = FET with MFN & NT (FET in ≠ §)	1997 model, exact	–	FET	investments of investors	V	–
Belgium–Lux	2005	2009	prot. art. / FET & FPS ≠ §	≠	–	FET	investments made by investors	–	–
Equatorial Guinea	2005	2006	double (!): art. 2: FET & disc. / art. 3: FET with MFN & NT (FET ≠ §) / no FPS	≠	–	FET	investments of investors	V	–
Guinea	2005	–	prot. art. / FET & FPS ≠ §	≠	–	FET	investors	V	–
Namibia	2005	–	= art. MFN / no FPS	≠	–	FET	investments by investors	V	–
North Korea	2005	2005	split: art. 2 = FPS & disc. / art. 3 = FET with MFN & NT (FET in ≠ §)	1997 model, exact	–	FET	investments of investors	V	–

Protection formulation	Protection object of coverage	Protection limitations	Discrimination prohibition	Object of coverage	Expressly covered activities	Subject to laws	Express exclusions / other
protection & security – constant	= FET	–	[1989 model]	investments by investors	[1989 model]	–	–
protection & security – constant	= FET	–	arbitrary or discriminatory	investments by investors	[1989 model]	–	–
protection & security – constant	invest-ments of investors	–	[1989 model]	= FET	[1989 model]	without prejudice to its laws & regulations	–
–	/	/	[1989 model]	= FET	[1989 model]	without prejudice to its laws & regulations	–
protection & security – full & com-prehensive	= FET	–	[1989 model]	investments	[1989 model]	without prejudice to its laws & regulations	–
–	/	/	[1989 model]	investments of investors	[1989 model] – management	without prejudice to its laws & regulations	–
protection & security – constant	= FET	–	[1989 model]	investments by investors	[1989 model]	without prejudice to its laws & regulations	= MFN only for FET

TABLE 22 FET, FPS, MST and PAD in Chinese IIAs (*cont.*)

Counterpart	Signed	In force	Location & relationship FET & FPS	Structure and key wording FET & FPS v PRC models	MST	FET formulation	FET object of coverage	FET at all times	FET other
Madagascar	2005	2007	FET art. / no FPS	≠	–	FET	investments of national or companies	–	in accordance with IL princ.
Czech Rep.	2005	2006	prot. art. / FET & FPS = §	1989 model, similar	–	FET	investments of investors	V	no less than MFN or NT
India	2006	2007	prot. art. / no FPS	≠	–	FET	investments of investors + returns	V	–
Pakistan [FTA]	2006	2007	split: art. 47 = FPS & disc. / art. 48 = FET with MFN & NT (FET in ≠ §)	1997 model, exact	–	FET	investments of investors	V	–
Vanuatu	2006	–	split: art. 2 = FPS & disc. / art. 3 = FET with MFN & NT (FET in ≠ §)	1997 model, similar	–	FET	investments of investors	V	subject to domestic laws
Russia	2006	2009	split: art. 2 = FPS in prot. art. / art. 3 = FET & disc. with MFN & NT (FET & disc. in = §)	≠	–	FET	investments made by investors & activities associated	–	–

Protection formulation	Protection object of coverage	Protection limitations	Discrimination prohibition	Object of coverage	Expressly covered activities	Subject to laws	Express exclusions / other
–	/	/	– *	= FET *	restrictions on investment–related purchases (FET context) *	/	FET: public order, public health, morality, environment
FPS	= FET	–	–	/	/	/	general: taxation
–	/	/	–	/	/	/	–
protection & security – constant	= FET	–	[1989 model]	= FET	[1989 model]	without prejudice to its laws & regulations	–
protection & security – constant	= FET	in accordance with domestic laws	[1989 model]	investments by investors	[1989 model]	without prejudice to its laws & regulations	–
protection – full	investments of investors	in accordance with domestic laws	[1989 model]	activities in connection with investments	management and disposal	without prejudice to its laws & regulations	–

TABLE 22 FET, FPS, MST and PAD in Chinese IIAs (*cont.*)

Counterpart	Signed	In force	Location & relationship FET & FPS	Structure and key wording FET & FPS v PRC models	MST	FET formulation	FET object of coverage	FET at all times	FET other
South Korea	2007	2007	prot. art. / FET & FPS = §	≠	–	FET	investments of investors	–	–
Seychelles	2007	–	prot. art. / no FPS	≠	–	FET	investments made by investors	–	in accordance with IL princ.
France	2007	2010	split: art. 3: FET / art. 5: FPS with exp.	≠	–	FET	investments made by investors	–	in accordance with IL princ. – generally recognized
Costa Rica	2007	2016	split: art. 2 = FPS & disc. / art. 3 = FET with MFN & NT (FET in ≠ §)	1997 model, exact	–	FET	investments of investors	V	in accordance with IL princ. – universally accepted
Cuba	2007	2007	= art. MFN / FET & FPS in = §	1984 model, exact	–	FET	investments & activities associated of investors	–	–
Mexico	2008	2009	= art. MST / FET & FPS = §	≠	V	FET	investments of investors	–	no > CIL MST

Protection formulation	Protection object of coverage	Protection limitations	Discrimination prohibition	Object of coverage	Expressly covered activities	Subject to laws	Express exclusions / other
protection & security – full & constant	= FET	–	[1989 model]	investments by investors	[1989 model] + "local content, technology transfer or export performance requirements"	–	–
–	/	/	–*	= FET *	restrictions on investment–related purchases (FET context) *	/	–
protection & security – full & comprehensive	= FET	–	–	/	/	/	–
protection & security – constant	= FET	–	[1989 model]	= FET	[1989 model]	without prejudice to its laws & regulations	–
protection	= FET	–	–	/	/	/	= MFN
FPS	= FET	= FET	–	/	/	/	BIT breach NO auto treat. breach

TABLE 22 FET, FPS, MST and PAD in Chinese IIAS (*cont.*)

Counterpart	Signed	In force	Location & relationship FET & FPS	Structure and key wording FET & FPS v PRC models	MST	FET formulation	FET object of coverage	FET at all times	FET other
Colombia	2008	2013	prot. art. / FET & FPS = §	≠	V	FET including denial of justice in judicial / admin. proceedings in accordance with generally accepted CIL principles	investments of investors	–	no > CIL MST
New Zealand [FTA]	2008	2008	FET art. / FET & FPS = §	≠	–	FET including denial of justice or unfair / inequitable treat. in legal / admin. proceedings in accordance with general principles of law	investments of investors	V	in accordance with commonly accepted IL rules
Peru [FTA]	2009	2010	FET & FPS art. / FET & FPS = §	≠	V	FET including denial of justice in judicial / admin. proceedings in accordance with generally accepted CIL principles	investments of investors	–	no > CIL MST
Switzerland	2009	2010	= art. MFN & NT / FET & FPS = §	1989 model, similar	–	FET	investments of investors + returns	V	–

Protection formulation	Protection object of coverage	Protection limitations	Discrimination prohibition	Object of coverage	Expressly covered activities	Subject to laws	Express exclusions / other
FPS	= FET	no > CIL MST; no > NT	[1989 model]	investments	[1989 model]	without prejudice to its laws & regulations	BIT breach NO auto treat. breach
FPS + def.: measures reasonably necessary	= FET	= FET	[1989 model]	investments by investors	[1989 model]	–	BIT breach NO auto FET breach
FPS	= FET	no > CIL MST; no > NT	–	/	/	/	BIT breach NO auto treat. breach
FPS	= FET	–	[1989 model]	investments	[1989 model] + extension	–	–

TABLE 22 FET, FPS, MST and PAD in Chinese IIAs (*cont.*)

Counterpart	Signed	In force	Location & relationship FET & FPS	Structure and key wording FET & FPS v PRC models	MST	FET formulation	FET object of coverage	FET at all times	FET other
Mali	2009	2009	split: art. 2 = FPS & disc. / art. 3 = FET with MFN & NT (FET in ≠ §)	1997 model, similar	–	FET	investments of investors	V	–
Bahamas	2009	–	split: art. 2 = FPS & disc. / art. 3 = FET with MFN & NT	1997 model, exact	–	FET	investments of investors	V	–
Malta	2009	2009	split: art. 2 = FPS & disc. / art. 3 = FET with MFN & NT (FET in ≠ §)	1997 model, similar	–	FET	investments of investors	V	–
ASEAN [CAIA/FTA]	2009	2010	prot. art. / FET & FPS = §	≠	–	FET + def.: obligation not to deny justice in any legal / admin proceedings	investments of investors	–	–
Libya	2010	–	split: art. 2 = FPS & disc. / art. 3 = FET with MFN & NT (FET in ≠ §)	1997 model, exact	–	FET	investments of investors	V	–

Protection formulation	Protection object of coverage	Protection limitations	Discrimination prohibition	Object of coverage	Expressly covered activities	Subject to laws	Express exclusions / other
protection & security – constant	invest-ments made by investors	–	[1989 model]	= FET	[1989 model]	without prejudice to its laws & regulations	–
protection & security – constant	= FET	–	[1989 model]	investments by investors	[1989 model]	without prejudice to its laws & regulations	–
protection & security – constant	invest-ments	–	[1989 model]	investments by investors	[1989 model] – maintenance	without prejudice to its laws & regulations	–
FPS + def.: measures reasonably necessary	= FET	–	–	/	/	/	BIT breach NO auto FET/ FPS breach
protection & security – constant	= FET	–	[1989 model]	investments by investors	[1989 model]	without prejudice to its laws & regulations	–

TABLE 22 FET, FPS, MST and PAD in Chinese IIAs (*cont.*)

Counterpart	Signed	In force	Location & relationship FET & FPS	Structure and key wording FET & FPS v PRC models	MST	FET formulation	FET object of coverage	FET at all times	FET other
Chad	2010	–	FET art. / FET & FPS = §	≠	–	FET includes willful denial of justice & obvious discriminatory or arbitrary measures	investors & investments	–	in accordance with domestic laws & general legal principles; no > NT
DR Congo	2011	–	FET art. / FET & FPS = §	≠	–	FET includes willful denial of justice & obvious discriminatory or arbitrary measures	investors and associated investments	–	no > NT
Uzbekistan	2011	2011	FET art. / FET & FPS = §	≠	–	FET + def.: willful denial of justice & obvious discriminatory or arbitrary measures	investors and associated investments	–	–
South Korea & Japan	2012	2014	prot. art. / FET & FPS = §	≠	V	FET	investments of investors	–	no > reasonable and appropriate standard in accordance with generally accepted IL rules

Protection formulation	Protection object of coverage	Protection limitations	Discrimination prohibition	Object of coverage	Expressly covered activities	Subject to laws	Express exclusions / other
FPS def.: reasonable & necessary police measures	= FET	no > NT	–	/	/	/	BIT breach NO auto treat. breach
FPS + def.: reasonable & necessary police measures	= FET	= FET	–	/	/	/	BIT breach NO auto treat. breach
FPS + def.: reasonable & necessary police measures	= FET	no > NT	–	/	/	/	BIT breach NO auto treat. breach
FPS	= FET	= FET	–	/	/	/	–

TABLE 22 FET, FPS, MST and PAD in Chinese IIAS (*cont.*)

Counterpart	Signed	In force	Location & relationship FET & FPS	Structure and key wording FET & FPS v PRC models	MST	FET formulation	FET object of coverage	FET at all times	FET other
Canada	2012	2014	= art. MST / FET & FPS = §	≠	V	FET	investments ('covered')	–	no > CIL MST
Chile [SAI/FTA]	2012	2014	= art. MST / FET & FPS = §	≠	V	FET	investments ('covered')	–	no > CIL MST
Tanzania	2013	2014	FET art. / FET & FPS = §	≠	–	FET + def.: denial of justice & obvious discriminatory or arbitrary treatment	investors and associated investments	–	–
South Korea [FTA]	2015	2015	= art. MST / FET & FPS = §	≠	V + def.: CIL princ. that protect economic rights and interests of aliens	FET: including obligation not to deny justice in judicial / administrative proceedings in accordance with due process of law	investments ('covered')	–	no > CIL MST
Australia [FTA]	2015	2015	/	/	/	/	/	/	/
Turkey	2015	–	prot. art. / FET & FPS = §	1989 model, similar	–	FET + def.: denial of justice & obvious discriminatory or arbitrary measures	investments of investors	V	in accordance with IL princ.

Protection formulation	Protection object of coverage	Protection limitations	Discrimination prohibition	Object of coverage	Expressly covered activities	Subject to laws	Express exclusions / other
FPS	= FET	= FET	–	/	/	/	BIT breach NO auto treat. breach
FPS	= FET	= FET	–	/	/	/	BIT breach NO auto treat. breach
FPS + def.: reasonable & necessary police measures	= FET	no > CIL MST	–	/	/	/	BIT breach NO auto treat. breach
FPS + def.: CIL level of police protection	= FET	= FET	[1989 model]	investors & investments (covered)	losses due to war, revolt, insurrection, riot, or other civil strife; performance requirements on export or transfer of technology	–	BIT breach NO auto treat. breach; no PD on NT subsidies/grants in case of war, revolt, insurrection, riot, or other civil strife
/	/	/	/	/	/	/	/
FPS + def.: reasonable & necessary police measures	= FET	–	[1989 model]	investments	[1989 model]	–	BIT breach NO auto treat. breach

G Conclusion

Moving from the detailed review in Chapter 2 of the definition of investment, Chapter 3 has provided a wider and more in-depth comparative and analytical study of China's treaty practice.

After having defined the pool of 120 Chinese IIAs considered best fit to produce a solid and novel piece of research on treaty making, the work focused on dissecting and comparing the various elements and components of seven key foreign investment protection clauses: ISDS, expropriation, MFN, NT, FET, FPS, and PAD.

The result of this review reveals a considerable degree of uniformity within China's IIA programme, also with respect to the corresponding BIT template, marked by certain 'evolutionary steps' roughly corresponding to the novel periodization proposed in Chapter One.

Out of all findings, however, it is important not to overlook the fact that in a considerable number of Chinese IIAs, ISDS is still significantly constrained, either by old-style clauses limiting consent to arbitration *ratione materiae* to disputes relating to the amount of compensation due to expropriation, or by the contemporary trend of including various exceptions and exclusions.

In this respect, in the context of the China-led *One Belt – One Road* transcontinental infrastructural project (involving many sovereign States stretching from East Asia to Europe), the related IIA-updating process currently underway could *inter alia* confirm whether China has indeed adopted a 'dual policy' in its IIA-making, namely granting narrower or wider standards depending on the negotiating counterpart. It could, in fact, be otherwise concluded that the greater flexibility China has shown in more recent stipulations is the result of the rapid expansion of its economy and global presence, hence of *ad hoc* adjustments (or 'experiments') with selected counterparts, with a view to determining future standard policy features.

While the variety of the findings of this Chapter may not be effectively resumed here, as a general assessment it may be said that, throughout its investment treaty practice, China has consistently demonstrated remarkable attention to aspects relating to sovereignty as opposed to other matters, considered perhaps 'ancillary', such as calculation methods (of damages) and rates (of interest).

Conclusion

The sheer size of China's economy and the corresponding out- and in-bound investment capacity, the manner in which such outbound investment is (or can be) directed (or influenced) by the State, and the vast investment treaty network already in place, arguably make China the most significant player in the field of international investment law today.

Next to preliminarily proposing a new periodization of China's investment law programme, the research presented in this book demonstrates that, overall, while maintaining certain typical features, China continues to build its foreign investment protection programme, borrowing from international best practices. Until well after the year 2000, this meant relying on models and practices of Western European States with a consistent volume of exported capital and significant experience with investment treaties (most notably, Germany and the UK). Since the turn of the millennium, and after 2008 especially, with the Chinese authorities progressively relaxing control over their investment treaty negotiators and the related gradual turn to more complex stipulations (in particular, investment chapters in FTAs, as well as investment agreements part of multi-stage FTAs established through framework agreements), China has begun enriching, partly through renegotiations, what was an already vast treaty network by cautiously borrowing from the North American models and practice – in particular, NAFTA, Canada, and the U.S. Today, China's international investment treaty making, while incomparably more flexible than that carried out before the year 2000, still maintains privileged features that the country seems unwilling to give up (such as the requirement to go through the domestic administrative review procedure before initiating arbitration), yet would concede if it deems so fit. The analysis of the treaties concluded over the last decade, especially when compared to earlier periods, seems to point to the adoption of a 'dual' treaty-making policy on the part of China, which pivots on the relative political strength and investment potential of the treaty counterpart.

China's Model BITS

With regard to China's three model BITS (1984, 1989, and 1997), reliance on perceived best practices resulted in significant borrowing from the German and British templates. The wording of each Chinese model provision is built

© KONINKLIJKE BRILL NV, LEIDEN, 2021 | DOI:10.1163/9789004443938_006

through a careful selection of the terms borrowed, with a criterion that seems to privilege simplicity and clarity, in the attempt to avoid expressions potentially leading to unwarranted interpretations or unexpected outcomes (in the eyes of China, at least). Not infrequently, when no foreign model was deemed sufficiently clear, China proceeded to crossbreed terms from different models, crafting new wordings (whose ties to the original templates nevertheless remain visible). On occasion, the result of these mergers has been further adjusted with the insertion of original elements, aimed at preserving what would consequently emerge as China's core interests, at least at the time (*e.g.*, the explicit, and reiterated, obligation to respect domestic laws and regulations). The 1997 model, finally, signals China's willingness to get past a 'defensive' policy – which, albeit welcoming of foreign investment, tended to restrain the investors' ability to initiate international claims against China, and circumscribed the jurisdiction and/or powers of arbitral tribunals. Such a willingness, however, for some time remained largely on paper, as China only employed this model on a stable basis after the year 2000.

China's Investment Treaty Practice

China's investment treaty-making developments emerge clearly from the in-depth comparative survey of the 120 investment treaties undertaken in this book. The survey dissected and contrasted the key procedural and substantive protection clauses (ISDS, expropriation, MFN, NT, FET, FPS, PAD) of each treaty against the Chinese models as well as those of the principal actors in the field from Western Europe (Germany, UK, the Netherlands, France, Italy) and North America (U.S., Canada). The results confirm that, next to a significant adherence of the treaty practice to any of the first two Chinese models up to year 2000, with the employment of the third model China has also become increasingly more available to consider variations to its text (all the while welcoming its reconfirmation whenever possible). Concurrently, China cautiously undertook a process of gradual modernization of its foreign investment protection standards. Once central references, the German and British model BITs are being replaced with contents borrowed from North American models. There, seeds of a 'dual policy' seem to have been planted: while throughout the 1990s innovations were tested with trusted (or innocuous) treaty partners with the goal of extending them to subsequent stipulations, the current trend sees China maintaining a simplified (or rigid) approach toward certain treaty counterparts, and a more sophisticated (or flexible) one with others, based on a variety of factors, including not only bilateral investment flow and potential but, also, geopolitical considerations.

The in-depth look at China's treaty practice illustrates that policy developments in treaty making have been undertaken gradually and cautiously: i) relying on more experienced counterparts or ii) choosing some with limited outward investment potential or, anyway, iii) with whom China has an advantage in the bilateral relationship (of an economic or geopolitical nature). In particular, in those cases where it consented to go beyond the model text, in terms of guarantees provided, China did so either: i) by reason of the reliance it placed on a trusted and more experienced State partner for the agreement (*e.g.*, the 2003 China-Germany BIT), or ii) by drawing from the experience of the latter, while negotiating a preliminary agreement with another State with which it enjoys close diplomatic ties, yet not overly significant economic relationship (*e.g.*, BITs with Seychelles and South Africa, FTA with Pakistan). Therefore, where the conclusion of the agreement is chiefly driven by a political rationale (*e.g.*, FTA with Pakistan), the stipulation may still be limited to reproduce the latest Chinese model BIT, thus simply updating the previous investment protection regime. Similarly, innovations in the text of the treaty are limited where trade and investment relationships are 'unilateral', with China in the position of key trade partner and capital-exporting State (*i.e.*, FTA with Peru). On the other hand, the conclusion of the agreements with New Zealand and Chile – both small yet developed OECD economies – produced more sophisticated results. The new investment discipline featured in these stipulations constituted preparatory ground for more complex negotiations with more significant (investment-wise) Western partners. Indeed, it is no coincidence that, at about the same time, negotiations for a long-sought BIT with Canada finally came to a successful end. Lastly, a considerable interplay of political, trade, and investment rationales underlie the China-ASEAN Agreement on Investment. It is with such an increasingly relevant partner (and regional neighbor) that China appears to have found a shared understanding of the investment protection treaty regime and, consequently, struck a balance between its conservative grasp of State sovereignty and consent, on the one hand, and the protection of foreign investment (incoming as well as outgoing), on the other.

Over the past 20 years, the progressive willingness to leap over a 'defensive' foreign investment policy has been dictated chiefly by the steep rise of Chinese outward investments, and the resulting need to offer to these a better framework protection. China's economic rise mirrors its progressive geopolitical repositioning, from modest player to global hegemon (in an unprecedented short period of time). As seen, in terms of international investment protection policy, this meant modeling the new stipulations by turning partly away from Western Europe and, instead, towards North America – mainly, NAFTA and Canada – especially in the case of investment regimes that are part of, or flow from, FTAs. Thus, the North American-styled updating of China's foreign investment protection standards has been carried out chiefly in connection with more complex arrangements that contemplate inter alia a regime for the protection of foreign investments. Targets of this approach have been strategic geopolitical partners (Pakistan), vital suppliers of raw materials (Chile, Peru, Canada), key regional partners to boost exports of domestic manufacturing (ASEAN), and a liberal small market-economy (New Zealand) that served as 'test-agreement' for subsequent negotiations with larger economies with which China carries more significant bilateral trade and investment relations (*e.g.*, Canada, Australia, the U.S., the EU).

The new structure and terminology have also often been employed in order to support – or prevent – further developments of certain interpretive trends in investment arbitration (*e.g.*, the adoption of the Salini criteria in the notion of investment; the punctual indication of the treaty provisions to which the MFN clause applies), as well as to retain interpretive control over future issues (*e.g.*, the Parties' binding interpretation of a treaty clause; the preliminary exception to dismiss manifestly frivolous claims). From the analysis of the texts, what ultimately emerges is an intertwined collection of cross-influences, amidst an overall trend in which the Pacific region (ASEAN and China) is on the rise, and the old European framework is recalibrated through the North American templates, in an attempt to regulate new issues in the field, both substantive (*i.e.*, environment) and procedural (ISDS). Therefore, while for the most part not proactive in this process, China has not been deaf to developments, including the ensuing doctrinal debate. In all, however, the 'North American turn' and the new IIAs represent, for the time being, more an update in structure and terminology than concrete substantive advancements in terms of protection standards (such as liberalization, for which China is still quite unprepared).[1] Similarly, despite more modern or refined wording, certain BITs maintained the concise European form (as opposed to the analytical North American; *e.g.*, Tanzania, Turkey).

1 Without pre-establishment protection, the BIT does not offer any guarantee toward restrictive establishment laws, or complex approval process. However, as noted by Kong, implementation of pre-establishment obligations would require the overhaul of much of China's foreign investment regime; see Kong Q, '*US – China Bilateral Investment Treaty Negotiations*' (Chapter 1, fn. 98).

The transitory nature of the current *status quo* is evident in all agreements concluded from 2012 onward. The process is still *in fieri*, and China seems to still be weighing certain fundamental policy choices on the matter of foreign investment protection – hence, the cautiousness so far displayed, *e.g.*, by not officially releasing a new template,[2] or that currently shown at UNCITRAL's table on ISDS reform.

China and the Proposal for an International Investment Court

China's political positioning and potential assertiveness, including via Chinese foreign investments abroad as well as a more proactive role in shaping investment protection standards, may prove critical to the ongoing negotiations at UNCITRAL for ISDS reform.

Specifically, it could determine the fate of the proposal that the EU has been pushing at various levels since 2015, *i.e.*, to replace investment arbitration with an *ad hoc* international investment court. This plan, push forth by the EU with increasing insistence, has met with significant resistance from countries ranging from the U.S. to Russia, Japan, and Chile. China has so far not taken a definite stance, arguably weighing not only the consistency of the U.S. opposition but also the benefits the EU proposal may bring to itself. However, while gains for China appear limited, disadvantages seem quite evident:

- With regard to foreign investment in China, the institutionalization of an international legal dispute settlement mechanism through a full-fledged court, quite entirely independent from the participation and control of the host State, would diminish China's pre-litigation bargaining position vis-à-vis foreign investors (a position uniquely strong, combining an unparalleled domestic market with a very specific political organization);
- In relation to both foreign investment in China and Chinese investment abroad, the consideration of specific Chinese interests and views is likely to lose weight in the context of an international court (as China would enjoy, at most, only one national in a body with a wider membership and composition, and in a field that it is likely to perceive as under the influence of 'Western thinking').[3]

2 Despite the repeated calls in this sense of authoritative doctrine on the point; see N. Gallagher, '*China's BIT's and Arbitration Practice*' (Chapter 3, fn. 12); this call follows that of 2008 from the same Gallagher which, jointly with Shan, drafted what they thought could be the text of the new model at the time (see Chapter 1, fn. 63).

3 As mentioned in the Introduction, China has long resented the 'unequal treaties' that it concluded with Western Powers in the XIX century, and has since been suspicious of the West

While the above concerns may be addressed in both theory and practice, at least to a certain extent, it remains to be seen why China should embark on radically changing a system that it has finally made itself comfortable with. Although it welcomes certain restraints to the power of arbitrators, limits to initiating claims, and proper consideration to protecting sovereign prerogatives of the State, China is arguably mindful that the significant Chinese investments abroad may be better guaranteed in a less-than-fully legalized context; as such, arbitration is preferable to an international court.

Indeed, the position China articulated at UNCITRAL in July 2019 (two years into the negotiations), seems pointing in this direction.[4] There, and chiefly, China stated its position that ISDS is overall worth maintaining – highlighting, notably, the essential right of appointing arbitrators – albeit certain improvements are desirable. Drawing a parallel with the WTO dispute settlement mechanism, China declared itself open to considering research on a permanent appellate mechanism aimed at "error correction and strengthening the coherence and legitimacy of the system".[5] Interestingly, the formalization of this lack of support from China to the EU-backed multilateral investment court has seen a corresponding softening of the EU, now open to the so-called 'open architecture' approach (in which various dispute settlement mechanisms would co-exist, and even overlap, as long as they are all working towards the goal of increasing the consistency and legitimacy of the system as a whole).[6]

China plays, however, its own game. On the one hand, the desired investment arbitration reforms it supports touch upon i) more objective and transparent rules on the selection and removal of arbitrators; ii) a shared understanding of what 'conflict of interest' means for arbitrators; and iii) an expansion of the pool of arbitrators to include more from developing countries. These proposals, in addition to facilitating Chinese adjudicatory participation to ISDS, impact quite favorably on the protection of Chinese investment abroad. On the other hand, China's focus on increased transparency on third-party funding and, chiefly, on strengthening pre-arbitral negotiations and mediation

---

use of international law, felt as a tool to keep China's ambitions and influence in check. While over the decades before and after the turn of the millennium, China has brought itself mostly in line, and complied with, most international legal standards, recently it has voiced its different stance – when not outright opposition – to certain interpretations felt led by the 'West'. Among the recent expressions of this sentiment is China's vehement refusal to acknowledge the 2016 UNCLOS award in the South China Sea arbitration (China v Philippines).

4 See also fn. 231 in Chapter 1.

5 *Ibid.*

6 Submission of the European Union and its Member States to UNCITRAL Working Group III, 18 January 2019; available at http://trade.ec.europa.eu/doclib/docs/2019/january/tradoc_157631.pdf.

mechanisms, are aimed at buttressing China's position as host/respondent-State, and thus are in opposition to Western-led calls for increased transparency in investor-State dispute settlement as a whole: what happens in the mediation room remains, of course, confidential – including the terms of any settlements.

The Contribution of This Work

In sum, the review carried out in this book offers an objective assessment of China's actual treaty-practice regarding a number of key investment clauses. As such, it not only can form a solid base for related research on this matter, but it also enables arbitral tribunals to reach sound conclusions regarding the interpretation of said key clauses. Further study on other important investment protection standards, such as transfer of personnel and capital, is both possible and recommended, with regard to China as well as other States.

The methodology employed in this research, and the analysis that ensued, take time and patience; however, neither can be delegated to automated systems, as these are still quite unable to deliver the prerequisite quality and certainty needed to develop proper academic research. As Leonardo da Vinci (seemingly) put it: "details make perfection, and perfection is not a detail".

Bibliography

Books & Treatises

Antkiewicz A and Whalley J, 'China's New Regional Trade Agreements', in Greenway D (ed.), *The World Economy*, vol. 28(10) (Blackwell Publishing, 2005).

Backhouse E and Bland JOP, *Annals and Memoirs of the Court of Peking (from the 16th to the 20th Century)* (Heinemann, 1914).

Bath V, 'ASEAN: The Liberalization of Investment through Regional Arrangements', in Trakman LE and Ranieri N (eds.), *Regionalism in International Investment Law* (Oxford University Press, 2013).

Bath V, 'The South and Alternative Models of Trade and Investment Regulation – Chinese outbound investment and approaches to international investment agreements', in Morosini F and Ratton Sanchez Badin M (eds.), *Recalibrating International Investment Law: Global South Initiatives* (Cambridge University Press, 2018).

Bernstein W, *A Splendid Exchange: How Trade Shaped the World* (Grove Press, 2008).

Bernstein TP and Xiaobo L, *Taxation Without Representation in Rural China* (Cambridge University Press, 2003).

Boisson de Chazournes L, 'The Growth in Investment Litigation: Perspectives and Challenges', in Echandi R and Sauvé P (eds.), *Prospects in International Investment Law and Policy* (Cambridge University Press, 2013).

Bonner SE, *Socialism Unbound: Principles, Practices, and Prospects* (Columbia University Press, 2013).

Bottini G, 'Protection on Essential Interests in the BIT Era', in Weiler TG (ed.), *Investment Treaty Arbitration and International Law*, vol. 1 (Jurisnet LLC, 2008).

Bottini G, 'Legality of Investments under ICSID Jurisprudence', in Waibel M, Kaushal A, Chung KL and Balchin C (eds.), *The Backlash against Investment Arbitration* (Wolters Kluwer, 2010).

Brown C (ed.), *Commentaries to Selected Model Investment Treaties* (Oxford University Press, 2013).

Brown C (ed), 'The Development and Importance of the Model Bilateral Investment Treaty', in *Commentaries on Selected Model Investment Treaties* (Oxford University Press, 2013).

Brødsgaard KE and Rutten K, *From Accelerated Accumulation to Socialist Market Economy in China* (Brill, 2017).

Bungenberg M and Titi C, 'The Evolution of EU Investment Law and the future of EU-China Investment Relations', in Shan W (ed.), *China and International Investment Law* (Brill Nijhoff, 2014).

Cai C, 'China', in Shan W (ed.), *The Legal Protection of Foreign Investment – A Comparative Study* (Hart Publishing, 2012).

Carreau D and Juillard P, *Droit international économique* (Dalloz, 2010).

Chaisse J, 'China's International Investment Policy: Formation, Evolution, and Transformation(s)', in Chaisse J and Nottage L (eds.), *International Investment Treaties and Arbitration across Asia* (Brill Nijhoff, 2018).

Chaisse J, 'Untangling the Triangle: Issues for State-controlled Entities in Trade, Investment, and Competition Law', in Chaisse J and Lin T (eds.), *International Economic Law and Governance* (Oxford, 2016).

Chaisse J and Jusoh S, *The ASEAN Comprehensive Investment Agreement* (Edward Elgar Publishing, 2016).

Chen A (ed.), 'Should the Four "Great Safeguards" in Sino-Foreign BITs be Hastily Dismantled? Comments on Critical Provisions Concerning Dispute Settlement in Model US and Canadian BITs', in *The Voice from China* (Springer, 2013).

Chi M, 'Sustainable Development Provisions in Investment Treaties' (UN ESCAP Report, UN Publications, 2018).

Chi M, *Integrating Sustainable Development in International Investment Law* (Taylor & Francis, 2017).

Cho S and Kurtz J, 'The limits of isomorphism: global investment law and the ASEAN Investment Regime', in Chaisse J and Nottage L (eds.), *International Investment Treaties and Arbitration across Asia*, (Brill Nijhoff, 2018).

Choi WM, 'Substantive Provisions of the East Asian Trilateral Investment Agreement and their Implication', in Chaisse J (ed.), *China's International Investment Law Strategy* (Oxford, 2019).

Collins D, *The BRIC States and Outward Foreign Direct Investment* (Oxford University Press, 2013).

Comeaux PE and Kinsella NS, *Protecting Foreign Investment under International Law: Legal Aspects of Political Risk* (Oceana Publications Inc., 1997).

De Mestral A and Falsafi A, 'Investment Provisions in Regional Trade Agreements: A more Efficient Solution?', in De Mestral A and Lévesque C (eds.), *Improving International Investment Agreements* (Routledge, 2013).

De Mestral A and Lévesque C (eds.), *Improving International Investment Agreements* (Routledge, 2013).

Dolzer R and Kim Y, 'Germany', in Brown C (ed.), *Commentaries on Selected Model Investment Treaties* (Oxford University Press, 2013).

Dolzer R and Schreuer C, *Principles of International Investment Law* (Oxford University Press, 2012).

Dolzer R and Stevens M, *Bilateral Investment Treaties* (Martinus Nijhoff Publishers, 1995).

Escobar A, *Encountering Development: The Making and Unmaking of the Third World*, Princeton University Press, 1995.

Finder S, 'The International Fraud and Corruption Sanctioning System – The case of Chinese SOEs', in Chaisse J (ed.), *China's International Investment Strategy* (Oxford, 2019).

Gallagher N, 'China's BIT's and Arbitration Practice: Progress and Problems', in Shan W (ed.), *China and International Investment Law* (Brill Nijhoff, 2014).

Gallagher N and Shan W, *Chinese Investment Treaties: Policies and Practice* (Oxford University Press, 2009).

Gallagher N and Shan W, 'China', in Brown C (ed.), *Commentaries on Selected Model Investment Treaties* (Oxford University Press, 2013).

Haftel YZ, 'BRICS and the Global Investment Regime', in Kim SY (ed.), *BRICs and Global Economy* (World Scientific Publishing, forthcoming 2019) <https://papers.ssrn.com/sol3/papers.cfm?abstract_id=2957721> accessed 31 Oct. 2019.

Hart HLA, *The Concept of Law* (Oxford University Press, 1961).

History of the ICSID Convention: Documents Concerning the Origin and the Formulation of the Convention on the Settlement of Investment Disputes Between States and Nationals of Other States, (ICSID Publishing, 1968).

Huang J, *International Business Law: Chinese and Comparative Perspectives* (Foreign Language Teaching and Research Press, 2017).

Khambata DJ and Mehta AN, 'Foreign Investment in India: The Unfolding Legal Story' in Esplugues C (ed.) *Foreign Investment and Investment Arbitration in Asia* (Intersentia, 2019).

Kueh YY, *China's New Industrialization Strategy: Was Chairman Mao Necessary?* (Edward Elgar Publishing, 2008).

Li S, 'Bilateral Investment Promotion and Protection Agreements: Practice of the People's Republic of China', in De Waart P, Peters P and Denters E (eds.), *International Law and Development* (Martinus Nijhoff, 1988).

Lim CL, Elms DK and Low P (eds.), *The Trans-Pacific Partnership: A Quest for a Twenty-First-Century Trade Agreement* (Cambridge University Press, 2012).

Lin C, *The Transformation of Chinese Socialism* (Duke University Press, 2006).

Liu C, 'The Evolution of Chinese Approaches to IIAs', in De Mestral A and Lévesque C (eds.), *Improving International Investment Agreements* (Routledge, 2013).

Manger MS, 'A Quantitative Perspective on Trends in IIA Rules', in De Mestral A and Lévesque C (eds.), *Improving International Investment Agreements* (Routledge, 2013).

Marti ME, *China and the Legacy of Deng Xiaoping: From Communist Revolution to Capitalist Evolution* (Brassey's Washigton DC, 2002).

McLachlan C, Shore L and Weiniger M, *International Investment Arbitration: Substantive Principles* (Oxford University Press, 2007).

Mercurio B, 'Bilateral and Regional Trade Agreements in Asia: A Skeptic's View', in Buckley RP, Weixing Hu R and Arner DW (eds.), *East Asian Economic Integration: Law, Trade and Finance* (Edward Elgar Publishing, 2011).

Moran TH, Graham EM and Blomström M, *Does Foreign Direct Investment Promote Development?* (Institute for International Economics Center for Global Development, Washington DC, 2005).

Newcombe A, 'Developments in IIA Treaty-Making', in De Mestral A and Lévesque C (eds.), *Improving International Investment Agreements* (Routledge, 2013).

Nottage L, Chaisse J, and Thanitcul S, 'International Investment Treaty Arbitration across Asia: a bird's eye view', in Chaisse J and Nottage L (eds.), *International Investment Treaties and Arbitration across Asia*, (Brill Nijhoff, 2018).

Papa M, 'BRICS and Politics of Reforming Global Governance: the Case of Investment Arbitration', in De Búrca G, Scott J and Kilpatrick C (eds.), *Critical Legal Perspectives on Global Governance: Liber Amicorum David M Trubek* (Hart Publishing, 2013).

Paulsson J, *The Denial of Justice in International Law* (Cambridge University Press, 2005).

Pekar E, 'The Chinese Investment Regime and the US-China Negotiations', in Shan W (ed.), *China and International Investment Law* (Brill Nijhoff, 2014).

Perkins DH, 'China's Economic Policy and Performance', in MacFarquhar R, Fairbank JK and Twitchett D (eds.), *The Cambridge History of China*, vol. 15 (Cambridge University Press, 1991).

Peterson L, 'Out of Order', in Waibel M, Kaushal A, Chung KL and Balchin C (eds.), *The Backlash against Investment Arbitration* (Wolters Kluwer, 2010).

Petrochilos G, Noury S and Kalderimis D, 'Annotated Commentary to the ICSID Arbitration Rules', in Mistelis L (ed.), *Concise International Arbitration* (Kluwer, 2010).

Pollan T, *Legal Framework for the Admission of FDI* (Eleven International Publishing, 2006).

Sacerdoti G, 'The Proliferation of BITs: Conflict of Treaties, Proceedings and Awards', in Sauvant P (ed.), *Appeals Mechanism in International Investment Disputes* (Oxford University Press, 2008).

Salacuse JW, 'Towards a Global Treaty on Foreign Investment: The Search for a Grand Bargain', in Horn N (ed.), *Arbitrating Foreign Investment Disputes: Procedural and Substantive Legal Aspects* (Kluwer Law International, 2004).

Schneiderman D, *Constitutionalizing Economic Globalization* (Cambridge University Press, 2008).

Shan W, *The Legal Framework of EU-China Investment Relations – A Critical Appraisal* (Hart Publishing, 2005).

Shan W (ed.), *The Legal Protection of Foreign Investment: A Comparative Study* (Hart Publishing, 2012).

Shan W, 'China and International Investment Law', in Trakman LE and Ranieri N (eds.), *Regionalism in International Investment Law* (Oxford University Press, 2013).

Shelley B, *Democratic Development in East Asia* (Routledge, 2004).

Soderberg M (ed.), *Changing Power Relations in Northeast Asia: Implications for Relations between Japan and South Korea* (Routledge, 2011).

Sornarajah M, *The International Law on Foreign Investment* (Cambridge University Press, 2004).

Sornarajah M, 'The Retreat of Neo-Liberalism in Investment Treaty Arbitration', in Rogers CA and Alford RP (eds.), *The Future of Investment Arbitration* (Oxford University Press, 2009).

Trakman LE and Ranieri NW (eds.), *Regionalism in International Investment Law* (Oxford University Press, 2013).

Vaccaro-Incisa GM, 'China's Policy Rationale and Treaty Making on the Protection of Foreign Investment: A Comparative Perspective, from the Model Bits to the Latest Stipulations' (Université de Genève, thèse doctorale, 2015) <https://archive-ouverte.unige.ch/unige:48427> accessed 23 Nov. 2019.

Vogel EF, *Deng Xiaoping and the Transformation of China* (Belknap Press, 2011).

Walder AG, *China Under Mao: A Revolution Derailed* (Harvard University Press, 2015).

Wang D, *China's Unequal Treaties: Narrating National History* (Lexington Books, 2005).

Wang HY and Miao L, 'China's Outward Investment – Trends and Challenges in the Globalization of Chinese Enterprises', in Chaisse J (ed.), *China's International Investment Strategy* (Oxford, 2019).

Wang L, 'Chinese SOEs Investment and the National Security under IIAs', in Chaisse J (ed.), *China's International Investment Strategy* (Oxford, 2019).

Wang Y, *Transformation of Foreign Affairs and International Relations in China, 1978–2008* (Social Sciences Academic Publisher, 2011).

Wee KH and Mirza H, 'ASEAN Investment Cooperation: Retrospect, Developments and Prospects', in Bartels F and Freeman N (eds.), *The Future of Foreign Investment in Southeast Asia* (RoutledgeCurzon, 2005).

Willems J, 'Investment Disputes under China's BITs', in Chaisse J (ed.), *China's International Investment Law Strategy* (Oxford, 2019).

Xiao J, 'Chinese BITs in the Twenty-First Century: Protecting Chinese Investments', in Chaisse J and Gugler P (eds.), *Expansion of Trade and FDI in Asia* (Routledge, 2009).

Xiao J, 'ASEAN-China FTA: A Pragmatic Approach to Regulating Services and Investment', in Chaisse J and Gugler P (eds.), *Competitiveness of the ASEAN Countries* (Edward Elgar Publishing, 2010).

Yen TH, 'East Asian Investment Treaties in the Integration Process: *Quo Vadis?*', in Buckley RP, Weixing Hu R and Arner DW (eds.), *East Asian Economic Integration: Law, Trade and Finance* (Edward Elgar Publishing, 2011).

Yuqing Z, 'The Case of China', in Moser MJ (ed.), *Investor-State Arbitration: Lessons for Asia* (Juris, 2008).

Zhao Y, 'Neoliberal Strategies, Socialist Legacies: Communication and State Transformation in China', in Chakravarty P and Zhao Y (eds.), *Global Communications: Toward a Transcultural Political Economy* (Rowman & Littlefield Publishers, 2008).

Articles

Alvarez J, 'The Return of the State' (2011) 20(2) *Minnesota Journal of International Law* 223.

Alvarez GA and Park WW, 'The New Face of Investment Arbitration: NAFTA Chapter 11', (2003) 28(2) *Yale Journal of International Law* 365.

Bath V, 'Foreign Investment, The National Interest and National Security: Foreign Direct Investment in Australia and China' (2012) 34(1) *Sydney Law Review* 5.

Beckley M, 'China and Pakistan: Fair-Weather Friends', (2012) 7(1) *Yale Journal of International Affairs* 9.

Cai C, 'China-US BIT Negotiations and the Future of Investment Treaty Regime: A Grand Bilateral Bargain with Multilateral Implications' (2009) 12(2) *Journal of International Economic Law* 457.

Carter J, 'The Protracted Bargain: Negotiating the Canada-China Foreign Investment Promotion and Protection Agreement', (2010) 47 *Canadian Yearbook of International Law* 197.

Chaisse J, 'The Regional Comprehensive Economic Partnership's investment chapter: One step forward, two steps back?' (Columbia FDI Perspectives, No. 271, Feb. 10th, 2020).

Chen H, 'China-Asean Investment Agreement Negotiations' (2006) 1(3) *Frontiers of Law in China* 423.

Clodfelter MA, 'The Adaptation of States to the Changing World of Investment Protection through Model BITs' (2009) 24(1) *ICSID Review* 165.

Côté CE, 'Investissment', (2012) 50 *Annuaire Canadien de Droit International* 363.

Denza E and Brooks S, 'Investment Protection Treaties: United Kingdom Experience' (1987) 36(4) *The International and Comparative Law Quarterly* 908.

Douglas Z, 'The MFN Clause in Investment Arbitration: Treaty Interpretation Off the Rails', (2011) 2(1) *Journal of International Dispute Settlement* 97.

Foster GW, 'Investors, States and Stakeholders: Power Asymmetries in International Investment and the Stabilizing Potential of Investment Treaties', (2013) 17(2) *Lewis & Clark Law Review* 361.

Gachùz GC, 'Chile's Economic and Political Relationship with China', (2012) 41(1) *Journal of Current Chinese Affairs* 133.

Hadley K, 'Do China's BIT Matter? Assessing the Effect of China's Investment Agreements on Foreign Direct Investment Flows, Investors' Rights, and the Rule of Law' (2013) 45 *Georgetown Journal of International Law* 255.

Heymann M, 'International Law and the Settlement of Investment Disputes Relating to China', (2008) 11(3) *Journal of International Economic Law* 507.

Huang J, 'Procedural Models to Upgrade BITs: China's Experience', *Leiden Journal of International Law* (2017), 1–23.

Huang PCC, 'Profit-Making State Firms and China's Development Experience: "State Capitalism" or "Socialist Market Economy"?' (2012) 38(6) *Modern China* 591.

Huiping C, 'China-ASEAN Investment Agreement Negotiations', (2006) 1(3) *Frontiers of Law in China* 423.

Huiping C, 'China-ASEAN Investment Agreement Negotiations: the Substantive Issues' (2006) 7(1) *The Journal of World Investment & Trade: Law, Economics, Politics* 143.

Kalderimis D and Tripp C, 'Investment Chapter of the NZ-China FTA', (May 2009) *New Zealand Law Journal* 156.

Kalicki J and Medeiros S, 'Investment Arbitration in Brazil: Revisiting Brazil's Traditional Reluctance towards ICSID, BITs and Investor-State Arbitration' (2008) 24 *Arbitration International* 423.

Kong Q, 'Bilateral Investment Treaties: The Chinese Approach and Practice' (1998/99) 8 *Asian Yearbook of International Law* 105.

Kong Q, 'US-China Bilateral Investment Treaty Negotiations: Context, Focus and Implications' (2012) 7(1) *Asian Journal of WTO and International Health Law & Policy* 181.

Kreindler RH, 'Investment Treaties and the Evolution in their Negotiation and Application: The New Germany-China BIT and its Relevance to International Financial Law Trends' (2009) 6(1) *Transnational Dispute Management* 1.

Langford M and Behn D, 'Managing Backlash: The Evolving Investment Treaty Arbitrator?', *European Journal of International Law* (forthcoming 2017) <https://papers.ssrn.com/sol3/papers.cfm?abstract_id=2835488> accessed Jul. 8th, 2017.

Li L, 'Chinese BIT Practice and Challenges' (2010) 17(4) *Chinese Journal of International and Economic Law* 114.

Masron TA and Yusop Z, 'The ASEAN Investment Area, other FDI Initiatives, and Intra-ASEAN Foreign Direct Investment', (2012) 26(2) *Asian-Pacific Economic Literature* 88.

Moloo R and Khachaturian A, 'The Compliance with the Law Requirement in International Investment Law', (2010–2011) 34 *Fordham International Law Journal* 1473.

Orrego Vicuña F, 'Reports of [Maffezini's] Demise Have Been Greatly Exaggerated', (2012) 3(2) *Journal of International Dispute Settlement* 299.

Paulsson J, 'Arbitration Without Privity', Vol. 10, Issue 2, Fall 1995, *ICSID Review – Foreign Investment Law Journal* 232–257.

Qi H, 'Investment Law in the China-ASEAN Free Trade Agreement', (2012) 5(2) *Journal of East Asia and International Law* 343.

Sacerdoti G, 'Bilateral Treaties and Multilateral Instruments on Investment Protection' (1997) 269 *Recueil des cours de l'Académie de Droit International de la Haye* 251.

Saleem O, 'The Spratly Islands Dispute: China Defines the New Millennium', (2000) 15(3) *American University International Law Review* 527.

Sauvant KP and Chen VZ, 'China Needs to Complement its "Going-Out" Policy with a "Going-In" Strategy' (Columbia FDI Perspectives, No. 121, May 12th, 2014).

Schill S, 'Tearing down the Great Wall: The New Generation Investment Treaties of the People's Republic of China', (2007) 15 *Cardozo Journal of International and Comparative Law* 73.

Schill S, 'W(h)ither Fragmentation? On the Literature and Sociology of International Investment Law', (2011) 22(3) *The European Journal of International Law* 875.

Schill S, 'Illegal Investments in International Arbitration', (2012) 11(2) *Law and Practice of International Courts and Tribunals* 281.

Schlemmer EC, 'Dispute Settlement in Investment-Related Matters: South Africa and the BRICS' (2018) 112 *AJIL Unbound* 212.

Schweickart D, 'China: Socialist or Capitalist?' (2015) 14 *Perspectives on Global Development and Technology* 13.

Shan W, 'From North-South Divide to Private-Public Debate: Revival of the Calvo Doctrine and the Changing Landscape in International Investment Law' (2007) 27(3) *Northwestern Journal of International Law and Business* 631.

Shan W & Wang L, The China-EU BIT: The emerging "Global BIT 2.0"? (Columbia FDI Perspectives, No. 128, August 18, 2014).

Smith G, 'Chinese Bilateral Investment Treaties: Restrictions on International Arbitration' (2010) 76 *Arbitration* 58.

Thompson TN, 'China's Nationalization of Foreign Firms: The Politics of Hostage Capitalism, 1949–57', (1979) 27(6) *Maryland Series in Contemporary Asian Studies* 1.

Trakman LE, 'The ICSID under Siege', (2012) 45(3) *Cornell Journal of International Law* 603.

Trakman LE, 'China and Foreign Direct Investment: Does Distance Lend Enchantment to the View?' (2014) 2(1) *The Chinese Journal of Comparative Law* 1.

Vaccaro-Incisa GM, 'Protection of Foreign Investment and the EU: Framework, Legal Risks, and First Fruits', in Mišcenic E and Raccah A, *Legal Risks in EU Law* (Springer, 2016), 111–133.

Vaccaro-Incisa GM, 'Arbitration clauses limited to compensation due to expropriation: Relevant case-law, interpretive trends, and the case of China's treaty policy and practice', in Chaisse J (ed.), *The Handbook of International Investment Law and Policy* (Springer, forthcoming).

Vaccaro-Incisa GM, *Objective criteria and* ratione legis *condition in the definition of investment: global trends and the Chinese practice*, in Nakagawa J (ed.), *Asian Perspectives on International Law* (Routledge, 2019).

Vandevelde KJ, 'The Bilateral Investment Treaties Program of the United States' (1988) 21(1) *Cornell Journal of International Law* 202.

Wang H, 'China's Approach to the Belt and Road Initiative: Scope, Character and Sustainability', (2019) 22(1) *Journal of International Economic Law* 29.

Wang H, 'The RCEP and its investment rules: learning from past Chinese FTAs' (2017) 3(2) *The Chinese Journal of Global Governance* 160.

Wang G, 'China's Practice in International Investment Law: From Participation to Leadership in the World Economy' (2009) 34 *Yale Journal of International Law* 575.

Zhang M, Enforceability: Foreign Arbitral Award in Chinese Courts, in 20 San Diego Int'l L.J.1 (2018).

Zheng Y, China's new Foreign Investment Law: deeper reform and more trust are needed, Columbia FDI Perspectives, No. 264, November 4, 2019.

Papers and Presentations

Berger A, 'China's New Bilateral Investment Treaty Programme: Substance, Rational and Implications for International Investment Law Making' (Paper for presentation at the American Society of International Law International Economic Law Interest Group Conference, Nov. 14th–15th, 2008) <https://www.die-gdi.de/uploads/media/Berger_ChineseBITs.pdf> accessed 20 Nov. 2019.

Berger A, 'Investment Rules in Chinese Preferential Trade and Investment Agreements: Is China Following the Global Trend towards Comprehensive Agreements?' (German Development Institute Discussion Paper n. 7, 2013), <http://www.die-gdi.de/uploads/media/DP_7.2013.pdf> accessed Jul. 15th, 2017.

Koleski K, 'The 13th Five-Year Plan' (US-China Economic and Security Review Commission Staff Research Report, Feb. 14th, 2017) <https://www.uscc.gov/Research/13th-five-year-plan> accessed 20 Nov. 2019.

Nakagawa J and Liang W, 'A Comparison of the FTA Strategies of Japan and China and their Implications for Multilateralism' (RCCPB Working Paper n. 11, Oct. 2011) <https://papers.ssrn.com/sol3/papers.cfm?abstract_id=2169361> accessed 20 Nov. 2019.

O'Neil J, 'Building Better Global Economic BRICs' (Goldman Sachs Global Economics Paper n. 66, Nov. 30th, 2001) <http://www.goldmansachs.com/our-thinking/archive/archive-pdfs/build-better-brics.pdf> accessed 20 Nov. 2019.

Rubinacci L, 'EU-China Investment Relationship, Update on State of Play' (DG Trade Civil Society Dialogue, Mar. 7th, 2012) <http://trade.ec.europa.eu/doclib/docs/2012/march/tradoc_149185.pdf> accessed 20 Nov. 2019.

Wang Y, 'New SASAC Rules to Enhance Risk Control of Chinese SOEs' Outbound Investments' (Norton Rose Fulbright Publications, Feb. 2012) <https://www.martindale.com/investments-law/article_Norton-Rose-Canada-LLP_1451278.htm> accessed 20 Nov. 2019.

Wehner L, 'Power, Governance, and Ideas in Chile's Free Trade Agreement Policy' (German Institute of Global and Area Studies Working Paper no. 102, May 2009) <https://www.giga-hamburg.de/en/publication/power-governance-and-ideas-in-chile%E2%80%99s-free-trade-agreement-policy> accessed 20 Nov. 2019.

Xiao J, 'The ASEAN-China Investment Agreement: A Regionalization of Chinese New BITs' (Society of International Economic Law, Jul. 8th–10th, 2010) <http://papers.ssrn.com/sol3/papers.cfm?abstract_id=1629202> accessed 20 Nov. 2019.

Official Reports and Statistics

EU Centre for Small and Medium Enterprise, 'Dispute Settlement with Chinese Companies' (2012) <http://www.eusmecentre.org.cn/guideline/dispute-settlement-chinese-companies> accessed 20 Nov. 2019.

Government of New Zealand, 'Two-Year Review Joint Report' (2011) <http://www.chinafta.govt.nz/4-Events-and-press/2-Press-releases/joint-report-feb2011.pdf> accessed 20 Nov. 2019.

Ministry of Foreign Affairs of the People's Republic of China, 'China's Initiation of the Five Principles of Peaceful Co-Existence' <http://www.fmprc.gov.cn/mfa_eng/ziliao_665539/3602_665543/3604_665547/t18053.shtml> accessed 20 Nov. 2019.

Ministry of the Treasury of New Zealand, 'New Zealand's External Debt – An International Comparison' (2013) <http://www.treasury.govt.nz/economy/mei/jan13/03.htm> accessed 20 Nov. 2019.

MOFCOM, '2010 Statistical Bulletin of China's Outward Foreign Direct Investment' (2011) <http://english.mofcom.gov.cn/article/statistic/foreigninvestment/201109/20110907742320.shtml> accessed 20 Nov. 2019.

OECD, 'Novel Features in Recent OECD Bilateral Investment Treaties' (OECD International Investment Perspectives 2006) <http://www.oecd.org/investment/internationalinvestmentagreements/40072428.pdf> accessed 20 Nov. 2019.

UNCTAD, 'Fair and Equitable Treatment' (UNCTAD Series on Issues in International Investment Agreements, 2012) <http://unctad.org/en/docs/unctaddiaeia2011d5_en.pdf> accessed 20 Nov. 2019.

UNCTAD, 'Recent Developments in International Investment Agreements (2007–June 2008)' (UNCTAD Series on Issues in International Investment Agreements, 2008) <http://unctad.org/en/docs/webdiaeia20081_en.pdf> accessed 20 Nov. 2019.

UNCTAD, 'Scope and Definition' (UNCTAD Series on Issues in International Investment Agreements, 2011) <http://unctad.org/en/pages/PublicationArchive.aspx?publicationid=354> accessed Jul. 15th, 2017.

UNCTAD, 'Taking Stock of IIA Reform: Recent Developments' (UNCTAD IIA Issues Note, Issue 3, June 2019) <https://unctad.org/en/PublicationsLibrary/diaepcbinf2019d5_en.pdf> accessed 11 Oct. 2019.

UNCTAD, 'The Role of International Investment Agreements in Attracting Foreign Direct Investment to Developing Countries' (UNCTAD Series on International Investment Policies for Development, 2009) <http://unctad.org/en/docs/diaeia20095_en.pdf> accessed 20 Nov. 2019.

UNCTAD, 'World Investment Report: Transnational Corporations, Agricultural Production and Development' (2009) <http://unctad.org/en/pages/PublicationArchive.aspx?publicationid=743> accessed 20 Nov. 2019.

UNCTAD, 'World Investment Report: Non-Equity Modes of International Production and Development' (2011) <http://unctad.org/en/PublicationsLibrary/wir2011_en.pdf> accessed Jul. 15th, 2017.

UNCTAD, 'World Investment Report: Global Value Chains: Investment and Trade for Development' (2013) <http://unctad.org/en/PublicationsLibrary/wir2013_en.pdf> accessed 20 Nov. 2019.

UNCTAD, 'World Investment Report: investment and the digital economy' (2017) <http://worldinvestmentreport.unctad.org/world-investment-report-2017> accessed 10 Oct. 2019.

UNCTAD, 'World Investment Report: investment and new industrial policies' (2018) <https://unctad.org/en/PublicationsLibrary/wir2018_en.pdf> accessed 18 Oct. 2019.

UNCTAD, 'World Investment Report: Special Economic Zones' (2019) <https://unctad.org/en/PublicationsLibrary/wir2019_en.pdf> accessed 18 Oct. 2019.

WTO, 'Report of the Working Group on the Relationship between Trade and Investment to the General Council', Dec. 9th, 2002 (WT/WGTI/6).

Online Sources

BBC, 'Deng Xiaoping', *BBC News* <http://news.bbc.co.uk/2/shared/spl/hi/asia_pac/02/china_party_congress/china_ruling_party/key_people_events/html/deng_xiaoping.stm> accessed 20 Nov. 2019.

Cary E., 'SOEs Declining Role in China's Foreign Investment', *The Diplomat* (Jul. 3rd, 2013) <http://thediplomat.com/2013/07/soes-declining-role-in-chinas-foreign-investment/> accessed 20 Nov. 2019.

Chidede T, 'Investment dispute resolution under the Amended Annex 1 of the SADC FIP', *Tralac Blog* (Oct. 1st, 2018) <https://www.tralac.org/blog/article/13526-investment-dispute-resolution-under-the-amended-annex-1-of-the-sadc-fip.html> accessed 31 Oct. 2019.

Chu W, 'China Takes Global Number Two Outward FDI Slot: Hong Kong Remains the Preferred Service Platform', *HKTDC Research* (Nov. 11th, 2016) <http://economists-pick-research.hktdc.com/business-news/article/Research-Articles/China-Takes-Global-Number-Two-Outward-FDI-Slot-Hong-Kong-Remains-the-Preferred-Service-Platform/rp/en/1/1X000000/1X0A804W.htm> accessed 10 Nov. 2019.

Citizens Trade Campaign, *Letter on the Korea Free Trade Agreement to President Obama from 550 organizations* (Sept. 22nd, 2010) <http://www.citizenstrade.org/pdf/Korea_Opposition_Final.pdf> accessed 14 Dec. 2019.

Deen T, 'China: Pakistan is our Israel', *Aljazeera* (Oct. 28th, 2010) <http://www.aljazeera.com/indepth/features/2010/10/2010102813572823512.html> accessed 20 Nov. 2019.

Huanxin Z, 'China names key industries for absolute state control', *China Daily* (Dec. 19th 2006) <http://www.chinadaily.com.cn/china/2006–12/19/content_762056.htm> accessed 31 Oct. 2019.

PublicCitizen.org, *Letter on the Korea Free Trade Agreement to President Obama from 110 members of Congress* (Jul. 22nd, 2010) <http://www.citizen.org/documents/KORUSLetterJuly2010.pdf> accessed 14 Dec. 2019.

Ritchie D, 'Chinese Outward Foreign Direct Investment', *China Go Abroad* (Dec. 4th, 2013) <http://www.chinagoabroad.com/en/commentary/chinese-outward-foreign-direct-investment> accessed 20 Nov. 2019.

Trakman LE, 'Enter the Dragon IV: China's Proliferating Investment Treaty Program', *UNSW Centre for Law, Markets and Regulation* (2011) <https://www.clmr.unsw.edu.au/article//enter-the-dragon-iv%3A-china%27s-proliferating-investment-treaty-program> accessed 20 Nov. 2019.

Online Databases and Media

China Daily online <http://www.chinadaily.com.cn> accessed 20 Nov. 2019.

Council of the European Union <http://www.consilium.europa.eu> accessed 14 Dec. 2019.

European Commission – Trade <http://trade.ec.europa.eu/> accessed 14 Dec. 2019.

European Court of Justice <http://curia.europa.eu> accessed 14 Dec. 2019.

European Parliament <http://www.europarl.europa.eu> accessed 14 Dec. 2019.

Foreign Trade Information System of the Organization of American States <http://www.sice.oas.org/> accessed 20 Nov. 2019.

ICSID <https://icsid.worldbank.org/en/> accessed 20 Nov. 2019.

Jean Monnet Centre for International and Regional Economic Law and Justice <http://www.jeanmonnetprogram.org> accessed 20 Nov. 2019.

OECD FDI Regulatory Restrictiveness Index, https://stats.oecd.org/Index.aspx?datasetcode=FDIINDEX accessed 14 Dec. 2019.

UNCTAD, 'International Investment Agreements Navigator' <https://investmentpolicy.unctad.org/international-investment-agreements> accessed 10 Oct. 2019.

US Government Publishing Office <http://www.gpo.gov> accessed 14 Dec. 2019.

US Trade Representative <http://www.ustr.gov/> accessed 20 Nov. 2019.

White House <https://www.whitehouse.gov> accessed 14 Dec. 2019.

World Bank <http://data.worldbank.org> accessed 20 Nov. 2019.

Index

NOTE: not included:

entries in tables & data summaries in Chapter 3 (including references to States mentioned only or chiefly there)

terms/concepts having a dedicated section in the table of contents and/or appearing throughout the text (e.g., China, national treatment, fair and equitable treatment, investment, investor-State arbitration)

Administrative
- Authorities 136, 174n
- Court/Tribunal 30n, 50, 68n, 136, 139, 162n, 173n
- Law/Regulation/Norm see law
- Proceedings 327, 344, 386
- Review 84, 135, 136, 145, 156–158n, 163n, 170, 391
- Special Regions (China) 4

Admissibility 80, 82, 83

ASEAN 2, 4, 5, 9n, 10, 39, 42, 57, 73, 89, 96, 101–103, 110, 130, 235, 394
- China-ASEAN Investment Agreement 16n, 18n, 29n, 32–33, 48, 132n, 138n, 142–143, 168, 230n, 233–234, 327, 331, 335, 339, 393

Australia 25, 42, 43, 55n, 57, 69, 102, 394
- China-Australia BIT (1988) 35, 65, 85, 97, 143, 330
- China Australia FTA (2015) 16n, 32, 34, 39, 41–42, 48, 89, 96, 100, 134–136, 138, 140, 141n, 164 175n, 230, 233, 287–288, 324
- Treaty practice 113

Bona fide see good faith

Brazil 15–18, 29, 106

BRICS 13, 15–18, 31

British see UK

Canada 9, 10, 12, 18n, 25, 28, 29, 32, 34, 36, 38–43, 48, 55–56n, 61, 73, 80, 89, 94, 99, 103–104, 107, 111–113, 116, 120–127, 137–141
- Model BIT 71, 73, 97, 103–105, 111–113, 133–134, 138, 228, 230, 231, 233, 282, 328, 331, 334, 335

compensation 19, 27, 61–62, 63, 99
- (amount of) due to expropriation 8, 27, 35, 46, 47, 49, 133–135, 139, 144–147, 167–170, 202–224, 390
- characteristics 167, 178–186

Domestic court 7, 30n, 135–140, 144n
- Administrative see administrative court/tribunal

Due process 19, 166–167, 173n

Economy
- Capital-exporting 2, 4, 6, 9n, 17, 23, 25, 28, 49, 60n, 70, 138–140, 166, 170, 393
- Capital-importing 1, 6, 28, 58, 60n, 70, 100n, 107, 138, 166
- Developed 12, 36, 26–27, 28n, 33, 36, 41, 70, 100n, 110, 135, 138, 165, 177, 393
- Developing 6, 8, 9n, 10, 12, 15, 19, 23, 25–27, 28n, 60, 70, 100n, 133, 165, 169, 177, 396
- Emerging 4, 15
- Liberal see Western
- Market 36, 43, 52–54, 102–103, 110, 394
- Most-promising see emerging
- OECD see Western
- Private 109
- Socialist 20n, 21–22, 52–54,
- Western 3, 43, 48, 55, 393

Enforcement 21n, 41, 49, 51

Environment 3, 12, 37–42, 44, 56, 394
EU (European Union) 10, 11n, 12, 13, 17n, 37–38, 50, 54n, 73, 92, 132, 232, 234, 285, 394–396
  China-EU BIT 4, 42–45

France 1, 2, 7, 9n, 10, 11n, 17n, 20n, 23, 25, 29n, 55n, 65n, 88, 95, 97, 101, 142, 229, 230, 283, 392
  Model BIT 62n, 81n, 97n, 134n, 138, 166, 167, 171, 174, 226n, 229, 281n, 325–326n, 328, 330–331, 339n
  Treaty practice 80

G7 8, 10, 62, 167
Germany 2, 6–11, 17–18n, 23, 25, 26n, 31, 87, 95, 101, 133, 142, 391
  China-Germany BIT (1983) 65, 67n, 69, 106, 129
  China-Germany BIT (2003) 28, 29, 48, 69, 74, 92, 93–94, 97–98, 100, 102, 105, 108, 110, 113, 139n,
  Legal system 50
  Model BIT 61, 62, 67, 68, 70, 72, 74, 76n, 79, 80, 82, 97–98, 102, 105, 106, 107, 112, 130, 134, 138, 164–170, 172–174, 226, 228, 230, 281–282, 325, 328, 330, 331, 334–336, 339–340, 391–393
  Treaty practice 66n, 71, 80, 92n, 105, 106, 129, 228
  West see Germany
Good faith 50, 82, 91, 93
Great Leap Forward 1, 21

Hull Rule 33, 164, 167

India 10n, 15–17, 29, 34n, 42, 60
Italy 7, 10, 17n, 23, 25, 26, 29, 34, 49, 55n, 80, 84, 132, 392
  Legal system 50n
  model BIT 66n, 71n, 81, 97n, 133–134, 138–139, 168, 169, 171, 226, 228, 230, 281n, 283, 325n, 326–327, 328, 330–331, 334–336, 339n
  treaty practice 72, 173

Japan 9n, 10, 16n, 25, 34n, 42, 48, 54n, 56, 80, 85, 100n, 135, 142, 395
  China-Japan-South Korea Investment Agreement 2, 18, 29, 32, 35, 40, 84, 89, 96, 99, 101, 104n, 132–133n, 141n, 165, 169, 172, 235n, 287–288, 329–330, 338
Jurisdiction 80, 82, 100, 392
  Administrative court see administrative court
  Arbitral tribunal see arbitral tribunal
  Domestic court see domestic court
  Ratione legis 65, 68–70, 72–73, 80–92, 102–104, 106, 107, 110, 131, 337
  Ratione loci 69–70, 72, 80, 106
  Ratione materiae 72–73, 100, 390
  Ratione personae 72–73, 80, 106
  Ratione temporis 69–70, 72–73

Law (incl. rule, regulation)
  Administrative 81, 83
  Domestic 23, 28, 31, 49–50, 67–68, 79, 81, 83–84, 103, 107, 118–127, 167, 177 187–201, 231–232, 240, 245–281, 324, 332, 337, 346, 352, 392
  Environmental see environment
  International 4, 19, 20 61, 93n, 164, 174n, 329, 347, 396n
    Customary 329, 331, 338, 346, 348, 349
    Principles 329, 338, 346, 380, 384
Liberalization 10, 24, 29, 31, 33, 44, 55, 71, 74n, 394

Market
  access see liberalization
  domestic 45, 395
  single 51
Mexico 60, 89, 96, 101, 138, 230, 233, 325, 329, 335, 338, 340n

NAFTA 10, 36, 38, 111n, 235, 283–284, 288n, 338, 391, 394
Netherlands 7, 8, 9n, 10, 11n, 17, 26, 142, 230
  China-Netherlands BIT (1987) 47

Netherlands (cont.)
  China-Netherlands BIT (2001) 77–78n, 84, 87, 149, 166, 169, 280
  Model BIT 26, 62, 71n, 80, 133–134, 138, 139n, 164, 166–167, 168n, 169, 171–174, 226, 228, 230, 281–283, 325–326n, 328, 330, 331–332, 333n, 334–336, 339, 392
  Treaty practice 72, 80
New Zealand 20, 42, 69, 102, 109, 394
  China-New Zealand FTA (2008) 2, 16n, 18n, 32–33, 36, 38n, 39–40, 48, 85, 89, 95, 98, 101, 108, 132n, 138n, 141n, 142, 229, 233–234, 327, 331, 339, 393
North America 10, 226
  BIT model / template / standard 18, 34, 40, 41, 48, 66, 73, 89n, 99, 104, 107, 113, 133, 137–139, 147, 227, 230n, 231–232, 235, 284, 285, 288, 325, 327, 328, 333, 335, 339, 353, 391–392, 394
  Treaty practice 282, 284, 338, 340, 391

Pacta sunt servanda 50
Property 19, 20n, 53, 71
  Right see right to property
public health 40–42, 56, 165, 353
public welfare 12, 42, 65

Ratione legis jurisdiction / requirement / condition see jurisdiction
Ratione loci jurisdiction / requirement / condition see jurisdiction
Ratione materiae jurisdiction / requirement / condition see jurisdiction
Ratione personae jurisdiction / requirement / condition see jurisdiction
Ratione temporis jurisdiction / requirement / condition see jurisdiction
Right
  Contractual 22, 71n, 73, 105–112
  Economic 338
  Environment see environment
  Human 12, 145n, 287
  In rem see contractual right
  Investor 29, 35, 43
  Labor 38, 40
  Procedural 41, 140, 396
  Property see contractual right
  To regulate 12, 19, 29 44n, 70, 80, 81n,
  To review 173–174
Regulation see law
Romania 7n, 25, 26n, 36, 65n, 97
Rule see law
Russia 15–16, 242n

Salini test 91n, 93, 229, 394
South Africa 11n, 17, 28, 47
South Korea 34, 133
  China-South Korea BIT (2007) 35, 95, 101, 142–143, 229
  China-South Korea FTA (2015) 2, 32, 35, 40–42, 48, 88–89, 96, 102, 135, 138n, 141n, 169, 287–288, 325, 327, 329–330, 336–338
  China-South Korea-Japan Investment Agreement (2012) see Japan
Sovereignty 8, 19, 22, 27, 67, 103, 113, 390, 393, 396
Soviet Union see USSR
Sweden 7, 10, 15, 22, 23, 25, 36, 46, 65, 69n, 80, 83, 105n, 128, 129, 132, 142, 171, 233
  China-Sweden BIT see Sweden
  Treaty practice see Sweden
Switzerland 2, 7n, 9n, 10, 17n, 25, 34–35, 80, 89, 96, 101, 141n, 142, 168, 230, 287
  China-Switzerland BIT see Switzerland
  Treaty practice see Switzerland

Transparency 51, 56–57, 396–397
Treaty of Friendship, Commerce and Navigation (FCN) 7, 9
Tribunal
  Arbitral 5, 21n, 41, 81n, 82, 91, 94, 130n, 138n, 139, 152n, 338, 392, 397
  Administrative see administrative court
  Domestic see domestic court

UNCITRAL 5, 12, 37, 44n, 59, 395–396
  Arbitration rules 137–139

UK (United Kingdom) 1, 2, 7, 9, 10, 20, 23, 25, 49, 84, 132, 391–392
China-UK BIT (1986) 26, 46, 69n, 280, 285, 330
Model BIT 26, 61–62, 63, 66n, 67–69, 70–72, 74, 76–80, 82, 97–98, 102, 105–110, 114–116, 120n, 129–130, 133–134, 138, 139n, 165–169, 171–174, 226, 227n, 228, 230, 232, 236n, 239n, 281–285, 325n, 326–328, 331, 334–337, 339, 391–392
Treaty practice 7n, 11n, 16, 17, 103n, 128, 130, 165, 228, 330, 334
US (United States) 1, 4, 61,
Model BIT 62, 66n, 70, 71n, 73, 76–78n, 79, 80, 90, 92, 93, 96n, 97, 100, 102–105, 106n, 107–127, 133–134, 137–138, 139n, 164–167, 169–173, 174n, 175, 226n, 228, 230–234, 235n, 239n, 281–284, 285n, 288, 289n, 325–326n, 327–328, 330–331, 334, 338
USSR 9, 16, 20n, 21, 54, 106, 166, 171, 242n, 327

Value
Economic 53, 75, 77, 106–108
Market 170, 171, 173, 180–181, 184–185, 203–225

www.ingramcontent.com/pod-product-compliance
Lightning Source LLC
Chambersburg PA
CBHW071231230926
51849CB00001B/70
* 9 7 8 9 0 0 4 4 4 3 9 0 7 *